Thomas Johansson

The King's Gambit
for the Creative Aggressor

Das Königsgambit
für den erfindungsreichen Angriffsspieler

Schachverlag Kania

Schachverlag Kania

Thomas Johansson
e-Mail: TalJechin@telia.com
Homepage:
http://hem.passagen.se/tjmisha/index.html
mit aktuellen Infos zum Königsgambit
King's Gambit - topic information

ISBN 3-931192-09-1

The King's Gambit for the Creative Aggressor! • Das Königsgambit für den inspirierten Angreifer!

bilingual English/German
zweisprachig englisch/deutsch

1. Auflage © 1998
2. Auflage © 2001
by:

Schachverlag Kania
Richard-Wagner-Str. 43
D-71701 Schwieberdingen
Tel./Fax 07150/37098
eMail Keilhack@aol.com
Internet: www.kaniaverlag.de

Satz & Layout: Harald Keilhack
Übersetzung der englischsprachigen Texte: Harald Keilhack
Druck: Tiskárna Akcent s.r.o., Vimperk Cz
Diagramme erstellt mit ***ChessOle!***
Umschlaggestaltung: Frank Stiefel

Contents *Inhalt*

Symbols *Zeichenerklärung*

+–	White is winning	*mit weißem Gewinn*
±	White has a clear advantage	*Weiß hat klaren Vorteil*
⩲	White is slightly better	*Weiß steht etwas besser*
=	equality	*mit Ausgleich*
=/∞	approximately equal	*mit ungefährem Ausgleich*
∞	unclear	*mit unklarem Spiel*
$\overline{\overline{\infty}}$	with compensation for the material	*mit Kompensation für das Material*
⩱	Black is slightly better	*Schwarz steht etwas besser*
∓	Black has a clear advantage	*Schwarz hat klaren Vorteil*
–+	Black is winning	*mit schwarzem Gewinn*
!!	a superb move	*Glanzzug*
!	a good move	*starker Zug*
!?	an interesting move	*beachtlicher, interessanter Zug*
?!	a dubious move	*zweifelhafter Zug*
?	a mistake	*Fehler*
??	a blunder	*grober Fehler*
Δ	with the idea, intending	*mit der Idee (... Plan, ... Drohung)*
→	with an attack	*mit Angriff*
↑	with initiative	*mit Initiative*
×	weak point	*Schwäche*
#	mate	*matt*
+	check	*Schach(gebot)*
⊕	time-trouble	*Zeitnot*
corr.	correspondence game	*Fernpartie*
1:0/27.	and White won after 27 moves	*und Weiß gewann im 27. Zug*
♥	Learn by heart! Indicates a variation worth remembering due to popularity or unsoundness *Auswendig lernen! Kennzeichnet eine Variante, die man sich wegen ihrer Beliebtheit oder ihrer Unkorrektheit einprägen sollte*	

Introduction

I wrote this book primarily for myself, which is why it focuses on a relatively narrow repertoire for White. Since the King's Gambit generally requires a high standard from White for the first ten moves or so, I think it's quite necessary to specialize in a few variations to avoid confusing them with similar variations. This approach - one major variation against each defence plus some interesting off-beat alternatives - has formed the book into a mixture of encyclopaedia, trends and repertoire book.

This selective approach also has the benefit of making the book ideal for those who wish to convert to the King's Gambit. They will soon be provided with an easily remembered repertoire which will enable them to start playing the KG with some confidence.

I've noticed that many players have a strange double-edged attitude towards the King's Gambit. They won't play it themselves since they fear they'll end up with the king on e2 in a very complicated position. And they won't play 1...e5 against someone they know plays it, since now they're afraid of various sacrifices on f7! This second fear is of course quite rational, but the first one isn't. There is no way for Black to force White's king to e2 or d2 without accepting a clearly worse position.

What does it take to become a King's Gambiteer? Well, the requirements aren't that different from the ones of other openings. It's important to be able to exploit the usual endgame advantages like: better pawn structure, more space, the bishop pair and especially the initiative that comes from having the more active pieces. The two most important personal qualities required are hinted in the title: Creativity and the Will to Attack!

Some might wonder: Why should I play the King's Gambit? I'll just mention a few reasons that spring to mind:

- Young and/or ambitious players will learn a lot about dynamic positions and the relation between time and material and also between structure and material.
- Practical players may appreciate just having to learn one opening against 1...e5 (those who play 2.♘f3 will have to learn the Petroff, the Philidor, the Latvian gambit, the Ruy Lopez etc).
- Entertainment, the King's Gambit provides fun positions full of strategical and tactical complexities which are a pleasure both to play and analyze.
- The surprise factor shouldn't be underestimated either, because this book considers many unusual and highly aggressive lines for White which most other books totally ignore.

Those players who wish to be well prepared but only have a limited time for opening preparations will appreciate the King's Gambit, since it's quite manageable to keep oneself up to date theoretically because this opening isn't continually showered by new TNs from grandmaster practise.

Some might feel a bit hesitant considering the openings unpopularity among grandmasters, but this is more due to fashion and the fact that they are professionals playing hundreds of games a year just to make a living and thus don't feel like taking any risks at all. And besides, they probably already know the Ruy Lopez and Petroff etc and have no desire to change their repertoire. But the rest of us non-grandmasters hardly play more than fifty competitive games a year so we can treat ourselves to not play the modern base-line chess and instead have some fun!

Historically, the King's Gambit has been championed by quite an impressive crowd of grandmasters and World Champions. In this book you'll find games or analysis by most of the following players: Morphy, Anderssen, Steinitz, Lasker, Capablanca, Alekhine, Chigorin, Rubinstein, Reti and more recently Fischer, Tal, Keres, Bronstein and Spassky.

Nowadays, the King's Gambit is still played regularly by a few very highly rated players like Illescas and Judit Polgar. Many British grandmasters also seem to fancy the sharp King's Gambit, most frequently Gallagher and Hebden but recently they've been joined by Nunn and Short. Time will tell if this new trend is here to stay.

Where possible the repertoire I'm recommending will consist of relatively new, less known variations which give both players, but especially White - who usually will be the best informed part - plenty of room to find new ideas. The variations I recommend will be covered in detail using all available information and where possible I've tried to supply many complete games as illustrations of how play may unfold and to help you acquire a 'feel for the positions' which is at least as important as the learning of variations. And besides it's more fun to learn from practical examples!

By the way, I've found that a good way to remember variations is to analyze the critical positions in search of new ideas. Even if you don't find any (very improbable), you will learn a lot about the position at hand and about similar structures.

In general, this book is structured like this: Each chapter begins with Black's worst defences and works it's way up to the best. A lot of space is saved by this arrangement of the material since you won't have to see the moves leading up to the positions of interest over and over again as you play through the games.

Unfortunately, all uncredited analysis is not mine, a large part is derived from Colin Leach's game collections but sadly enough he doesn't cite the sources of the variations.

Thomas Johansson

Malmö, February 1998

Einführung

In erster Linie habe ich dieses Buch für mich selbst niedergeschrieben, was erklären mag, daß hier lediglich ein recht schmales Repertoire für den Anziehenden aufgezeigt wird. Da im Königsgambit die ersten zehn Züge recht hohe Anforderungen an den Weißspieler stellen, ist es meiner Ansicht nach aber ohnehin sinnvoll, sich auf einige wenige Varianten zu konzentrieren, um Verwechslungen mit ähnlichen Varianten zu vermeiden. Durch diese Methode - ausführliche Erläuterung einer Hauptvariante gegen jede schwarze Verteidigung sowie Erwähnung einiger interessanter Nebengleise - ist dieses Buch zu einer Mischung aus Enzyklopädie, "Trends"-Büchlein und Repertoirewerk geworden.

Diese Vorauswahl sollte auch demjenigen, der auf das Königsgambit umsatteln will, den Einstieg erleichtern. Ihm wird ein leicht einprägsames Repertoire geboten, das gleichzeitig ein hinreichendes Vertrauen in das Königsgambit schafft.

Mir ist aufgefallen, daß viele Spieler eine merkwürdige ambivalente Einstellung gegenüber dem Königsgambit an den Tag legen. Selbst würden sie es niemals anwenden, da sie fürchten, in einer komplizierten Stellung mit dem König auf e2 zu verbleiben. Auf der anderen Seite vermeiden Sie den Zug 1...e5 gegen Königsgamit-Spieler, da ihnen nun vor Opferwendungen auf f7 Angst und Bange wäre! Die Furcht vor letzterem ist begründet, die vor ersterem hingegen nicht. Es gibt keine Möglichkeit für Schwarz, den weißen König nach e2 oder d2 zu zwingen, ohne anderweitig klaren Nachteil hinzunehmen.

Was gehört dazu, um zu einem erfolgreichen Ritter des Königsgambits zu werden? Nun, eigentlich stellt das Königsgambit keine anderen Anforderungen als jede andere Eröffnung auch. Es ist wichtig, in der Verwertung folgender typischer Endspielvorteile versiert zu sein: Bessere Bauernstruktur, Raumvorteil, Läuferpaar und insbesondere einer von aktivem Figurenspiel herrührenden Initiative. Doch die beiden wichtigsten individuellen Eigenschaften haben wir schon in unserem Buchtitel angedeutet: Erfindungsreichtum und Entschlossenheit zum Angriff!

Man mag die Frage stellen: Wieso soll ich ausgerechnet das Königsgambit spielen? Hier ein paar augenfällige Gründe:

- *Junge und/oder aufstrebende Spieler lernen hier eine Menge über dynamische Stellungen, das Verhältnis zwischen Zeit und Material und auch über das Verhältnis zwischen Struktur und Material.*
- *Der Pragmatiker mag es schätzen, nur eine einzige Eröffnung gegen 1...e5 lernen zu müssen (wer mit 2.♘f3 fortsetzt, muß die Russische - und die Philidor-Verteidigung, das Lettische Gambit, die Spanische Eröffnung lernen, usw.)*
- *Kurzweil und Abwechslung. Das Königsgambit sorgt für anregende Positionen voller strategischer und taktischer Finessen, die sowohl beim Spiel als auch bei der Analyse Freude bereiten.*
- *Der Überraschungseffekt sollte gleichfalls nicht unterschätzt werden. Zumal etliche ungebräuchliche und hochgradig aggressive Varianten, die andere Bücher uns vorenthalten, hier zur Sprache kommen.*

Wer sich gut vorbereitet ans Brett setzen will, andererseits aber nur begrenzte Zeit für das Eröffnungsstudium hat, wird das Königsgambit gleichfalls schätzen, zumal man hier recht gut auf dem laufenden bleiben kann, ohne von fortwährenden Neuerungen aus der GM-Praxis erschlagen zu werden.

Zum Zögern mag der Umstand veranlassen, daß diese Eröffnung in Großmeisterkreisen alles andere als beliebt ist. Doch dies ist einerseits Mode, und zum anderen animiert die Tatsache, daß Profispieler Hunderte Partien pro Jahr absolvieren müssen, bloß um halbwegs ihr Leben fristen zu können, diese nicht gerade zur Inkaufnahme zusätzlicher Risiken. Und außerdem beherrschen die Profis Spanisch, Russisch usw., und ihnen steht nicht der Sinn nach Veränderung. Doch wir, der große Rest an Nicht-Großmeistern, absolvieren pro Jahr kaum mehr als fünfzig Turnierpartien, und wir können es uns leisten, anstelle des modernen Grundlinienschachs ein wenig Spaß zu haben!

Dabei finden sich in der Geschichte des Königsgambit zahlreiche namhafte Verfechter bis hin zu Groß- und Weltmeistern. In unserem Buch tauchen Partien und/oder Analysen von Morphy, Anderssen, Steinitz, Lasker, Capablanca, Aljechin, Tschigorin, Rubinstein, Keres sowie aus neueren Zeiten Fischer, Tal, Keres, Bronstein und Spasski auf.

Doch auch heutzutage wird das Königsgambit von einigen Spielern mit hoher Elozahl regelmäßig angewandt, wie z.B. Illescas oder Judit Polgar. Viele britische Großmeister scheinen an das Königsgambit zu glauben, vor allem Gallagher und Hebden, die jüngst mit Nunn und Short weitere Mitstreiter für ihre Leidenschaft gefunden zu haben scheinen. Die nächste Zukunft wird zeigen, ob dieser Trend anhält.

Soweit möglich, besteht das von mir empfohlene Repertoire aus verhältnismäßig jungen, weniger bekannten Varianten, welche beiden Spielern, insbesondere aber dem Weißen - der in der Regel besser informiert als sein Kontrahent sein sollte - Raum für eigene, neue Ideen lassen. Die von mir empfohlenen Varianten werden ausführlich und unter Auswertung aller verfügbaren Quellen besprochen. Soweit sinnvoll, sind komplette Partien aufgeführt, um zu zeigen, wie sich das Spiel weiterentwickeln kann, und um Ihnen beim Erwerb eines "Stellungsgefühls" zu helfen - ein solches ist ja bekanntlich mindestens ebenso wichtig wie exakte Variantenkenntnis. Zudem macht es mehr Spaß, anhand von praktischen Beispielen zu lernen!

Eine gute Möglichkeit, sich Varianten einzuprägen, besteht übrigens darin, die kritische Stellung auf der Suche nach neuen Wegen zu analysieren. Selbst wenn sich keine neue Idee finden läßt (was äußerst unwahrscheinlich ist), lernt man viel über die vorliegende Stellung und solche mit vergleichbaren Strukturen.

In der Regel ist der Aufbau des Buches folgendermaßen: Jedes Kapitel beginnt mit der schwächsten Verteidigung von Schwarz und arbeitet sich dann bis zur besten Verteidigung vor. So ließ sich viel Platz sparen, und man muß sich nicht mühsam bis zu den interessantesten Stellungen durchkämpfen.

Leider stammen längst nicht alle Analysen ohne Quellenangabe von mir. Viele davon habe ich aus Leachs Partiensammlung übernommen, der selbst leider keinerlei diesbezüglichen Angaben macht.

Chapter I *Kapitel I*

King's Gambit Declined - Various Second Moves
Abgel. Königsgambit - Verschiedene zweite Züge

1.e4 e5 2.f4

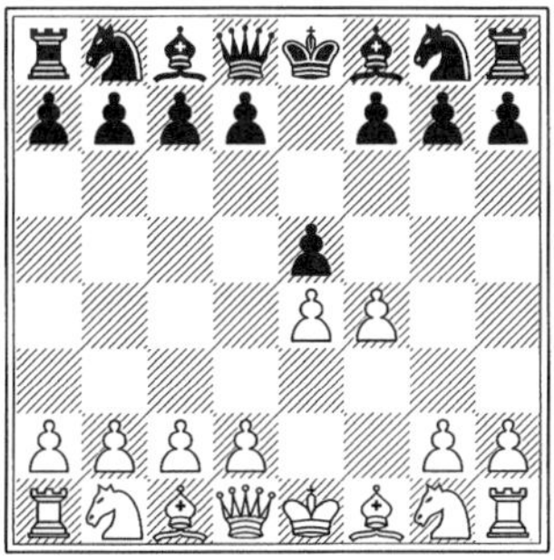

I

2...d6

This 'Philidor approach' gives White a small advantage, almost instantly, in control of the centre and easy development.

Dieser "Philidor'sche Ansatz" gibt Weiß praktisch sofort einen kleinen Vorteil, bestehend in größerem Zentrumseinfluß und unkomplizierter Entwicklung.

2...c6 3.♘f3! d5 4.♘:e5 de4 5.♗c4 ♘h6 6.♘c3 f6 7.♕h5+ g6 8.♘:g6 h:g6 9.♕:g6+ ♔d7 10.♘:e4 ♕e7 11.0-0 ♔c7 12.d3 f5 13.♘c3 ±.

3.♘f3 ♘d7

Missing the last chance to transpose to something respectable with 3...e:f4! - see The Fischer defence.

Verpaßt die letzte Chance, mit 3...e:f4! zu einer anerkannten Spielweise - nämlich der Fischer-Verteidigung - überzuleiten.

- 3...♘f6 4.♘c3 ♘c6 5.♗b5! ♗d7 6.d3 (6.d4!?) e:f4 (6...♗e7 7.♗:c6 ♗:c6 8.f:e5 ±) 7.♗:f4 ± Rabinovitch.
- 3...f5 4.♗c4! f:e4 (4...♘f6 5.d3 f:e4 6.d:e4 ♗g4 7.f:e5 ♗:f3 8.♕:f3 d:e5 9.♗e3 ±, 4...e:f4 5.d3 ♘f6 6.♘c3 ♘h5 7.0-0 f:e4 8.d:e4 c6 9.♘d4 ±) 5.♘:e5 d:e5 6.♕h5+ ♔d7 7.♕f5+ ♔c6 8.♕:e4+ ♔b6 9.♘c3 ± c6 10.f:e5 a6 11.d4 ♔a7 12.♗e3 ♘d7 13.d5+ (Δ 0-0-0, d6, e6).

4.d4 ♘gf6 5.f:e5 ♘:e4 6.♗d3 d5 7.♘c3!? ♘:c3 8.b:c3 ♗e7 9.0-0 0-0 10.♕e1 ♖e8 11.♕g3 ♘f8 12.♘g5 f6 13.e:f6 ♗:f6 14.♗d2 c5

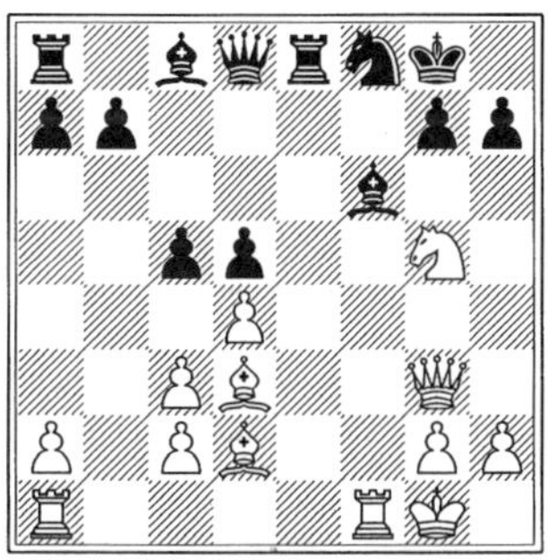

15.♖:f6! ♕:f6 16.♖f1 ♕e7 17.♖:f8+ ♔:f8 18.♕f3+ ♔g8 19.♗:h7+ ♔h8 20.♕h5 ♗g4 21.♕h4 ♕f6 22.♗g6+ ♔g8 23.♗f7+ ♔f8 24.♕:g4 ♖e4 25.♘h7+ ♔:f7 26.♘:f6 ♖:g4 27.♘:g4 +–, Uritsky - Lepman, Simferopol 1986.

II

2...♘f6 3.♘f3 ♘:e4

The 'Petroff approach' doesn't give Black much, either. The same kind of position can be seen in the Schallopp, after 2...e:f4 3.♘f3 ♘f6 4.e5 ♘e4; where White will at least have to spend a tempo taking back on f4.
Der "Russische Ansatz" verspricht Schwarz gleichfalls nicht viel. Derselbe Stellungstyp ist in der Schallopp-Verteidigung zu sehen, wo Weiß aber mindestens ein Tempo in das Zurückschlagen auf f4 investieren muß.

3...d5 4.f:e5 d:e4? (Black must transpose with 4...♘:e4 - *Schwarz muß überleiten mit 4...♘:e4*) 5.e:f6 e:f3 6.♕:f3 ♘c6 7.♗b5! ♕f6 8.♕:f6 g:f6 9.d4! ±.

4.f:e5 d5 5.d3 ♘c5 6.d4 ♘e6

Anderssen once said 'You can't lose with a knight on e6!'. I don't think he was speaking about this exact position, but it is a strong piece and if Black is allowed to end his development it may turn into a thorn in White's side ...
Anderssen behauptete einst, "mit einem Springer auf e6 könne man gar nicht verlieren". Ich glaube natürlich weniger, daß er dabei ausgerechnet von der vorliegende Position sprach, doch der ♘e6 ist eine ansehnliche Figur und mag dem Anziehenden ein Dorn im Auge sein, wenn er den Schwarzen seine Entwicklung vollenden läßt ...

6...♘e4 7.♗d3 ♗e7 (7...c5 8.c4 c:d4 9.0-0 ±) 8.0-0 0-0 9.c4! ♗e6? (9...c6 10.♕c2 f5 11.e:f6 ♘:f6 12.♘g5 h6 13. ♘f3 ± Δ ♘c3) 10.♕c2 c6 11.♘c3 ♘:c3 12.♗:h7+ ♔h8 13.b:c3 +– (1:0/17.), Bronstein - Kostro, Tbilisi 1970.

7.c4!

Creating tension in the centre before Black has time to consolidate!
Schafft einen Spannungsherd im Zentrum, bevor Schwarz die Gelegenheit erhält, sich zu konsolidieren.

7... ♗b4+

7...c6 8.♘c3 ♗e7 9.♗e3 0-0 10.♕d2 b6 11.♗d3 ♘a6 12.c:d5 c:d5 13.♖d1 f5 14.e:f6 ♖:f6 15.0-0 ♘ac7 16.♘e5 ±, Bronstein - Holmov, Vilnius 1975.

8.♗d2!

Black has some potentially weak black squares around his king, so why not exchange their key defender!
Der Nachziehende hat ein paar potentielle schwarzfeldrige Felderschwächen am Königsflügel. Was spräche also dagegen, deren Hauptverteidigungsfigur abzutauschen!?

8...♗:d2+ 9.♕:d2 c6 10.♘c3 0-0 11.♖c1

Black is so far behind in development that white can afford this quiet escalation.
Schwarz ist so weit mit der Entwicklung im Rückstand, daß der Anziehende sich mit einer allmählichen Zuspitzung der Ereignisse zufriedengeben kann.

11...♘c7?!

A better defence would be 11...b6 Δ ♗a6.
Eine bessere Verteidigung würde in 11...b6 Δ ♗a6 bestehen.

12.c:d5 c:d5

12...♘:d5 13.♘:d5 ♕:d5 14.♗c4 ♕e4+ 15.♕e2 ♕:e2+ 16.♔:e2 ±.

13.♗d3 ♗g4 14.♘g5! f5

14...h6 15.♘h7! ♖e8 16.0-0 (Δ♘f6+) +–.

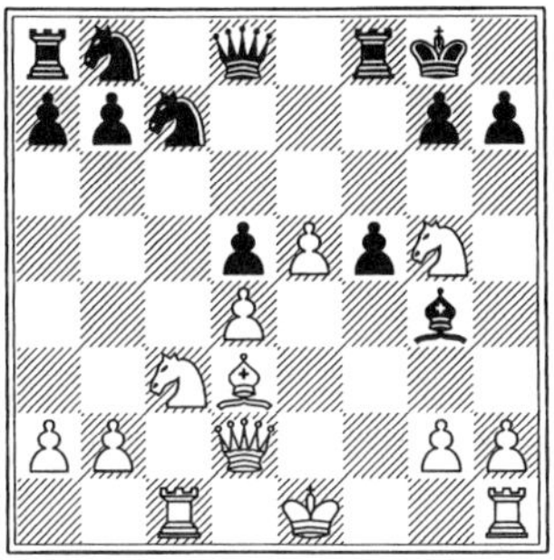

15.h3 ± (1:0/48.), Bronstein - Jusupov, SSSR 1981.

There's even more to be taken by:
Noch mehr zu holen wäre mit:

15.0-0! h6 16.♘:d5! ♘:d5 17.♘e6 ♕e7 18.♘:f8 ♔:f8 19.h3 ♗h5 20.♖:f5+ +−.

III

(1.e4 e5 2.f4)

2...♕h4+

Keene's defence, popularized in the early 70s, almost extinct nowadays.
Die Keene-Verteidigung, zu Anfang der siebziger Jahre progagiert und heutzutage beinahe ausgestorben.

3.g3 ♕e7 4.d3!

A system which has done quite well in it's limited practise.
In der beschränkten vorliegenden Praxis fuhr Weiß mit diesem System recht gut.

Gallagher offers some interesting but untested analysis:
Gallagher bietet hier einige interessante, jedoch unerprobte Analysen an:
4.♘c3 e:f4!? (4...d6 5.♘f3 [5.♘d5!? ♕d8 6.d4 c6 7.♘c3] 5...♗g4 6.h3 ♗:f3 7.♕:f3 ♘f6 8.d3/8.♗c4 ⩲) 5.d4 f:g3 6.♗f4!? (The little guys don't matter, as usual - *Die kleinen Bäuerchen spielen keine Rolle, wie üblich*) 6...d5! (6...♘f6 7.e5 d6 8.♕e2!/!? ∞/⩲) 7.h:g3⩲ (Gallagher).
I'm not all that convinced about White's compensation here, though. How should 7...♗e6 be met? 8.e5 definitely feels wrong, but what else?
Ich bin alles andere als überzeugt von der weißen Kompensation. Wie soll 7...♗e6 beantwortet werden? 8.e5 ist bestimmt verkehrt, aber was sonst?

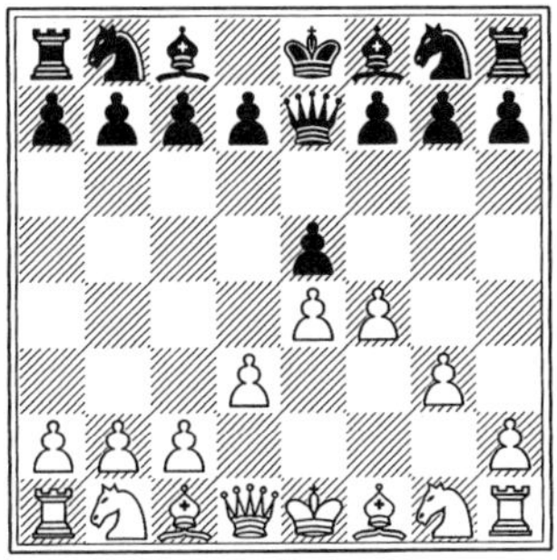

Position after 4.d3/*Nach 4.d3*

- **4...f5 5.♘c3 ♘f6 6.f:e5 ♕:e5 7.♗f4 ♕e7 8.♕d2 f:e4 9.0-0-0 d5 10.d:e4 ♘:e4 11.♘:e4 d:e4 12.♗g5** ±.

- **4...d5 5.♘c3!?**

•• 5...d4? 6.♘d5 ±.

•• 5...d:e4 6.d:e4 ♘f6 (6...e:f4 7.♗:f4 ♘f6 8.♕e2 ♗g4 9.♘f3 ♗:f3 10.♕:f3 c6 11.e5 Δ ♗c4) 7.f:e5 ♕:e5 8.♘f3 ♕a5 9.♗d2 ∞ (9.♗g5!?).

•• 5...c6 6.f:e5 d:e4 7.♘:e4 ♕:e5 8.♘f3 ♕d5 9.♕e2 ♗e7 10.♘fg5!? f5!? (10...h6 11.♗g2 ⩲)

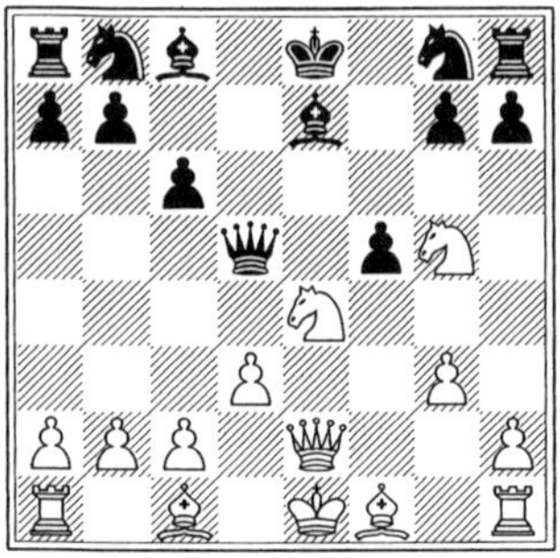

11.♘c3! ♕:h1 12.♗f4 ♗d7 (12...c5 13.0-0-0 ♕c6 14.♗g2 ♕d7 15.♘d5 ♔f8 16.♘:e7 ♘:e7 17.♕h5 ♕e8 18.♘:h7+ →) 13.0-0-0 ♘f6? (13...♘a6 14.♗h3) 14.♗d6! 0-0 15.♕:e7 ♘a6 16.d4 ♕:h2 17.♗c4+ ♔h8 18.♘f7+ ♖:f7 19.♗:f7 ± c5 20.♗e5! ♘b4 21.♖d2 ♕h1+ 22.♘d1 ♘e4 23.♗:g7+! ♔:g7 24.♗e8+ 1:0, Krantz - Dehmelt, corr. 1986.

It's mate in a few more moves.

Mit Mattsetzung in wenigen Zügen.

• • 5...e:f4 6.♗:f4 c6 7.♗h3 or *(oder)* 7.♘ge2.

• **4...d6 5.♘c3 ♘f6 6.♗h3 ♗:h3 7.♘:h3 h6**

7...♘c6 8.0-0 0-0-0 9.♘d5 ♘:d5 10.e:d5 ♘b4 11.c4 e4 12.♘f2 ±, 7...g6 8.0-0 ♗g7 9.f5 0-0 10.♗g5 c6 11.♕d2 (11.g4!?) ♘bd7 12.g4 ♕e8 13.♘f2 d5 14.♗:f6 ±.

8.♗e3 ♘bd7 9.0-0 ♘b6 10.a4 ♕d7, Christiansen - Gibbons, Los Angeles 1980, 11.♘f2 ♕c6 12.♘g4! Δ f:e5 ±.

IV

(1.e4 e5 2.f4)

2...♕f6

The Nordwalder variation named and extensively analyzed by Stefan Bücker. I suppose that most of the analysis in this section is his although I found it in one of Leach's books.

Die Nordwalder Variante, erforscht von und benannt nach Stefan Bücker. Ich vermute, daß die meisten Analysen in diesem Passus auf ihn zurückgehen, auch wenn ich diese dem Buch von Leach entnommen habe.

3.♘c3 ♕:f4 4.♘f3

One have to be careful not to over-reach while chasing the queen, but Black must be even more careful not to get trapped! Those who don't feel like chasing Black's king and queen in exchange for a piece sac, can try 4.d4 ♕h4+ 5.g3 ♕d8 6.d:e5 ± which, by the way, is the critical variation at least according to Bücker.

Man muß aufpassen, daß man sich bei der Jagd auf die schwarze Dame nicht ins eigene Fleisch schneidet, doch Schwarz muß natürlich noch mehr aufpassen, daß er nicht in die Grube fällt! Wem nicht der Sinn danach steht, eine Figur zu investieren, um ♕ und ♔ von Schwarz einzukreisen, dem sei 4.d4 ♕h4+ 5.g3 ♕d8 6.d:e5 ± nahegelegt, was Bücker selbst übrigens für die kritische Variante hält.

4...♗b4

4...d6(!) 5.d4 ♕g4 6.d:e5 d:e5 7.♗c4 ♗e6 =, Bücker.

Here should be room for improvements for White, 5.♗c4 ♘f6 6.0-0 ♕g4 7.d3

♗e7 is about equal too. But 5.♗e2!? (Δ ♘d5) may offer White some advantage:
Hier sollte es jedoch Raum für weiße Verbesserungen geben, 5.♗c4 ♘f6 6.0-0 ♕g4 7.d3 ♗e7 wäre gleichfalls etwa ausgeglichen. Jedoch könnte 5.♗e2!? (Δ ♘d5) dem Weißen einen gewissen Vorteil geben:
5...♕f6 6.d4 e:d4 (6...♗g4 7.0-0) 7.♗g5 ♕g6 8.♘d5 ±.

5.♗c4 ♗:c3 6.0-0!

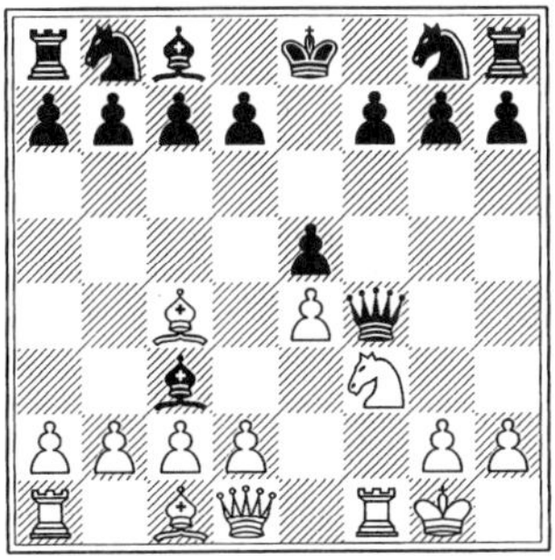

A

6...♗a5 7.d4 ♕:e4 8.♗:f7+!

Thematic, combining threats against both king and queen. Besides, the attack on f7 is what the King's gambit is all about!
Thematisch, verbindet Drohungen gegen König und Dame von Schwarz miteinander. Ganz davon abgesehen, um den Angriff auf f7 geht es ja im Königsgambit!

8...♔d8

8...♔f8? 9.♘g5 ♕:d4+ 10.♕:d4 e:d4 11.♗:g8+ ♔:g8 12.♘f7 ♗b4 13.♘:h8 ♔:h8 14.♗d2 ♗c5 15.b4 ♗d6 16.♖ae1 +–.

9.♗:g8!

The cleanest kill! Black's got no time to deviate since 10.♘g5 is also threatened.
Der klarste Gewinn. Schwarz erhält keine Gelegenheit auszuweichen, da 10.♘g5 auch noch droht.
9.♘:e5 ♗b6 10.♗:g8 ♕:e5 11.♖f8+ ♔e7 12.♖:c8 ♕:d4+ 13.♕:d4 ♗:d4+ 14.♔h1 ♔f6! 15.c3! ♗e5 16.h4! g5 (16...h6 Δ g5 looks like a more stubborn defence - *sieht nach einer hartnäckigeren Verteidigung aus*) 17.♗:g5+ ♔g7 18.♖f1 h6 (18...♖:g8 19.♗h6+) 19.♗f4! +–.

9...♖:g8 10.♗g5+ ♔e8 11.♘:e5 h6 12.♕h5+ g6 13.♕:h6 ♕:d4+ 14.♔h1 ♕:e5 15.♕h7 ♕g7

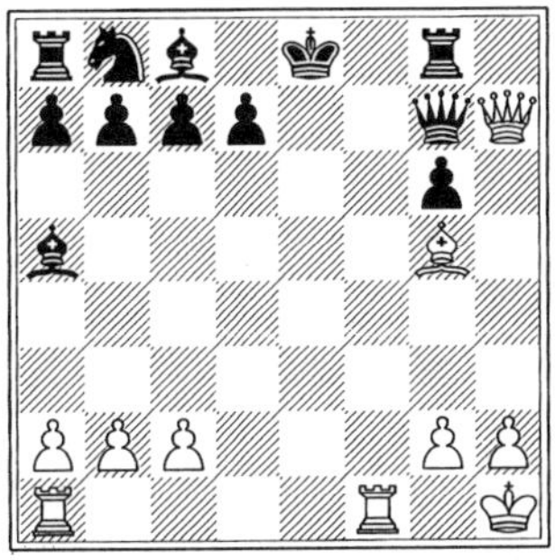

16.c3!! d5 17.♖ae1+ ♔d7 18.♖f7+ 1:0, Sanchez Almeyra - Lugo, Matanzas 1992.

B

(1.e4 e5 2.f4 ♕f6 3.♘c3 ♕:f4 4.♘f3 ♗b4 5.♗c4 ♗:c3 6.0-0)

6...♗d4+ 7.♘:d4 ♕:e4 8.♗:f7+ ♔d8 9.♘f5 ±.

C

(1.e4 e5 2.f4 ♕f6 3.♘c3 ♕:f4 4.♘f3 ♗b4 5.♗c4 ♗:c3 6.0-0)

6...♗b4 7.d4 ♕:e4

7...♕g4 8.♗:f7+ ♔d8 9.h3 ♕g3 10.♘:e5 ♘f6 11.♗f4 ♕h4 12.♘d3 ♗e7 13.g3 ♕:h3 14.♘f2 +–.

8.♗:f7+ ♔d8 9.c3! ♗e7 10.♘:e5

Δ ♖f4.

10...g5 11.g4!

Insisting on courting Her Majesty, now with ♖e1!
Umgarnt Ihre Majestät weiterhin! (Δ♖e1)

11...b6

11...h6 12.♗g6 +–.

12.♖e1 ♕b7 13.♗:g5 ±

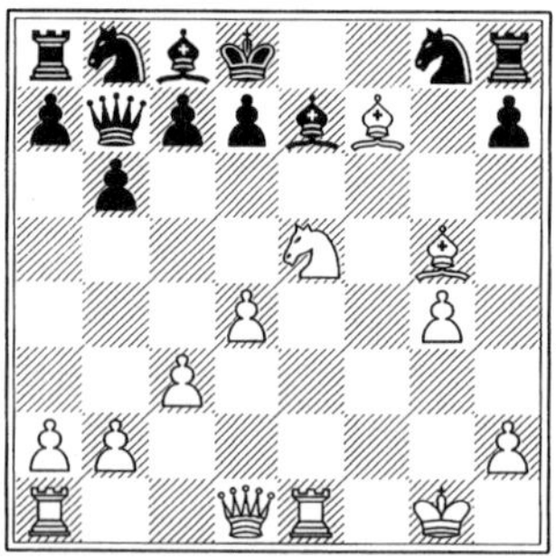

13...♗:g5? 14.♘c6+ d:c6 15.♖e8+ ♔d7 16.♕e2 +–.
On *(auf)* 13...♘f6 *(wirkt)* 14.♕e2 looks decisive *(entscheidend)*.

D

(1.e4 e5 2.f4 ♕f6 3.♘c3 ♕:f4 4.♘f3 ♗b4 5.♗c4 ♗:c3 6.0-0)

6...f6! 7.d:c3! ♕:e4

7...♕g4 8.♗f7+ ♔e7 9.h3! ♕g3 10.♘g5!? A strange-looking move, the knight doesn't threaten anything but it can't be taken and White's queen can now enter the action *(Ein merkwürdig aussehender Zug. Der Springer droht nichts, darf jedoch nicht geschlagen werden und ebnet der Dame den Weg zum Gefecht)*. 10...♘h6 (10...f:g5 11.♗:g8 ♖:g8 12.♖f3 ♕h4 13.♕d5 +–) 11.♕h5! d6 12.♗b3 ♗d7 13.♖:f6! ♗e8 14.♕f3 ♕e1+ 15.♕f1 ♕:f1 16.♖:f1 ±.

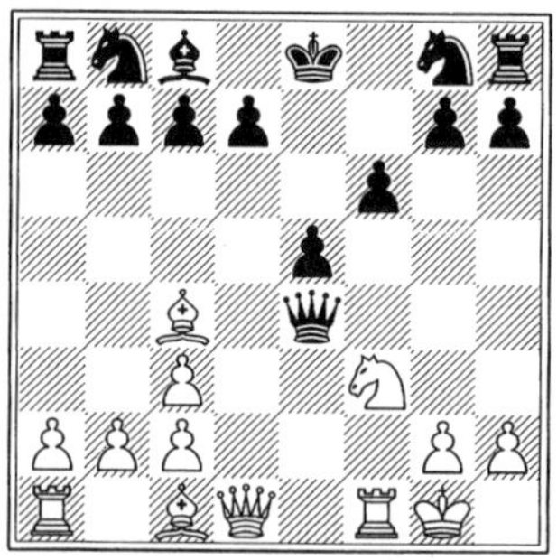

Position after 7...♕:e4/*Nach 7...♕:e4*

8.♘:e5! ♘e7

8...f:e5 9.♕h5+ g6 10.♗f7+ ♔d8 11.♗g5+ ♘e7 12.♗:e7+ ♔:e7 13.♕g5+ +–.

9.♖e1 ♕h4

9...♕f5 10.g4 ♕:e5 11.♖:e5 f:e5 12.♗g5 ±.

10.g3 ♕h3 11.♕e2 f:e5 12.♕:e5 ♘bc6 13.♕:g7 ♖f8 14.♗h6 ♕f5 15.♖f1 ♕c5+ 16.♔h1 ♖:f1+ 17.♖:f1 d5 18.♖f8+ ♔d7 19.♕g4+ +−.

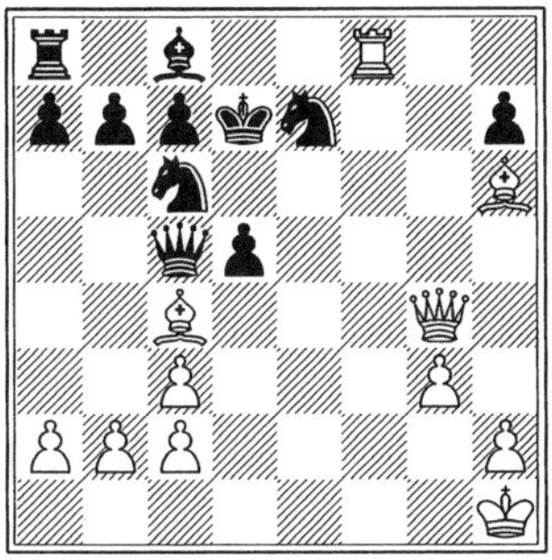

A long but more or less forced variation! *Eine lange, aber mehr oder weniger zwangsläufige Variante!*

I strongly recommend that you spend a few hours just making sure why some pieces can't be taken and how to continue the attack if the king takes a road less travelled by. It's not that hard and it will make it easier to reconstruct the theory that sunny day when you finally encounter this defence!

Ich empfehle Ihnen von Herzen, sich - auch wenn es einige Stunden lang dauert - selbst davon zu überzeugen, warum diese oder jene Figur nicht geschlagen werden darf und wie jeweils der Angriff zu führen ist. So schwer ist es nicht, und es wird Ihnen umso leichter fallen, sich der Varianten an jenem Glückstag zu entsinnen, an welchem Ihnen diese Verteidigung vorgesetzt wird!

Chapter II *Kapitel II*

King's Gambit Declined - Counter-Gambits
Abgel. Königsgambit - Die Gegengambits

1.e4 e5 2.f4

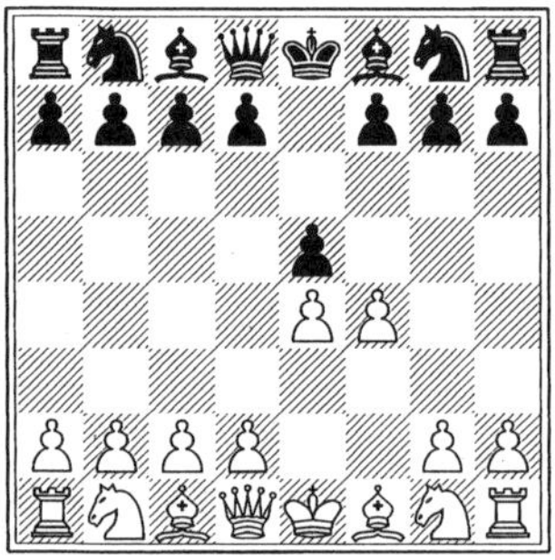

I

2...♘c6 3.♘f3 f5!?

3...d5?! 4.e:d5 ♕:d5 5.♘c3 ♕e6 6.♗b5! e:f4+ 7.♔f2 ♘e7? (7...♗e7 8.♖e1 ♕h6 9.d4 ♗d7 10.♘d5 ±, von Bardeleben), Blackburne - Ledger, Glasgow 1882, and here White should have played 8.d4! ± *(und nun sollte Weiß 8.d4! ± spielen).*

4.e:f5 e4!? ♥

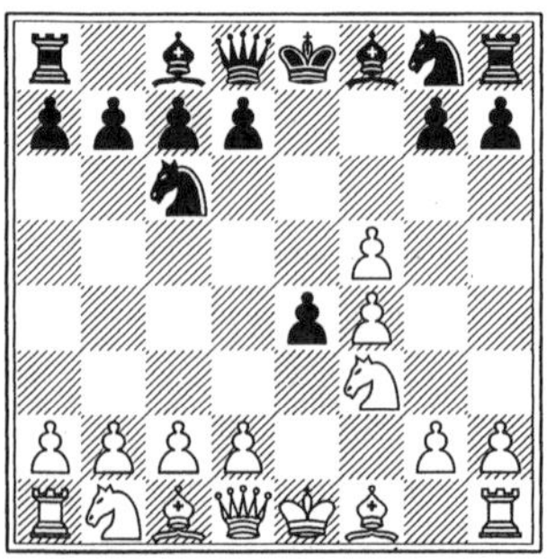

The Adelaide Counter-Gambit
Das Adelaide-Gegengambit.

In Wahls' article in NiC Yearbook 38, which this section is based on, he claims that it's the refutation of the King's gambit! When you've read this section you will probably wonder what the fuss is all about, since Black doesn't even have equality in any line!
Nevertheless it will increase in popularity partly simply because it's new and partly because most people tend to decline it with 4.d3 or not allow it with 3.♘c3. However, there hasn't been much action in this line lately as far as I know.

In Wahls' Artikel im NiC-Jahrbuch 38, auf dem der vorliegende Abschnitt beruht, behauptet der Autor, hiermit die Widerlegung des Königsgambits gefunden zu haben! Nachdem Sie diesen Abschnitt studiert haben, werden Sie sich allerdings fragen, wozu soviel Lärm um nichts!? Nicht einmal Ausgleich erreicht Schwarz hier in irgendeiner Variante.
Dennoch wird die Beliebtheit dieses Gegengambits steigen. Zum einen, weil es neu ist, und zum anderen, weil die meisten Weißspieler dazu neigen, das Gambit mit 4.d3 abzulehnen oder mit 3.♘c3 zu verhindern. Danach war jedoch - sowohl in theoretischer wie in praktischer Hinsicht - zuletzt nicht viel "los".

4...e:f4

This might actually be Black's best if he's determined to get a draw.
Zumindest im Remissinne wohl das Beste.

5.d4 (5.♕e2+!?) d5 6.♗:f4 (I can't help feeling that White can improve here. - *Mich läßt das Gefühl nicht los, daß Weiß sein Spiel hier verstärken kann.* 6.♗d3 looks interesting e.g. - *scheint interessant, z.B.* - 6...♗d6 7.0-0 ♕f6 8.♘c3 ♘ge7 9.♘e2± or - *oder* - 6...♕e7 7.♔f2 ♘f6 8.♘c3 ♘g4 9.♔f1±) 6...♗:f5 7.♗b5 (7.♗d3 is a good move according to Wahls, but then he illustrates with a variation where everything is traded down to an equal ending ... - *laut Wahls ist 7.♗d3 ein guter Zug. Anschließend führt er aber eine Variante an, bei dem das Spiel gnadenlos zu einem Remisendspiel abgeholzt wird* ...) 7...♗d6 8.♗:d6 (8.♗g5 ♘f6 9.0-0 Δ ♘e5 or - *oder* - 8...♗e7 9.♕e2 seems to give White something to work with, at least - *gibt Weiß zumindest eine Stellung, aus der man etwas machen könnte.* Black's best might be - *Möglicherweise die beste Antwort ist* - 8...♘e7 9.♘c3 h6 10.♗h4 g5 11.♗g3 ♗:g3+ 12.h:g3 ♕d6 13.♗:c6+ ♘:c6 14.♕e2+ ♘e7 15.0-0-0 0-0-0 16.♘e5 =/∞) 8...♕:d6 9.0-0 ♘ge7 10.♘h4 ♗d7 11.♘d2 0-0-0 (11...♘:d4 12.♕h5+ g6 13.♗:d7+ ♔:d7 14.♕g4+ ♘df5) 12.♘b3 g5 13.♘f3 ♘f5 14.♕d3 g4? 15.♗:c6 g:f3? (15...♗:c6 16.♕:f5 ♗d7 17.♕e5 g:f3 18.♕:d6 should be winning too, but Black can still feel some hope here ... *dürfte ebenfalls für Weiß gewinnen, doch bliebe dem Nachziehenden zumindest etwas Hoffnung*) 16.♗:d7+ ♕:d7 17.♘c5 ♕f7 18.♖:f3 1:0, Pigott - Gottschalk, Islington 1975.

5.♘e5

White's knight is forced to an att
central field, which is one of the r
why I don't fear this gambit.
Der weiße Springer wird auf ein a
liches Zentrumsfeld gezwungen
Grund dafür, daß ich dieses G
keineswegs fürchte.

A

5...♘f6

Wahls variation.
Die Wahls-Variante.

6.♘c3!

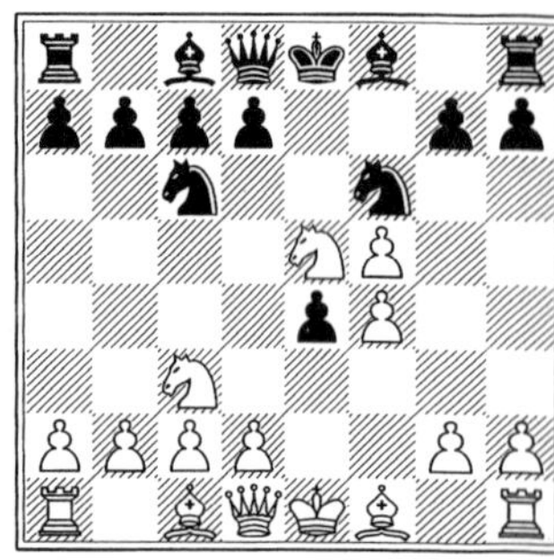

As usual in The King's Gambit, Bla
has a plethora of options:
Wie so oft im Königsgambit, h
Schwarz jetzt eine große Auswahl:

a

6...d5? 7.♗b5 ♕d6

7...♗d7 8.d3 +–.

8.g4± d4 9.g5 d:c3 10.g:f6 +–.

b

(1.e4 e5 2.f4 ♘c6 3.♘f3 f5 4.e:f5 e4 5.♘e5 ♘f6 6.♘c3)

6...♗c5? 7.♘:e4!

A central diversion making a blitzkrieg on the wing possible - an idea we'll see again and again!
Ein Ablenkungsmanöver im Zentrum ermöglicht einen Blitzkrieg am Königsflügel - eine Idee, die uns immer wieder begegnen wird!

7...♘:e4 8.♕h5+ g6 9.♘:g6

9.f:g6? ♗f2+ Δ ♕h4.

9...h:g6 10.♕:h8+ ♗f8 11.f:g6 ♕e7 12.♕h7 ♕e6 13.♕f7+ ♕:f7 14.g:f7+ ♔:f7 15.♗c4+ +−.

c

(1.e4 e5 2.f4 ♘c6 3.♘f3 f5 4.e:f5 e4 5.♘e5 ♘f6 6.♘c3)

6...♘d4? 7.♗c4 c6 8.♘f7 ♕b6 9.♘:h8 d5± 10.♗e2 ♗:f5 11.g4

11.d3 looks safer and more natural.
11.d3 macht einen natürlicheren und sichereren Eindruck.

11...♘:e2 12.g:f5 ♘d4 13.d3±.

d

(1.e4 e5 2.f4 ♘c6 3.♘f3 f5 4.e:f5 e4 5.♘e5 ♘f6 6.♘c3)

6...♗b4? 7.♗c4± ♗:c3

7...♕e7? 8.♘d5! ♕d6 9.♘:f6+ ♕:f6 10.♕h5+ +−.

8.d:c3 ♕e7 9.♘g4 d6 10.♘e3±.

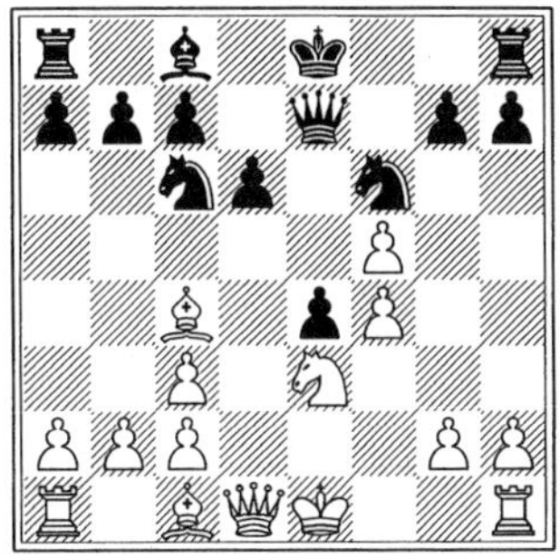

After a long journey this knight has found a wonderful place to dwell!
Nach einer langer Reise hat der Springer seinen Platz zum Wohlfühlen gefunden!

e

(1.e4 e5 2.f4 ♘c6 3.♘f3 f5 4.e:f5 e4 5.♘e5 ♘f6 6.♘c3)

6...♕e7? 7.♘g4! ♘:g4 8.♕:g4 ♘d4 9.♕h5+ ♔d8 10.♘d5 ♕d6 11.♕g5+ ♔e8 12.♘e3±.

f

(1.e4 e5 2.f4 ♘c6 3.♘f3 f5 4.e:f5 e4 5.♘e5 ♘f6 6.♘c3)

6...d6 7.♘:c6 b:c6 8.d3 ♗:f5 9.d:e4 ♘:e4 10.♘:e4 ♗:e4 11.♗d3 ♗:d3

11...♗:g2? 12.♕h5+ g6 13.♗:g6+ h:g6 14.♕:g6+ ♔d7 15.♕g4+ ♔e8 16.♕:g2 +−, 11...♕h4+ 12.g3 ♕e7 13.0-0 ♗:d3 14.♕:d3 ♕d7±.

12.♕:d3 ♕h4+ 13.g3 ♕e7 14.♗e3 ♕f7 15.♗d4

15.0-0±.

15...c5 16.♗c3 ♗e7 17.0-0-0

17.♕b5+!?. Why allow castling?! - *Wie-*

so dem Nachziehenden die Rochade erlauben?!

17...0-0 18.♖he1 ♖fe8 19.♔b1 ±.

g

(1.e4 e5 2.f4 ♘c6 3.♘f3 f5 4.e:f5 e4 5.♘e5 ♘f6 6.♘c3)

6...♗d6

So this 'beginner's move' is supposedly the refutation of the King's Gambit?!
Dieser "Anfängerzug" soll also die Widerlegung des Königsgambits darstellen?!

7.d4 ♗b4 8.♗e2 ♘d5(!)

- 8...d6?! 9.♘:c6 b:c6 10.0-0 h5 (10...♗:f5 would run into 11.g4! - *würde in 11.g4! hereinlaufen*) 11.♘:e4!? or *(oder)* 11.♗d2 Δ ♘:e4.
- 8...0-0 9.d5
- 8...♘e7 9.0-0 d6 (9...0-0 10.g4!) 10.♗h5+! ♔f8 11.♘f7 ♕e8 12.♘:h8 ♘:h5 13.♘:e4 ♗:f5 14.♘g5 ±. Play might continue: *(Es könnte folgen:)* 14...h6 15.♘gf7 ♘f6 16.c3 ♗a5 17.b4 ♗b6 18.c4 and both the black-squared bishop and d6 are in dire straits *(und sowohl der schwarzfeldrige Läufer als auch der ♙d6 sind in Nöten)*.

9.♗c4!

S. Bücker.

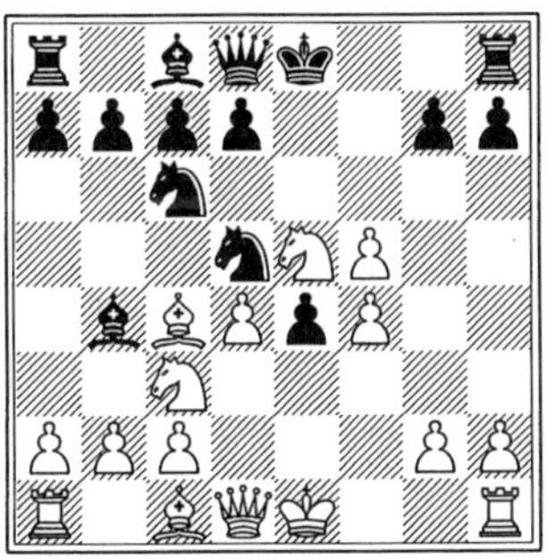

If your opponent breaks a general rule - like moving the same piece twice in the opening - you're justified in breaking the same rule yourself! I think it was Alekhine who said something like that. Anyway, it's a nice rule about breaking rules!
Wenn Ihr Kontrahent gegen allgemeine Prinzipien verstößt - etwa indem er in der Eröffnungsphase zweimal dieselbe Figur zieht -, haben Sie durchaus das Recht, dasselbe zu tun! Ich denke, Aljechin war der erste, der sich dahingehend geäußert hatte. Jedenfalls ist dies eine schöne Regel über das Brechen von Regeln!

Wahls only considers *(Wahls berücksichtigt lediglich)* 9.♗h5+ ♔f8 10.♘f7 ♕f6 ∞.

9...♕h4+

9...♘:c3? 10.♕h5+ ♔e7 11.♕f7+ ♔d6 12.b:c3 ♗:c3+ 13.♔d1 ♕f8 14.♗a3+ ♘b4 15.♕d5+ ♔e7 16.♕:e4+ +−.

10.g3 ♘:c3 11.b:c3 ♗:c3+ 12.♗d2 ♗:d2+ 13.♕:d2 ♕f6 14.♗f7+

14.♕e3! seems even stronger e.g: *(scheint noch stärker zu sein, z.B.:)* 14...♕:f5 15.♗d5! ♘:e5 16.f:e5 ♖f8 17.♗:e4 ♕h5 18.♔d2 c5 19.d5 b6 20.d6 ♖b8 21.♖af1 ♖:f1 22.♖:f1 ♗a6 23.♖f2 ♗c4 24.♕f4 ♕h6 25.♗:h7 ♕:f4 26.♖:f4 ♗f7 27.h4 +−, Johansson - Computer (blitz).

14...♔f8 15.♗d5 ♕:f5 16.0-0 d6 17.g4 ♕f6 18.♘:c6

Since the knight isn't really threatened yet White may have time to pick up a pawn with 18.♗:e4!?; or try to trap the ♖a8 with 18.♖ab1!?.
Da der ♘e5 nicht wirklich bedroht ist, könnte sich Weiß die Zeit nehmen, mit

18.♗:e4!? einen Bauern zu schlagen oder mit 18.♖ab1!? zu verhindern, daß der ♖a8 ins Spiel kommt.

18...b:c6 19.♗:c6 ♖b8 20.f5± (Bücker).

B

(1.e4 e5 2.f4 ♘c6 3.♘f3 f5 4.e:f5 e4 5.♘e5)

5...♘:e5!?

Miles variation
Die Miles-Variante.

6.f:e5 ♕e7

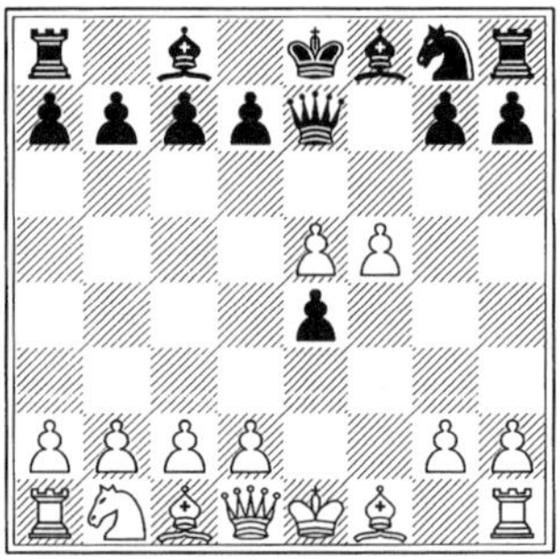

7.♕h5+ ♔d8 8.♗c4

The stem game Gallagher - Wohl, Kuala Lumpur 1992 went *(Die Stammpartie Gallagher - Wohl, Kuala Lumpur 1992, verlief wie folgt:)* 8.d4 e:d3 9.♗:d3 ♕:e5+ 10.♔d1 ♘f6 11.♕f3 and Black got the better game but White still won in 62 moves *(wonach Schwarz das bessere Spiel erhielt, dennoch 1:0/62.)*. I thought *(Zunächst hielt ich ...)* 11.♗g5 ♕:b2 12.♕f7 ♕:a1 13.c3 looked interesting until I realized that Black can postpone taking the rook and play *(... für interessant, bis mir klar wurde, daß Schwarz das Schlagen des Turmes aufschiebt und zunächst ...)* 12....c6! 13.c3 ♔c7! −+ *(... spielt).*

8...♕:e5 9.♗:g8 g6

9...♖:g8? 10.♕:h7 ♕d5 11.♘c3 ♕f7 12.♘e4 +−.

10.♕h3!

Bücker.

10.♕h4+ ♗e7 11.♕h6 ♖:g8 12.♕:h7 ♖h8 13.♕:g6 d5 ∞. But why let Black gain a tempo? *(Wieso dem Schwarzen ein Tempo schenken?)*

10...♖:g8 11.♕:h7 ♖h8 12.♕:g6 d5 13.♖f1 ♖:h2 14.♘c3 c6

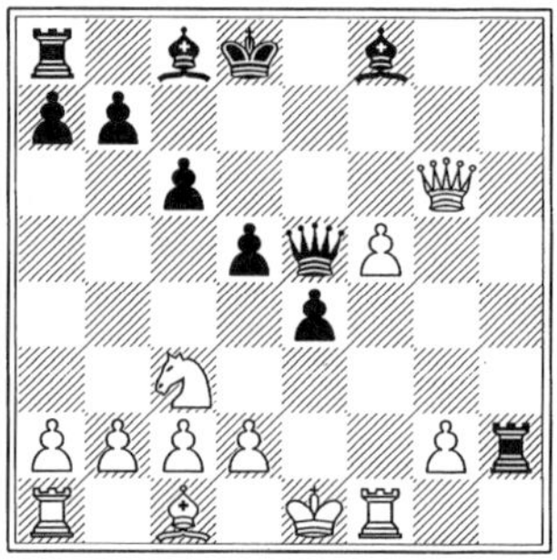

15.d4!?

15.Se2.

15...e:d3+ 16.♔d1 d:c2+ 17.♔:c2 ♗d7 18.♗d2 ♗e8 19.♕g4 ♗h5 20.♕g5+ ±

e.g: *(z.B.:)* 20...♗e7 (20...♕e7 21.♕g3 ♕h7 22.♗f4! +−) 21.♕g8+ ♗e8 22.f6! ♗:f6 23.♖ae1.

II

(1.e4 e5 2.f4)

2...d5 3.e:d5 e4 ♥

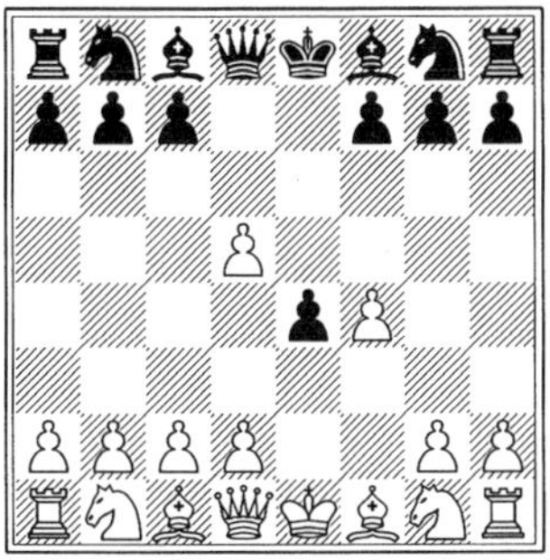

The Falkbeer Counter-Gambit
Das Falkbeer-Gegengambit.

A gambit which has lost it's attraction among the top players, since White ends up with an advantageous endgame in most variations. However, it's still very popular among ordinary mortals, because 2...d5 looks like a strong active blow in the centre, besides, it's often used to transpose into the Modern or the Nimzowitsch Counter-Gambit which are two of the most common defences for Black together with 3...g5 and 2...♗c5.

Dieses Gambit hat unter Spitzenspielern seine Anziehungskraft eingebüßt, da Weiß in den meisten Varianten Endspielvorteil behält. Unter gewöhnlichen Sterblichen ist seine Beliebtheit jedoch ungebrochen, zumal 2...d5 wie ein starker Schlag gegen das weiße Zentrum anmutet. Davon abgesehen, wird 2...d5 häufig gebraucht, um zur Modernen Verteidigung oder Nimzowitschs Gegengambit überzuleiten - was beides, gemeinsam mit 3...g5 und 2...♗c5, zu den beliebtesten Verteidigungsmethoden gehört.

- 3...♗c5 (Δ 4.♘f3 e4 5.♘e5 ♘h6! Δ ...f6) 4.♘c3! ♘h6 5.♘f3 ♗g4 6.f:e5 ♘f5, Hebden - Miles, England 1981, 7.♗d3! ♘d4 (7...♘h4 8.♕e2) 8.♗e2 ♘f5 9.♘e4 Miles.
- 3...e:f4 transposes to the Modern defence or the Nimzowitsch.
mit Überleitung zur Modernen Verteidigung oder zum Nimzowitsch-Gegengambit.
- 3...♕:d5 4.♘c3 ♕a5
This is actually unmentioned by theory as far as I know, but I've faced it several times in blitz. I think White should keep the tension with 5.♘f3! e.g.
Findet sich meines Wissens in der Tat nicht in den Büchern, ich wurde damit aber gelegentlich im "Blitzen" konfrontiert. M.E. sollte Weiß die Zentrumsspannung mit 5.♘f3! aufrechterhalten, z.B.:
5...e:f4 6.♗b5+ c6 7.♕e2+ ♘e7 8.♗c4 ±.

4.d3!

It's important to consistently challenge Black's control of e4.
Es ist wichtig, konsequent die schwarze Kontrolle über d4 zu unterminieren.

A

4...e:d3

- 4...f5? 5.d:e4 f:e4 6.♕h5+ g6 7.♕e5+ ♕e7 8.♕:h8 ♘f6 9.f5 ♔d7! 10.♗b5+ c6 11.d6! (Δ ♗g5) +–, Johansson - Sörensson, Malmö 1996.
- 4...e3? 5.♕f3
This seems most prudent, since 5.c4 c6 gives Black some activity and 5.♗:e3 ♘f6 (Δ ♗d6, 0-0, ♖e8) gives Black some initiative on the e-file.

Der umsichtigste Zug. 5.c4 c6 würde Schwarz einige Aktivität geben, und 5.♗:e3 ♘f6 (Δ♗d6, 0-0, ♖e8) gäbe dem Nachziehenden Initiative auf der f-Linie. 5...♘f6 6.♘c3 c6 (6...♗c5 7.♘e4!) 7.♕:e3 ♗e7 8.d6 (the greedy 8.d:c6 may be good too, but here Black will still have some hope of counter-play - *das habgierige 8.d:c6 mag ebenfalls gut sein, überließe dem schwarzen jedoch Hoffnungen auf Gegenspiel*) 8...♕:d6 9.♘e4!, and White will be a pawn up for nothing *(und Weiß behält ersatzlos einen Bauern mehr).*

5.♗:d3 ♕:d5

5...♘f6 6.♘c3 ♗e7 (6...♘:d5 7.♗b5+) 7.♘f3 0-0 8.0-0 ♘bd7 9.♗c4 ♘b6 10.♗b3 ♗b4 11.♘e5 ♗:c3 12.b:c3 ♘b:d5 13.♗a3 ♖e8 14.♕d4 ±, Keres - Lilienthal, Moscow 1941.

6.♘c3 ♕e6+

6...♗b4 (6...♕:g2? 7.♗e4) 7.♗d2 ♗:c3 8.♕e2+! ±.

7.♘ge2 ♘h6 8.f5! ♘:f5 9.0-0 ♘e3 10.♗:e3 ♕:e3+ 11.♔h1 ♗d6 12.♘f4

With such an enormous lead in development, the position plays itself!
Mit solch einem gewaltigen Entwicklungsvorsprung spielt sich die Stellung von alleine!

12...0-0 13.♕h5 g6

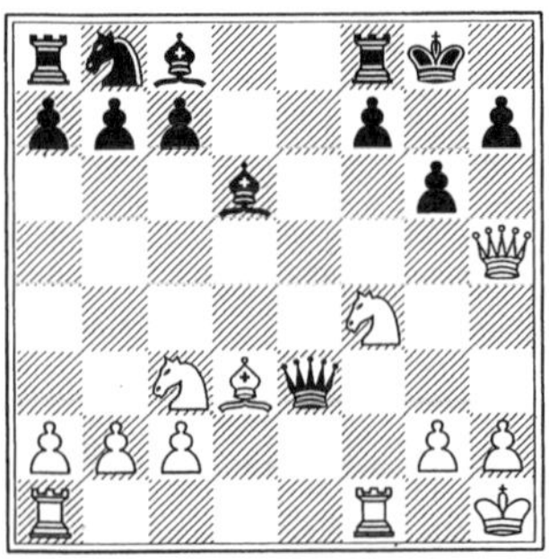

14.♘:g6! h:g6 15.♗:g6 f:g6 16.♕:g6+ ♔h8 17.♘d5 ♖:f1+ 18.♖:f1 ♕e2 19.♕h6+ ♔g8 20.♘f6+ 1:0 (20...♔f7 21.♕h7+ ♔e6 22.♕g8+), Murey - Nikitin, UdSSR 1970.

B

(1.e4 e5 2.f4 d5 3.e:d5 e4 4.d3)

4...♕:d5 5.♕e2 ♘f6

5...f5 (5...♗f5 6.g4) 6.♘c3 ♗b4 7.♗d2 ♗:c3 8.♗:c3 ♘f6 9.0-0-0! (or - *oder* - 9.d:e4 ♕:e4 [9...f:e4 10.♕c4, 9...♘:e4 10.♗:g7] 10.♕:e4+ f:e4 11.♗c4 ± Keres) 9...♕:a2 10.d:e4 ♘:e4 11.b3 0-0 12.♕c4+ ♔h8 13.♗b2 → (Reti).

6.♘c3

Targeting both queen and the VIP (Very Important Pawn) on e4, forcing Black to give up the bishop pair.
Nimmt die Dame und auch den VIP (Very Important Pawn) auf e4 ins Visier, was Schwarz zwingt, das Läuferpaar aufzugeben.

Some books recommend:
Einige Bücher empfehlen:
6.♘d2 ♗f5 7.de4 ♗:e4 8.g4 ♗e7 9.♘:e4 ♕:e4 10.♗g2! ♕:e2+ 11.♘:e2 c6 12.g5 ±, but don't mention: *(erwähnen aber nicht)* 8...♘c6!? 9.♗g2 0-0-0 10.♘:e4 ♘d4 11.♘:f6 ♕a5 12.♗d2 ♘:c2 13.♔d1 ♗b4 14.♘f3 ♘:a1 15.♘e4.
Leach quotes it as unclear but I, and probably most of you readers too, I guess, would rather play Black in this position!
"Unklar" laut Leach, ich hingegen - und wie ich vermute, die meisten Leser ebenfalls - würde hier lieber mit Schwarz spielen!

So I decided to recommend something more easily played and that is 6.♘c3! which soon enters a better endgame for White. As you will see again and again, the antidote to the Falkbeer is a better endgame!
Somit habe ich mich entschieden, etwas pflegeleichteres zu empfehlen, und dies ist 6.♘c3!, was bald zu einem besseren Endspiel für Weiß führt. Wie immer wieder zu sehen sein wird - das beste Gegengift gegen das Falkbeer-Gambit ist das bessere Endspiel!

6...♗b4 7.♗d2 ♗:c3 8.♗:c3 ♗g4

- 8...♘bd7 9.d:e4! ♘:e4 10.♗:g7 ♖g8 11.♖d1 (or - *oder* - 11.♗e5 ♘:e5 12.f:e5 ♕:e5 13.0-0-0 ♗e6 ± Kortchnoi) 11...♕e6 12.♗e5 f5 13.♕h5 ±.
- 8...0-0 9.♗:f6 e:d3 10.♕:d3 ♕:d3 (10...♖e8+ 11.♗e5 ±) 11.♗:d3 g:f6 12.0-0-0 ±, e.g. *(z.B.)* 12...♘c6 13.♗e4, 12...♗g4 13.♖e1 Δ h3, 12...♗e6 13.♘e2 Δ f5, ♘c3.

9.d:e4!

The beginning of a wonderful ending, and finally getting rid of the VIP!
Damit brechen herrliche Zeiten im Endspiel an. Und der VIP ist beseitigt!

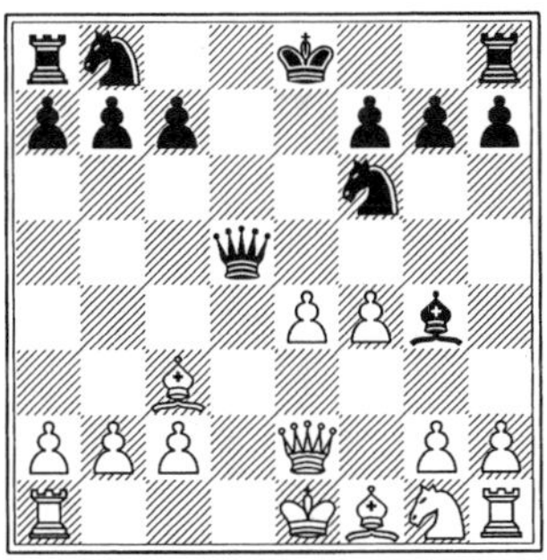

a

9...♕:e4 10.♕:e4 ♘:e4 11.♗:g7 ♖g8 12.♗e5 ♘c6 13.♗d3

13.♘f3!?.

13...♘:e5 14.♗:e4 ♘c4 15.♗:b7! ♖b8 16.♗c6+

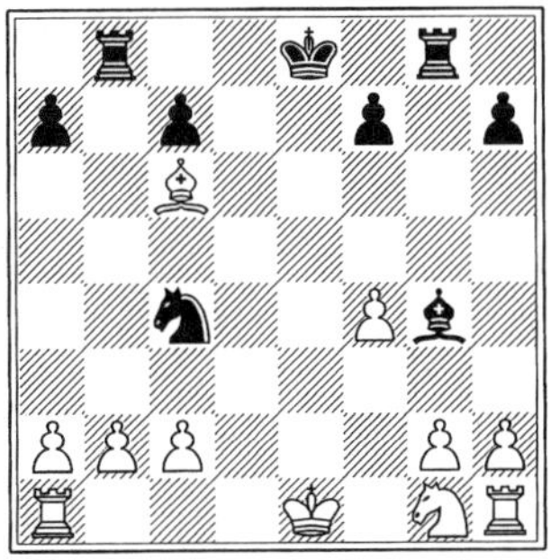

- 16...♗d7 17.♗:d7+ ♔:d7 18.0-0-0+ ±, e.g. *(z.B.)* 18...♔c8 19.b3 ♘e3 20.♖d3 ♘:g2 21.♖g3.
- 16...♔e7 17.b3 ♖b6 18.♗f3! ♗:f3 19.♘:f3 ♘e3 20.♔f2 ±.

b

(1.e4 e5 2.f4 d5 3.e:d5 e4 4.d3 ♕:d5 5.♕e2 ♘f6 6.♘c3 ♗b4 7.♗d2 ♗:c3 8.♗:c3 ♗g4 9.d:e4)

9...♗:e2 10.e:d5 ♗:f1

10...♗g4 11.♗:f6 g:f6 12.♗e2 ♖g8 13.♔f2 ±.

11.♔:f1 ♘:d5 12.♗:g7 ♖g8 13.♖e1+ ♔d7 14.♖d1 ♔c6

14...♔e6 15.f5+!.

15.♗d4 ♘:f4 16.♘f3 ♘d7 17.g3 ♘e6

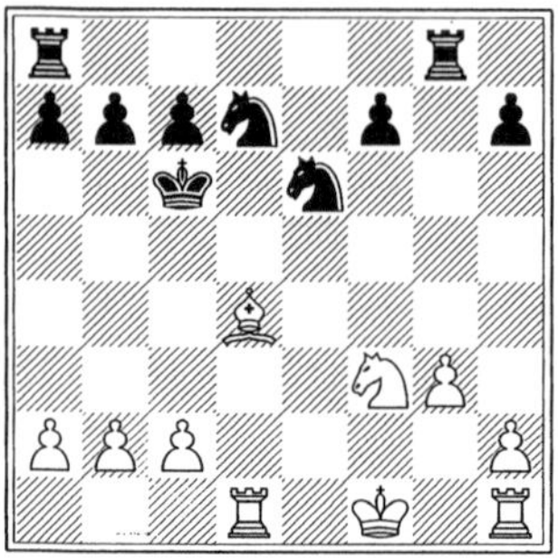

18.♗e3 ±

Or *(oder)* 18.♔f2 ± ♘g5 19.♘:g5 ♖:g5 20.♖he1 ♘f8 21.♖e7 ♖f5+ 22.♔e3 ♘g6 23.♖e4 ♖d8 24.g4 ♖e5 25.♖f1 ♖:e4+ 26.♔:e4 ♖e8+ 27.♔f5 ♖e6 28.♔g5 1:0, Reti - Spielmann, Stockholm 1919.

18...b6 19.♔g2 ♖ae8 20.♖hf1 f5 21.♘h4 ♘g7 22.♗d4 ♖e2+ 23.♖f2 ♖:f2+ 24.♔:f2 ♘e8 25.♖e1! ♘d6 26.♖e7 ♘f8 27.♗e5 ♘g6 28.♗:d6 ♘:e7 29.♗:e7 ♔d5 30.♔f3 ♔e6 31.♗b4 ♖d8 32.♔e2 ♔f6 33.♗c3+ ♔g5 34.h3 ♖e8+ 35.♔f2 ♖d8 36.♘f3+ ♔h5 37.♘d4 ♔g6 38.♘e6 ♖d1 39.♘:c7 ♖c1 40.♔f3 ♖:c2 41.♘b5 a6 42.♘c7 a5 43.a4 ♖c1 44.♘d5 ♖f1+ 45.♔g2 1:0, Bronstein - Szabo, Moscow 1949.

c

(1.e4 e5 2.f4 d5 3.e:d5 e4 4.d3 ♕:d5 5.♕e2 ♘f6 6.♘c3 ♗b4 7.♗d2 ♗:c3 8.♗:c3 ♗g4 9.d:e4)

9...♕e6 10.♕c4 ♕e7?!

10...♕:c4.

11.♗d3 ♘c6 12.♘f3 0-0-0 13.0-0 ♗e6 14.♕a4 ♕c5+ 15.♔h1 ♘g4 16.♗e1 f6 17.b4 ♕h5

17...♕e3 or *(oder)* 17...♕d6 is safer *(wären sicherer)*.

18.♗g3 ♔b8 19.b5 ♘e7 20.f5 ♗f7 21.♖ab1 ♘c8 22.♘d4! ♖d6 23.♘c6+ ♔a8 24.b6! ♖:c6

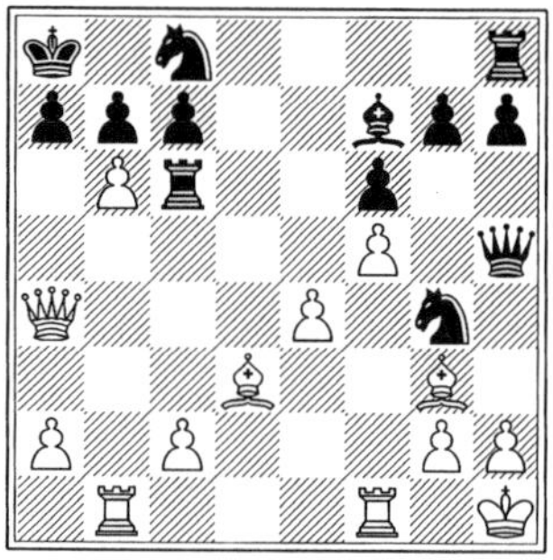

25.♕:c6!! ♘:b6 26.♕:c7 ♖c8 27.♕d6 ♘e3 28.♖:b6 ♘:f1 29.♗:f1 ♗e8 30.♖:b7 ♔:b7 31.♕a6+ 1:0, Spielmann - Wadling, Västerås 1940.

C

(1.e4 e5 2.f4 d5 3.e:d5 e4 4.d3)

4...♘f6 5.d:e4 ♘:e4 6.♘f3 ♗c5

- 6...♗e7!? 7.♗e3 (A better try would be 7.♘bd2! As usual White should fight for e4! e.g.: - *Ein besserer Ansatz wäre 7.♘bd2! Wie gewöhnlich sollte Weiß um e4 kämpfen! z.B.: 7...*♗h4+?! 8.g3 ♘:g3 9.♗b5+ c6 10.h:g3 ♗:g3+ 11.♔f1 c:b5 12.♘e4!) 7...0-0 8.♘c3 ♘:c3 9.b:c3 ♗f6 10.♕d2 ♘d7 ∞/∓, Gallagher - Meyers, Passau 1993.
- 6...c6 7.♘bd2! ♘:d2 8.♗:d2 ♕:d5 9.♗d3 ±.
- 6...♗f5 7.♗e3 c6 (7...♗e7 8.♗c4 ♗h4+?! 9.g3 ♗f6 10.♘d4 ±, 1:0/28., Hölscher - Berg, Gausdal 1995) 8.♗c4 b5 9.♗b3 c5 10.d6! (Concrete calcu-

lation, Alekhine's trademark, ensuring White of a clear pawn up - *Konkrete Berechnung - Aljechins Markenzeichen - sichert ihm einen klaren Mehrbauern).* 10...c4 11.♕d5 ♘d7 12.♕:f5 ♘:d6 13.♕d5±, Alekhine - Tarrasch, Sankt Petersburg 1914.

7.♕e2

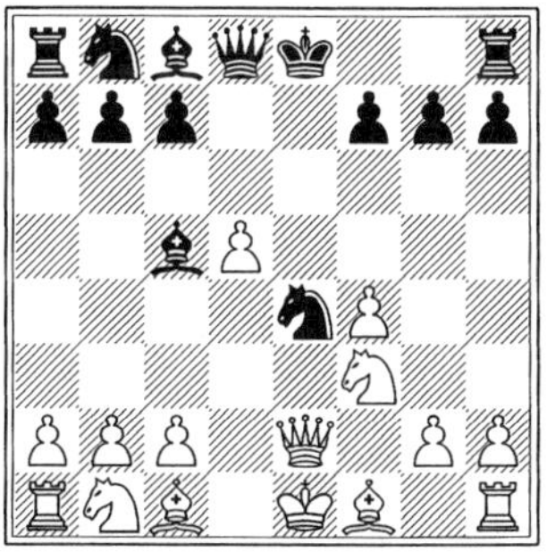

a

7...♗f2+? ♥

Most likely Black's most common mistake in the Falkbeer.
Wahrscheinlich der am meisten verbreiteste Fehler im Falkbeer-Gambit.

8.♔d1 ♕:d5+ 9.♘fd2! f5 10.♘c3 ♕d4 11.♘:e4 f:e4 12.c3 ♕e3 13.♕h5+ ±

There is of course nothing wrong with the ending a pawn up either, e.g:
Ebensogut kann Weiß natürlich in ein Endspiel mit Mehrbauer abwickeln, z.B.: 13.♘:e4 ♕:e2+ 14.♗:e2 ♗b6 15.a4 ♘c6 16.♖e1 ♗f5 17.♗h5+ ±, Yoos - Björnsson, Reykjavik 1996.

b

(1.e4 e5 2.f4 d5 3.e:d5 e4 4.d3 ♘f6 5.d:e4 ♘:e4 6.♘f3 ♗c5 7.♕e2)

7...♕:d5?

Also a very common mistake similar to a) above, be sure to study these and you won't miss an easy point in the future!
Ganz ähnlich wie a) ein sehr verbreiteter Fehlgriff. Studieren Sie diese Varianten, und Sie werden an einem in Zukunft möglichen leichten Punkt nicht achtlos vorbeigehen!

8.♘fd2! ♔d8 9.♘:e4 ♖e8 10.♘bc3 ♗b4

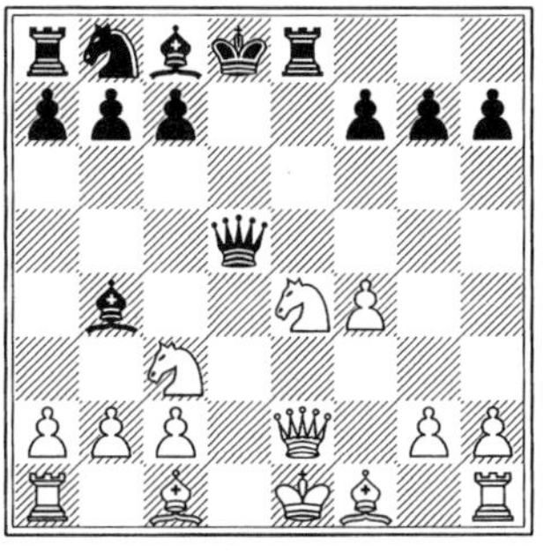

11.♗e3!

A very useful move in most variations of the Falkbeer, as you've probably noticed!
Ein im Falkbeer-Gambit zumeist sehr nützlicher Zug, wie Sie wahrscheinlich schon bemerkt haben!

11...♗d7 12.♔f2 ♕a5 13.♖d1 f5 14.♘g5 ♘c6 15.♕d3 ♖e7 1:0, P. Bücker - Schuh, Dortmund 1989.

16.♘d5 is of course decisive.
16.♘d5 ist natürlich entscheidend.

c

(1.e4 e5 2.f4 d5 3.e:d5 e4 4.d3 ♘f6 5.d:e4 ♘:e4 6.♘f3 ♗c5 7.♕e2)

7...f5 8.♗e3

8.♘fd2 also looks good since 8...♕:d5 or 8...♗f2+ will transpose to the variations above.
8.♘fd2 wirkt gleichfalls stark, zumal 8...♕:d5 oder 8...♗f2+ zu den ebengenannten Varianten überleitet.

8...♕:d5 9.♗:c5 ♕:c5 10.♘c3 ±, Spielmann - Wolf, Düsseldorf 1908.

d

(1.e4 e5 2.f4 d5 3.e:d5 e4 4.d3 ♘f6 5.d:e4 ♘:e4 6.♘f3 ♗c5 7.♕e2)

7...♕e7 8.♗e3 ♗:e3 9.♕:e3 ♘d7 10.♘bd2 ♘df6 11.♘:e4 ♘:e4 12.0-0-0 0-0 13.♗d3 ±.

e

(1.e4 e5 2.f4 d5 3.e:d5 e4 4.d3 ♘f6 5.d:e4 ♘:e4 6.♘f3 ♗c5 7.♕e2)

7...0-0!?

This was formerly thought to be a mistake, nowadays it seems to be Black's best chance!
Früher hielt man dies für einen Fehlgriff, heutezutage scheint dies die beste Chance für Schwarz zu sein!

8.♕:e4 ♖e8 9.♘e5 f6

Now White has three options and I'm not completely certain which is best of them:
Weiß hat nun drei Möglichkeiten, und ich könnte nicht mit Sicherheit sagen, welches die stärkste ist:

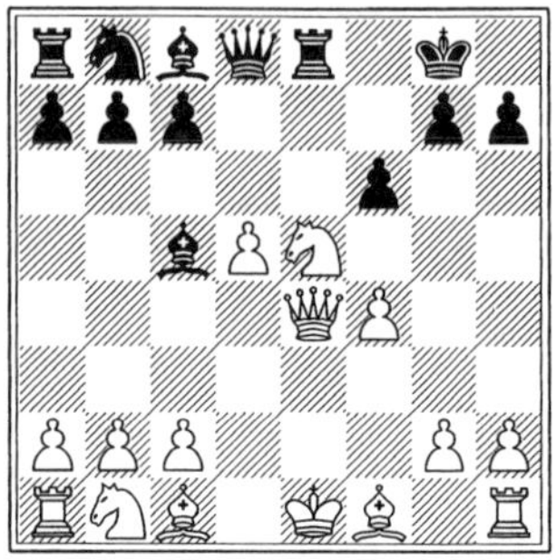

e1

10.♗d3 g6 11.♕c4! ♘a6!

Bücker.
11...♗d6? 12.0-0 f:e5 13.f5!, 11...♕d6? 12.♘c3 Δ ♘e4, Bilguer.

12.♘c3

12.b4!?/?! b5 (12...♗:b4+ 13.♘d2 b5 14.♕b3 f:e5 15.0-0 c6 ∞ Bücker) 13.♕b3 ♘:b4 14.♗:b5 ♗d7 15.♗:d7 ♕:d7 16.d6+ ♔g7 17.♗e3 ♖:e5 18.f:e5 ♗:e3 19.♕:b4 f:e5 20.♕e4 +–, Werner - Marder, Stockholm 1994 (½:½ ⊕).

12...f:e5

12...b5!? 13.♘:b5 f:e5 14.♘c3 e:f4+ 15.♗e2! ♘b4 ∞ Bücker.

13.♘e4 e:f4 14.♗:f4 ♕f6

14...b5! Bücker, e.g. *(z.B.)* 15.♕b3 ♗f5 16.d6+ ♔g7 17.♕c3+ ♔g8 18.d:c7 ∞: 18...♕c8 19.♗e5 or *(oder)* 19.0-0-0, 18...♕d5 19.0-0-0 ♗:e4 20.♗:b5 Δ ♗c4.

15.d6+ ♔g7 16.♗d2 b5 17.♕c3 ♗d4 18.0-0-0! ♗:c3 19.♗:c3 ♕:c3 20.♘:c3 c6 ± (1:0/40.), Joakimidis - Messedi, Graz 1981.

e2

(1.e4 e5 2.f4 d5 3.e:d5 e4 4.d3 ♘f6 5.d:e4 ♘:e4 6.♘f3 ♗c5 7.♕e2 0-0 8.♕:e4 ♖e8 9.♘e5 f6)

10.d6! ♕:d6

Another move order *(eine andere Zugfolge ist)* is 10...♗e6 11.♗c4 ♕:d6 (11...♘c6? 12.d7 +–).

11.♗c4+

Or *(oder)* 11.♗e3.

11...♗e6 12.♗e3!

Black has to be well booked up just to survive in this variation!
Schwarz muß bestens präpariert sein, um hier knapp zu überleben.

12.♗:e6+ ♕:e6 13.♘c3 ♘d7! 14.♗d2 f:e5 15.f5 ♕f7 16.0-0-0 ♘f6! 17.♕:b7 e4 18.♗g5, Kindermann - Eckert, Bundesliga 1979, here Black should've played: *(und nun hätte Schwarz spielen sollen:)* 18...♖ab8 19.♕c6 ♕c4! 20.♕a4 ♖b4 –+ Bücker.

12...♗:e3

12...♘d7 13.f5 ♕:e5 14.♕:e5 ♘:e5 15.♗e6+ ♖:e6 16.f:e6 ♗:e3 17.♘c3 ±.

13.f5!

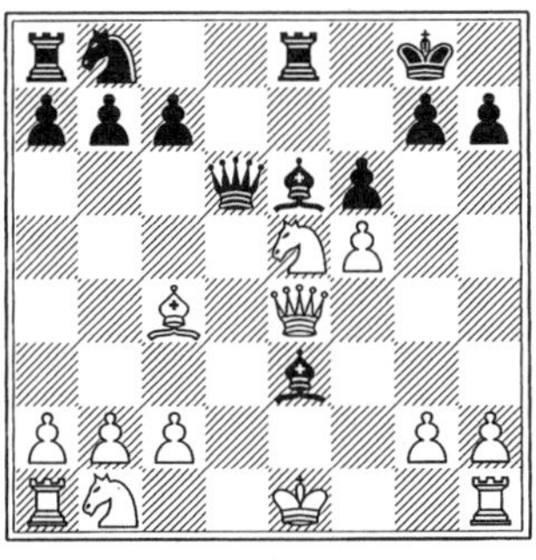

13...♕d4

The only move *(Der einzige Zug)*.

14.♕:d4 ♗:d4 15.♗:e6 ♖:e6 16.f:e6 ♗:b2 17.♘d3 ♗:a1 18.c3 a5! 19.a4 c6 20.♔f2!? b5 21.a:b5 c:b5 22.♖c1 b4 23.c:b4 ♔f8! ± Bücker.

However, there seems to be a third, little known but quite promising, option for White; the unpretentious 10.♗b5! which, as far as I can tell, wins some material without giving Black too much compensation e.g:
Es gibt jedoch eine dritte, zwar kaum bekannte, doch vielversprechende Alternative: Das bescheidene 10.♗b5!, was, soweit ich sagen kann, etwas Material gewinnt, ohne dem Nachziehenden sehr viel Kompensation zu geben:

e3

(1.e4 e5 2.f4 d5 3.e:d5 e4 4.d3 ♘f6 5.d:e4 ♘:e4 6.♘f3 ♗c5 7.♕e2 0-0 8.♕:e4 ♖e8 9.♘e5 f6)

10.♗b5!

This disturbs Black's piece coordination and thereby sharpens the ideas known from e*1)* and e*2)*:
*Stört die Koordination der schwarzen Figuren und pointiert damit die aus **e1)*** and ***e2)** bekannten Ideen:*

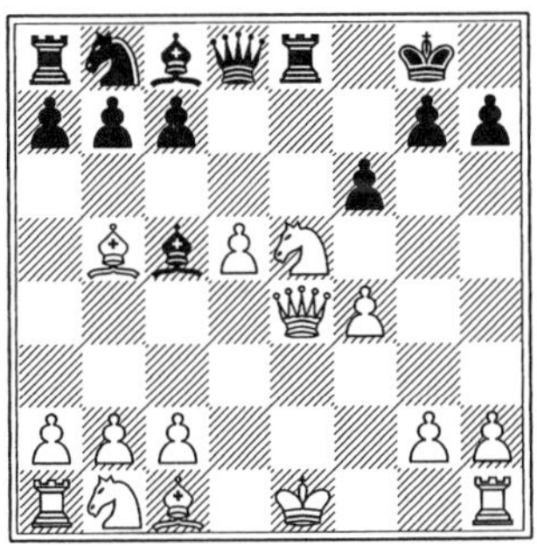

- **10...♖e7**

On 10...c6? both 11.♗d3 and 11.d:c6 should give White a clear advantage.
Nach 10...c6? sollte Weiß sowohl mit 11.♗d3 als auch durch 11.d:c6 klaren Vorteil erhalten.

11.d6 c:d6 12.♗c4+ d5 13.♗:d5+ ♔f8 14.♖f1 ±.

- **10...♘d7 11.♘c3!**

I leave it to the greedy reader to explore the consequences of *(die Untersuchung der Folgen von ...)* 11.d6 f:e5 12.♕c4+ ♔h8 13.♗:d7 ♗:d7 14.♕:c5 e:f4+ 15.♔f1 c:d6 or *(oder)* 13...♕h4+ 14.g3 e:f4+ 15.♗:e8 ♗f2+ *(... überlasse ich dem geneigten Leser).*

11...f:e5 12.♗:d7 ♗:d7 13.f:e5 ±, for example: *(z.B.:)* 13...♖f8 14.♖f1 ♖:f1+ 15.♔:f1 ♕f8 16.♕f3 ♗f5 17.♗e3! ±.

- **10...♗d7**

This is supposed to be Black's best defence, and it's not all that easy proving an advantage, for example:
Dies gilt als stärkste schwarze Verteidigung, und ein weißer Vorteil ist hiernach alles andere als leicht nachzuweisen, zum Beispiel:

11.♗d3

Bücker gives *(Bücker gibt an:)* 11.♗c4 f:e5 12.f:e5 ♗f5! 13.♕f4 ♗d6 14.0-0 ♖:e5 ∞. This is by the way the only analysis I've found on 10.♗b5 so it may come as quite a shock for our opponents ... *(Dies ist übrigens die einzige Analyse, die ich betreffs 10.♗b5 gefunden habe. Entsprechend schockierend dürfte die Wirkung dieses Zuges auch auf einen gutvorbereiteten Gegner sein!)* 11.d6 looks logical, but *(wirkt logisch, doch)* 11...♗:b5! is at least equal for Black, e.g: *(gibt Schwarz mindestens Ausgleich, z.B.:)* 12.♕d5+ ♔h8 13.♕:c5 ♗c6.

11...g6 12.♘c3!

This seems to give White the advantage since the d7 bishop suddenly has become an obstruction (Compare with 10.♗d3 g6 11.♘c3 where Black has 11...♘d7! threatening 12...♘:e5).
Dies scheint Weiß einen Vorteil zu überlassen, da der Läufer auf d7 dem Schwarzen im Weg herumsteht (man vergleiche mit 10.♗d3 g6 11.♘c3, wo 11...♘d7! mit der Drohung 12...♘:e5 möglich ist)

12...♗d6

This passive move seems safest for Black.
Dieser passive Zug dürfte am sichersten für Schwarz sein.

12...♗f5 13.♕c4 ♗:d3 14.c:d3 ♗d6 15.d4 ±, 12...f:e5 13.f:e5 ♗f5 14.♕e2 ♗d4 15.♗f4 ♗:e5 16.♗:e5 ♘d7 17.♗:f5 g:f5 18.0-0 ♖:e5 19.♕f2 ♕e7 20.♖ae1 ±.

13.0-0 f:e5 14.♕c4 a6

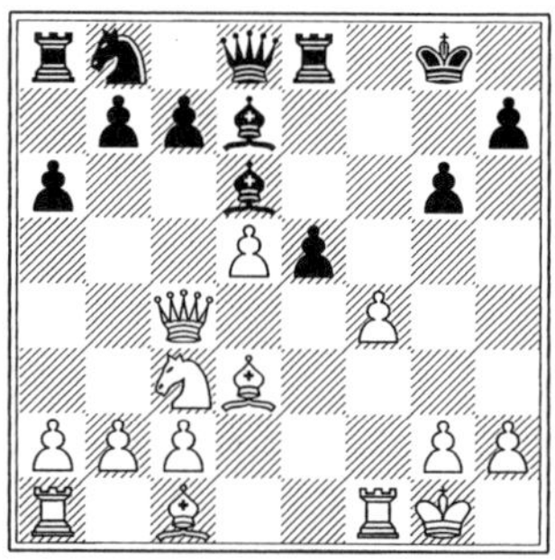

Now White has two promising continuations:
Und nun verfügt Weiß über zwei vielversprechende Fortsetzungen:

15.♗e3 b5 16.♕b3 c5!? 17.♘e4 c4 18.♕c3 ♗e7 19.f:e5 c:d3 20.e6 ± or *(oder)* 15.♘e4 ♗b5 16.♕b3 ♗:d3 17.♕:d3 ±.

f

(1.e4 e5 2.f4 d5 3.e:d5 e4 4.d3 ♘f6 5.d:e4 ♘:e4 6.♘f3 ♗c5 7.♕e2)

7...♗f5 8.♘c3 ♕e7

8...0-0?! 9.♘:e4 ♖e8 10.♘e5 ♗:e4 11.♕:e4 f6 12.d6!, and now Black has no ...♗e6 defence as in *e1)* and *e2)* above *(und dem Schwarzen fehlt die Verteidigung ...♗e6 aus* ***e1)*** *und* ***e2)***. 12...♕:d6 (12...♗:d6/12...c:d6 13.♗c4+ ♔f8 14.♕:h7) 13.♗e3! ♗:e3 14.♕c4+ ♕e6 15.♕:e6+ ♖:e6 16.♗c4 +– e.g. *(z.B.)* 16...f:e5 17.♗:e6+ ♔f8 18.♗c8!.

9.♗e3!

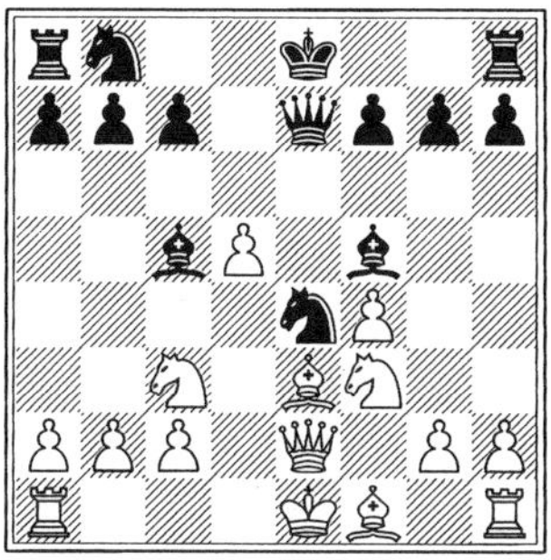

f1

9...♗b4 10.♗d4 0-0 11.0-0-0

11...♖e8 12.♘:e4 ♗:e4 13.♗e5 ♗g6 14.♕c4 ±, Sembukhov - Brichkov, corr. 1985/86.

11...♗:c3 12.♗:c3 ♕c5

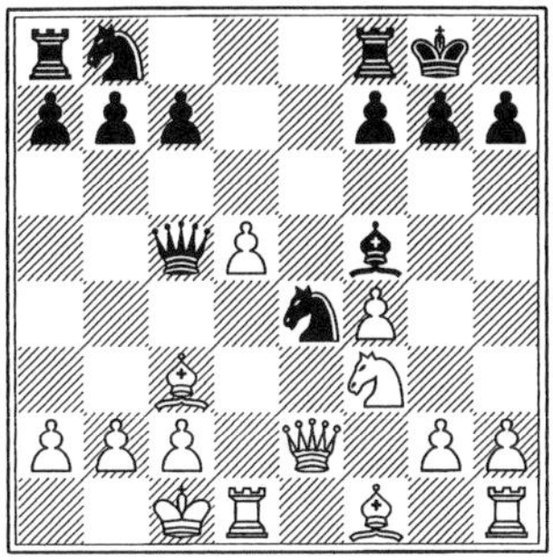

13.♗:g7! 13.♔:g7 14.♘h4 +–

f2

(1.e4 e5 2.f4 d5 3.e:d5 e4 4.d3 ♘f6 5.d:e4 ♘:e4 6.♘f3 ♗c5 7.♕e2 ♗f5 8.♘c3 ♕e7 9.♗e3)

9...♘:c3 10.♗:c5 ♘:e2 11.♗:e7 ♘:f4 12.♗a3! ♘d7

12...♘:d5 13.0-0-0 c6 14.♘g5! Δ♖e1+.

13.0-0-0 ♗e4

13...0-0-0? A losing 'natural' move! *(ein natürlicher Zug, der indes verliert!)* 14.♖d4! ♘g6 15.g4 +–.

14.♘g5 ♗:d5

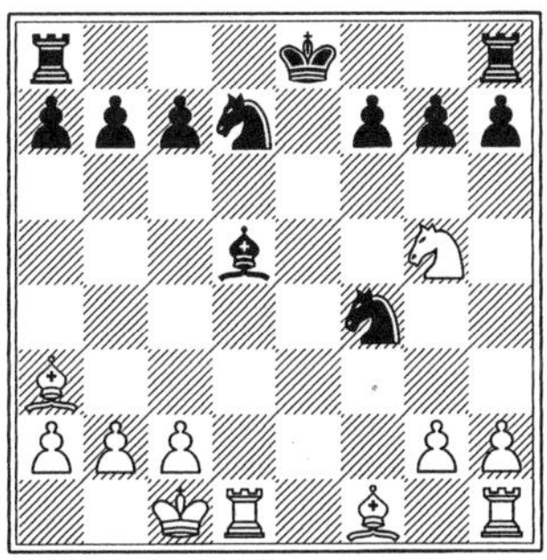

15.g3!?

15.♖e1+! ± There really is no need to show off! *(Es gibt keinen Grund, so dick aufzutragen!)*

15...♗:h1 16.g:f4 c5 17.♗c4 ♗c6 18.♘:f7 b5 19.♘d6+ ♔e7 20.♘:b5 ♖hf8?

20...♗:b5 ±.

21.♘d4! (1:0/43.), Bronstein - Tal, Riga 1968.

f3

(1.e4 e5 2.f4 d5 3.e:d5 e4 4.d3 ♘f6 5.d:e4 ♘:e4 6.♘f3 ♗c5 7.♕e2 ♗f5 8.♘c3 ♕e7 9.♗e3)

9...♗:e3 10.♕:e3 ♘:c3 11.♕:e7+ ♔:e7 12.b:c3

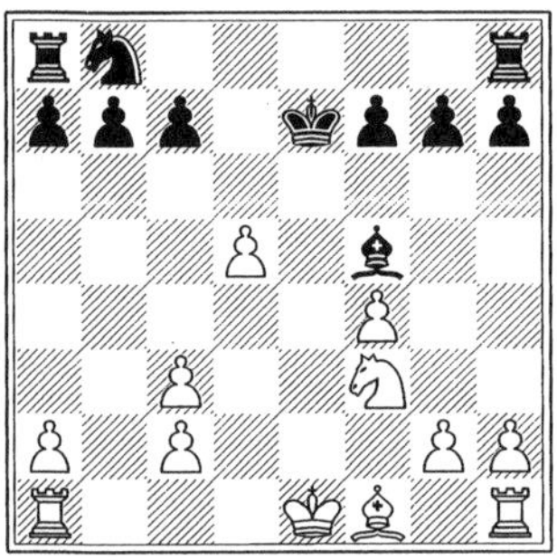

12...♗e4

Black can try many variations of the same bad endgame, but he can't change the fact that White has a lead in development and will be first to create tangible threats.

Der Nachziehende kann in diesem traurigen Endspiel allerlei probieren, doch der Umstand, daß Weiß großen Entwicklungsvorteil hat - und somit als erster reale Drohungen aufzustellen vermag -, läßt sich nicht aus der Welt schaffen!

12...♗:c2 13.♔d2:

- 13...♗f5 14.♖e1+ ♔f6 15.♘d4 ♘d7? (15...♗d7 16.h3 ±) 16.♘:f5 ♔:f5 17.♖e7 ♖ad8 18.♖:f7+ ♔g6 19.♖e7 ♘c5 20.c4 c6 21.♖e5 c:d5 22.c:d5 ♘d7 23.♗d3+ ♔f7 24.♖f5+ 1:0, Roscher - Foerster, corr. 1990.
- 13...♗a4 14.♖e1+ ♔d6 15.♘g5 ♗e8 16.♖e5 b6 (16...f6 17.♘e4+ ♔d7 18.♘c5+ ±) 17.♗c4 h6 18.♘e4+ ♔d7 19.♖e1 ♔d8 20.d6 ♘d7 21.♖e7 f5 22.♘g3 g6 23.♗d5 ♖c8 24.♗b7 ♖b8 25.♖:e8+! +−, Opychaneyj - Skigin, Buenos Aires 1996.
- 13...♗g6 14.♖e1+ ♔d6 15.♘d4 (15.♘g5!?) h5 (15...♔:d5 16.f5 Δ g4, Lg2+) 16.f5 ♗h7 17.♖b1! b6 ±, Analysis by *(Analyse von)* Gallagher.

13.♘g5! ♗:c2

13...♗:d5 14.0-0-0!:

- 14.♗:a2 15.c4 b5 16.c:b5 a6 17.♗d3!? (17.♔b2 Glaskov) 17...a:b5?! 18.♖he1+ ♗e6 19.f5 ♔f6 20.f:e6 ♔:g5 21.e:f7 ♖f8 22.♖e8 ♖:f7 23.♔b2! c6 24.♗:h7 ♖fa7 25.♖dd8 +−, Foune - Mathieu, corr. 1985
- 14...♗e6 15.♘:e6 (15.♗d3!?) f:e6 16.♗c4 ♖f8 17.♖he1 ♖f6 18.f5! ±.
- 14...c6 15.♗d3! (Gallagher gives - *Gallagher gibt an* - 15.c4 ♗e6 16.♗d3 but - *doch* - 16...h6! 17.♘:e6 f:e6 18.♖he1 ♖f8 secured equality for Black in - *sicherte Schwarz Ausgleich in* - Tarmak - Burkett, corr. 1996; e.g. - *z.B.* - 19.f5 ♖f6 20.♖:e6+ ♖:e6 21.f:e6 ♘a6! =) 15...h6? (15...g6 16.♖he1+ ♔f6 17.g4 Δ ♖e3, ♖de1, ♘e4/c4 ±; 15...♗:g2? 16.♖he1+ Δ ♘h7+; 15...♘d7?! 16.♖he1+ ♔f8 17.c4 ♗:g2? 18.♖d2 h6 19.♘h7+ +−) 16.♖he1+ ♔d6 17.♘:f7+! ♗:f7 18.♗a6+ ♔c7 19.♖e7+ ♔b6 20.♗:b7 1:0 (20...♘a6

21.♗:a8 ♗h5 22.♖dd7 +–), Szymanski - Petrik, Warsaw 1971.

- 14...♖d8 15.c4 ♗e6 16.♖:d8 ♔:d8 17.♘:e6+ f:e6 18.♗d3 h6 19.♖e1! ♔d7 20.♖e3 ♘c6 21.♖g3 +– (Kortchnoi /Zak).

14.♔d2 ♗g6 15.♖e1+ ♔f8

- 15...♔d6 16.f5!.
- 15...♔f6 16.g4! ♖d8 17.c4 c6 18.♘h3 +–/±.
- 15...♔d7 16.♗d3 f6 17.♘e6 ±.

16.♗b5!?

16.g4.

16...c6 17.f5!

Trying to open an attack route on the f-file!
Versucht, die f-Linie zur Angriffsmagistralen zu erheben!

17...♗h5

17...♗:f5 18.♖hf1 g6 19.g4 +–.

18.d:c6 ♘:c6 19.♗:c6 b:c6 20.c4 g6

20...h6 21.♘e4 f6 22.♔c3 ♗f7 23.♘c5±.

21.f6 h6 22.♘e4 ± ♗g4 23.♔c3 ♔g8 24.♘c5 g5 25.♖e7 ♔h7 26.♖:f7+ ♔g6 27.♖g7+

Finally getting rid of his own obstructing f-pawn!
Damit wird Weiß endlich seinen störenden eigenen f-Bauern los!

27...♔:f6 28.♖c7 ♖hc8 29.♖f1+ ♔e5

29...♔g6 30.♖cf7 +–.

30.♘d3+ ♔d6 31.♖h7 ♖h8 32.c5+ ♔d5 33.♖e7! ♖ae8 34.♖fe1 ♖:e7 35.♖:e7 ♗e6 36.♘b4+ ♔e5 37.♘:c6+ ♔f6 38.♖:a7 ♗d5 39.♖a6 ♗:g2 40.♘d4+ ♔e7 41.♖:h6 ♖a8 42.♖g6 ♖:a2 43.♖:g5 ♗h3 44.♘c2 ♔f6 45.♖h5 ♗f5 46.♘b4 1:0, Bangiev - Gutgarch, corr. SSSR 1985/87.

III

(1.e4 e5 2.f4)

2...d5 3.e:d5 c6 ♥

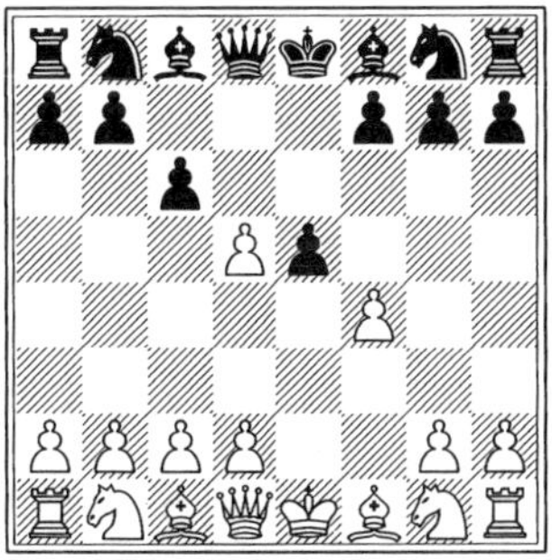

The Nimzowitsch Counter-Gambit
Das Nimzowitsch-Gegengambit.

White has an interesting off-beat option in Metz's Attack 4.♕e2!? which brings about positions quite different from the ones we'll encounter in the main-lines. I'm actually a bit surprised that it hasn't been played more often since it seems very strong indeed ... I'll give a brief coverage for those who feel ready to boldly go where few have gone before:

Mit dem Metz-Angriff 4.♕e2!? steht dem Weißen eine ausgefallene Möglichkeit offen, welche gänzlich andere Stellungen als die arrivierten Varianten hervorbringt. Tatsächlich bin ich ein wenig überrascht, daß der Metz-Angriff nicht häufiger gespielt wird, da er zudem recht stark zu sein scheint ... Für diejenigen, die kühn auf noch recht jungfräulichen Pfaden wandeln wollen, gebe ich eine kurze Zusammenstellung:

A

4.♕e2!? c:d5

4...e4 5.♕:e4+ ♗e7 6.d6! ♕:d6 7.♘f3!? (7.d4 ♘f6 8.♕d3 may be a sounder set-up - *wäre vielleicht eine gesündere Aufstellung*) 7...♘f6 8.♕e5 ♕d8 9.♗c4 0-0 10.0-0, and White had no problems in *(und Weiß hatte keine Sorgen in)* Krutihin - Zilin, Novosibirsk 1962 (1:0/39.).

5.f:e5 ♘c6 6.♘f3!

This is Metz's improvement on Alekhine - Johner, Karlsbad 1911, which went:
Die Metzsche Verbesserung im Vergleich zur Partie Aljechin - Johner, Karlsbad 1911, die folgendermaßen weiterging:
6.c3?! d4 7.♘f3 ♘ge7 8.d3 ♘g6 9.♕e4 ♗c5 10.♘bd2 0-0 11.♘b3 f5! (0:1/28.).

6...♗g4 7.♕f2!

Δ d4, Δ ♗b5.

7.♘c3 also keeps a slight advantage for White, and may actually transpose to Zuse - Kraft in *B, a*.
7.♘c3 mit möglicher Überleitung zur Partie Zuse - Kraft (siehe ***B, a****) ist gleichfalls für leichten Vorteil gut.*

7...♗:f3 8.♕:f3 ♘d4

8...♘:e5? 9.♗b5+ ♘c6 10.0-0±.

9.♕d3

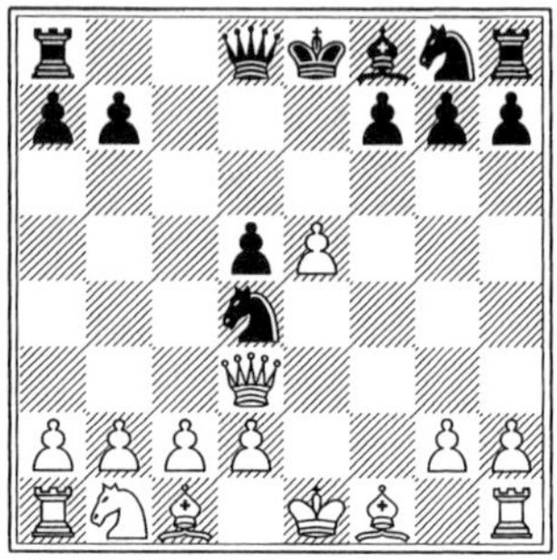

a

9...♗c5 10.c3 ♘c6

10...♘e6? 11.♕b5+ ♔f8 12.d4 ♕h4+ 13.♔d1±.

11.♕g3

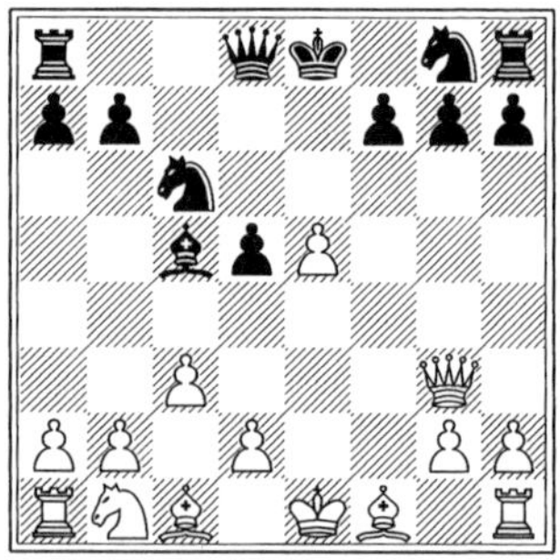

• 11...♔f8 12.d4 ♗e7 13.♕f3 ♖c8 14.♘d2 ♗g5 15.♗d3± ♘h6 16.0-0 ♖c7 17.♘b3 g6 18.♕g3 (18.♘c5!?) ♗:c1 19.♘:c1 ♔g7 20.♘e2 ♖f8 21.♘f4 ♔h8 22.♕h3 (22.♕f3! is a cleaner kill - *wäre ein klarerer Gewinn*) 22...♔g7 23.♖f3 ♖e7 24.♖g3 ♘g8 25.♘h5+ ♔h8 26.♘f6 ♘:f6 27.e:f6 +– ♖ee8 28.♖f1 h5 29.♖f5 ♔g8 30.♕:h5 ♘e7 31.♖f4 (31.♖h3! results in a very pretty mate: *hätte zu einem hübschen Matt geführt:* 31...g:h5 32.♖f:h5 ♘g6 33.♖h8+ ♘:h8 34.♗h7#) 31...♘c8 32.♖:g6+ 1:0, H.

Metz - J. Schlenker-Pape, Bundesliga 1987.
Isn't it striking how little Black gained from chasing White's queen?
Ist es nicht verblüffend, wie wenig Schwarz mit seiner Hatz auf die weiße Dame erreicht?

• 11...d4 12.♕:g7 ♕h4+ 13.♔d1 0-0-0? (13...♕h5+ 14.♗e2 ♕:e5 15.♕:e5 ±) 14.♕:h8 ♕g4+ 15.♗e2 ♕:g2 16.♖e1 d3 17.♗:d3 (Forced, but quite good all the same! - *erzwungen, aber auch stark!*) 17...♖:d3 18.♕:h7 ♖f3 19.♕e4 f5 (19...♗f2 20.e6!?) 20.e:f6 (20.♕e2 ♖f2 21.♕h5) 20...♘:f6 21.♕e2 ♖f2 22.♕c4 ♕f3+ 23.♔c2 ♕f5+ 24.♕d3 ♕h5 25.b3! ♘e5 26.♖:e5 +– (1:0/50.), H. Metz - J. Schlenker-Pape, Kuppenheim 1990.

b

(1.e4 e5 2.f4 e:f4 3.e:d5 c6 4.♕e2 c:d5 5.f:e5 ♘c6 6.♘f3 ♗g4 7.♕f2 ♗:f3 8.♕:f3 ♘d4 9.♕d3)

9...♕h4+ 10.g3 ♕e4+ 11.♕:e4 d:e4 12.♔d1 0-0-0

12...♖c8 13.♘c3 ♘h6 14.♗h3 ♖c5 15. ♖e1 ♖:e5 16.♖:e4 ±.

13.♗h3+

Metz prefers *(Metz bevorzugt)* 13.♗g2 f5 (13...e3 14.♘c3) 14.e:f6 ♘:f6 15.♖e1 ♘f3 16.♖e2(!) but *(doch)* 16...♘d4 17.♖e3 ♔b8 isn't all that clear *(ist keineswegs klar)*, however 15.♘c3! looks quite good for White *(jedoch sieht 15.♘c3! recht gut für Weiß aus)*.

13...♔b8 14.c3?!

I would prefer 14.♖e1 here.
Ich würde hier 14.♖e1 bevorzugen.

14...♘f3 15.♗f5 ♘:e5 16.♗:e4 ♘f6 17.♗g2 ♘d3!

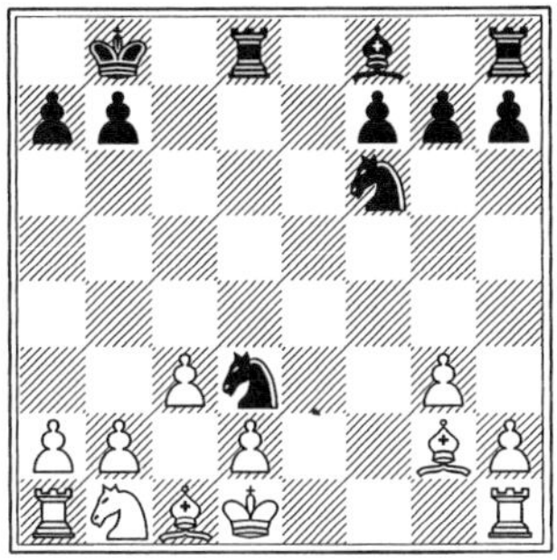

And Black's d3-blockade gave him some compensation for the pawn in *(Die Blockade auf d3 gab dem Nachziehenden gewisse Kompensation für den Bauern in)* Metz - Happe, corr. Germany 1989/90 (1:0/46).

B

(1.e4 e5 2.f4 d5 3.e:d5 c6)

4.♘c3

Taking control of e4 and thereby threatening to capture on e5. This prudent move is almost the only one played in this position.
Nimmt e4 unter Kontrolle und droht damit, auf e5 zu schlagen. Dieser umsichtige Zug wird hier praktisch ausschließlich angewandt.

a

4...c:d5

4...♗b4 5.♘f3 ♗:c3 6.d:c3 e4 7.♘e5 c:d5? 8.♗b5+ ♔f8 9.♗e3± (Rubinstein).

5.f:e5

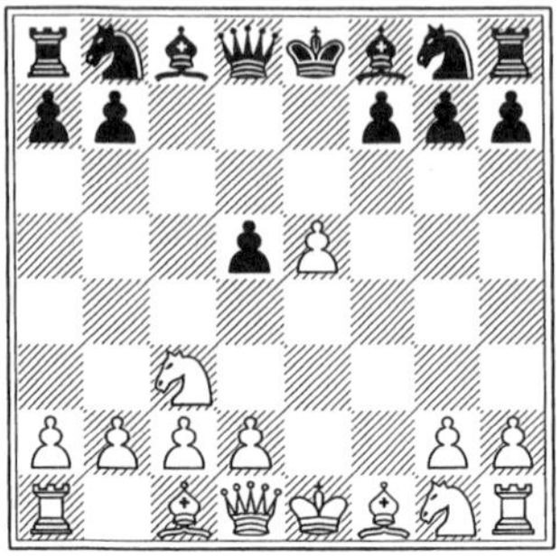

5...♘c6

5...d4 6.♘e4

- 6...♘c6 7.♘f3 ♕d5 8.♘f2! The position is reminiscent of a reversed Staunton gambit, if you play the Dutch you'll recognize the importance of keeping d3 open for your minor pieces, especially for the f2-knight! - *Die Stellung erinnert, bei vertauschten Farben, an das Staunton-Gambit. Wenn Sie "Holländisch" spielen, werden Sie bereits wissen, daß es wichtig ist, daß Feld d3 für die Leichtfiguren, insbesondere den ♘f2, freizuhalten!* 8...♗f5 (8...♘:e5 would of course run into 9.♕e2 Δ ♕b5+ and d4 is doomed - *auf 8...♘:e5 würde natürlich 9.♕e2 Δ ♕b5+ folgen, und der ♙d4 ist verloren*) 9.♗d3 ♗g6 10.0-0 ±, Teichmann - Marshall, Baden-Baden 1914.

- 6...♕d5
- • 7.♗d3 ♘c6 8.♕e2 ♘h6 (8...♘:e5 9.♗b5+ ♗d7 10.♗:d7+ ♔:d7 Marco) 9.♗c4 ♕a5 10.♘f3 ♗g4 11.♘d6+ ±, Opocensky - Johner, Baden-Baden 1914.
- • A recent game went: *(eine kürzlich gespielte Partie verlief wie folgt:)* 7.♕e2!? ♘c6 8.♘f3 ♗g4 9.♘f2 ♗:f3 10.g:f3 ♘ge7 11.f4 ♘g6 12.c4 d:c3 13.d:c3 ♗c5 14.♘e4 ♘h4 15.♕d3 ♕:d3 16.♗:d3 ♗b6 17.♘d6+ ♔e7 18.♗e4 f6 19.♘:b7 ♖ac8 20.♘d6 ♖c7 21.♘c4 ♔e6 22.e:f6 ♔:f6 23.♘:b6 a:b6 24.0-0 +– (1:0/42.), Zuse - Kraft, Konstanz 1997.

6.d4

It may look like a blunder, but White gets some activity and the pawn back. However, 6.♘f3 would be a better choice - most likely transposing to the variations above.
Sieht wie ein grober Schnitzer aus, doch Weiß gewinnt den Bauern zurück und erlangt eine gewisse Aktivität. Dennoch wäre 6.♘f3 - was wahrscheinlich zu den soeben gesehenen Abspielen führt - eine bessere Wahl.
But *(Doch)* 6.♗b5 may also be worth a closer look e.g. *(wäre gleichfalls eines näheren Blickes würdig, z.B.:)* 6...d4 7.♘e4 ♕d5 8.♕e2.

6...♕h4+ 7.g3 ♕:d4 8.♗f4! ♗b4! 9.♕:d4 ♘:d4 10.0-0-0 ♗:c3 11.b:c3 ♘c6! 12.♖:d5 ♘ge7 13.♖d6 ♗e6 14.♘f3 =/∞

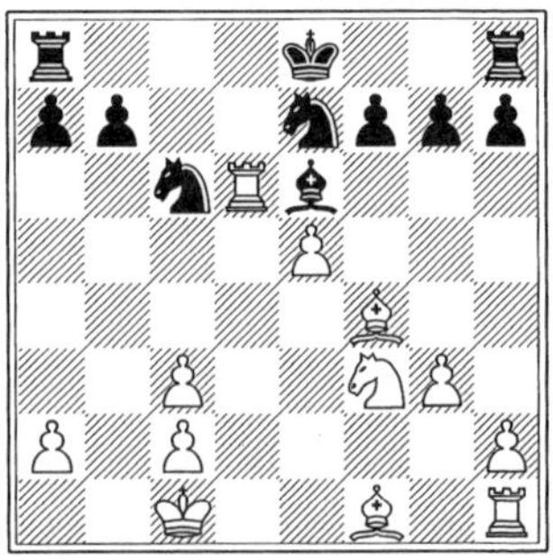

14...h6? 15.♘d4 ♘:d4 16.c:d4 ♘f5 17.♗b5+ ♔f8 18.♖:e6 ± (1:0/46.), Gallagher - Milanovic, 1990.

b

(1.e4 e5 2.f4 d5 3.e:d5 c6 4.♘c3)

4...e:f4

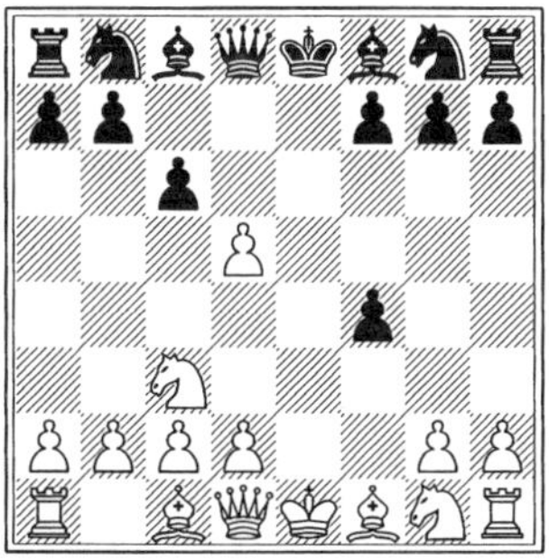

5.♘f3

The most natural move, developing a piece and ruling out the check at h4.
Der natürlichste Zug. Weiß entwickelt eine Figur und schließt das Schach auf h4 aus.
But *(Doch)* 5.♕e2+!? may be worth a closer look e.g: *(mag eines zweiten Blickes würdig sein, z.B.:)* 5...♗e7 6.d4 ♘f6 7.♗:f4 ♘:d5 8.♘:d5 ♕:d5 9.♘f3±. If you'd like to explore some more unknown ground you might consider the provocative *(Wenn Sie gerne in unbekannten Gefilden auf Erkundungsreise gehen, mögen Sie in Betracht ziehen:)* 5.d4!? ♕h4+ (This check should be the critical test - *dieses Schachgebot sollte der kritische Test sein.* 5...♗d6?! 6.♗c4 ♘f6 7.♕e2+ [7.♘ge2] 7...♕e7 8.d:c6 [or *oder* 8.♕:e7+ ♔:e7 9.♘ge2! ♘h5 10.♘e4, 9...♗f5 10.0-0 ±] 8...♘:c6 9.♘b5 ♗b8 10.c3) 6.♔e2 ♗g4+ 7.♘f3 c:d5? (7...♗d6 ∞) 8.♘:d5 ♗:f3+ 9.g:f3 ♗d6 10.♕e1 ♕h6 (10...♕:e1+ 11.♔:e1 ♘c6 12.c3 g5 13.h4 ±) 11.♔d1+ ♔f8 12.♗:f4 ♗:f4 13.♕b4+ ♕d6 14.♕:b7 ♘e7 15.♘:f4 ♕:f4 16.♕:a8 +–, Nikitin - Baranov, Moscow 1958.

5...♗d6

Black's plan is to hold his outpost on f4, hoping that his freer piece play will compensate for White's better queenside pawnstructure.
Schwarz spielt auf Behauptung seines Vorpostens auf f4, in der Hoffnung, daß sein freieres Figurenspiel einen Ausgleich für die weiße Bauernmasse am Damenflügel darstellt.

5...c:d5 6.d4 ♗d6 7.♘:d5 ♕a5+ 8.♘c3 ♘f6? (8...♘e7) 9.♗b5+ ♗d7 10.♕e2+ ♔d8?! 11.0-0 ♖e8 12.♘e5! ♗:e5 (12...♘c6 13.♘:f7+ ♔c7 14.♕c4 ♗e6 15.♘:d6! ♗:c4 16.♘:c4 ♕b4 17.♗:f4+ ♔d8 18.♗d6! Gallagher) 13.d:e5 ♘c6 14.♗:f4 ± 1:0 Gallagher - Barczay, Kecskemet 1990.

5...♘f6 6.d4 ♘:d5 7.♘:d5 ♕:d5 8.♗:f4 ♗d6 9.♗:d6 ♕:d6 10.♗d3 ♗e6 11.0-0 ♘d7 12.c3 h6 13.♕d2 0-0 14.♗c2 ♖fe8 15.♘h4 c5 16.♕d3 ♘f8 17.♘f5 ♕c7 18.♖f3 ♗:f5 19.♖:f5 c:d4 20.♗b3 ♘e6 21.♖af1 d:c3 22.♖:f7 ♕c5+ 23.♔h1 c:b2 24.♗c2 +– ♘g5 25.♖:g7+ ♔:g7 26.♕g6+ ♔h8 27.♕:h6+ ♔g8 28.♗b3+ ♘e6 29.♗:e6+ +– (1:0/45.), Fedorov - Yandemirov, Minsk 1995.

6.d4

b1

6...♘f6

This is a bit inconsistent since this knight should support f4 from g6.
Ein wenig inkonsequent, der Springer sollte f4 von g6 aus überdecken.

7.♕e2+

An awkward check for Black, since he's got no non-committal answer.
Ein für den Nachziehenden, der über keine unverbindliche Antwort verfügt, ziemlich unangenehmes Schachgebot.

7...♕e7

7...♔f8 8.♘e5!

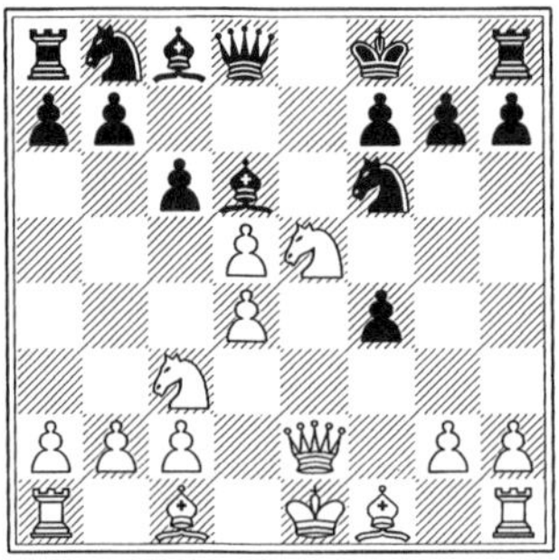

- 8...c:d5 9.♗:f4 ♘c6
  - 10.♕f2 ♘g4 11.♘:g4 ♗:g4 12.♗d3 ♗:f4 13.♕:f4 h5 14.0-0 ±/±, Gallagher - Nemet, Suhr 1990.
  - 10.0-0-0!? ♗:e5 11.d:e5 ♗g4 12.♕d2 ♗:d1 13.e:f6 ♗h5 14.f:g7+ ♔:g7 15.♗h6+ ♔g8 16.♕:d5 ♗g6 17.♗c4 ±/± (Glaskov).
- 8...♘:d5 9.♘:d5 c:d5 10.♗:f4 ♕c7 11.♕f2 (defending both f4 and d4 in advance - *verteidigt vorsorglich sowohl f4 als auch d4)* 11...♘c6 12.♘d3 ♗:f4 13.♘:f4 ♗g4 14.♗e2! ♖e8 (14...♗:e2 15.♘e6+) 15.0-0 ♗:e2 16.♘:e2 ±, Gallagher - Fedorov, Saverne 1990.
White is practically a rook up, and on top of that d5 is very weak!
Weiß hat praktisch einen Turm mehr, und darüberhinaus ist d5 sehr schwach!
- 8...g5 9.h4 ♘:d5 10.♘:d5 c:d5 11.♕h5 ♕e7 12.♕h6+ ♔e8 13.♕g7 ♗:e5 14.d:e5 ♖f8 15.♕:g5 ♕b4 16.c3 ♕e4+ 17.♗e2±/∞ (½:½/48.; 17.♔f2!?), Nunn - Anand, Monaco (rapid/*Schnellschach*) 1995.

8.♕:e7+ ♔:e7 9.♘e5 ♘:d5 10.♘:d5 c:d5 11.♗:f4

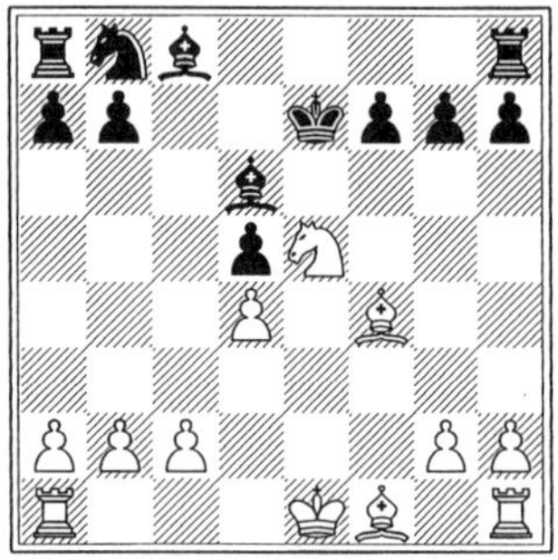

11...♘c6

11...♗e6 12.♗b5 h6 13.0-0-0 ♖c8 14.♖he1 a6 15.♗a4 b5 16.♗b3 ♘c6 17.♗:d5!? ♗:e5 18.d:e5 ♗:d5 19.♖:d5 ♘b4 20.♖d2 ♘:a2 21.♔b1 ♘b4 22.e6 (1:0/82.) with a small edge for White due to the better minor piece *(mit leichtem Vorteil für Weiß dank der wirkungsvolleren Leichtfigur)*, Yoos - Gustafson, Reykjavik 1996.

12.0-0-0 ♗e6 13.c3 ♖ac8 14.♘:c6+

Making sure of getting an ending with the superior bishop, since the ♗e6 is hemmed in by its own pawns.
Sichert sich ein Endspiel mit besserem Läufer. Der ♗e6 wird von seinen eigenen Bauern gehemmt.

14...b:c6 15.♗:d6+ ♔:d6 16.♗d3 ± c5?! 17.d:c5 ♔:c5+ 18.♗c2

With a clear advantage for White in *(mit klarem weißen Vorteil in)* Ermenko - Kurguz, corr. 1982/83 (1:0/48.).

b2

(1.e4 e5 2.f4 d5 3.e:d5 c6 4.♘c3 e:f4 5.♘f3 ♗d6 6.d4)

6....♘e7

b21

7.♗d3!?

A less common alternative to 7.d:c6 and 7.♗c4 which both lead to approximately the same thing.
Im Vergleich zu 7.d:c6 und 7.♗c4, was beides in etwa auf das gleiche herausläuft, eine weniger geläufigere Alternative.

7...0-0

7...h6!?
Black scored an easy win in Olsson - Moynihan, Kilkenny 1996 after
In der Partie Olsson - Moynihan, Kilkenny 1996, kam Schwarz damit zu einem leichten Gewinn nach
8.0-0 ♗g4 9.♘e4 c:d5 10.♘:d6+ ♕:d6 11.♕d2 g5 12.♘e5 ♗e6 13.♕e2 ♘bc6 14.♘:c6 ♘:c6 ∓.
8.d:c6 ♘b:c6 9.♘e4 may be a better try *(dürfte ein besserer Versuch sein).*

8.d:c6

8.0-0 ♘:d5?! (8...c:d5) 9.♘:d5 c:d5 10.♘e5 ♘c6 11.♘:c6 b:c6 12.♗:f4 ±, J. Polgar - S. Jackson, Thessaloniki 1988.

8...♘b:c6 9.♘e4?!

This is premature. Usually it's better to finish development before playing actively, unless of course you're punishing Black for the same mistake!
Verfrüht, normalerweise sollte man vor der Einleitung aktiver Operationen erst die Entwicklung abschließen - außer natürlich, wenn man den Nachziehenden für ebendiesen Fehler bestrafen möchte!

9.0-0 ♘f5 (9...♘b4 10.♘e1) 10.♘e4 ♘c:d4 11.♘:d4 ♘:d4 12.♘:d6 ♕:d6 13.♗:f4 ±.

9...♘b4 10.♘:d6 ♘:d3+ 11.♕:d3 ♕:d6 12.0-0 ♗f5 13.♕d2 ♘d5! 14.♕f2 ♖ac8 15.c3 ♖fe8 16.♘e1

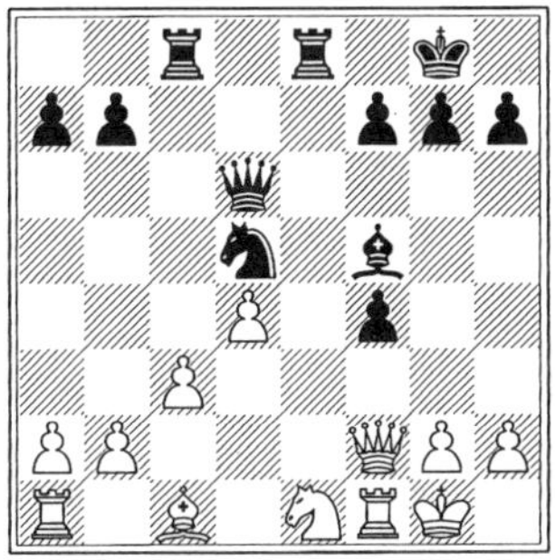

Going through the motions, White is worse but can there be counter-play?
Nach den bisherigen Geschehnissen steht Weiß schlechter, aber vielleicht gibt es ja Gegenspiel?

16...g5 17.h4 h6 18.g3

18.h:g5 h:g5 19.g3 runs into *(würde erwidert mit)* 19...♗g4 20.g:f4 ♗e2.

18...♘e3?!

18...♗h3! 19.♘g2 ♕a6 ∓.
I guess White was hoping for *(Ich vermute, Weiß hoffte hier auf)* 19...f:g3 20.♕:f7+ ♔h8 21.♗:g5! ±.

19.♗:e3 ♖:e3 20.g:f4 g:f4 21.♘g2 ♕g6?!

21...♖g3 =/∞.

22.h5! ♕:h5??

22...♕g7 ±.

23.♘:e3 ♖c6 24.♕:f4 ♕g6+ 25.♔f2 ♖f6 26.♘d5! 1:0, Depasquale - Levi, Melbourne 1991.

This game is a fine example of 'the fighter's King's Gambit' coming back despite the odds, here probably thanks to the opponents time-trouble. Just as a reminder never to lose hope!
Ein schönes Beispiel dafür, wie der kampfeslustige Königsgambit-Ritter zurückschlägt, trotz diverser Ungereimtheiten. Zeitnot war hier wahrscheinlich auch im Spiel. Mit dem Gedanken an derartige Partien sollten Sie nie die Hoffnung aufgeben!

b22

(1.e4 e5 2.f4 d5 3.e:d5 c6 4.♘c3 e:f4 5.♘f3 ♗d6 6.d4 ♘e7)

7.d:c6 ♘b:c6 8.♗c4

8.d5?! just weakens the black squares around the king, and with so many minor pieces still on the board in an open position it would be quite foolhardy to risk having one's king caught in the cross-fire.
Mit 8.d5?! würde Weiß nur das schwarzfeldrige Feldernetz um seinen König schwächen, was in Anbetracht der noch zahlreich vorhandenen Leichtfiguren in solch einer offenen Stellung einem Spiel mit dem Feuer gleichkäme.

8...0-0 9.0-0

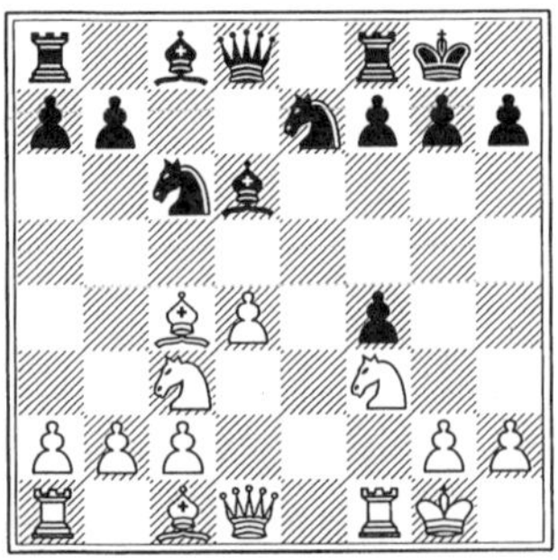

• **9...♗g4 10.♘e4**
10.♘e2!? ♘g6 11.c3 ♕c7 12.♗d3 ♖fe8 13.h3 ♗h5 14.♕b3! ♘f8 15.♔h1! ♖e7 16.♘g1 ♘e6 17.♕b5 ♗g6 18.♗:g6 h:g6 ± 19.d5? a6!, Hector - Hellsten, Stockholm 1995.

10...♗c7
10...♖c8 11.♗b3 ♗b8 12.c3 ♘g6 13.h3 ♗f5 14.♘fg5 h6 15.♕h5 h:g5 16.♘:g5 ♘h8 17.♗:f4?? (17.♘:f7!, Compare Westerinen - Motwani at the end of this chapter - *vgl. die Partie Westerinen - Motwani ganz am Schluß dieses Kapitels*), 0:1/26., Johansson - Hellsten, Malmö 1995.

11.c3 ♘g6
11...♘d5?! 12.♘c5! ♖b8 13.♕e1! (Since White has the clearly better pawn structure he aims for an ending - *In Anbetracht seiner klar besseren Bauernstruktur strebt Weiß ein Endspiel an*) 13...♖e8 (13...g5 14.♘:g5! ♕:g5 15.♘e4! ♕f5 16.♗:d5 ♖be8 17.♕f2 ♖:e4 18.♗:e4 ♕:e4 19.♗:f4 ♗:f4 20.♕:f4 ♕:f4 21.♖:f4 ♗e6 22.b3 b5 23.♖d1 ± Mikhalchisin) 14.♕h4 ♕:h4 (Avoiding the queen trade seems unwise: - *Es scheint unklug, dem Damentausch auszuweichen:* 14...♘f6?! 15.♘g5 ♗h5 16.♗:f4 ♗g6 17.♗:c7 ♕:c7 18.♗:f7+! ♗:f7 19.♖:f6 g:f6 20.♕:h7+ ♔f8 21.♘ge6+ +–, Baudin - Nielsen, Viborg 1996) 15.♘:h4 ♘e3 16.♗:e3 ♖:e3 17.♖ae1 ♖:e1 18.♖:e1 ±, Illescas - Nunn, Dubai 1986.
There's no reason to fear *(Es gibt keinen Grund, ...)* 11...♗:f3?! 12.♖:f3! ♘e5? since *(... zu fürchten, da)* 13.♖h3 is close to winning for White: *(fast schon für Weiß gewinnt:)* 13...♘:c4 14.♘f6+ g:f6 15.♕h5 +– or *(oder)* 13...h6 14.♘f6+ g:f6 (14...♔h8 15.♗:f4! ♘:c4 16.♗:h6 g:h6 [there's no escape anyway/*auch anders kann Schwarz nicht*

entkommen: 16...g:f6 17.♕h5 +–, 16...♕c8 17.♕d3! +–] 17.♕c1! +–) 15.♕h5 ♕c8 16.♕:h6 ♕:h3 17.♕:h3 ♘:c4 18.♕d7 ♗d8 19.♗:f4 ±.

12.♘f2

Compare this with 7.♗c4 and 13.♘f2 where the ♗c4 is on b3.

Vergleiche mit 7.♗c4 und 13.♘f2, wo der ♗c4 sich auf b3 befindet.

12...♗h5 13.♕d3 ♖c8 14.♕f4 ♗:f3 15.g:f3 ♗b8 16.♗d3 ♘ce7 17.♕h5 f5 18.♘h3 ♖f6 19.♔h1 ♕d7 20.♗d2 ♘d5 21.♗c2 ♘f8 22.♖ae1 b5 23.♖g1 ♔h8 24.♘g5 ♔g8 25.♗b3 ♖d8 26.♘h3 ♘e6 27.♘g5 ♘:g5 28.♕:g5 ♖f7 29.♖e2 ♔f8 30.♖ge1 ♗c7 31.♕h5 g6 32.♕h6+ ♔g8 33.♗:d5 1:0, Olesen - Gretarsson, Gausdal 1995.

- 9...♗f5 10.♘h4! ♖c8 (10...♕b6 11.♘d5!) 11.♔h1 ♗b8 12.♗:f4 ♘:d4 13.♘:f5 ♘e:f5 14.♗d3 ♘e7 15.♗:b8 ♖:b8 16.♕h5 f5 17.♖ad1 ⩲ ♕b6 18.♗c4+ ♔h8 19.♘a4 ♕f6 20.♘c5 ♕c6 21.b4 ♘:c2 22.♕e2 ♕e4 23.♘:e4 1:0, Hellers - Välkesalmi, Thessaloniki 1988.

- 9...♘g6 10.♘e4 ♗f5 11.♘:d6 ♕:d6 12.c3 a6?! 13.♗d3 ♗:d3 14.♕:d3 ♖fe8 15.♗d2 ±, Popovych - Shahade, 1989.

Another case of better pawn structure.

Ein weiteres Mal hat Weiß die bessere Bauernstruktur.

- **9...♗c7 10.♘e4 ♘d5!?**

An attempt to improve on Illescas - Nunn above, where *(Ein Versuch, die oben gesehene Partie Illescas - Nunn zu verbessern, wo Weiß nach ...)* 9...♗g4 10.♘e4 ♗c7 11.c3 ♘d5?! 12.♘c5! allowed White to gain a tempo on the b7-pawn. But then there is the question if the knight really belongs on d5 at all? *(... ein Tempo durch Angriff auf den ♙b7 gewann. Doch ist es die Frage, ob der Springer überhaupt nach d5 gehört?)*

11.c3 f6?!

Defends e5 and g5 but loosens the king's defence.

Nimmt e5 und g5 unter Kontrolle, schwächt aber die Königsstellung.

12.♕b3 ♘ce7 13.♗d2 ♔h8 14.♖ae1 ♖b8 15.♗:d5!

Trying to hold on to this beautiful bishop with 15.♗d3 would allow 15...b5 slowing down White's pawn push in the centre.

Der Versuch, mit 15.♗d3 diesen schönen Läufer zu behalten, würde 15...b5 ermöglichen, was die weißen Zentrumsbauern einstweilen im Zaum halten würde.

15...♘:d5 16.c4 ♘e7 17.♗b4 ♖e8 18.d5 ♘f5

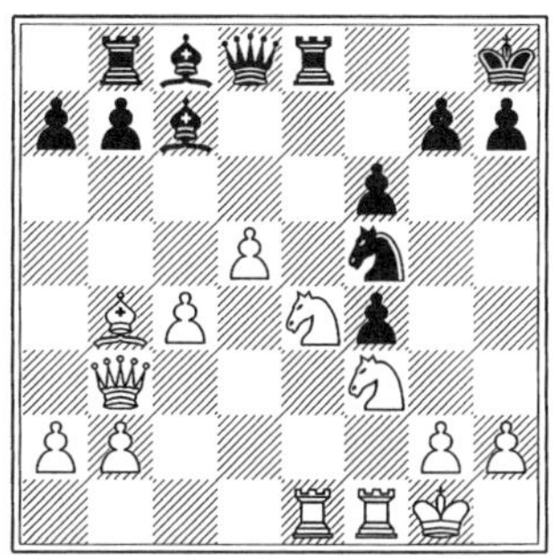

19.d6!

These pawns are made for walking!

Solche Bauern sind zum Vormarschieren geschaffen!

19...♗b6+ 20.c5 ♘e3 21.c:b6 a5

21...♖:e4 22.b:a7 ♖a8 23.♗c5 ♗e6 24.♕:b7 ♗d5 25.♕:d5! ♘:d5 26.♖:e4 ♕a5 27.b4 ♕:a2 28.♖d4 ♘e3 29.♖d2 ♕c4 30.♖e1 ±.

22.d7!

Making room for the knight.
Schafft Platz für den Spinger.
22...♕:d7 23.♘d6 ♖e6 24.♘:c8 a:b4
24...♖:c8 25.♖d1 ♘:d1 26.♖:d1 ♕e8 27.♗:a5 ±.
25.♘a7 ♖:b6 26.♖f2 ♖a6 27.♖d2 ♕e8 28.♕:b4 ♖a4 29.♕b6 ♖a8 30.♕c7 f5 31.♖d7 +−, Popovych - Valvo, New York 1990.

b23

(1.e4 e5 2.f4 d5 3.e:d5 c6 4.♘c3 e:f4 5.♘f3 ♗d6 6.d4 ♘e7)

7.♗c4 c:d5

7...0-0 8.0-0 ♗g4 9.d:c6 see *(siehe)* 7.d:c6.

8.♗:d5 0-0

8...♘:d5?! (this knight is needed in the defence of the f4-pawn - *dieser Springer wird zur Verteidigung von f4 benötigt*) 9.♘:d5 ♕a5+ 10.♘c3 0-0 11.0-0 ♗g4 12.♘e4 ♗c7 13.♘f2 ♗h5 14.♘h3!? ♕f5 15.♕d2 ±, Gallagher - Brito, Las Palmas 1990 (15...♗:f3 16.♖:f3 g5 17.♘:g5! ♕:g5 18.♖g3 +− Gallagher).

9.0-0 ♘bc6 10.♗b3 ♗g4 11.♘e4 ♗c7 12.c3 ♘g6

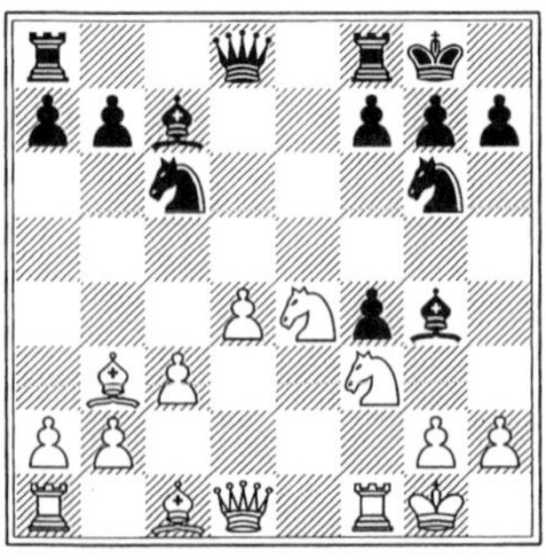

• **13.♘f2!**
This is the consistent continuation of the long-term plan of pressurizing the f4-pawn, it also seems to be the best since 13.h3!? is under a cloud due to van Perlo's improvements in the 15...♘:d4 line, see below.
Die konsequenteste Fortsetzung; Weiß arbeitet an dem langfristigen Vorhaben, Druck gegen den ♙f4 auszuüben. Gleichzeitig dürfte es sich auch um die stärkste Fortsetzung handeln, da sich über 13.h3!? seit van Perlos Verstärkung in der 15...♘:d4-Variante dunkle Wolken zusammengezogen haben.
13...♗f5 14.♘d3 ♘a5 15.♘fe1 ♘:b3
15...♕g5 16.♕f3 ♗g4 17.♕f2 ♘:b3 18.a:b3 ♕b5 19.♘:f4 ♗:f4 20.♗:f4 ♗e2 21.c4 ♕e8 22.♗d6 ♗:f1 23.♔:f1 ♘e7 24.♕e2 ♘f5 25.♗:f8 ♕:f8 26.♘c2 ♕d6 27.♔g1 ♘:d4 28.♕d3 ± Mikhailchisin.
16.a:b3 ♕h4
16...♕g5 17.♕f3! ♖ae8 18.♘:f4 ♗g4 19.♕g3! ♖:e1 20.♖:e1 ♘:f4 21.♖e4 ♘e2+ 22.♖:e2 ♕:c1+ 23.♖:c1 ♗:g3 24.♖e7 ± Nunn.
17.♕f3 ♖ae8 18.♗:f4 ♘:f4 19.♘:f4 ♗e4 20.♕h5 ♕d8 21.g3 ⩲, Hebden - Nunn, London 1987.

• **13.h3!?**
This modest pawn-push gives rise to some amazing tactics. A foretaste of the complexities to come, is, as pointed out by Gallagher, that 13.h3 is not available in the 7.d:c6 variation - i.e. with the bishop on c4 instead of b3 - because Black can play:
Dieser bescheiden anmutende Bauernzug hat einige verblüffende taktische Komplikationen zur Folge. Ein kleiner Vorgeschmack auf die folgenden Verwicklungen ist, daß - wie Gallagher aus-

geführt hat - 13.h3 in der 7.d:c6-Variante (♗c4 statt ♗b3) nicht spielbar ist wegen:
13...♗:f3 14.♕:f3 (14.♖:f3 ♘e5!) 14...♘:d4! 15.♕h5 ♘e5 16.♘g5 h6 17.♘:f7 ♘:f7 18.♗:f4 ♗:f4 19.♖:f4 ♘e6! −+.

13...♗f5

13...♗h5 14.♕d3.

14.♘fg5!? h6

14...♗:e4 15.♘:e4 ♖e8 16.♕f3! ♘h4 17.♕d3 ♘e5 18.♕b5! a6 (18...♘g6 19.♘g5!) 19.♕d5 ♕:d5 20.♗:d5 ♘d3 21.♖d1! ♘:c1 22.♖a:c1 ♖e7 23.♖e1 ♖ae8 24.♔f2 ♔f8 25.♘c5 f3 26.♖:e7 ♖:e7 27.♗:f3 ±, Gallagher - Almada, Chiasso 1991.

15.♕h5

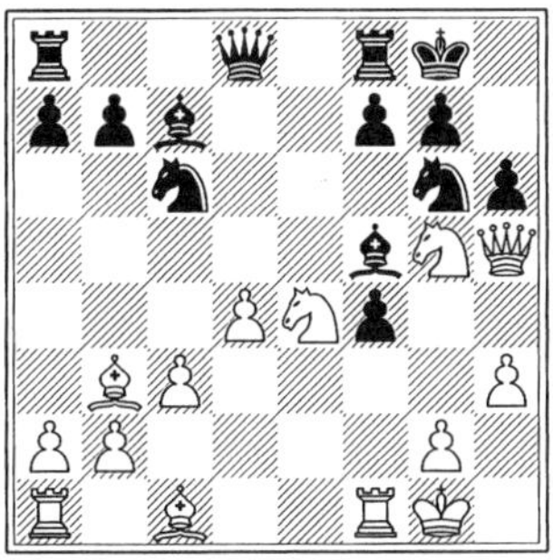

• • 15...♘:d4!?

This is the critical variation, in the light of van Perlo's new ideas below.

Im Lichte von van Perlos neuer Idee die kritische Variante.

16.♗:f7+

Taking with the knight would be an obvious improvent, trying to force Black to take twice at f7, unfortunately Black can 'sacrifice' his queen instead:

Mit dem Springer zu nehmen (um Schwarz zum zweimaligen Schlagen auf f7 zu bewegen), wäre eine ins Auge fallende Verstärkung, doch unglücklicherweise kann Schwarz stattdessen seine Dame "opfern":

16.♘:f7 ♘:b3! 17.♘:d8 ♘:a1 18.♘:b7 ♗:e4 19.♘c5 ♗b6 20.♔h2 ♗:c5 21.♕:c5 ♔h7 22.♕d4 ♖ae8! 23.♕:a7 f3 24.g:f3 ♘h4! −+, Sowray - van Perlo, corr. 1994.

16...♖:f7 17.♘:f7 ♔:f7?!

Much better is 17...♕h4! (∞ van Perlo). Unclear even seems to be a rather modest evaluation, I think it's at least slightly better for Black: e.g.

Viel stärker ist 17...♕h4! (∞ van Perlo), wobei "unklar" eher noch eine bescheidene Einschätzung ist. Meines Erachtens steht Schwarz zumindest leicht besser, z.B.:

18.♘:h6+ g:h6 19.c:d4 ♗:e4 20.♕:h4 ♘:h4 21.♗:f4 ♗b6 22.♗e5 (Δ♖f4) ♖d8 23.♖f4 ♘g6 24.♖:e4 ♘:e5 25.♖ae1 ♘c6 or *(oder)* 18.♕:h4 ♘e2+! 19.♔f2 ♘:h4 20.♘fd6 (20.♔:e2 ♖e8) 20...♘g3 21.♘:g3 f:g3+ 22.♔:g3 g5 23.♗f4 g:f4+ 24.♔:h4 ♗:d6.

I would love to be wrong about this, because it's such a cool variation! But it's no disaster for the King's Gambiteer if Black really is better off here, since it's only 13.h3 that should be avoided in that case.

But why is 13.h3 covered in such detail then? Well it's worth knowing about and it contains some beautiful tactical ideas which may be applicable in similar variations. For example in Johansson - Hellsten (variation *b22*). Besides, there may still be an improvement for White somewhere ...

Liebend gern würde ich mich hier geirrt haben! Doch wäre es keineswegs eine Katastrophe für den Königsgambit-Spieler, wenn Schwarz hier tatsächlich

besser stehen sollte. Denn lediglich um 13.h3 sollte man in diesem Fall einen Bogen machen.
*Doch wieso habe ich dann 13.h3 so ausführlich untersucht? Nun, man sollte diesen Zug kennen, und er enthält einige Ideen, die man vielleicht in ganz ähnlichen Varianten zur Anwendung bringen kann - vgl. z.B. Johansson - Hellsten (unter **b22**). Ganz davon abgesehen, vielleicht findet sich eine Verbesserung für Weiß?*

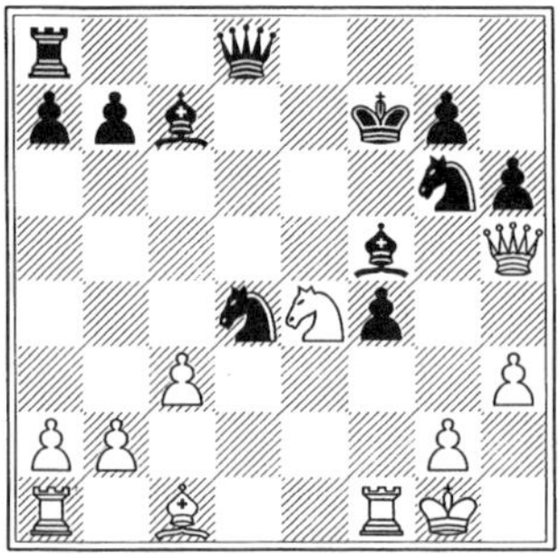

Position after 17...♔:f7/*Nach 17...♔:f7*

18.♘g3!!
A kind of magic that works!
Magische Kräfte scheinen hier am Werk zu sein!

•••18...♗d3 19.♗:f4 ♔g8 (19...♗:f1 20.♖:f1 ⩲) 20.♗:c7 ♕:c7 21.c:d4 ♗:f1 22.♕:g6! (Queen and knight often cooperate better than queen and bishop - *häufig wirken Dame und Springer besser zusammen als Dame und Läufer*) 22...♗b5 23.♘f5 ♔h8 24.♘d6 ♕d7 25.♘f7+ ♔g8 26.♘:h6+ ♔h8 27.♘f7+ ♔g8 28.♘g5 ♕:d4+ ±, Gallagher - Sorin, Biel 1992.
•••18...f:g3 (18...♕h4 19.c:d4) 19.c:d4 ♕:d4+ 20.♔h1 ♔g8 21.♕:f5 ♖f8 22.♗e3! ♕d6 23.♕c2 ♖f2?! 24.♗:f2 g:f2 25.♕b3 ♔h7 26.g3 ± Gallagher.

• • **15...h:g5?!**
Calling White's 'bluff', but he turns out to have a full hand ...
Sollte Weiß bluffen? - Nein, er hat ein "Volles Haus" auf der Hand!
16.♘:g5 ♘h8

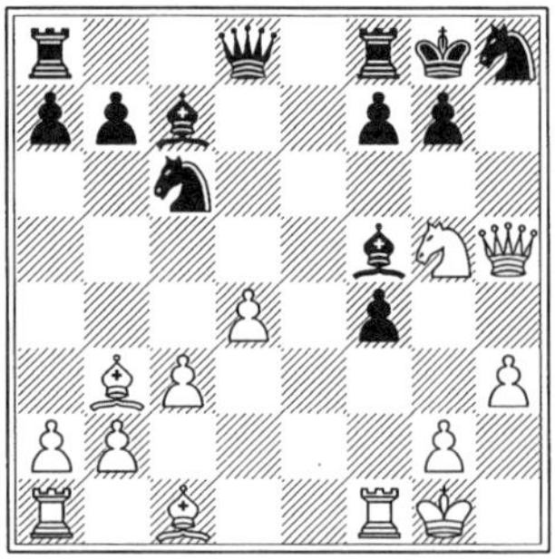

17.♘:f7! ♘:f7 18.♕:f5 ♕f6 19.♕:f6!?
19.♕g4.
19...g:f6 20.♗:f4 ♗:f4 21.♖:f4 ♔g7 22.♖g4+ ♔h6 23.♖f1 ± ♘g5 24.h4 ♘h7 25.♗c2! ♘e7 26.♖e1 ♖f7 27.♗b3 ♖af8 28.♗:f7 ♖:f7 +– 29.♖ge4 ♘g6 30.g3 f5 31.♖e6 ♘f6 32.c4 ♔h5 33.♖f1 ♘g4 34.d5 f4 35.d6 f3 36.c5 ♘6e5 37.♖e7 ♖f8 38.d7 f2+ 39.♖:f2 ♘:f2 40.♖:e5+ ♔g4 41.♖g5+ ♔h3 42.d8♕
1:0, Westerinen - Motwani, London 1988.

Chapter III *Kapitel III*

King's Gambit Declined - The Classical Defence
Abgel. Königsgambit - Die Klassische Verteidigung

1.e4 e5 2.f4 ♗c5

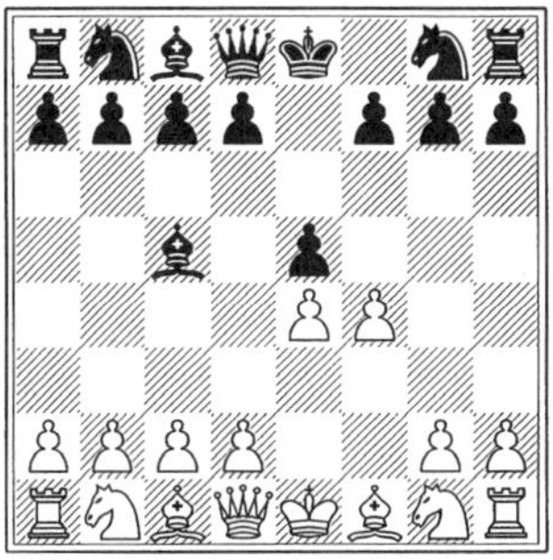

I have decided to cover The Classical very thoroughly because:

- it's very common among solid players who wish to avoid the craziness of the KGA and therefore it's important for White to know how to create similar Chaos in this quieter line!
- the variation I recommend can also be reached via the Bishop's Opening or the Vienna, which may be familiar territory for Black, which means that White has to be quite familiar with it too.

Ich habe mich entschlossen, die Klassische Verteidigung äußerst gründlich abzuhandeln, da:

- *sie bei soliden Spielern, die die aberwitzigen Komplikationen des Angen. Königsgambits umgehen wollen, sehr beliebt ist. Umso wichtiger ist es für Weiß zu wissen, wie sich in den vorliegenden ruhigeren Gewässern ein vergleichbares Durcheinander schaffen läßt!*
- *die von mir empfohlene Variante gleichfalls über das Läuferspiel oder die Wiener Partie herbeigeführt werden kann. Dies mögen dem Schwarzen vertraute Gefilde sein, also sollte man sich auch als Anziehender hier keinesfalls fremd fühlen.*

3.♘f3

This is the usual move order, but 3.♘c3 is an interesting try to provoke Black into entering unknown territory (3...d6 4.♘f3 just transposes to the usual move order).

Die normale Zugfolge. 3.♘c3 wäre ein interessanter Versuch, den Nachziehenden in unbekannte Gefilde zu locken (3...d6 4.♘f3 leitet zum Haupttext über).

3...♗:g1 4.♖:g1

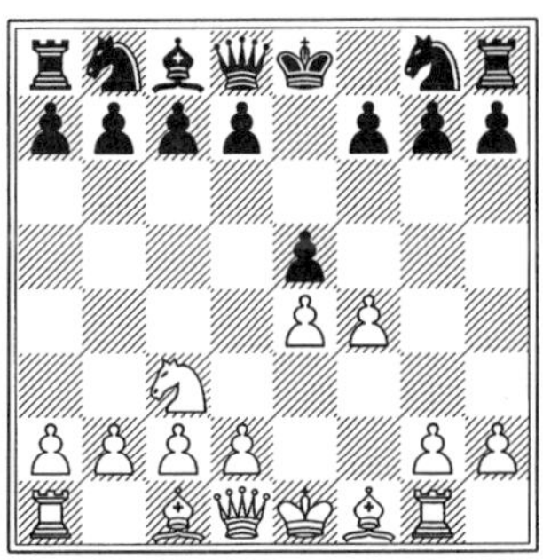

- 4...d6 5.d4 e:d4 6.♕:d4 ♘f6, Steinitz - Barry, Dublin 1865, 7.e5! ±.
- 4...c6 5.f:e5 d6 6.e:d6 ♕:d6 7.g3 f5 8.♕e2 ♘e7 9.d3 0-0 10.♗f4 ♕d4 11.♗e3 ♕f6 12.0-0-0 ±, Steinitz - Rousseau, Paris 1867.
- 4...e:f4 5.d4 ♕h4+ 6.g3 ∞, Tsai - Dubinsky, SSSR 1964.
- 4...♕h4+? 5.g3 ♕:h2 6.♖g2 ♕h1 7.f:e5 h5 8.♕e2 h4 9.♖h2 ♕g1 10.♕g2 ♕:g2 11.♗:g2 ♘c6 12.♖:h4 ±, Chikovani - Beradze, SSSR 1962.

3...d6

3...d5!? is a hard move to run into unprepared, so here's the refutation!

Unvorbereitet ist 3...d5 schwer zu parieren, deshalb hier die Widerlegung!

4.♘:e5! ♘f6 (4...d:e4? 5.♕h5 ♕e7 6.♗c4 g6 7.♕e2 ♘h6 8.♘c3 ♘d7 9.♘d5 ♕d6 10.♕:e4 0-0 11.b4! c6 12.b:c5 ♘:c5 13.♘:f7!! ♘:f7 14.♘e7+ ♔g7 15.♗b2+ ♔h6 16.♕e3 ♘a4 17.f5+ g5 18.♕h3#, Zelevinsky - Ravinsky, Moscow 1962) 5.d4 ♗b6 6.e:d5! ♕:d5 7.♗e3 ♘c6 8.♘c3 ♗a5

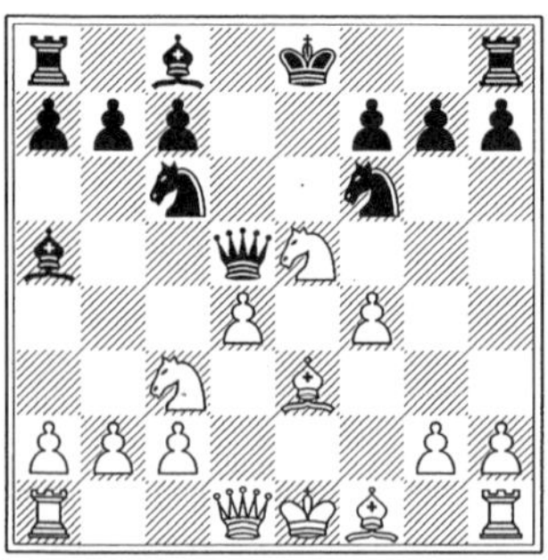

And now 9.♕d2 is enough for a clear edge but Gallagher's 9.♗e2! seems to be even better, e.g:

9.♕d2 genügt nun bereits für einen klaren Vorteil, doch Gallaghers 9.♗e2! scheint fast noch stärker, z.B.:

9...♗:c3+ (9...♘e4 10.0-0 ♗:c3 11.♗c4! →) 10.b:c3 ♕e4 11.♕d3 ♘:e5 12.f:e5 ♕:g2 13.0-0-0 ± Gallagher.

4.♘c3!

Fast development is never wrong in the King's Gambit. White gets a solid yet aggressive position quite easily. As a matter of fact it's reminiscent of a mirrored Queens Gambit, but here Black has no Slavs or Tarraschs since ...f6 or ...f5 would be close to suicide for Black.

Rasche Entwicklung ist im Königsgambit niemals verkehrt. Weiß erhält recht einfach eine sichere, aber auch aggressive Position. Ein Grund hierfür ist, daß wir hier praktisch ein spiegelverkehrtes Damengambit vorliegen haben, wobei dem Schwarzen aber keine Slawische oder Tarrasch-Verteidigung zur Verfügung steht, da ...f6 oder ...f5 hier praktisch gleichbedeutend mit Selbstmord wäre.

4.c3 is the other main line, but I feel that I can't recommend it since Black gets a lead in development while White is buzy building a large balloon centre which must be nursed very tenderly or else it will be exploded!

Die andere Hauptvariante beginnt mit 4.c3, was ich jedoch gefühlsmäßig nicht empfehlen kann. Schwarz kommt mit der Entwicklung in Vorteil, während der Weiße um den Aufbau eines aufgeblähten Zentrums bemüht ist, welches anschließend äußerst zarter Pflege bedarf, um nicht in die Luft gejagt zu werden.

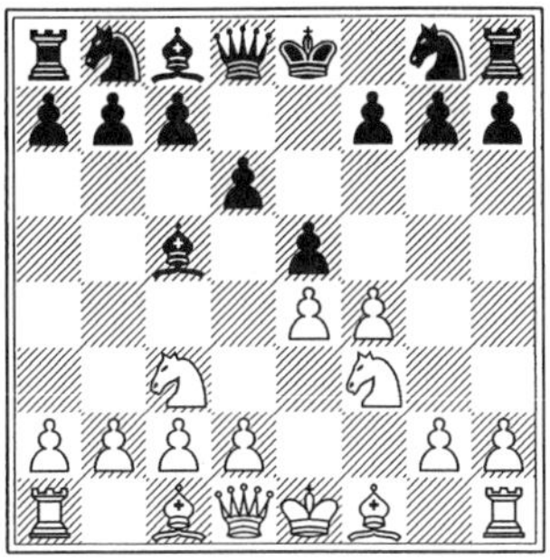

I

4...♗g4 5.♘a4!?

When the ♗c5 is chopped off, White usually gets an easy game.

Ist der ♗c5 erst einmal eliminiert, dann spielt sich die weiße Stellung meist sehr bequem.

5.h3 is a good alternative, if you don't want to insist on gambiting the f-pawn. For example:

5.h3 ist eine gute Alternative, sofern Weiß nicht auf dem Opfer seines f-Bauern besteht. Hier ein Partiebeispiel:

5...♗:f3 6.♕:f3 ♘c6 7.♗b5 ♘ge7 8.f5!? a6 9.♗c4 b5 10.♗b3 ♘d4 11.♕g4 0-0 12.f6 ♘g6 13.♘d5 c6 14.♘e7+ ♔h8 15.f:g7+ ♔:g7 16.♘f5+ ♘:f5 17.e:f5 h5 18.♕:h5 ♖h8 19.♕f3 e4 20.♕c3+ ♘e5 21.♕g3+ ♔f8 22.d4! ♗:d4 23.♗g5 ♕a5+ 24.♗d2 ♕b6 25.f6 ♔e8 26.0-0-0 a5 27.♗c3 ♗:c3 28.♕:c3 b4 29.♕d2 d5 30.♗:d5! e3 31.♗:c6+ ♘:c6 32.♕d7+ ♔f8 33.♖d6 e2 1:0, Fedorov - Najer, Moscow 1996.

A

5...e:f4 6.d4 ♗:f3 7.g:f3 ♕h4+ 8.♔e2 ♗b6 9.♘:b6 a:b6 10.♕d2 g5 11.♔d1

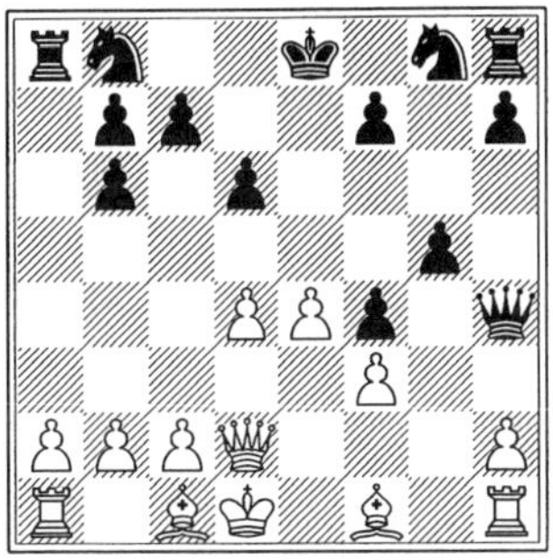

With the bishop pair and a large stable centre as compensation for the pawn, e.g.

Läuferpaar und fester Zugriff auf das Zentrum bieten genügend Ersatz für den Bauern, z.B.:

11...♘e7 12.♗d3 0-0 13.♖g1 ♘g6 14.♕g2 ♘c6 15.c3 h6 16.♗d2 ♕h5 17.♔c2 ♔h8 ±/∞ (1:0/37.), Hebden - Schärer, Lugano 1984.

B

(1.e4 e5 2.f4 ♗c5 3.♘f3 d6 4.♘c3 ♗g4 5.♘a4)

5...♘f6 6.f:e5 ♘:e4 7.d4 ♗b6 8.♘:b6 a:b6 9.♗d3 f5 10.e:d6 ♕:d6 11.0-0 0-0 12.♗e3 ♘c6 13.c3 ♖ae8 14.♕b3+ ♔h8 15.♖ae1 h6 16.♕c2 ♖f6? 17.♘e5! ♗h5

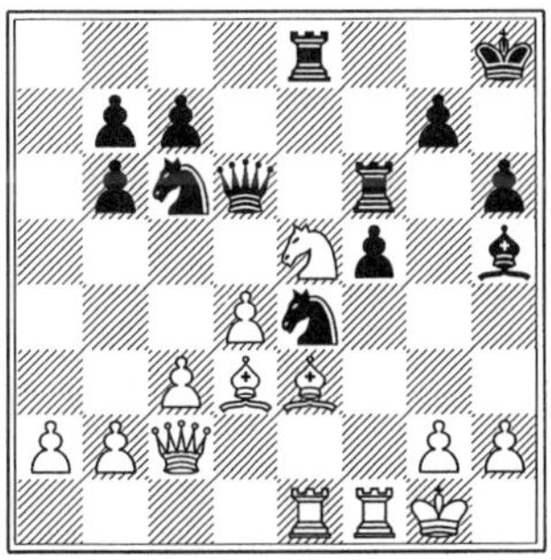

18.g4!

The proud knight on e4 has suddenly been turned into a mortal weakness!
Plötzlich hat sich der "ewige" ♘e4 in einen normalen Sterblichen mit all seinen Fehlern und Schwächen verwandelt!

18...♖:e5 19.d:e5 ♘:e5 20.♗:e4 ♗:g4 21.♗g2 ♖g6 22.♗f4 +– (1:0/28.), Winawer - Wemmers, Berlin 1881.

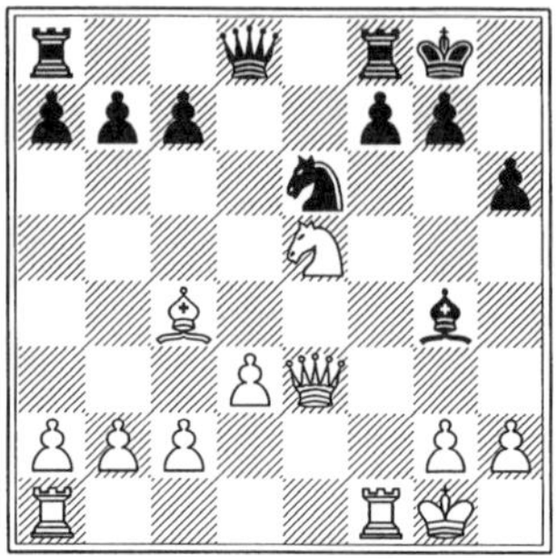

C

(1.e4 e5 2.f4 ♗c5 3.♘f3 d6 4.♘c3 ♗g4 5.♘a4)

5...♗:f3 6.♕:f3 e:f4 7.♘:c5 d:c5 8.♕:f4 ♘f6 9.d3 0-0 10.♗e2 ♘c6 11.♗e3 ♘d4 12.♗d1 ♖e8 13.0-0 ♕d6 14.♕f2 ♖ad8 15.♗g5 ♖e6 16.♗f4 ♕b6 17.♖b1 ♖d7 18.♔h1 ♕a6 19.a3 c4?

19...♖de7.

20.e5! c:d3

20...♘d5 21.♗g4.

21.e:f6 d:c2 22.♗:c2 ♖e2 23.♕g3 ♕:f6 24.♗:h7+ ♔f8 25.♗d3 +– (1:0/30.), Lipschütz - Gossip, New York 1889.

D

(1.e4 e5 2.f4 ♗c5 3.♘f3 d6 4.♘c3 ♗g4 5.♘a4)

5...♘d7 6.♗c4 ♘gf6 7.d3 h6 8.♘:c5 ♘:c5 9.0-0 e:f4 10.♗:f4 ♘e6 11.♗e3 d5 12.e:d5 ♘:d5 13.♕d2 0-0 14.♘e5 ♘:e3 15.♕:e3 ±

White has achieved the usual pressure on f7 ...
Wie üblich übt Weiß Druck auf f7 aus ...

II

(1.e4 e5 2.f4 ♗c5 3.♘f3 d6 4.♘c3)

4...♘c6 5.♗b5!

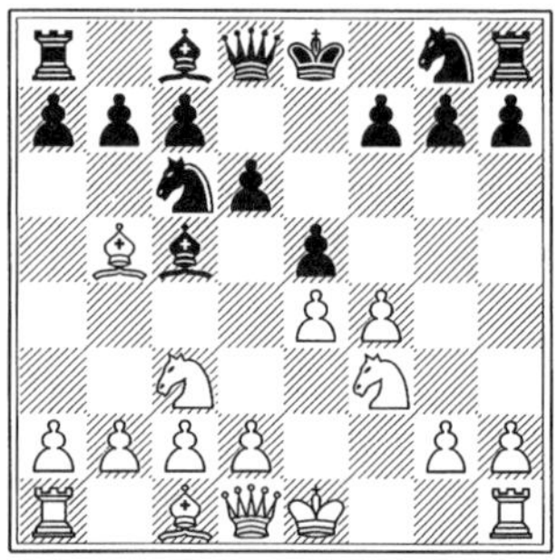

Taking advantage of the King's Gambit move order by making Black worry about his pawn structure!
Versucht, aus der Zugfolge Nutzen zu ziehen - der Nachziehende muß sich nun um seine Bauernstruktur sorgen!

A

5...♗g4 6.♗:c6+

Doubling the c-pawns!
Verdoppelt zunächst den c-Bauern ...

6...b:c6 7.f:e5

And now ripping the pawns apart!
... um anschließend die schwarzen Bauern voneinander zu trennen.

7...d:e5 8.h3 ♗:f3 9.♕:f3 ♘e7 10.d3 ♘g6 11.♗d2 ±

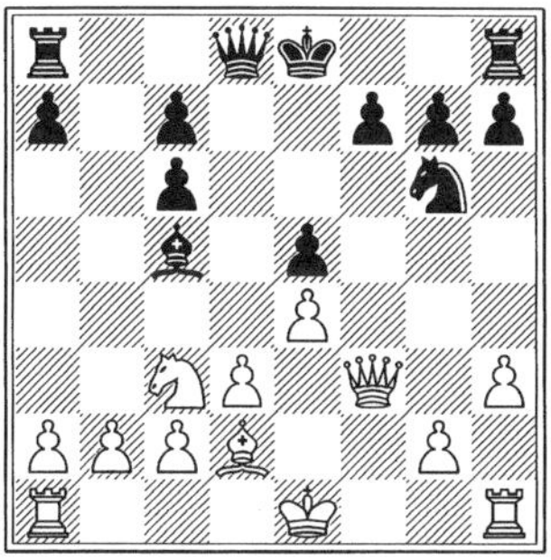

Schlechter - Tietz, Karlsbad 1906.

Black will have a hard time creating enough counter-play to compensate for his dreadful pawn structure!
Schwarz stehen schwierige Zeiten bevor. Er muß versuchen, irgendein Gegenspiel zuwege zu bringen, um von seiner gräßlichen Bauernstruktur abzulenken!

B

(1.e4 e5 2.f4 ♗c5 3.♘f3 d6 4.♘c3 ♘c6 5.♗b5)

5...♘ge7 6.♘a4 ♗b6 7.♘:b6 a:b6 8.d3

8.f:e5!?.

8...0-0 9.0-0 e:f4 10.♗:f4 d5 11.e:d5 ♘:d5 12.♕d2 ±

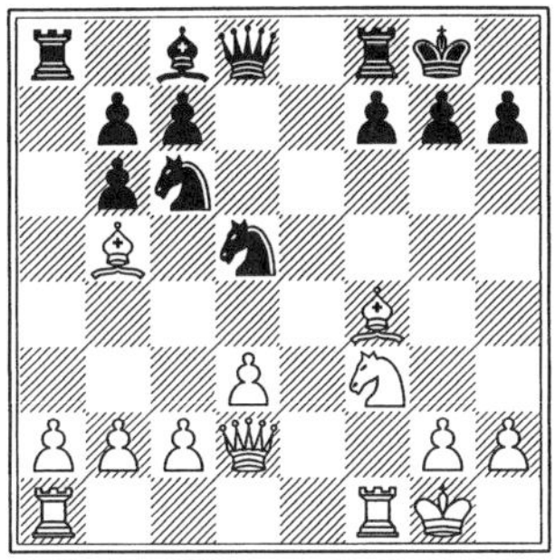

12...♘:f4?! 13.♕:f4 ± Δ ♘g5, ♗c4

C

(1.e4 e5 2.f4 ♗c5 3.♘f3 d6 4.♘c3 ♘c6 5.♗b5)

5...♘f6 ♥ 6.d3!

White should avoid rushing things at this early stage.
Weiß sollte sich hüten, die Dinge zu diesem frühen Zeitpunkt zu forcieren.

a

6...0-0 7.f5!?

This is often a good move, especially when Black has castled kingside, intending to drown the Black king in a tidewave of pawns! However it's often a difficult judgement call what to do with the ♙f4, ripping apart with f:e5; tidewave with f5; or just wait for a better moment.
Häufig ein starker Zug, insbesondere wenn der Nachziehende kurz rochiert hat. Der schwarze König soll unter der Flutwelle der weißen Bauern ertrinken! Gleichwohl ist häufig schwer zu entscheiden, was mit dem ♙f4 geschehen soll: f:e5, um die schwarze Bauernkette zu zerreißen; f5 nebst Bauernsturm

oder einfach ausharren und auf einen günstigen Augenblick für das eine oder andere warten.

7.♗:c6 b:c6 8.f:e5 d:e5 9.♕e2 ♖e8 10.♗d2 or *(oder)* 10.♗e3 Δ 0-0-0 ±.

7...♘g4 8.♕e2 g6 9.h3 ♘d4

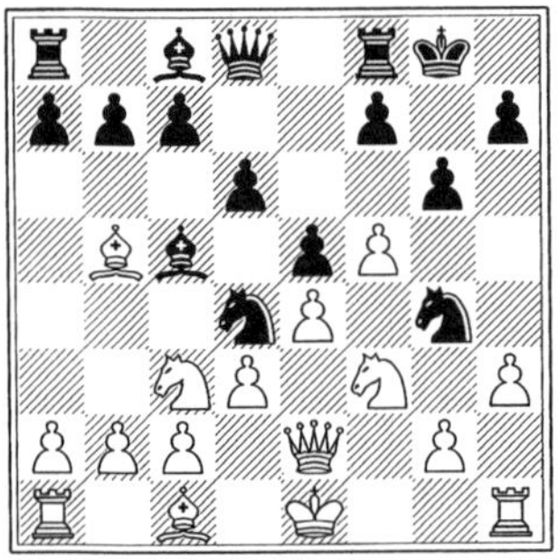

10.h:g4!! ♘:e2 11.♔:e2! g:f5 12.g:f5 c6 13.♗c4 d5 14.♗b3 ♖e8 15.♘g5 ♕f6 16.♘:h7 ♕g7 17.♗g5 ♕:h7 18.♖:h7 ♔:h7 19.♗f6 1:0, Maroczy - Jakoby, Budapest 1896.

A fine example of the strength of White's central pawn formation! Despite his material superiority, Black had nothing to attack and got strangled.
Ein herrliches Demonstrationsbeispiel für die Stärke der weißen Zentrumsformation! Der Nachziehende kann mit seinem Materialvorteil nichts anfangen und wird schließlich stranguliert.

b

(1.e4 e5 2.f4 ♗c5 3.♘f3 d6 4.♘c3 ♘c6 5.♗b5 ♘f6 6.d3)

6...♘g4?!

A tempting sortie, but if White doesn't panic it will turn out to be just a blow in the air and a waste of tempi!
Ein verlockender Ausfall. Doch wenn Weiß kühlen Kopf bewahrt, wird er sich als Schlag ins Wasser und reiner Zeitverlust erweisen!

7.♕e2 ♗f2+ 8.♔f1 ♗d4 9.h3 ♘f6 10.♘:d4 e:d4 11.♘d1 ♗d7 12.c3 ♕e7? 13.♗:c6 ♗:c6 14.c:d4 0-0-0 15.d5 ♗b5 16.♔f2 ♖he8 17.♘c3 ±/+− (1:0/30.), Burn - Watkinson, Bradford 1871.

c

(1.e4 e5 2.f4 ♗c5 3.♘f3 d6 4.♘c3 ♘c6 5.♗b5 ♘f6 6.d3)

6...♗g4 7.♘a4!

These two moves seem to belong to each other like thunder and lightning!
Diese beiden Züge scheinen zusammenzugehören wie Blitz und Donner!

7...♗b6 8.♘:b6 a:b6 9.0-0 0-0 10.c3 ± **e:f4 11.♗:f4 ♘e5 12.d4 ♘:f3+ 13.g:f3 ♗h3 14.♖f2 ♘h5 15.♗e3** ±

15...f5 16.♗f1!.

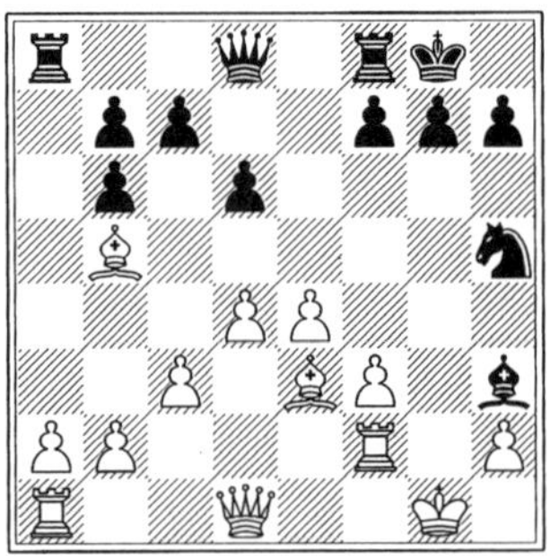

Chigorin - Salwe, Karlsbad 1907 (½:½/82.).

D

(1.e4 e5 2.f4 ♗c5 3.♘f3 d6 4.♘c3 ♘c6 5.♗b5)

5...♗d7 6.♘a4 ♗b6 7.♘:b6 a:b6 8.d3

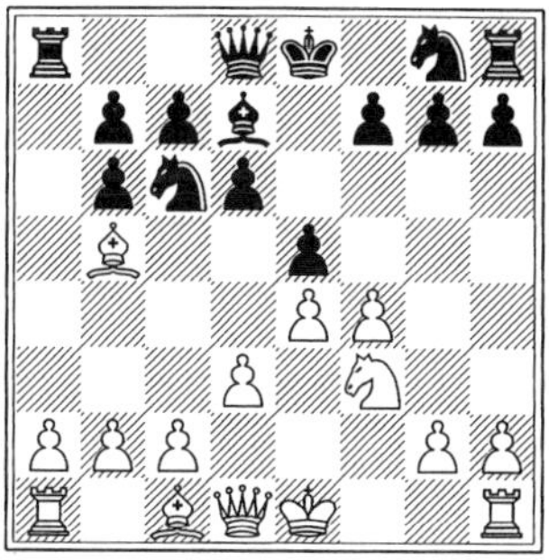

a

8...♕e7 9.0-0 ♘f6 10.♔h1 h6 11.♕e1 0-0-0?! 12.a4 e:f4 13.♗:f4 ♘b8 14.♘d4 c6 15.♕c3 ♘e8 16.a5 b:a5 17.♖:a5 ♘c7 18.♗c4 b5?

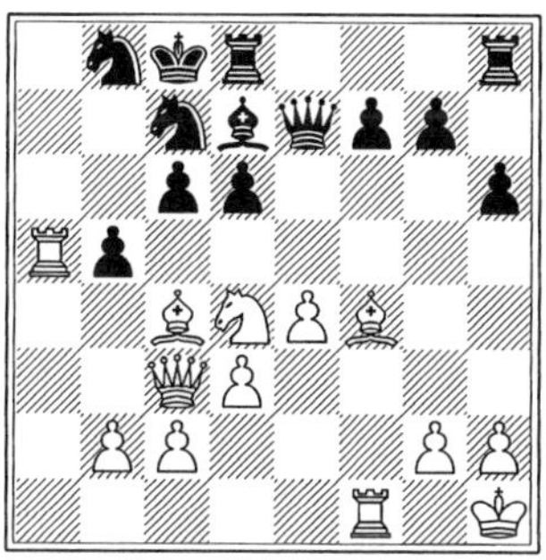

19.♗:b5! c:b5 20.♖a7 (20...♗e8 21.♘f5 +–) 1:0, Hebden - Lane, London 1987.

b

(1.e4 e5 2.f4 ♗c5 3.♘f3 d6 4.♘c3 ♘c6 5.♗b5 ♗d7 6.♘a4 ♗b6 7.♘:b6 a:b6 8.d3)

8...♘ge7 9.0-0 0-0 10.f5! f6 11.♗c4+ ♔h8 12.a3

Giving the bishop a hide-out in case of ...♘a5.
Gibt dem Läufer ein Versteck für den Fall von ...♘a5.

12.c3 ±, Capablanca - Molina, New York 1906.

12...♗e8 13.♗e6

13.♗a2! ♗h5 14.♕e1 ♗f7 14.c4! seems to save some tempi on the text *(scheint im Vergleich zur Partiefolge zwei Tempi einzusparen).*

13...♗h5

13...♗f7? 14.♗:f7 ♖:f7 15.♘h4 Δ ♕h5 →.

14.♕e1 ♕e8

14...♗f7 is better since White's queen can't reach h5 now, Capablanca.
Besser wäre 14...♗f7; im Unterschied zur vorigen Anmerkung gelangt die weiße Dame jetzt nicht gleich nach h5 (Capablanca).

15.♕h4 ♘d8 16.♗a2 ♗f7 17.c4 c5?!

17...b5.

18.g4 ♘g8 19.♗d2 b5 20.g5 f:g5 21.♘:g5 ♘f6 22.♖f3 b:c4

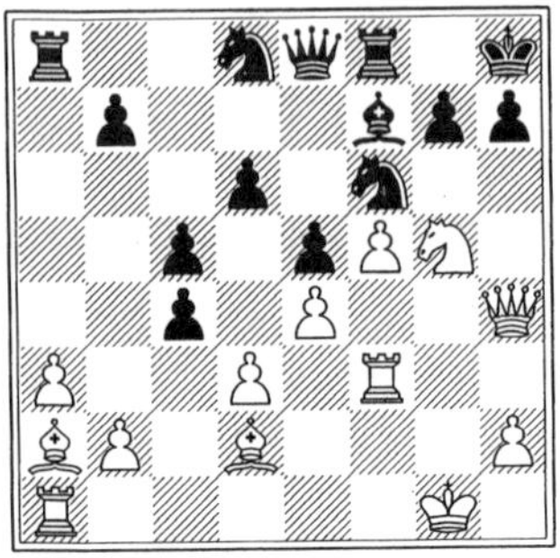

23.♘:h7!! ♘:h7 24.♖h3 ♗g8 25.♗:c4 ♖f7

25...♘f7 26.f6! g5 27.♕h5 ♘d8 28.♕h6 ♖f7 29.♗:g5 ♕f8 30.♔h1! ♕:h6 31.♗:h6 ♖:f6 32.♖g1 +– (Capablanca).

26.♔h1 b5 27.♗d5 ♖aa7 28.♖g1 ♖f6 29.♗g5 ♖af7 30.b3! ♕f8 31.a4 b:a4 32.b:a4 ♕e8 33.a5 ♘c6 34.a6 ♘b4 35.♗:f6 ♘:d5 36.♗:g7+ ♖:g7 37.♖:g7 ♔:g7 38.♕h6+ ♔h8

38...♔f7 39.♖g3 +–.

39.♕:d6 +–, Capablanca - Molina & Ruiz, Buenos Aires 1914.

A classic game!
Eine klassische Partie!

C

(1.e4 e5 2.f4 ♗c5 3.♘f3 d6 4.♘c3 ♘c6 5.♗b5 ♗d7 6.♘a4 ♗b6 7.♘:b6 a:b6 8.d3)

8...e:f4 9.♗:f4 ♕f6 10.♕c1 ♘ge7 11.0-0 ± ♕g6 12.d4 0-0 13.e5 d:e5 14.♗:e5 ♖ac8 15.♕d2 ♕h5 16.♖ae1 ♘g6 17.♗e2 f6 18.♗g3 (0:1/40.), Grekov - Pavlov & Panov, Moscow 1920.

III

(1.e4 e5 2.f4 ♗c5 3.♘f3 d6 4.♘c3)

4...a6

Trying to preserve his favourite bishop!
Schwarz möchte seinen Lieblingsläufer behalten!

5.♗c4

A good rule for White is to always complete development before beginning active play. Unless, of course, Black forces us to counter-attack!
Eine nützliche Faustregel besagt, daß Weiß, bevor er zu aktiven Kampfhandlungen schreitet, zunächst die Entwicklung beenden sollte - außer natürlich, wenn ein hyperaggressiver Schwarzer uns zum Gegenschlag zwingt!

5.f:e5!? d:e5 6.♘:e5 (This is seldom good before White is developed - *vor Abschluß der Entwicklung ist dies nur selten gut*) 6...♕d4 7.♘d3 ♗b6 8.♕f3 ♘f6 9.♘f2 ♘c6 ∞ (1:0/57.), Chigorin - Martinez, New York 1889.

A

5...♘c6 6.d3 ♗g4?!

6...♗e6.

7.h3 ♗:f3 8.♕:f3 ♘d4 9.♕g3! ♥

Thematic in many variation of this defence, but also very sharp demanding some accuracy from White.
Ein in diesem Verteidigungssystem thematischer Zug. Seine Schärfe verlangt jedoch gleichzeitig einige Genauigkeit von Weiß.

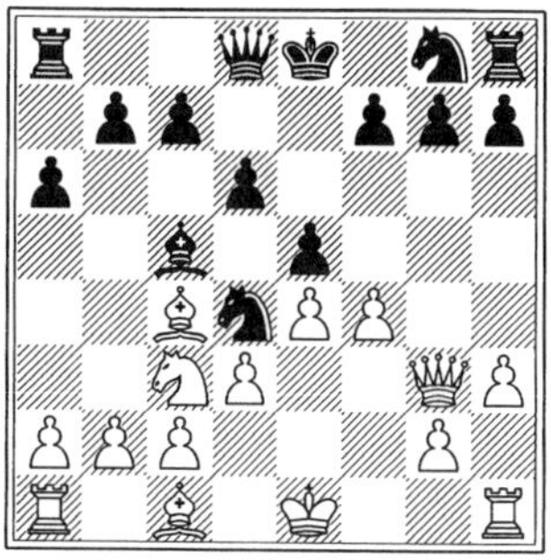

9...♘:c2+ 10.♔d1 ♘:a1 11.f:e5! d:e5

11...♔f8!? looks like a more stubborn defence *(gäbe dem Angreifer eine härtere Nuß zu knacken)*: 12.♖f1 f6 13.e:f6 ♘:f6 (13...g:f6 14.♕g5! c6 15.♗:g8 ♖:g8 16.♖:f6+ ♔e7 17.♕f5! ♕c8 18.♖f7+ ♔e8 19.♕f6 d5 20.♖:h7 +−) 14.♘d5 ♗d4 15.♕g5! (15.♘f4 ♔e8!) 15...b5 (15...c5 16.♘f4 ♕e7 17.♘e6+ ♔e8 18.♘:g7+ ♔d7 19.♘f5! +−) 16.♘f4 ♔e8 17.♘e6 ♕e7 18.♗d5! ♘:d5 19.♕:d5 ♖b8 20.♘:d4 ♕d7 21.♗h6!! ♖b6 22.♘e6 ♕c6? (22...c6 23.♕d4 ♕:e6 24.♕:b6 ♕d7 25.♗:g7 ±) 23.♕f5! +−.

12.♖f1!

White's reluctance to play the 'obvious' ♕:g7 until it's decisive is definitely worthy of imitation! 'All good things to he who waits'.

Weiß wartet mit dem offensichtlichen ♕:g7, bis dies mit entscheidender Wirkung geschehen kann - ein leuchtendes Beispiel für schöpferische Phantasie! "Alles Glück fällt dem zu, der zu warten versteht".

12...♘f6 13.♕:g7 ♔d7 14.♖:f6 ♔c8 15.♖:f7 ♗d6 16.♗g5! ♕e8 17.♘d5 +− ♖g8 18.♖:c7+ ♔b8 19.♖:b7+ ♔c8 20.♘b6#, Chigorin - Martinez, New York 1889.

B

(1.e4 e5 2.f4 ♗c5 3.♘f3 d6 4.♘c3 a6 5.♗c4)

5...♗g4 6.h3 ♗:f3 7.♕:f3 ♘c6 8.♕g3 g6 9.d3 ♘f6 10.f5! ♕d7 11.♗g5 ♘h5 12.♕h4 h6 13.f:g6! ± (1:0/30.), Fisher - Goldsmith, Melbourne 1875.

IV

(1.e4 e5 2.f4 ♗c5 3.♘f3 d6 4.♘c3)

4...♘f6 5.♗c4

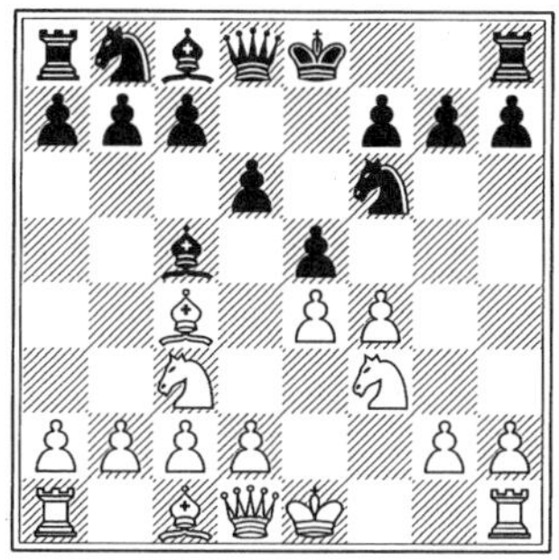

A

5...♗e6 6.♗:e6 f:e6 7.f:e5 d:e5 8.♘:e5

This seems quite safe here since Black has squandered his whitefielder and weakened his king.

Dies kann hier ziemlich gefahrlos geschehen, da Schwarz seinen weißfeldrigen Läufer weggeschenkt und seine Königsstellung geschwächt hat.

8...♕d4 9.♘d3 ♘:e4?

9...♗b6 10.♕e2 ♘c6 11.b3 ±, Melikhov - Sachisyan, corr. 1953/54.

10.♕e2 ♘:c3

10...♘g5? 11.♕h5+ +−.

11.♕:e6+ ♔d8 12.d:c3

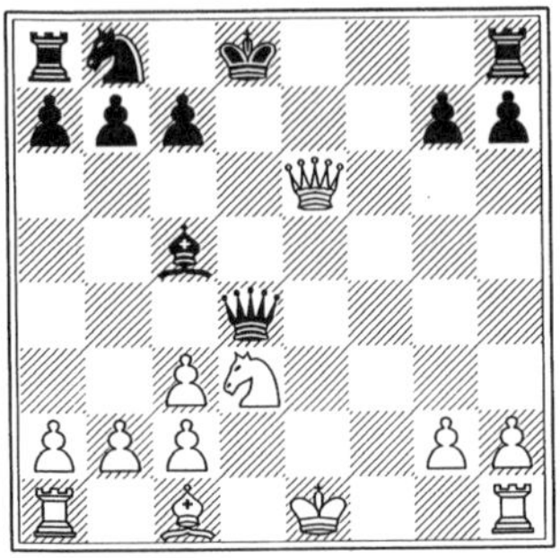

+−, e.g. (z.B.) 12...♕h4+ 13.g3 ♕h5 14.♘e5 ♖e8? 15.♗g5+ +−.

B

(1.e4 e5 2.f4 ♗c5 3.♘f3 d6 4.♘c3 ♘f6 5.♗c4)

5...♘g4 6.d4

6.♕e2.

6...e:d4 7.♘:d4 ♕h4+ 8.g3 ♕h3 9.♗f1 ♕h5 10.♘d5 ♗b6

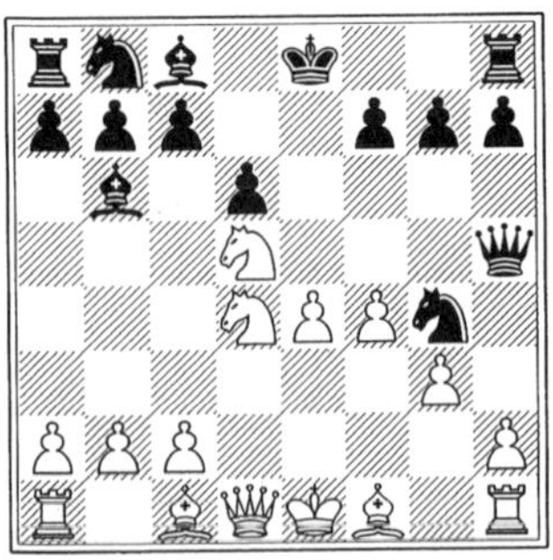

11.f5! 0-0 12.♗e2 ♖e8 13.♘:b6 a:b6 14.♗:g4 ♖:e4+ 15.♗e2 c5 16.0-0 ♕h3 17.♘b5 ♗:f5 18.♖:f5 ♕:f5 19.♘:d6 1:0, Schmid - Reiff, Leipzig 1877.

C

(1.e4 e5 2.f4 ♗c5 3.♘f3 d6 4.♘c3 ♘f6 5.♗c4)

5...c6 6.d3

a

(1.e4 e5 2.f4 ♗c5 3.♘f3 d6 4.♘c3 ♘f6 5.♗c4 c6 6.d3)

6...b5 7.♗b3 a5 8.a4!

Forcing the issue, which is usually good when you're ahead in development. *Forciert die Geschehnisse, was meist vorteilhaft ist, wenn man in der Entwicklung voran ist.*

8...b4 9.♘e2 ♘bd7 10.♘g3 0-0 11.♕e2

11.♖f1 may be more exact e.g: *(könnte noch genauer sein, z.B.:)* 11...♕b6 12.♕e2 Δ f:e5, Δ f5, ♗g5.

11...♗a6 12.f:e5 d:e5 13.♘f5 ♕c7 14.♖f1 ♖ae8 15.♘g5 h6 16.♘h3 ♔h7 17.♖f3

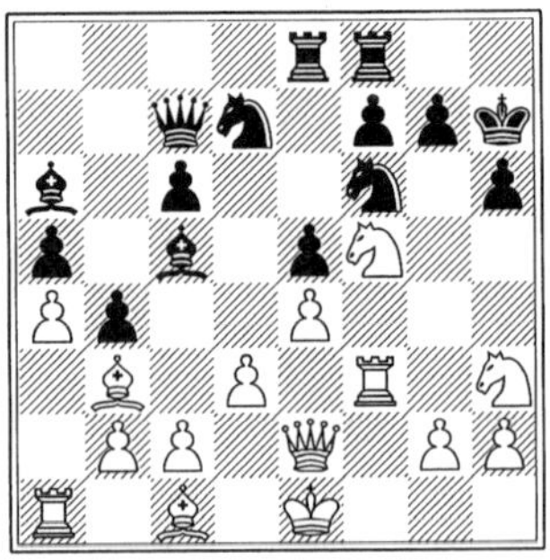

17...♘:e4

Desperation. If 17...♘h5 18.♘g5+!. *Verzweiflung. Auf 17...♘h5 folgt 18.♘g5+!.*

18.♕:e4 ♘f6 19.♕h4 e4 20.♘g5+ ♔g8 21.♘:e4 ♘:e4 22.d:e4 ♕e5 23.♗:h6 ♕:e4+ 24.♕:e4 ♖:e4 25.♗e3 ♗:e3 26.♘:e3 ♖fe8 27.♔f2 1:0, Zukertort - Anderssen, Berlin 1871.

b

(1.e4 e5 2.f4 ♗c5 3.♘f3 d6 4.♘c3 ♘f6 5.♗c4 c6 6.d3)

6...♘bd7 7.♕e2

This with the idea ♗e3 is far from as usual as one might think and it's mostly used when castling queenside is out of the question.
Dieses Manöver - in Verbindung mit ♗e3 - ist längst nicht so geläufig wie man meinen könnte. Es kommt meist dann zur Anwendung, wenn die lange Rochade außer Diskussion steht.

7...b5

7...0-0 8.f:e5 (8.f5) 8...d:e5 9.♖f1 ± ♕e7 10.♗g5 (provoking a weakness in the king's defensive wall - *provoziert eine Schwächung der schwarzen Königsstellung*) 10...h6 11.♗e3 ♗:e3 12.♕:e3 ♘g4 13.♕e2 ♕c5 14.♔d2 ± (Black will be pushed back by h3 and g4 eventually - *demnächst wird Schwarz mit h3 und g4 zurückgedrängt*).

8.♗b3 a5 9.a4 b4 10.♘d1 ♗a6 11.f:e5! d:e5 12.♘e3! ♗:e3

12...♘:e4 13.♘c4! or *(oder)* 13.♘f5!?.

13.♕:e3 ♘g4?

13...0-0.

14.♕e2 0-0 15.♗g5! ♘gf6 16.0-0 h6

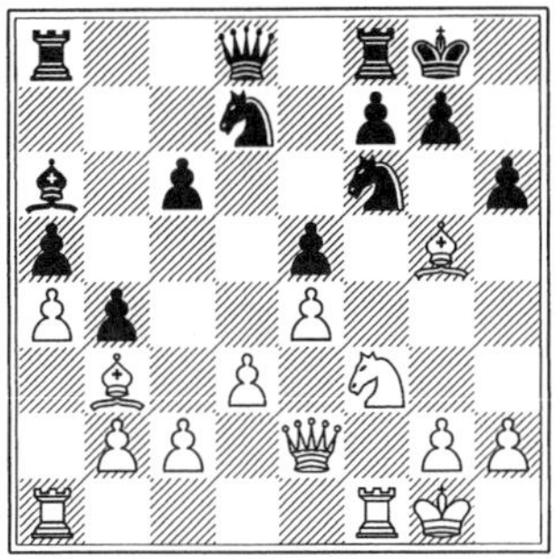

The rest is a fine illustration of White's slow, burning pressure on the f-file suddenly becoming a forest fire!
Der weitere Verlauf ist eine schöne Illustration für das stetige Anwachsen des weißen Drucks auf der f-Linie, der sich von einer lodernden Flamme plötzlich zu einem Flächenbrand ausweitet.

17.♗h4 ♕c7 18.♘d2 ♕d6 19.♔h1 g5?

19...♘h7!?.

20.♗g3 ♔g7 21.♖f5 ♘g8 22.♘f1 ♖ae8 23.♘e3 ♕g6 24.♖af1 f6 25.h4! ♘c5 26.h5 ♕h7 27.♗c4 ♗c8

27...♗:c4 28.♘:c4 Δ ♘:a5, Δ ♘:e5.

28.♕f2! ♘e6

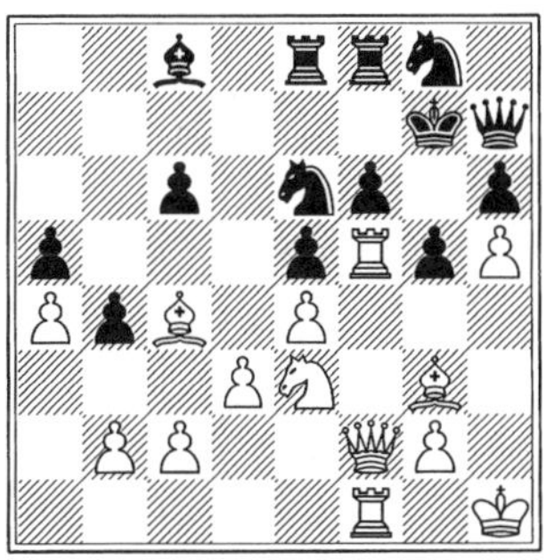

29.♖:e5! 26.f:e5 30.♗:e5+ ♘f6 31.♘g4! ♘f4 32.♕a7+ ♔h8 33.♗:f6+ 1:0, Chigorin - Marco, Ostend 1905.

c

(1.e4 e5 2.f4 ♗c5 3.♘f3 d6 4.♘c3 ♘f6 5.♗c4 c6 6.d3)

6...♕e7 7.♕e2 ♘bd7

7...♗g4 8.f:e5 d:e5 9.♗e3 ♘bd7 10.♘d1 ±, Honfi - Hardicsay, Hungary 1975.

8.f5 b5

8...h6 9.♗d2 Δ 0-0-0.

9.♗b3 a5 10.a4 b4 11.♘d1 ♗b6 12.♗g5 ♗a6 13.♘e3 ♘c5 14.♗c4 ♗b7 15.0-0 0-0?! 16.♔h1 ♗d8 17.♘g4 d5? 18.♗a2 d:e4

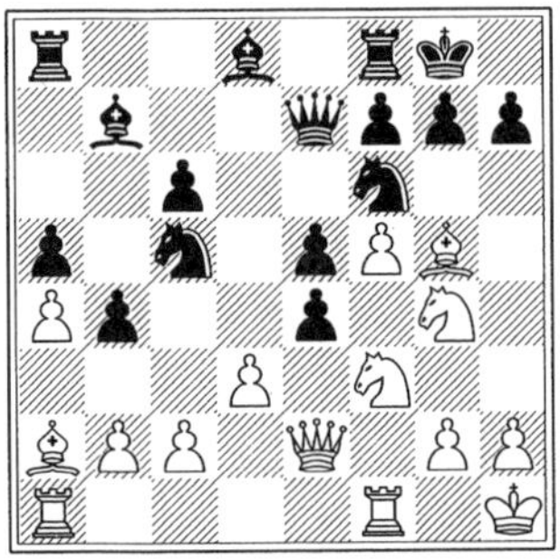

19.♘:f6+! g:f6 20.♗h6 e:f3 21.♖:f3 ♔h8 22.♖g3 ♗b6 23.♗g7+ ♔g8 24.♗:f6#, Gossip - Hanham, New York 1889.

D

(1.e4 e5 2.f4 ♗c5 3.♘f3 d6 4.♘c3 ♘f6 5.♗c4)

5...e:f4!?

Incredibly enough, this seems to be a recent novelty!

Es ist kaum glaublich, doch dieser Zug soll eine Neuerung aus einer kürzlich gespielten Partie sein!

6.d4 ♗b4 7.0-0 0-0 8.♘d5

8.e5!? d:e5 9.♘:e5 looks natural *(macht einen natürlicheren Eindruck)*.

8...♘:d5 9.♗:d5 c6 10.♗b3 d5 11.♗:f4 ♗e7 12.♕d2

12.e:d5 c:d5 13.♕d3 Δ c3, ♗c2 also looks natural *(wirkt wieder natürlicher)*.

12...♗e6 13.♘g5 ♗:g5 14.♗:g5 f6 15.♗h4 ♕d7 16.e:d5 c:d5 (0:1/55.), Shulman - Giorgadze, Linares 1997.

White eventually went down in the ending after spurning a perpetual in the middle game.
Der Anziehende zog schließlich im Endspiel den kürzeren, nachdem er im Mittelspiel ein Dauerschach verschmäht hatte.

E

(1.e4 e5 2.f4 ♗c5 3.♘f3 d6 4.♘c3 ♘f6 5.♗c4)

5...♘c6 6.d3

a

6...♘g4 ♥

6...♕e7 7.f5 ♘d4 (7...h6 8.♘a4) 8.♗g5 ±.
6...h6 (Δ ♘g4) 7.♘a4 ♗b6 8.♘:b6 a:b6 9.0-0 0-0 10.f:e5 d:e5 11.♕e1 ♘e8 12.♕g3 ♕d6 13.a3 b5 14.♗b3 ♖a6 15.♗e3 ♔h7 16.♖f2 ± (0:1/75.), Teichmann - Gunsberg, Hastings 1895.

7.♘g5!

If you panic this can be a hard move to find at the board, but if you remember it you'll see that it's even harder to meet!
Schwer zu finden, wenn man sich am Brett von 6...♘g4 erschrecken läßt. Umso schwerer ist dann 7.♘g5 zu erwidern, wenn einem dieser Zug wieder einfällt!

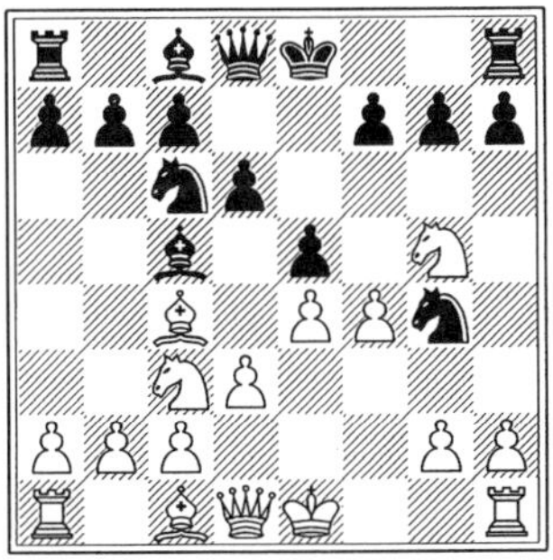

- 7...e:f4 8.♗:f4 ♘f2 9.♕h5 g6 10.♗:f7+ ♔d7 11.♕h6 ♘:h1? 12.♕h3+ ♔e7 13.♘d5+ ♔f8 14.♕h6#, Burgess - Miller, corr. 1974.
- 7...♘f2 8.♕h5 g6 9.♗:f7+ ♔e7? (9...♔f8 10.♕h6+ ♔e7 11.♘d5+ ♔d7 12.♗e6+ ♔e8 13.♕g7 ±, 9...♔d7 10.♗e6+ ♔e8 11.♕h6 ♘d4 12.♕g7±) 10.♘d5+ ♔d7 11.♗e6+ ♔e8 12.♕h6 +–.
- 7...h6 8.f5! ♘e3 (8...♘f2 9.♕h5, 8...♗f2+ 9.♔f1 ♗e3 10.♗:f7+ ♔f8 11.♕:g4±) 9.♗:f7+ ♔f8 10.♗:e3 ♗:e3 11.♘e6+ ♗:e6 12.f:e6 ♕f6 13.♕e2 ♘d4 14.♘d5 ±, Dresden - Prague, corr. 1891.
- 7...0-0 8.f5! ♗f2+ (8...♘f2 9.♕h5 h6 10.♘:f7 ♖:f7 11.♕:f7+ ♔h8 12.h4! ♘:h1 13.♗g5 +–) 9.♔f1 ♘e3+ 10.♗:e3 ♗:e3 11.h4! → ♗:g5 12.h:g5 ♕:g5 13.♖h5 ♕g3 14.♘d5

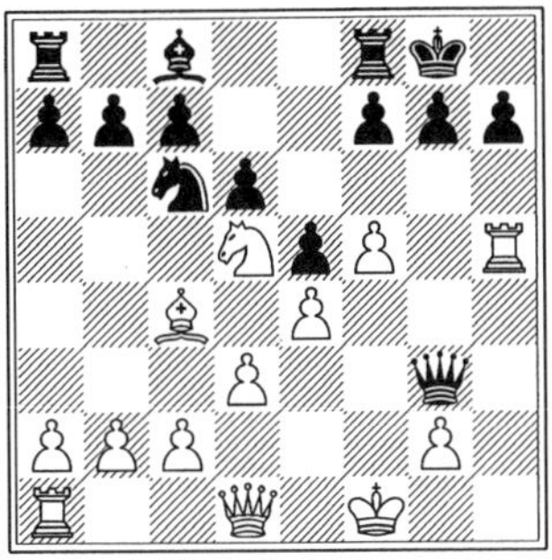

14...g6 (14...♘d4?? 15.♘e7+ ♔h8 ♖:h7+) 15.♖h3 ♕g5 16.♔f2! ♘d4 17. c3 ♘e6! 18.♕h1 ♕d2+ 19.♔g1 ♘g5 20.♖g3 ♔g7 21.f6+ ♔h8 22.♘e3 (Δ ♕h6) h5 23.♖d1 ♕e2 24.d4 +– (1:0/ 36.), Kamyshov - Panov, Moscow 1945.

b

(1.e4 e5 2.f4 ♗c5 3.♘f3 d6 4.♘c3 ♘f6 5.♗c4 ♘c6 6.d3)

6...♘a5

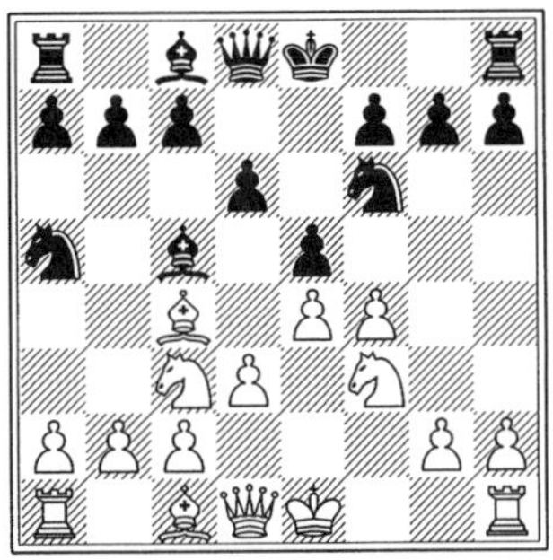

- 7.♕e2!? ♘:c4 8.d:c4

This increases White's presence in the centre and Black will find it very hard to liberate himself since d5 is firmly in White's hands.
Die weiße Präsenz im Zentrum ist nun noch stärker betont. Der Nachziehende

wird es sehr schwer haben, sich zu befreien, da d5 fest in weißer Hand ist.
8...♕e7 (8...e:f4) 9.f5! ♗b4 10.♗d2 ♗d7 11.0-0-0 a6 12.♖he1 h6 13.h3 ♗c6 14.♕d3 ♗:c3 15.♗:c3 0-0-0 ±/± (1:0/39.), Alekhine - Grunberg, Odessa 1916.

- 7.♗b3 ♘:b3 8.a:b3 a6 9.h3! h6 10.♘e2 ♕e7 (10...d5 11.♘:e5! d:e4 12.d4 ♗a7 13.c4) 11.f:e5 d:e5 12.♗d2! ♗d7 13.♗c3 ♗d6 14.0-0 ±, Spielmann - Fleischmann, Barmen 1905.

c

(1.e4 e5 2.f4 ♗c5 3.♘f3 d6 4.♘c3 ♘f6 5.♗c4 ♘c6 6.d3)

6...♗e6 7.♗b5!

Improving the bishop's position, similar to 4...♘c6 5.♗b5 since the ♗e6 will soon be forced to move again.
Verbessert die Stellung des Läufers; vgl. 4...♘c6 5.♗b5. Der ♗e6 muß ohnehin bald weder ziehen.

7...0-0

- 7...a6 8.♗:c6+ b:c6 9.f:e5! d:e5 10.♕e2 ±.
- 7...♗d7 8.♘a4 ♗b6 (8...e:f4 9.♘:c5 d:c5 10.♗:f4, 8...♘d4 9.♗:d7+! ♘:d7 10.♘:c5 ♘:f3+ 11.♕:f3 ♘:c5 12.♕g3! ±) 9.♘:b6 a:b6 10.♗:c6 Δ f:e5.

8.f5 ♗d7 9.♗g5 ♘d4 10.♗:d7! ♕:d7 11.♗:f6 (± ECO) **g:f6 12.♘:d4 ♗:d4 13.♘d5 ♕d8 14.♕g4+ ♔h8 15.♕h4 ♔g7 16.♖f1 c6 17.♖f3** ±

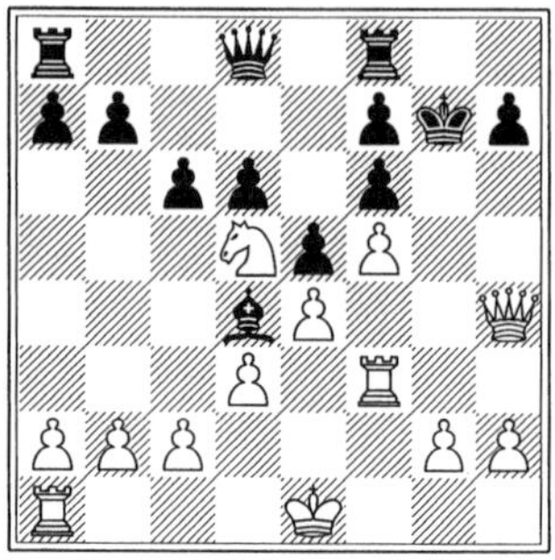

d

(1.e4 e5 2.f4 ♗c5 3.♘f3 d6 4.♘c3 ♘f6 5.♗c4 ♘c6 6.d3)

6...0-0 7.f5!

7.f:e5 d:e5 8.♗g5 ♗e6 9.♗b3 ♗:b3 10.a:b3 ♘b4 11.♘a4 ♗d6 12.0-0 Δ ♘h4 ±.

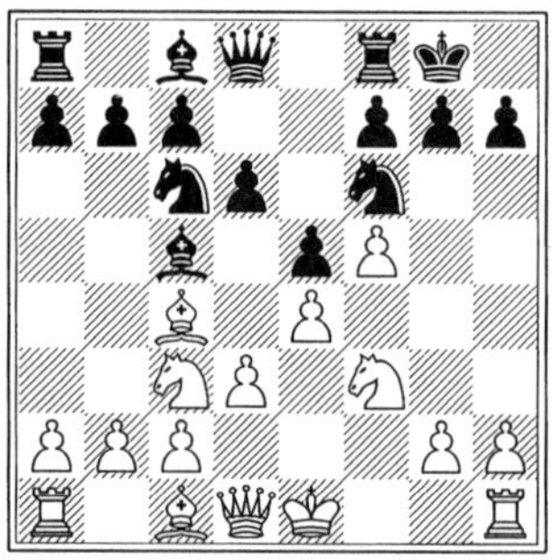

d1

7...h6 8.♘d5! ♘d4

8...♘a5 9.♘:f6+ ♕:f6 10.g4!.

9.♘:d4 ♗:d4 10.♘:f6+ ♕:f6 11.c3 ♗b6 12.♕h5 (± Gallagher) **c6 13.♖f1!?**

13.g4!?.

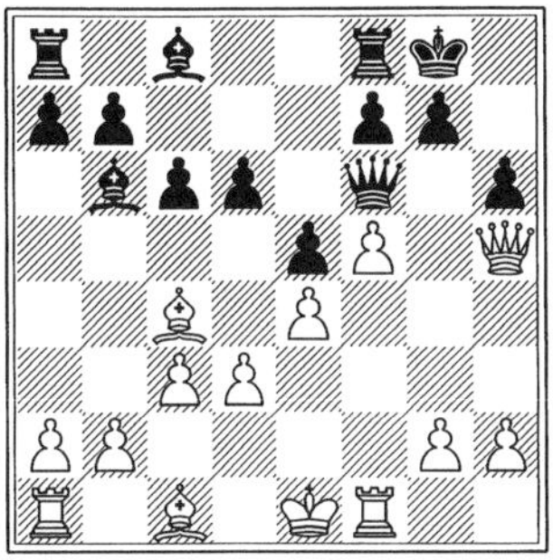

13...d5 14.e:d5 e4! 15.d4 c5 16.g4 e3! 17.d:c5 ♗:c5 18.♔e2 b5 19.♗d3 ♖e8 20.g5!? ∞ (1:0/70.), Hebden - Martinovsky, London 1986.

d2

(1.e4 e5 2.f4 ♗c5 3.♘f3 d6 4.♘c3 ♘f6 5.♗c4 ♘c6 6.d3 0-0 7.f5)

7...♘d4 8.♗g5 c6 9.a3 h6 10.♗h4 b5 11.♗a2 a5 12.g4

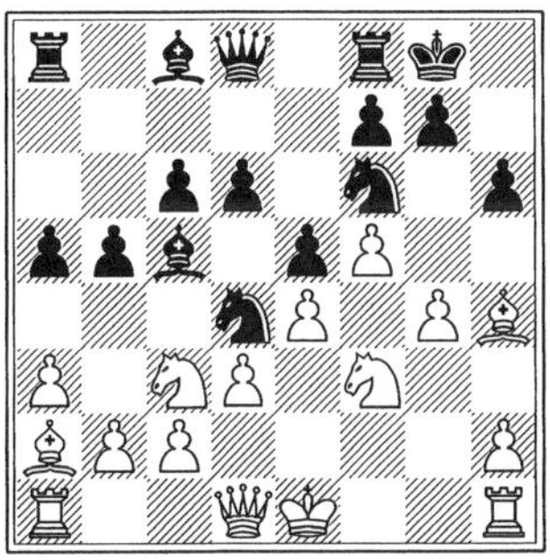

12...g5 13.f:g6 ♗:g4 14.♗:f7+ ♔g7 15.♘:d4 ♗:d4, A. Fischer - Pluto, Chicago 1964 (0:1/21.), 16.♗:f6+! ♕:f6 17.♕:g4 ♕f2+ 18.♔d1 +–.

d3

(1.e4 e5 2.f4 ♗c5 3.♘f3 d6 4.♘c3 ♘f6 5.♗c4 ♘c6 6.d3 0-0 7.f5)

7...a6 8.♗g5 h6 9.♗h4 ♔h7 10.♘d5 b5 11.♘:f6+ g:f6 12.♗d5 ♗d7 13.c3 ♖b8 14.♗g3 ♘e7 15.♗b3 d5 16.♕e2 d:e4 17.d:e4 ♗c6 18.♖d1 ♕c8 19.♖d3!

This humble move is actually the start of a renewed attack on the king!
Mit diesem unterwürfigen Zug läßt Weiß seinen Königsangriff wieder aufleben!

19...♕b7 20.♘d2 a5 21.♗h4 a4 22.♗c2 ♘g8 23.♖h3 ♖fd8 24.♕h5 ♖d6

24...♖d7 25.♗:f6.

25.♕:f7+ ♔h8 26.♕g6 ♗e8

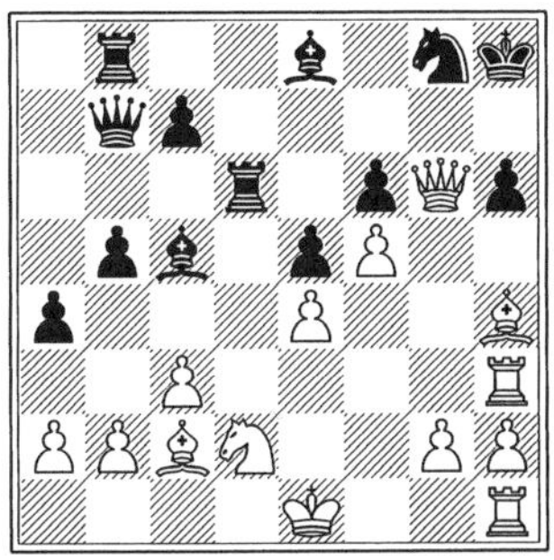

27.♗:f6+! ♖:f6 28.♖:h6+ ♘:h6 29.♕:f6+ ♔h7 30.♘f3 ♕b6 31.♘g5+ ♔g8 32.♘e6 +– (1:0/36.) Lamothe - Figueroa, Novi Sad 1990.

d4

(1.e4 e5 2.f4 ♗c5 3.♘f3 d6 4.♘c3 ♘f6 5.♗c4 ♘c6 6.d3 0-0 7.f5)

7...♘a5 8.a3 ♘:c4 9.d:c4 h6 10.♕d3 ♘g4 11.♖f1 c6 12.♗d2 ♖e8 13.h3

♘f6 14.g4 d5 15.0-0-0 d4 16.♘e2 b5 17.c:b5 c:b5 18.g5 h:g5 19.♗:g5 ♕b6 20.♖g1 ♔f8

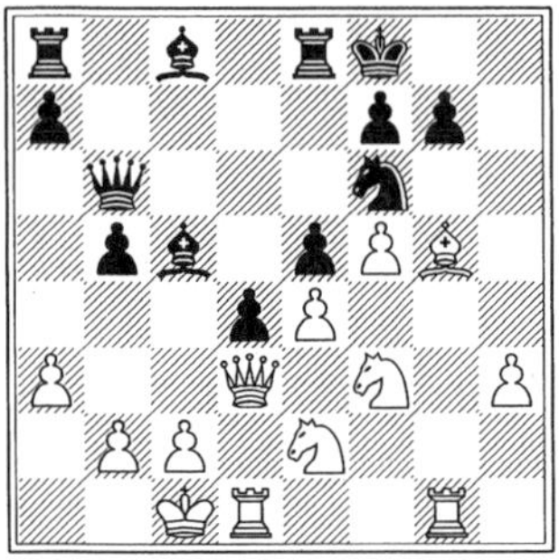

21.b4!?

A brave move, exposing his own king to eventually get at the Black king.
Ein couragierter Zug. Weiß entblößt seinen eigenen König, um anschließend an den gegnerischen heranzukommen.

21...♗d6 22.c3 ♗b7 23.♗:f6 g:f6 24.c:d4 ♖ac8+ 25.♔b2 e:d4 26.♕:d4 ♖:e4 27.♕d2 ♖e3 28.♘fd4 ♖:h3 29.♘f4 ♖h4 30.♘de6+ ♔e7 31.♖ge1 1:0, Mai - Pap, Rimavsk 1996.

Sometimes the pair of knights can outweigh the bishop pair, even in an open position!
Mitunter kann ein Springerduo das Läuferpaar ausstechen, selbst in einer offenen Stellung!

e

(1.e4 e5 2.f4 ♗c5 3.♘f3 d6 4.♘c3 ♘f6 5.♗c4 ♘c6 6.d3)

6...♗g4 7.♘a4!

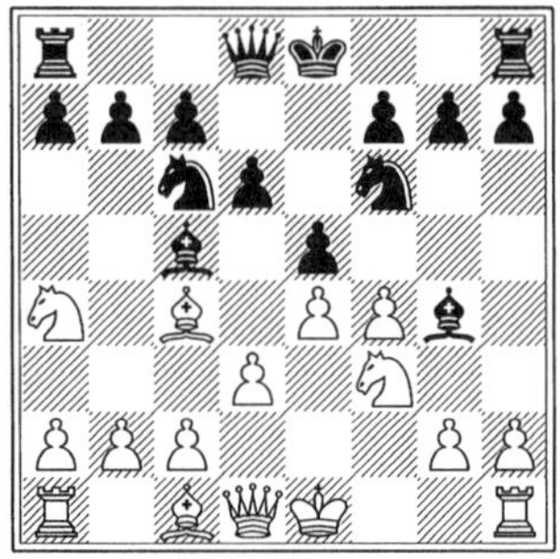

e1

7...♗:f3?! ♥ 8.♕:f3 ♘d4

e11

9.♕d1!? b5 10.♗:f7+! ♔:f7 11.♘:c5 d:c5

11...e:f4 12.♘b3 ♘e6 13.0-0 g5 14.g3 f:g3 15.♗:g5! →, Lane - Jackson, Plymouth 1989.

12.f:e5 ♘d7 13.c3 ♘e6 14.0-0+

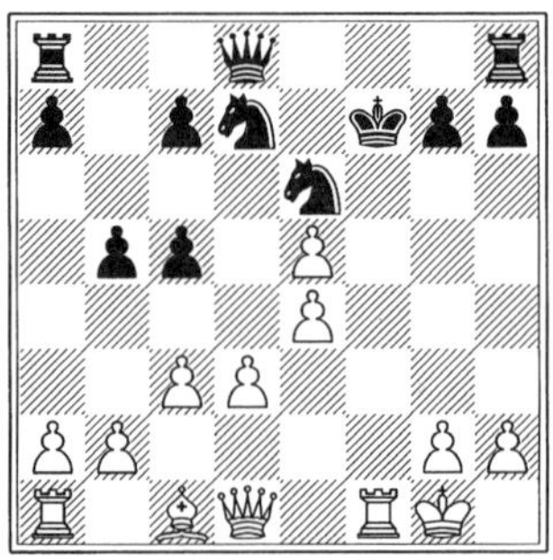

14...♔e8

14...♔g8 15.d4! c:d4 16.c:d4 h6 (16...♘:e5?! looks premature - *scheint verfrüht* 17.d:e5 ♕:d1 18.♖:d1 ♔f7 19.♗e3 ♖hd8 20.♖d5 a6 21.♖c1 ♔e7 22.♖c6 ♖d7 23.♔f2 ±, Rahman - Lodhi,

Dhaka 1995) 17.♕b3 ♕e8 18.♗e3 ∞ Kortchnoi.

15.d4 c:d4 16.c:d4 ♕e7?

16...♘:e5! 17.d:e5 ♕:d1 18.♖:d1 ♔e7 ±/=.

17.♗e3 ♖f8 18.d5 ♖:f1+ 19.♕:f1 ♘d8 20.e6 ±/+– (1:0/27.), Balashov - Matanovic, Skopje 1970.

e12

(1.e4 e5 2.f4 ♗c5 3.♘f3 d6 4.♘c3 ♘f6 5.♗c4 ♘c6 6.d3 ♗g4 7.♘a4 ♗:f3 8.♕:f3 ♘d4)

9.♕g3!

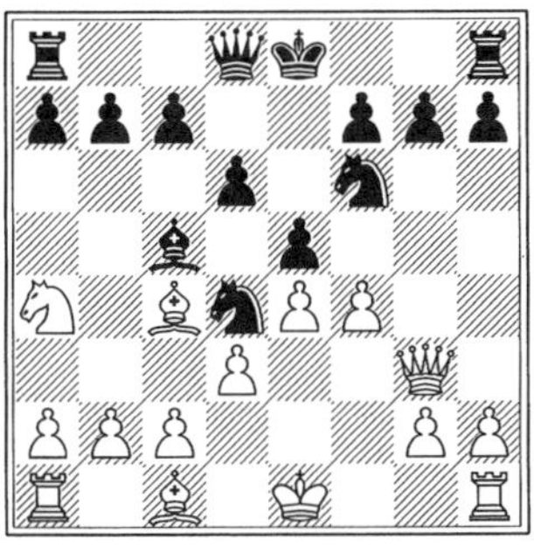

The best! However, it requires a high standard from White, because there are plenty of opportunities to go wrong.

Das Beste! Doch stellt diese Fortsetzung höchste Ansprüche an den Weißen, der im Folgenden viele Möglichkeiten hat fehlzugreifen.

• **9...♘:c2+ 10.♔d1 ♘:a1 11.♕:g7 ♖f8**

11...♕d7 12.♘:c5! d:c5 13.♕:h8+ ♔e7 14.♕g7! (14.♕:a8 ♕g4 –+) 14...♖f8 15.♗e3 b6 16.f:e5! ♘g4 (16...♘:e4 17.♔c1!) 17.♗g5+ ♔e8 18.e6 f:e6 19.♗b5!.

12.♘:c5 d:c5 13.fe5 ♘:e4 14.♖f1 ♕e7

14...♕d7 15.♗:f7+!.

15.♗h6 ±/± Keres (15...0-0-0 16.♕g4+).

• 9...e:f4 10.♕:g7 ♖f8 11.♘:c5 d:c5 12.♗:f4 b5 13.♗:b5+ ♘:b5 14.♗g5 ♖g8 15.♕:f6 ♖:g5 16.♕c6+ ♔f8 17.♕:b5± ♖b8 18.♕c4 ♖:b2 19.♖f1! ♕d7 20.0-0-0 ♖b4 21.♕c3 ♕d4 22.♕:d4 c:d4 23.♖d2 ±, Honfi - Salm, corr. 1958/60.

• 9...♘h5 10.♕g4 g6 11.♗b3 e:f4 12.♘:c5 d:c5 13.♗:f4 ±

As always, White has the more harmonious pawn structure.

Wie immer verfügt Weiß über die harmonischere Bauernstruktur.

• **9...0-0 10.f:e5! ♘:c2+**

10...♘h5 11.♕f2 ♘b3 12.♘:c5 ♘:a1 13.♘:b7 ♕b8 14.♗d5, 10...d:e5 11.♘:c5 ♘:c2+ 12.♔d1 ♘:a1 13.♗g5 ♕d6 14.♗:f6 Δ ♘d7.

11.♔d1 ♘:a1 12.e:f6 ♕:f6 13.♘:c5 d:c5 14.e5 ♕b6 15.♖f1 ± Δ ♖f6, ♗h6.

e2

(1.e4 e5 2.f4 ♗c5 3.♘f3 d6 4.♘c3 ♘f6 5.♗c4 ♘c6 6.d3 ♗g4 7.♘a4)

7...♘d4 8.♘:c5 d:c5 9.c3! ♘:f3+ 10.g:f3 ♗h5!

10...♗h3 11.f:e5±, 10...♘:e4 11.0-0! +–.

11.♕e2 ♕d6 12.f:e5 ♕:e5 13.f4 ♕e7 14.♕g2 0-0-0 15.0-0 ± Bogoljubov.

e3

(1.e4 e5 2.f4 ♗c5 3.♘f3 d6 4.♘c3 ♘f6 5.♗c4 ♘c6 6.d3 ♗g4 7.♘a4)

7...♘a5?! 8.♘:c5 ♘:c4 9.♘:b7 ♕b8 10.♘:d6+ c:d6 11.d:c4 ♕b4+ 12.c3

♕:c4 13.♕:d6 ♕:e4+ 14.♔f2 ♗:f3 15.♕:e5+ ±.

e4

(1.e4 e5 2.f4 ♗c5 3.♘f3 d6 4.♘c3 ♘f6 5.♗c4 ♘c6 6.d3 ♗g4 7.♘a4)

7...a6?! 8.♘:c5 d:c5 9.0-0 ♕e7 10.h3 ♗:f3 11.♕:f3 0-0 12.♗e3 e:f4 13.♕:f4 ♘e5 14.♗b3 ♖ae8?!

14...♖ad8.

15.♕f2!

Δ ♗:c5, Δ ♗g5.

15...♘fd7 16.♖ad1 b6 17.c3 ♘g6

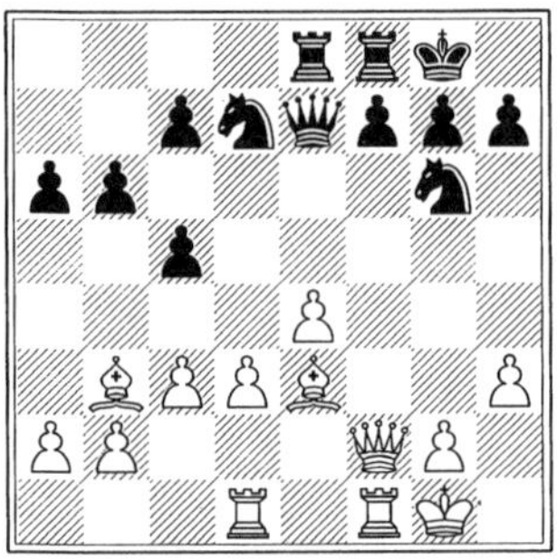

18.♕f5! ♔h8 19.♗f2! ♖d8 20.♗g3 ♘de5 21.d4 c:d4 22.c:d4 ♘c6 23.d5 ♘ce5 24.h4! ♕c5+ 25.♔h2 f6 26.♖c1 ♕d6 27.♖c6 ♕e7 28.♖e6 ♕d7 29.h5 ♘e7 30.♕h3 ♘f7 31.♗f4 h6 32.♕c3 ♘d6

[see diagram next column]

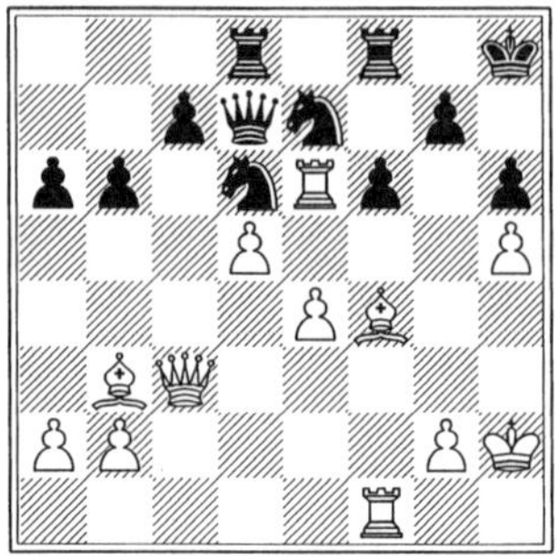

33.♗:h6! ♘:e4 34.♖:e4 ♘:d5 35.♕c1 1:0 (35...g:h6 36.♗:d5), Alekhine - Teichmann, Berlin 1921.

e5

(1.e4 e5 2.f4 ♗c5 3.♘f3 d6 4.♘c3 ♘f6 5.♗c4 ♘c6 6.d3 ♗g4 7.♘a4)

7...♕e7 8.♘:c5 d:c5 9.♗b5 e:f4 10.♗:c6+ b:c6 11.♗:f4 c4 12.0-0 0-0 13.♕e2 ±

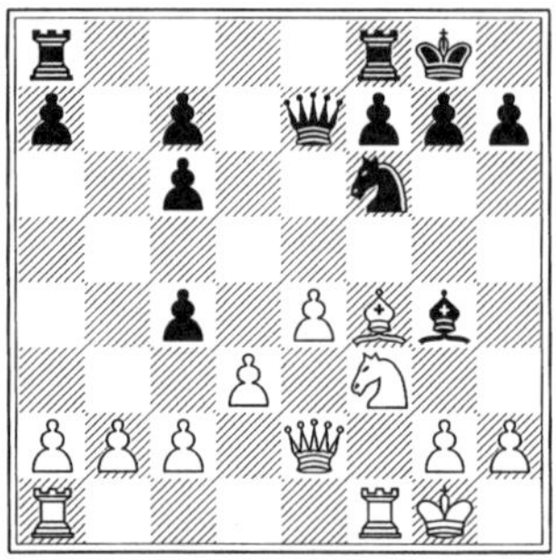

13...c:d3

Black can't rid himself of his tripled pawns without exposing his remaining doubled pawns, that's what I call really bad pawn structure!

Schwarz kann seinen Trippelbauern nur loswerden, indem er den verbleibenden Doppelbauern bloßlegt - das nenne ich eine wahrhaft schlechte Bauernstruktur!

14.c:d3 ♖ad8 15.♕c2 ♗:f3 16.♖:f3 ± (1:0/43.), Milner-Barry - Ed. Lasker, TV-match 1976.

e6

(1.e4 e5 2.f4 ♗c5 3.♘f3 d6 4.♘c3 ♘f6 5.♗c4 ♘c6 6.d3 ♗g4 7.♘a4)

7...0-0 8.♘:c5 d:c5 9.0-0

9.h3!? ♗:f3 10.♕:f3 ♘a5 11.♗b3 ♘:b3 12.a:b3 ±.

9...♘d4 10.f:e5 ♘d7 11.♗f4 ♕e7 12.c3 ±.

e7

(1.e4 e5 2.f4 ♗c5 3.♘f3 d6 4.♘c3 ♘f6 5.♗c4 ♘c6 6.d3 ♗g4 7.♘a4)

7...♘d7 8.♘:c5 d:c5

8...♘:c5 9.h3 ♗:f3 (9...♗d7 10.♘g5 ±) 10.♕:f3 ♘d4 11.♕f2 0-0 12.0-0 ♕e7 13.a4 ± Δ b4, c3, f5, g4.

9.0-0

9.h3! ♗:f3 10.♕:f3 ♘a5 11.♗b3 ♘:b3 12.a:b3 ⩲ 0-0 13.0-0 f6 14.f5 Δ ♗e3, g4, ♔h2, ♖g1-g3 etc.

9...e:f4 10.♗:f4 ♘ce5

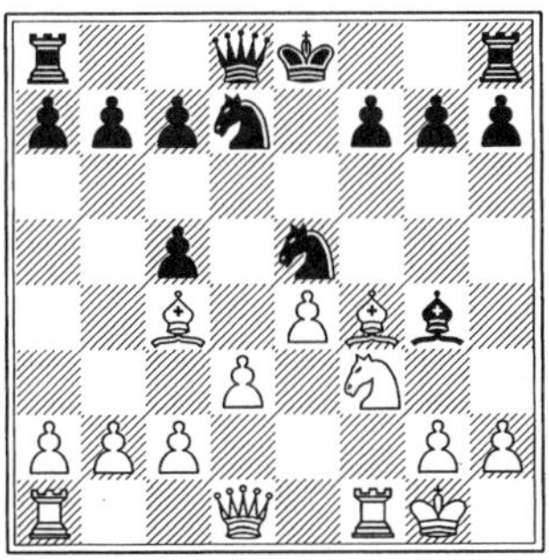

11.♘:e5!?

A wonderful intuitive sacrifice!
Ein herrliches intuitives Opfer!

11...♗:d1

11...♘:e5 12.♗:f7+ ♔f8 13.♗:e5 ♗:d1 ∞.

12.♘:f7 ♕f6 13.♖a:d1 ♖f8 14.♗:c7 ⩲ ♕:b2 15.e5! (Δ e6), Spielmann - Maroczy, Vienna 1907 (½:½/44.).

e8

(1.e4 e5 2.f4 ♗c5 3.♘f3 d6 4.♘c3 ♘f6 5.♗c4 ♘c6 6.d3 ♗g4 7.♘a4)

7...e:f4 8.♘:c5 d:c5 9.♗:f4 ♘h5 10.♗e3 ♘e5?

10...0-0 11.0-0 ♘e5 12.♗:c5 ♗:f3 13.g:f3 ♕g5+ 14.♔h1 ♘:c4 15.♗:f8 ♘e3 16.♖g1 ♕f4 17.♗:g7! ♘:g7 18.♕e2 ⩲ Glaskov.

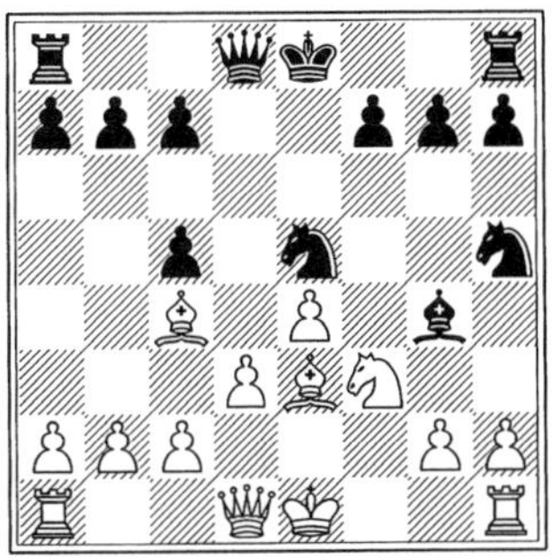

11.♘:e5! ♗:d1 12.♗:f7+ ♔e7 13.♗:c5+ ♔f6 14.0-0+ ♔:e5

14...♔g5 15.♗e3+ ♔h4 16.♖a:d1 ♕e7 17.♘f3+ ♔g4 18.♔f2 Δ h3#.

15.♖f5#, Alekhine - Tenner, Köln 1907.

e9

(1.e4 e5 2.f4 ♗c5 3.♘f3 d6 4.♘c3 ♘f6 5.♗c4 ♘c6 6.d3 ♗g4 7.♘a4)

7...♗b6 8.♘:b6 a:b6 9.c3 e:f4

- 9...d5 10.e:d5 ♘:d5 11.h3! ±.
- 9...0-0 10.0-0 ♘a5 11.♗b5 ±.

10.♗:f4

10.0-0 ♘a5 11.♗b5+ ±.

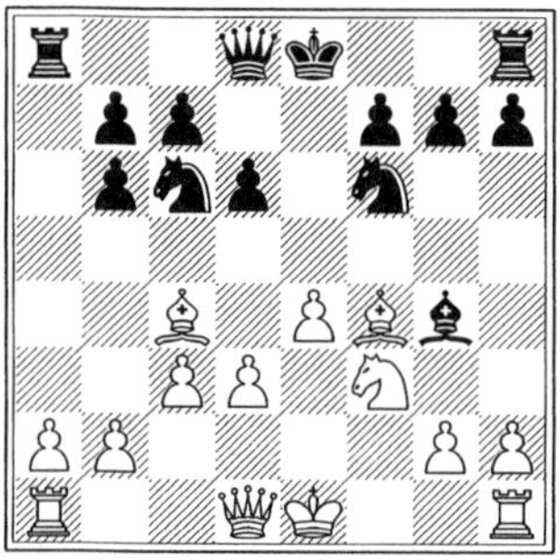

- 10...♘h5 11.♗e3 ♘e5 12.♗b3 ♗:f3 13.g:f3 ♕h4+ 14.♔d2 ±

Isn't it striking how often White ends up with the bishop pair and a big centre? Especially, since it's normally the result of Black's attempts to punish White!

Ist es nicht auffallend, wie oft der Anziehende mit Läuferpaar und einem gewaltigen Zentrum verbleibt? Insbesondere, da dies das normale Ergebnis von schwarzen "Strafexpeditionen" ist!

- 10...0-0 11.0-0 d5 12.e:d5 ♘:d5 13.♕d2 ♗:f3 14.♖:f3 ♘a5 15.♗:d5 ♕:d5 16.♖af1 c5 17.a3 ♖ae8 18.b4 ±, Kuijf - Mikhalevski, Leeuwarden 1995.

f

(1.e4 e5 2.f4 ♗c5 3.♘f3 d6 4.♘c3 ♘f6 5.♗c4 ♘c6 6.d3)

6...a6

Saving his blackfielder seems to be Black's best choice. The question is how White should try to exploit this non-developing move, brute force or measure for measure?

Sich den schwarzfeldrigen Läufer zu bewahren, scheint die beste Option für Schwarz zu sein. Die Frage ist, wie der Anziehende diesen nicht der Entwicklung dienlichen Zug ausnutzen soll: Mit brachialer Gewalt oder Schritt für Schritt?

f1

7.♖f1!?

Realizing that castling kingside is not in the cards, White chooses to just get on with it, rook to the f-file and then either a pawn storm or a blitz-krieg at the poor Black monarch.

Im Bewußtsein, daß die kurze Rochade ohnehin nicht möglich ist, versucht Weiß, das beste daraus zu machen und stellt seinen Turm auf die f-Linie. Es soll entweder ein Bauernsturm oder aber ein Blitzkrieg gegen den armseligen schwarzen Monarchen folgen.

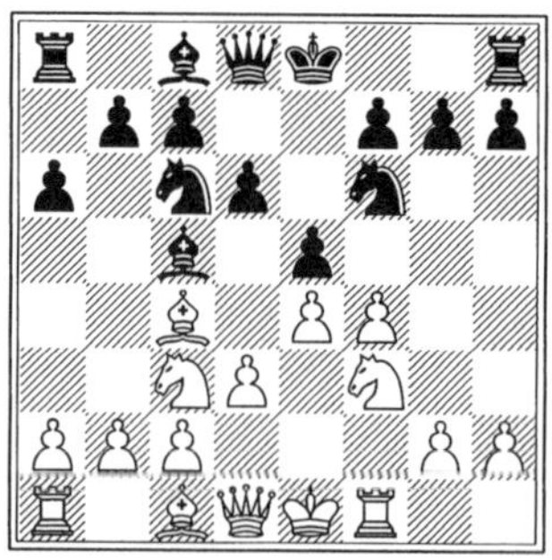

- 7...e:f4 8.♗:f4 ♘a5 9.♗g5 ♘:c4 10.d:c4 h6 11.♗h4 ♗e6 (11...c6 12.♘d4) 12.♕d3 ♖g8 13.0-0-0 g5

14.♗f2 (14.♗g3! Δ e5 Bangiev) ♗:f2 15.♖:f2 g4! 16.♘d4 ♘d7 17.♘d5 ♕g5+ 18.♕d2!? 0-0-0 19.♘f5 ♖h8 20.♘fe3 ♖de8 ∞ (0:1/64.), Bangiev - Malaniuk, Tallinn 1986.

- 7....♗g4 8.h3 ♗:f3 9.♕:f3 ♕e7 10.♕g3 ♘d4 11.f:e5 d:e5 12.♔d1 (12.♕:g7! ±) ♘e6 13.♕e5 ♗d4 14.♕f5 ♗:c3 15.b:c3 h6 16.♗e3 0-0-0 17.♔e2 ♖d7 18.♕a5 c6 19.♖ab1 ♘c7 20.♖:b7 ♔:b7 21.♖b1+ ♘b5 22.♕b6+ ♔c8 23.♕:c6+ ♖c7 24.♕:a6+ ♔d8 25.♖:b5 ♘d7 26.♖d5 1:0 Bangiev - Weigend, corr. 1985/86.

- 7...♕e7 8.f5 ♘a5 9.a3 ♘:c4 10.d:c4 ♗d7?! (10...h6) 11.♗g5 c6 12.♕d3 ♗b6 13.0-0-0 ♗c7 14.♘g1 0-0-0 15.♘ge2 ♔b8 16.♘g3 ♗c8 17.♔b1! (17.♘h5 ♕f8!) 17...b5 18.♘h5 ♖hg8 19.♖f3 ♕f8 20.g4! ♘:g4 21.♗:d8 ♕:d8 22.♖g1 ♘:h2 23.♖h3 g6 24.♖:h2 g:h5 25.♖:g8 ♕:g8 26.♖:h5 f6 27.c:b5 a:b5 28.♖h1 (not giving Black any hope of counter-play - *raubt dem Schwarzen jede Hoffnung auf Gegenspiel*) 28...♗d7 29.♕h3 d5 30.♕:h7 ♕c8 31.e:d5 ♗:f5 32.♕g7 ♗d8 33.♖h8 c:d5 34.♕f8 d4 35.♕d6 1:0, Maroczy - Exner, Budapest 1899.

- 7...0-0 8.f5

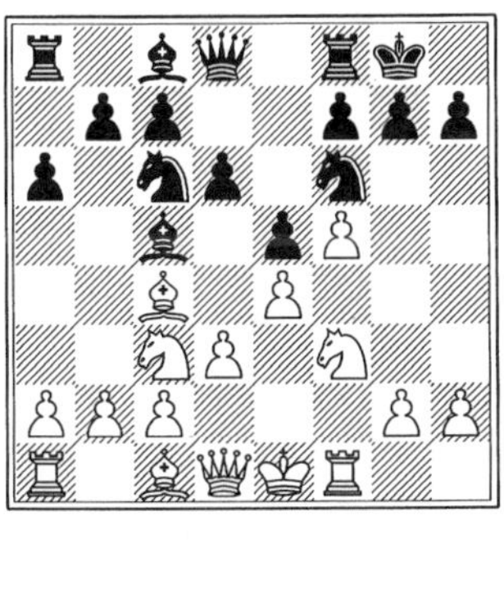

•• 8...b5 9.♗b3 ♘a5 10.♘d5 ♘:d5 11.♗:d5 c6 12.♘g6!? ♕f6 (12...c:d5 13.♕h5 h6 14.f6!) 13.♕h5 h6 14.♗:f7+ ♖:f7 15.♘:f7 ♕:f7 16.♕g4 ♔h7 17.♖f3 ♘b7 18.♖h3 d5 19.♕h4 ♗e7 20.♗g5 ♗:g5 21.♕:g5 ♘d6 22.♕e3 d4 23.♕d2 ♕f6 24.g4 ♘f7 25.0-0-0 ♕g5 26.♕:g5 ♘:g5 27.♖g3 ♗d7 28.h4 ♘f7 29.g5 h:g5 30.h:g5 ♔g8 31.♖h1 ♖f8 32.g6 ♘h6 33.♖gh3 c5 34.♔d1 ♖f6 35.♔e2 c4 36.♔f3 ♔f8 37.♖:h6 g:h6 38.♖:h6 ♗:f5 ½:½, Pullinger - Jackson, St Heliers 1997.

A slightly surprising draw, since White seems to get a clearly better ending after:
Ein etwas überraschender Remisschluß. Weiß dürfte ein klar überlegenes Endspiel erhalten nach:
39.e:f5 ♖:f5 40.♔e4 ♖g5 41.g7 ♔:g7 42.♖:a6

•• 8...h6 9.♘d5!
A thematic thrust when deprived of the ♗g5 pin.
Ein thematischer Vorstoß, falls Weiß der Fesselmöglichkeit ♗g5 beraubt ist.
9...♘d4 10.♘:d4 ♗:d4 11.♘:f6+ ♕:f6 12.♕h5

White's pieces are almost playing themselves by now!
Die weiße Stellung spielt sich jetzt fast von alleine!

12...d5 13.♗:d5 ♗c5 14.♖f3 ♗e7 15.♖g3 ♕b6 16.♗:h6 ♕g1+ 17.♔e2 ♕:a1 18.♖:g7+ 1:0, Gallagher - Giertz, Switzerland 1992.

• 7...h6 8.♘d5 ♘:d5 9.♗:d5 e:f4 10.d4 ♗a7 11.♗:f4 ♗e6 12.♗:e6 f:e6 13.c3 0-0 14.♗g3 ♕e7 15.♕b3 ♗b6 16.0-0-0 ♔h7 17.♕c2 e5=/∞ (½:½/38.), Kavalek - Smejkal, Kettler Cup 1996.

f2

(1.e4 e5 2.f4 ♗c5 3.♘f3 d6 4.♘c3 ♘f6 5.♗c4 ♘c6 6.d3 a6)

7.f5

Getting on with the pawn storm!
Der Bauernsturm macht Fortschritte!

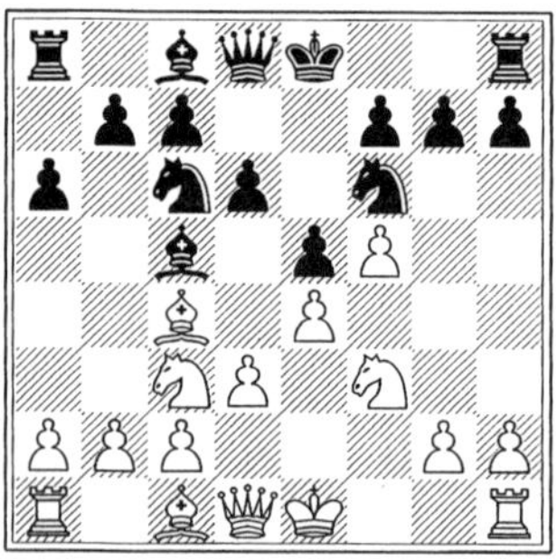

• **7...h6 8.♘d5**

Insisting on castling kingside gives Black time to break in the centre:
Wenn Weiß unbedingt kurz rochieren möchte, kann der Nachziehende in der Zwischenzeit einen Durchbruch im Zentrum organisieren:
8.♕e2?! ♗d7 9.♗e3 ♘d4 10.♗:d4 e:d4 11.♘d1 0-0 12.0-0 d5∓ Kortchnoi/Zak.

8...♘a5

8...♘d4 9.c3 ♘:f3 ♕:f3 c6 11.♘:f6 ♕:f6 12.♗e3 ♗:e3 13.♕:e3 ♗d7 14.0-0 0-0 =/∞ (½:½/46.), Hebden - Richardson, London 1983.

• • 9.♕e2 b5 10.♗b3 ♘:b3 11.♘:f6+ ♕:f6 12.a:b3 ♗b7 13.♗e3 ♗:e3 14.♕:e3 0-0-0?! (Christmas came early that year! - *Weihnachten ist dieses Jahr aber zeitig!*) 14.c4! ±, Gallagher - Davidovic, Szolnok 1987.

• • 9.b4! ♘:d5 (9...♘:c4 10.♘:f6+ ♕:f6 11.b:c5 Conquest) 10.b:c5 ♘f6 (10...♘:c4 11.e:d5 ♘a5 12.♗d2 b6 13. c6 ♗:f5 14.0-0 0-0 15.♕e1 Conquest) 11.♗b3 d:c5 12.♘:e5! ♘:b3 13.a:b3 ♕d4 14.♗f4 ♘:e4 (14...♗:f5 15.♘f3 ♗g4 16.♘:d4 ♗:d1 17.♘b5 ±) 15.d:e4 ♕:e4+ 16.♕e2 ♕:e2+ 17.♔:e2 ♗:f5 18.♔d2 ± f6 19.♘d3 0-0-0 20.♖a5! ♖d7 21.♖e1 ♗:d3 22.c:d3 ♖hd8 (22...g5!?) 23.♖:c5 ♖:d3+ 24.♔c2 c6 25.♖e7 ♖3d7 26.♖e2 ♖d1? 27.♗d2! ± ♖f1 28.♗a5 ♖d6 29.♖c3 ♖a1 30.♖e8+ ♔d7 31.♖ce3 c5 32.♖3e7+ ♔c6 33.♖c8+ ♔d5 34.♗c7 +−, Conquest - Smejkal, Germany 1996.

• 7...♘d4 8.♗g5 (8.♘d5!?) 8...c6 9.♘:d4 ♗:d4 10.♕f3 ± Gallagher.

• 7...♘a5 8.a3 ♘:c4 9.d:c4 h6 10.♕e2 ♗d7 11.♗e3 ♗:e3 12.♕:e3 b5 13.c5 0-0 14.0-0-0 ♕b8 15.g4! ♘:g4 (15...b4 16.a:b4 a5 17.g5) 16.♕d2 ♔h8 17.♖hg1 ♘f6

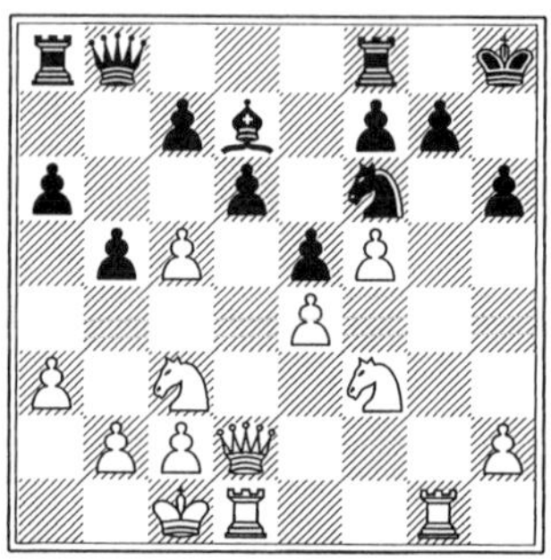

18.♖:g7! ♔:g7 19.♖g1+ ♔h7 20.♘g5+ ♔h8 21.♘e6! ♘h7 22.♕:h6 ♖g8 23.♖g7 ♖:g7 24.♕:g7#, Hartston - Richardson, Westergate 1983.

f3

(1.e4 e5 2.f4 ♗c5 3.♘f3 d6 4.♘c3 ♘f6 5.♗c4 ♘c6 6.d3 a6)

7.a3!?

If Black can spare a tempo to retain his king's bishop, why shouldn't White do the same?
Wenn Schwarz ein Tempo für die Erhaltung seines Königsläufers aufwendet, wieso sollte der Anziehende dann nicht das gleiche tun dürfen?

7...♗g4 8.h3 ♗:f3 9.♕:f3 ♘d4 10.♕g3 ♘h5 11.♕g4 g6 12.♖f1! e:f4

12...♘f6 13.♕d1, 12...f5 13.e:f5 ♘:f5 14.f:e5 ♘hg3 15.♖f3 d:e5 16.♖:g3 ♘:g3 17.♗g5 +−.

13.♗:f4 f6?

13...♘:f4 Δ 0-0.

14.0-0-0 c6 15.♖de1 ♘:f4 16.♕:f4 ♖f8 17.b4 ♗b6

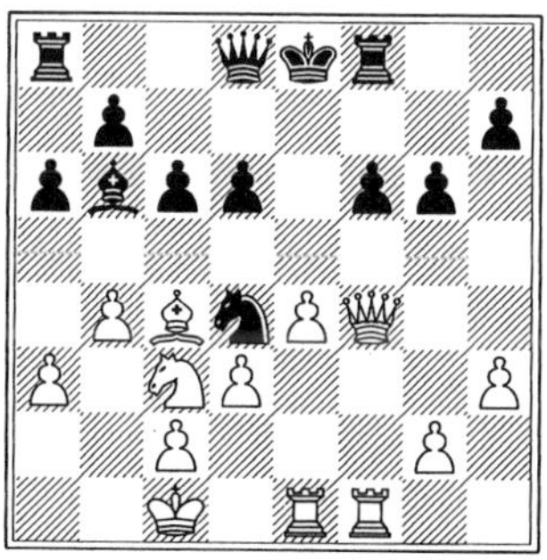

18.e5! d5 19.e:f6+ ♔d7 20.♗:d5 c:d5 21.♘:d5 ♘f5 22.♕e4 ♘d6 23.♕e6+ ♔c6 24.♖f4 a5 25.♖e5 a:b4 26.♖c4+ +− (1:0/33.), Rabinovich - Salwe, Vilna 1909.

f4

(1.e4 e5 2.f4 ♗c5 3.♘f3 d6 4.♘c3 ♘f6 5.♗c4 ♘c6 6.d3 a6)

7.♘g5!?

Definitely the most brutal! Black moved a rook pawn one step, and now he's gonna die!
Definitiv das Brutalste! Der Nachziehende hat sich einen "Eselsohrenzug" erlaubt (...a6), und nun soll er dafür bereits hingerichtet werden!

7...0-0

- 7...♗g4 8.♗:f7+ ♔f8 (8...♔d7 9.♕d2) 9.♘e6+!.
- 7...♖f8!? 8.f5 ♕e7 ∞.

8.f5

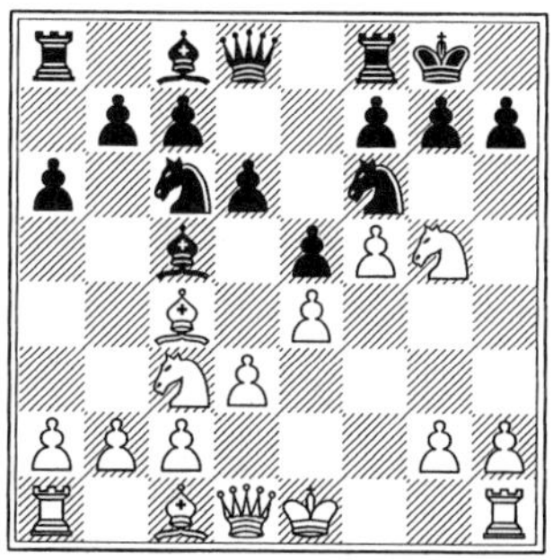

- 8...h6 9.h4!.
- 8...♘a5 9.♗:f7+ ♖:f7 10.♘:f7 ♔:f7 11.g4 h6 12.h4 h5 13.g5! ♘g4 14.g6+ ♔g8 15.♗g5 ♕d7 16.♖h2! ♗b4 17.♖g2 ♕c6 18.♖:g4 ♗:c3+ 19.b:c3 h:g4 20.♕:g4 ♕:c3+ 21.♔f2! ♗:f5 (21...♕:c2+? 22.♔g1 ♕:d3 23.♖e1)

22.e:f5 ♕d4+ 23.♕:d4 e:d4 24.♖e1 ♘c6 25.♖e6 ♖f8 26.f6! g:f6 27.♗h6 ♖c8 28.♖:f6 ♘e5 29.♔g3 ♖e8 30.h5 1:0 (30...a5 31.♗g5 ♖f8 32.h6 ♖:f6 33.h7+! +– Karker), Karker - Kalivoda, corr. 1987/88.

• 8...♘d4 9.g4 b5? (Just asking for White's reply! *Fordert die weiße Antwort geradezu heraus!* 9...c6 ∞) 10.♗:f7+ ♖:f7 11.♘:f7 ♔:f7 12.g5 ♘e8 13.♕h5+ ♔g8 14.♘d5 c6 (14...♘:f5?! 15.e:f5 ♗:f5 16.♕f3! 1:0 Leisebein - Krabbe, corr. 1986) 15.g6 ♘f6 16.♘:f6+ ♕:f6 17.♕:h7+ ♔f8

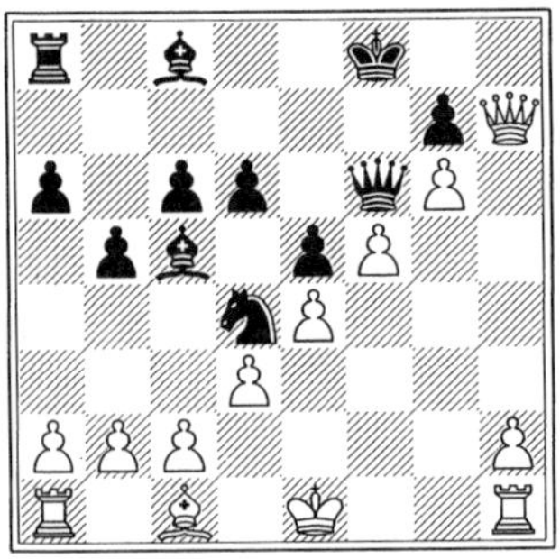

18.h4! +– Δ ♗g5.

• 8...b5 9.♗:f7+ ♖:f7 10.♘:f7 ♔:f7 11.♗g5?! (This may be too slow. 11.g4!? looks better but hasn't been tried in practise as far as I know, e.g: - *Wahrscheinlich zu langsam. 11.g4 dürfte besser sein, harrt jedoch meines Wissens noch der praktischen Erprobung z.B.:* 11...h6 12.h4, 11...♘h5 12.h4 ♘f4 13.♗:f4 e:f4 14.♘d5 ∞) 11...♗b7 (11...♘e7 12.♕f3 ♗b7 13.0-0-0 c6 14.g4 ♕g8 15.♔b1 ♗b6 16.♗c1 ♖f8 ∞, Hergott - Reyes, Dubai 1986) 12.♘d5 ♘b4 13.♘:f6 g:f6 14.♗h6 ♕d8 15.♕e2 and Black had the advantage *(und Schwarz hatte den Vorteil)* in Messere - Timmerman, corr. 1986 (0:1/43.).

f5

(1.e4 e5 2.f4 ♗c5 3.♘f3 d6 4.♘c3 ♘f6 5.♗c4 ♘c6 6.d3 a6)

7.h3!?

Stopping ...♗g4 and preparing the usual pawn wave.
Verhindert ...♗g4 und bereitet den üblichen Bauernsturm vor.

7.f:e5?! (This is White's only bad option it seems! - *Anscheinend die einzige ungünstige Möglichkeit von Weiß!*) 7...d:e5 8.♗g5 h6 9.♗:f6 ♕:f6 10.♘d5 ♕d6 11.♕d2 ♗e6 =.

7...0-0 8.f5 ♘d4 9.g4 b5 10.♗b3 ♗b7 11.g5 ∞ **♘:b3 12.g:f6 ♘bd4**

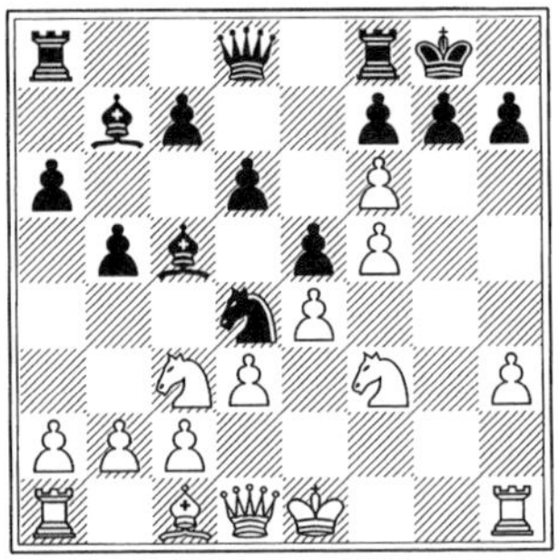

±, Gottschall - Jacob, Munich 1900.

Unfortunately, I haven't got the complete game, but it certainly started promising!

Leider ist mir der weitere Verlauf dieser so vielversprechend begonnenen Partie nicht bekannt!

Chapter IV *Kapitel IV*

King's Gambit Accepted - Various non-Main Lines
Angen. Königsgambit - Diverse Nebenvarianten

1.e4 e5 2.f4 e:f4 3.♘f3

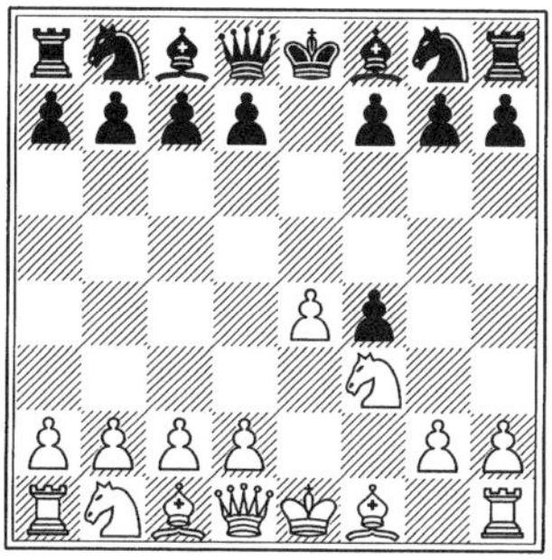

I

3...♘e7 4.d4

4.♗c4 d5 5.e:d5 ♘:d5
transposes to the Modern Defence, which however, enjoys a much better reputation than 3...♘e7.
leitet zur Modernen Verteidigung über - eine Variante, die in einem viel besseren Ruf als 3...♘e7 steht.

4...d5

4...♘g6 5.h4!.

5.♘c3 d:e4 6.♘:e4

A

6...♘g6 7.h4!

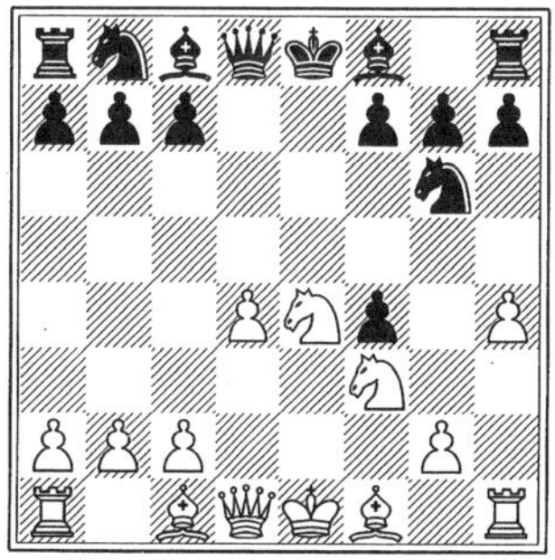

• **7...♗e7 8.h5 ♘h4 9.♗:f4 ♗g4 10.h6**±, Kuznetsov - Bonsch-Osmolovsky, Moscow 1964.

• **7...♕e7 8.♔f2!**
A frequent tactical motive in the KGA, if 8...♕:e4 9.♗b5+ ♔d8 10.♖e1 winning either the queen or the king.
Ein im Ang. KG immer wieder vorkommendes Motiv: falls 8...♕:e4, so 9.♗b5+ ♔d8 10.♖e1 mit Gewinn von Dame oder König.
8...♗g4 9.h5 ♘h4 10.♗:f4 ♘c6 11.♗b5! 0-0-0 12.♗:c6 b:c6 13.♕d3 ♘:f3 14.g:f3 ♗f5 15.♕a6+ ♔b8 16.♘c5 ♗c8 17.♕:c6 ♖:d4 18.♖ae1! ♖:f4
Otherwise, Black won't be able to stay defending the ♙c7.
Andernfalls könnte Schwarz nicht länger den ♙c7 verteidigen.
19.♕b5+ ♔a8 20.♕c6+ ♔b8 21.♖:e7 ♗:e7 22.♖d1 ♖f6

22...♗:c5 23.♕:c5 ♗b7 24.♖d3!. **23.♘d7+ ♗:d7 24.♕:d7 ♖d8 25.♕b5+ ♔c8 26.♖:d8+ ♗:d8 27.♕a4 g5 28.♕:a7 ♖f4 29.♕a6+ ♔b8 30.♕d3 ♗e7 31.♕:h7 g4 32.♔g3** 1:0, Spassky - Seirawan, Montpellier (ct) 1985.

• **7...♗f5!? 8.♗d3**

8.♕e2!

seems surprisingly strong:

scheint überraschend stark:

8...♗e7 9.h5 ♘h4 (9...♘f8 10.h6!, 9... ♗h4+ 10.g3! +–) 10.♘f6+ ♔f8 11. ♖:h4± or *(oder)* 11.♘:h4!? ♗c8 12.♘f3±.

8...♕e7 9.♕b5+ ♗d7 10.♕:b7 ♗c6 11.♕c8+ ±.

8...♗:e4 9.♕:e4+ ♕e7 10.♕:e7+ ♗:e7 11.h5 ±.

8...♗e7 9.h5 ♘h4 10.♘:h4 ♗:h4+ 11.♔f1 0-0 12.c3 ♖e8 13.♕f3 ♕d5 14.♖:h4

14.♘f6+?? g:f6 15.♕:d5 ♖e1#.

14...♗:e4 15.♗:e4 ♖:e4 16.♖:f4 ♕b5+, Carbonnel - Rausis, Enghien les Bain 1995.

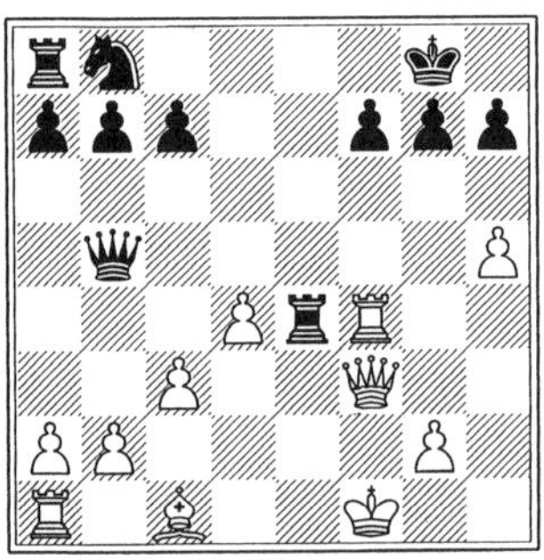

I think White should play 17.♔g1! here, instead of 17.♔f2?! ♖:f4 18.♗:f4 ♕:b2 (0:1/58.), for example:

Statt der Partiefortsetzung 17.♔f2?! ♖:f4 18.♗:f4 ♕:b2 (0:1/58.) sollte Weiß hier m.E. 17.♔g1! spielen, z.B.:

• • 17...♖:f4 18.♗:f4 ♕:b2 19.♖f1 ♘c6 20.♗:c7 ±

• • 17...♖e1+ 18.♔h2 ♕e8 (18...♘c6? 19.♖:f7 ♖ae8 20.h6 ♖1e7 21.♖f5! ♕b6 22.♗g5 ♖d7 23.♖f1 +–; 18...♖e7 may be Black's best however unenterprising it looks ... *18...♖e7 wirkt nicht gerade unternehmungslustig, ist aber vielleicht dennoch das Beste*) 19.♖g4 ♖e6 20.d5 ♖a6 21.♕g3! ♕f8 22.♗g5 (Δ♗e7) ♘d7 23.♕:c7 ♘f6 24.♗:f6 ♖:f6 25.♕e5 +–.

B

(1.e4 e5 2.f4 e:f4 3.♘f3 ♘e7 4.d4 d5 5.♘c3 d:e4 6.♘:e4)

6...♘d5!?

The latest try to revive this old variation. If you compare it with the Modern defence 3...d5, White has got his knight to e4 for free which must be good. However, one drawback is that if White continues as in the Modern with ♗c4:d5 then ♗:f4 may not be available since Black will threaten the ♘e4 when he recaptures on d5, gaining time for ...♗e7 and ...♗e6. Therefore I prefer the harder

7.c4!?

which looks very promising although it hasn't been tried in practise yet, e.g:

Der jüngste Versuch, diese alte Variante wiederzubeleben. Im Vergleich mit der Modernen Verteidigung hat Weiß seinen Springer "umsonst" nach e4 befördert bekommen, was günstig für ihn sein muß. Ein Nachteil zeigt sich jedoch, wenn der Anziehende analog zu jener Variante zu spielen versucht: Nach ♗c4:d5 könnte ♗:f4 undurchführbar sein, weil nach Zurückschlagen auf d5 zunächst der ♘e4 hängt, womit der Schwarze Zeit für ...♗e7 und ...♗e6 gewinnt. Deswegen bevorzuge ich das schärfere

7.c4!?,

was aussichtsreich scheint, obgleich es in der Praxis noch nicht erprobt worden ist, z.B.:

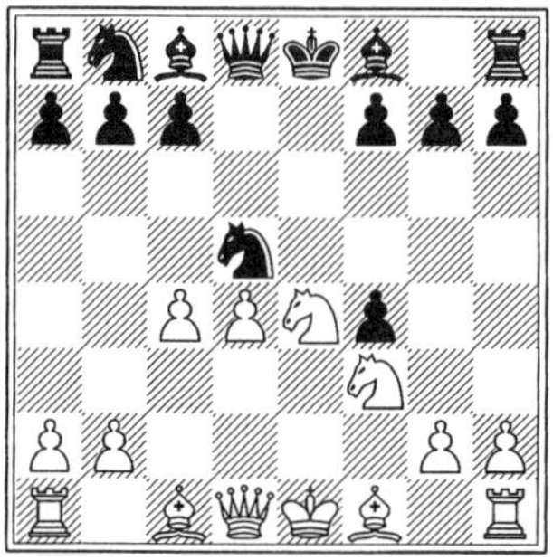

- 7...♗b4+ 8.♔f2 ♘e3 9.♕e2 (9.♕a4+?! ♘c6 10.d5 ♘g4 →) 9...♘g4+ 10.♔g1 0-0 11.♗:f4 ♖e8 12.♕c2 ♗f5 13.♗d3 ± (Bangiev).

- **7...♘e3 8.♗:e3**

Bangiev recommends 8.♕e2 but 8...♕e7 looks uncomfortable.
Bangiev empfiehlt 8.♕e2, doch danach scheint 8...♕e7 unangenehm.

8...f:e3

(Amazingly enough, Ivan Sokolov here gives the verdict '∓' in Informator. I can't say that I understand why, unless it's a misprint ...)
White seems to get a massive lead in development for a pawn that can't be held in the long run, e.g:
(Zur allgemeinen Verwunderung fällt Ivan Sokolov im Informator zu dieser Stellung das Urteil "∓". Daß dies ein Druckfehler ist, wäre für mich die einzig vernünftige Erklärung ...)
Als Gegenwert für den Bauern, welcher ohnehin auf Dauer verlorengehen dürfte, erhält Weiß offensichtlich einen großen Entwicklungsvorsprung, z.B.:

9.♕b3 ♕e7 10.♗d3 ♕b4+ 11.♔e2! f5 12.♘c3 ♕:b3

12...c6 13.c5!? ♕:b3 14.a:b3 f4 15.b4Δ d5/b5.

13.a:b3 c6 14.♔:e3 ±.

II

(1.e4 e5 2.f4 e:f4 3.♘f3)

3...f5 4.e5!

A

4...g5 5.d4 g4

5...d5 6.c4
Sometimes it's necessary to increase the tension in the centre by repeating the offer of a bishops pawn for a centre pawn. (See the Schallopp defence for similar positions.)
Zwecks Erhöhung der Spannung im Zentrum ist es mitunter notwendig, nochmals mit einem Läuferbauern einen Zentrumsbauern anzuknabbern (vgl. die Schallopp-Verteidigung)
6...♗e6 7.♘c3 ♗b4 8.h4 ±.

6.♗:f4! g:f3

This kind of sacrifice is usual in the Muzio-Polerio gambit after 3...g5 4.♗c4 g4 5.0-0, in the MacDonnell gambit 5.♘c3 and in the Rosentreter gambit 3...g5 4.d4 g4 5.♗:f4. These are not covered in this book, mainly because White seems to have certain difficulties if Black doesn't play ...g4! After 3...f5 the sacrifice gains even more in strength since Black has weakened his king by moving his f-pawn.

Ein analoges Figurenopfer charakterisiert das Muzio-Polerio-Gambit 3...g5 4.♗c4 g4 5.0-0 wie auch das MacDonnell-Gambit (5.♘c3) und das Rosentreter-Gambit (3...g5 4.d4 g4 5.♗:f4). Diese Gambitspiele behandeln wir in unserem Buch nicht - hauptsächlich deswegen, weil der Anziehende auf gewisse Probleme stößt, wenn Schwarz ...g4 unterläßt! Nach ...f5 gewinnt dieses Opferspiel hingegen noch an Stärke, da der Nachziehende seine Königsstellung durch den Aufzug des f-Bauern geschwächt hat.

7.♕:f3 ♕h4+ 8.g3 ♕g4 9.♕e3 ♘c6 10.♗e2 ♕g6 11.♘c3 ♗b4 12.d5! ♘d8 13.0-0-0 h6 14.g4!

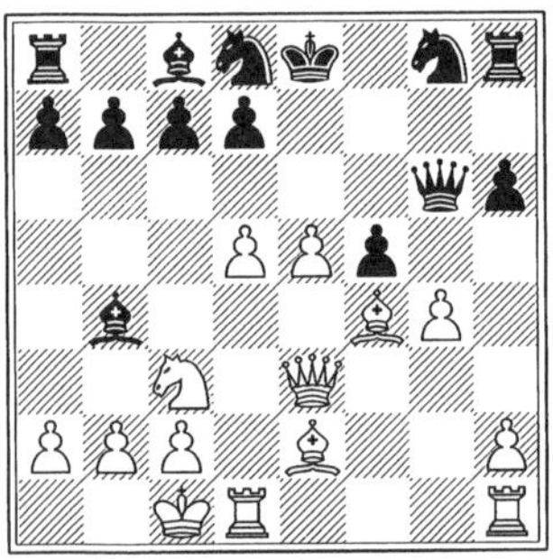

14...♘e7 15.d6 ♘e6

15...♘ec6? 16.g:f5/16.♘d5 +−

16.d:e7 ♗c5 17.♕g3 ♗:e7 ± 18.g:f5 ♕:f5 19.♗e3 ♗g5 20.♘d5 ♗:e3+ 21.♕:e3 ♔d8 22.♖hg1 ♕f8 23.♖df1 ♕c5 24.♕f3 ♖f8 25.♖g8! 1:0 (25...♖:g8 26.♕f6 Δ ♕f7), Schlechter-Teichmann, Vienna 1903.

B

(1.e4 e5 2.f4 e:f4 3.♘f3 f5 4.e5)

4...d6 5.♕e2! ♗e7

5...d:e5 6.♘:e5 ♕e7 7.d4 g5 8.♕h5+ ♔d8 9.♕:g5! Alapin.

6.d4 ♘c6 7.♗:f4 d:e5 8.d:e5 ♘d4 9.♕c4 ♘e6

9...♘:f3+ 10.g:f3 ♗h4+ 11.♔e2 ⩲ Gallagher.

But I don't see what's wrong with 11.♗g3 e.g.

Ich wüßte indes nicht, warum nicht 11.♗g3 geschehen soll, z.B.:

11...♗:g3+ 12.h:g3 ♕g5 13.♔f2 ♕c1? 14.♗g2 ♕g5 15.♖:h7!.

10.♗d3 ⩲

C

(1.e4 e5 2.f4 e:f4 3.♘f3 f5 4.e5)

4...d5 5.d4

5.h4!? ♗e7 6.d4 ♘h6 7.♗:f4 ♘g4 8.♘c3 0-0 9.♕d2 c6, Gunsberg - Swiderski, Vienna 1903, 10.0-0-0 ⩲/±.

5...g5 6.h4 g4 7.♘g1 f3 8.♗g5!

8.g:f3 ♗e7 ∞.

8...f:g2 9.♗:g2 ♗e7 10.♘c3 ♗e6

10...♗:g5 11.h:g5 ♕:g5 12.♘d5 ♘a6 13.♘e2 c6 14.♘df4 h5 15.d5!.

11.♘ge2 ♕d7

11...h6 12.♘f4! h:g5 13.♘:e6.

12.♘f4 c6 13.♗f1

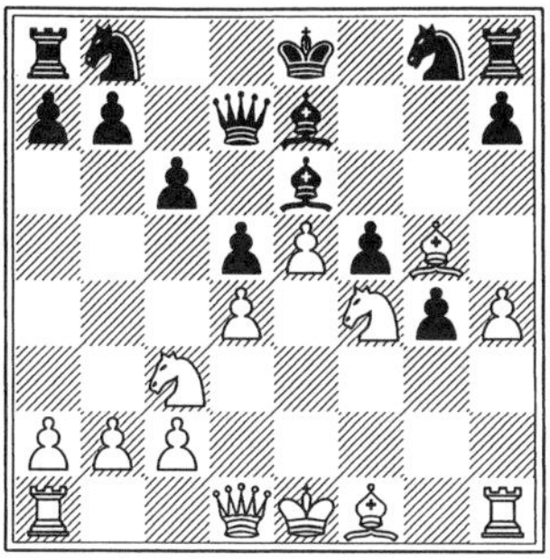

± (Kortchnoi/Zak)

III

(1.e4 e5 2.f4 e:f4 3.♘f3)

3...g6 4.d4 d6 5.♗:f4 ♗g7 6.♗d3 ♘e7 7.0-0 0-0 8.♘c3! ♘bc6 9.♘e2 ♗g4 10.c3 d5 11.e5 ♕d7 12.♘g3 ♘d8 13.♕d2 ♘e6 14.♗h6 ♗:f3 15.♖:f3 c6 16.♗:g7 ♔:g7 17.♖af1

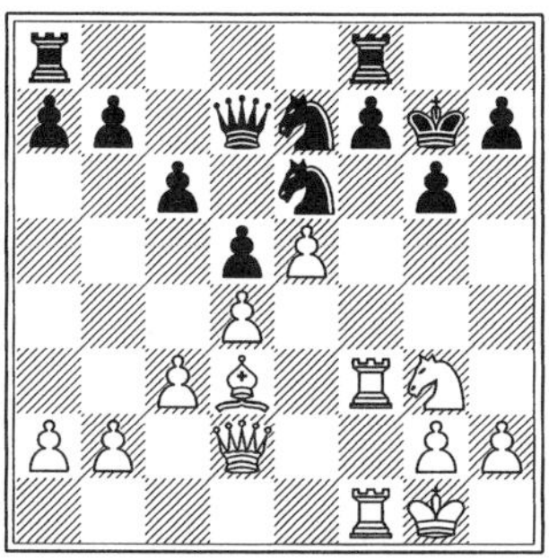

17...♕c7 18.♘e2 c5 19.♖h3 h5 20.♕e3 c4 21.♗c2 ♖h8 22.♕f2 ♖af8 23.♕f6+ ♔g8 24.g4 ♘g7 25.♘f4 ♘e8 26.♕g5 ♘g7 27.g:h5 ♕d8 28.h:g6 ♘:g6 29.♖:h8+ ♘:h8 30.♕g3 f5 31.♘e6 ♕e7 32.♘:f8 ♔:f8 33.♗:f5 ♔e8 34.♗g6+ ♘:g6 35.♕:g6+ ♔d8 36.♖f7

+–, Jaeg - Arnauld, Clichy 1991.

A nice illustration of how to deal with early deviations: grab the centre, take back the gambit pawn as you bring your pieces out and then exploit your advantage in centre control, mobility and space. Sounds very easy, doesn't it?

Ein schönes Beispiel dafür, wie mit frühzeitigen Abweichungen umzuspringen ist: Das Zentrum besetzen, den Gambitbauern zurückerobern und dabei gleichzeitig die eigenen Figuren ins Spiel bringen; anschließend werden dann die Vorteile - Zentralisierung, Beweglichkeit, Raumvorteil - umgesetzt. Hört sich alles schön einfach an, nicht wahr?

Chapter V *Kapitel V*

The Kieseritzky Gambit
Das Kieseritzky-Gambit

1.e4 e5 2.f4 e:f4 3.♘f3 g5

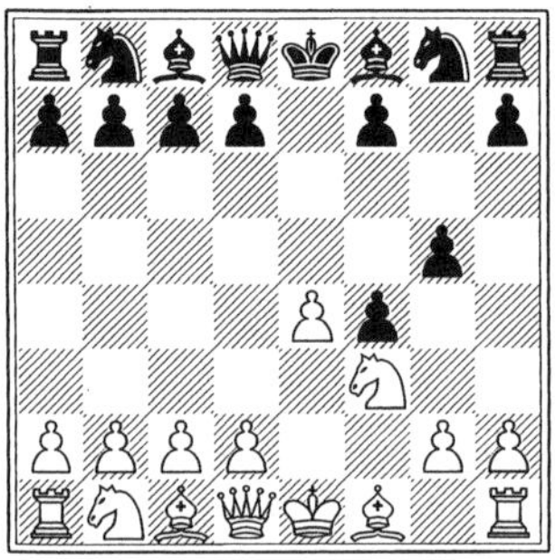

This old move is probably Black's best defence, at least theoretically speaking. But among players below 2300 ELO it's not very common and when it's played it's often mishandled at an early stage by Black!
Nevertheless, I advice you to read this chapter thoroughly, since the kind of positions you'll find here are often typical for the King's Gambit, especially note the way White handles his d, e, g and h-pawns to counter Black's different plans.

Dieser altehrwürdige Zug stellt - zumindest in eröffnungstheoretischer Hinsicht - die stärkste schwarze Verteidigung dar. Doch bei Spielern unterhalb der Elo 2300 ist er selten anzutreffen, und wenn doch, mißhandeln die Schwarzspieler die Stellung häufig bereits in der Anfangsphase gründlich!

Nichtsdestotrotz rate ich Ihnen, dieses Kapitel gründlich zu studieren, denn die entstehenden Stellungen sind grundlegend für das Königsgambit. Ein besonderes Augenmerk sei dabei auf die - in Abhängigkeit von den schwarzen Plänen differierende - weiße Handhabung seiner d-, e-, g- und h-Bauern gelegt.

4.h4 g4

The pawn chain can't be held intact e.g: 4...f6? This move is almost never any good.
Schwarz kann seine Bauernkette nicht mit beispielsweise 4...f6? - ein Zug, der praktisch nie gut ist - intakt halten:
5.♘:g5! f:g5 6.♕h5+ ♔e7 7.♕:g5+ ♔e8 8.♕e5+ ♔f7 9.♗c4+ d5 10.♗:d5+ ♔g6 11.h5+ ♔h6 12.♕:f4+ ♕g5 13.♕:f8+ ♕g7 14.d4#, W. Lutes - Jackson, Columbus 1962.

5.♘e5

This is the start of the Kieseritzky, 5.♘g5 would be the Allgaier gambit.
Leitet das Kieseritzky-Gambit ein. 5.♘g5 wäre das Allgaier-Gambit.

Those who like to break new ground or just surprise their opponents might like to try 'The Sorgenfri Gambit' [so:rjenfre:] **5.♘d4!?/?!** (named after the neighbourhood I live in, it may be translated to something like 'free from sorrows'), a move never tried in practice as far as I know.

Demjenigen, der gerne jungfräuliches Gebiet betritt oder auch nur seinen Gegner verblüffen will, sei das "Sorglos-Gambit" ***5.♘d4!?/?!*** *- ein Zug, welcher meines Wissens völlig unerprobt ist - ans Herz gelegt.*

However a modern trend seems to be to reserve d4 for the Knight in variations where e5 isn't available, for example: after 5.♘d4 d6 6.d3 (There are few alternatives for White: 6.♕e2? ♗g7 ∓, however, 6.♘e2!?/?! ♗e7 7.♘:f4 ♗:h4+ may be an alternative if you don't want to transpose) we've entered a minor variation of the Fischer defence which is more unclear than equal (There is a short coverage of this in Chapter VII).

Doch zumindest in Varianten, wo das Feld e5 unzugänglich für den Springer ist, scheint es ein moderner Trend zu sein, dem Springer das Feld d4 vorzubehalten, z.B. 5.♘d4 d6 6.d3 (es gibt kaum Alternativen: 6.♕e2? ♗g7 ∓, vielleicht 6.♘e2!?/?! ♗e7 7.♘:f4 ♗:h4+, wenn man partout nicht überleiten will), und wir befinden uns in einer Nebenvariante der Fischer-Verteidigung (in Kapitel VII widmen wir uns kurz dieser Stellung).

5.♘d4 d5 6.e:d5 ♕:d5 7.♕e2+
seems logical.
scheint logisch.

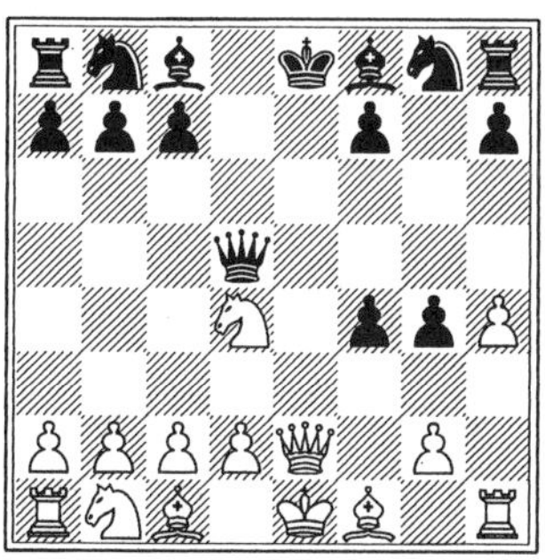

- 7...♗e7 8.♘b5 ∞.
- 7...♘e7 8.♘b5 ♘a6 9.♘1c3 ♕e6 (9...♕c6 10.♕f2) 10.d4 ♕f5 11.♕c4 ♕:c2 (11...f3 12.♗e3) 12.♗:f4! ♕:b2 13.♖b1 ♗:b5 14.♕:b5+ ♕:b5 15.♗:b5+ c6 16.♗e5! ±, Johansson - Computer (blitz).
- 7...♔d8!?

is probably the critical variation, e.g.
vermutlich die kritische Variante, z.B.:
8.♘b5 (Δ ♕e8+!) ♗e7 9.♘1c3 ♕f5 (9...♕h5 10.d4 c6 11.♗:f4 c:b5 12.♘:b5 ♘a6 13.d5!? ♗:h4+?! 14.g3 ♗:g3+ 15.♗:g3 ♕:h1 16.♘d6 ♘h6 17.♕e5 +−, Johansson - Computer, blitz) 10.♕c4 ♕e5+ 11.♔d1 c6 12.♘d4 ♗d6 13.d3 ♘f6 14.♘de2 f3 15.g:f3 g:f3 16.♘d4 ♗g4 17.♗g5
with some compensation.
mit gewisser Kompensation.

There is still a lot to discover in this variation!
Hier gibt es noch viel zu entdecken!

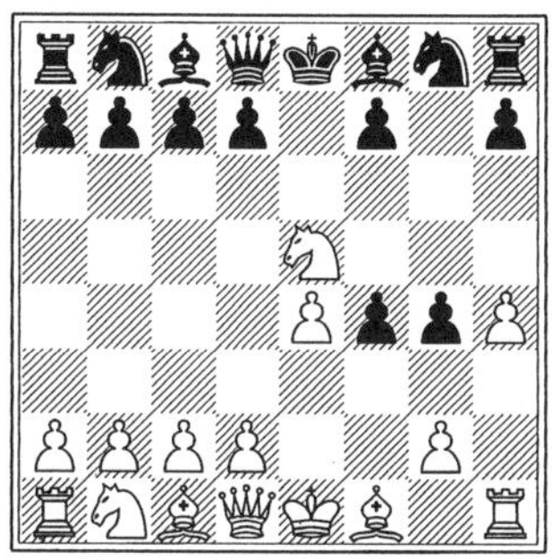

Position after 5.♘e5/*Nach 5.♘e5*

I

5...♕e7

The Rosenthal defence.
Die Rosenthal-Verteidigung.

6.d4!

Never back down in the earliest phase if it isn't strictly forced!
Gib in der Anfangsphase niemals klein bei - außer wenn es wirklich unabdingbar ist!

A

6...f5?! 7.♗c4

Black's position is already going downhill fast!
Mit der schwarzen Position geht es nunmehr bereits rasch bergab!

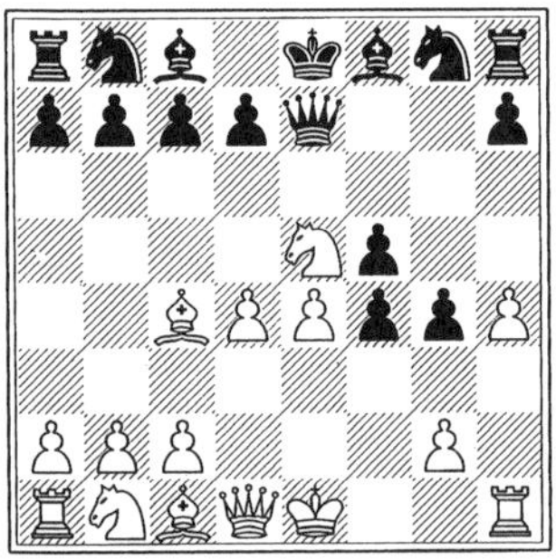

• **7...♘f6 8.♘c3 d6 9.♗f7+ ♔d8 10.♗:f4 ♘bd7 11.♗b3 ♔e8 12.♘f7 ♖g8 13.♘g5 ♖g7 14.♘e6** +–, Cozio (1766).
What a difference a knight makes!
Was ein Springer so alles anrichten kann!

• **7...c6 8.♗:f4 d6 9.♗g5 ♘f6 10.♗f7+ ♔d8 11.♘:g4!**

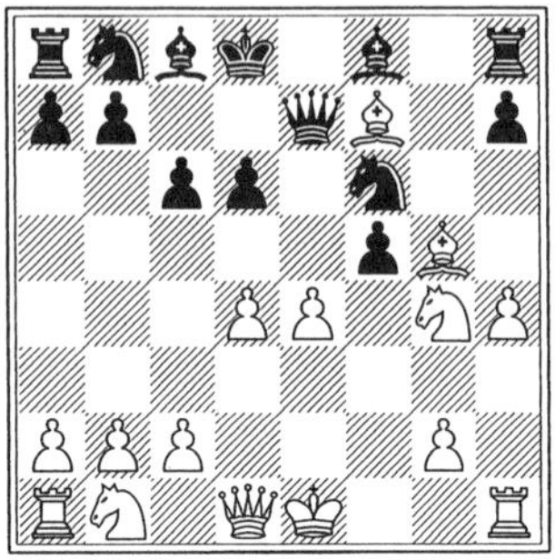

11...f:g4 12.0-0 ♗g7 13.e5 ♕:f7 14.♖:f6 ♗:f6 15.♗:f6+ ♔e8 16.♗:h8 ±.

• **7...♘h6 8.♗:f4 ♕b4+ 9.♘c3 d6 10.a3 ♕b6**
10...♕:b2 11.♘a4
11.♘d5 ♕:b2 12.♘:c7+ ♔d8 13.♘b5 +–, Szewczak - Donato, corr. 1980 (1:0/19.).

B

(1.e4 e5 2.f4 e:f4 3.♘f3 g5 4.h4 g4 5.♘e5 ♕e7 6.d4)

6...d6 7.♘:g4 f5

7...♕:e4+ 8.♕e2 d5 (8...♗f5 9.♗:f4 ♕:e2+ 10.♗:e2 ♗:c2 11.♘c3 ♗f5 12.♘d5 ♔d7 13.0-0 → Euwe) 9.♘e5 ♘h6 10.♘c3 ♗b4 11.♕:e4 d:e4 12.♗:f4 ♘f5 13.0-0-0 ♗:c3 14.b:c3 ♘d6 15.c4! f6 16.c5 f:e5 17.♗:e5 ♘f7 18.♗:h8 ♘:h8 19.♖e1±, Steinitz - Lord Churchill, Oxford 1870 (1:0/33.)

8.♘f2 ♘f6 9.♗:f4 ♘:e4

9...f:e4 10.d5!.

10.♕h5+ ♔d8 11.♗e2 ♘f6 12.♕f3 ♘c6 13.c3 ±/±

C

(1.e4 e5 2.f4 e:f4 3.♘f3 g5 4.h4 g4 5.♘e5 ♕e7 6.d4)

6...♘f6 7.♗c4 d6

7...♘:e4 8.♕:g4!. 7...d5 8.e:d5 is pointless since Black can't block the ♙d5 with ♗d6.
macht hier keinen Sinn, da Schwarz den ♙d5 nicht mit ♗d6 blockieren kann.

8.♗:f7+!

Obviously thematic, and worth remembering, because when one encounters an inferior move one is often tempted to play safe but it's this hard move that makes it inferior!
Ein thematischer Einschlag, den man sich merken sollte. Wenn der Kontrahent zu einem minderwertigen Zug greift, ist man oft geneigt, vorsichtig zu spielen, doch gerade dieser entschlossene Zug weist hier die Minderwertigkeit nach!

8...♔d8 9.♗:f4 d:e5 10.d:e5+ ♗d7 11.♗b3! ♕b4+ 12.♘d2 ♘:e4 13.c3 ♘:c3 14.♗g5+ ♗e7 15.b:c3 ♕:c3 16.♗:e7+ ♔:e7 17.0-0 ♕d4+ 18.♔h1 ♗e8

18...g3 19.♕h5 +–.

19.♖c1 ±

Δ ♖c4:g4.

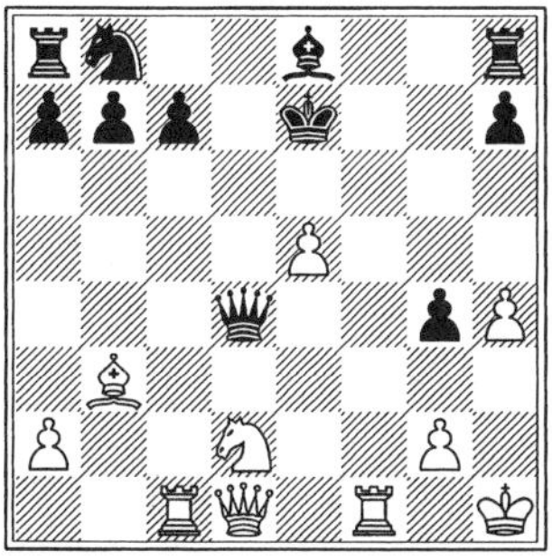

For the moment Black is a pawn up, but that's the only positive thing there is to say about Black's position!
Im Moment hat Schwarz noch einen Bauern mehr, aber das ist auch wirklich das einzig Positive, was man von seiner Stellung sagen könnte!

II

(1.e4 e5 2.f4 e:f4 3.♘f3 g5 4.h4 g4 5.♘e5)

5...♗e7

The Polerio defence.
Die Polerio-Verteidigung.

6.♗c4!

The h-pawn is frequently given up for a tempo or two. Besides, after Black takes on h4 the ♖h1 is ready for action immediately! Compare this with the Cunningham, where White must spend some time to get this rook to the f-file.
Der h-Bauer wird häufig für ein oder zwei Tempi geopfert. Außerdem ist der ♖h1 jetzt einsatzbereit! Man vergleiche mit der Cunningham-Verteidigung, wo Weiß einige Zeit benötigt, um seinen Turm auf der f-Linie ins Spiel zu bringen.

6...♗:h4+ 7.♔f1 d5

A vital pawn sac! Black must get his pieces out before White's initiative wipes him off the board!
Ein lebensnotwendiges Bauernopfer! Der Nachziehende muß ein paar Figuren herausbringen, bevor er von der weißen Initiative vom Brett gefegt wird!

7...♘h6 8.♘:g4 ♘:g4 9.♕:g4 ♗g5 (9...d5 10.♕:f4 d:c4 11.♖:h4 ±) 10.♕h5!? ♕f6 (10...♕e7 11.d4) 11.♘c3 c6 12.e5 ♕g6 13.♕:g6 f:g6

14.♘e4 ♗e7 15.d4 b5 16.♗b3 a5 17.a3 g5 18.♗d2 ♘a6 19.♖e1 ♘c7 20.♘d6+ ±, Kolisch - Schulten, Paris 1860 (1:0/30.).

White' bishop pair will have a major impact on the position.

Im weiteren Verlauf wird das Geschehen fest im Griff des weißen Läuferpaares sein.

8.♗:d5 ♘h6 9.d4 ♗g5

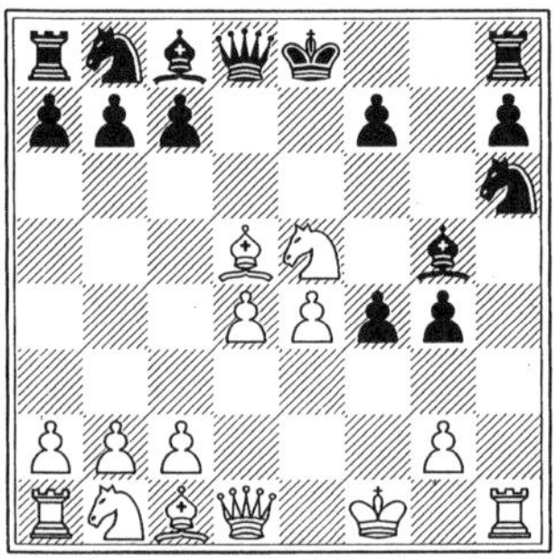

- **10.♘c3 c6 11.♗b3 f6?!**

11...f3? 12.♖:h6 ♗:h6 13.♗:f7+ +–; 11...♘d7!.

12.♘d3 ± ♕:d4 13.♗:f4 ♗:f4 14.♘:f4 ♕:d1+ 15.♖:d1 ♘f7 16.♘g6 ♖g8 17.♖:h7 +–.

- **10.g3!**

Getting access to the black holes on the kingside the KG way!

Eine Königsgambit-typische Methode, aus den Löchern am schwarzen Königsflügel Nutzen zu ziehen!

10...♕f6

10...c6!?; 10...f:g3 11.♗:g5 ♕:g5 12.♕d2! +–

11.g:f4 ♗:f4 12.♔g2

Thanks to his pieces great activity, the white king is quite safe here.

Dank der großen Aktivität seiner Figuren steht der weiße König hier ziemlich sicher.

12...c6 13.♗:f4 ♕:f4 14.♕d2!

Consistently getting rid of black square defenders!

Fährt mit der Eliminierung der die schwarzen Felder schützenden Figuren fort!

(14.♖f1 ♕g5 15.♗:f7+ ♘:f7 16.♘:f7 ♕h5 17.♘:h8 ♕h3+ =)

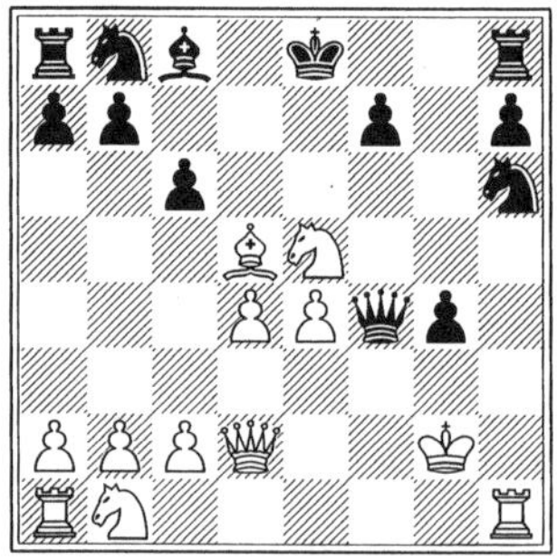

14...♕:d2 15.♘:d2 c:d5 16.♖:h6± ♗e6 17.c4! d:e4 18.♘:e4 ♘d7 19.♘:d7 ♗:d7 20.♘d6+ ♔e7 21.♖e1+ ♗e6 22.♘:f7! ±.

III

(1.e4 e5 2.f4 e:f4 3.♘f3 g5 4.h4 g4 5.♘e5)

5...♘c6

The Viennese defence.

Die Wiener Verteidigung.

6.d4!

This is always the right move if the knight is attacked by another piece, just concentrate on getting ahead in development!

Stets der korrekte Zug, wenn der Springer von einer schwarzen Figur angegriffen wird - man bemühe sich um Entwicklungsvorsprung!

6.♘:g4 d5 7.e:d5 ♕e7+ 8.♗e2 ♘d4 gives Black the initiative.
würde Schwarz die Initiative überlassen.

A

6...♘:e5 7.d:e5 d6

7...f3!? 8.g:f3 ♗e7, Powe - Schiller, USA 1991, 9.♗d3?! ♗:h4+ 10.♔f1 g3 11.f4 d5,
and Black won comfortably in 19 moves.
und Schwarz siegte gemütlich in 19 Zügen.
I think 9.♗c4 looks more critical, e.g.
Meines Erachtens ist viel eher 9.♗c4 kritisch, z.B.:
9...♗:h4+ 10.♔f1 d6 (10...g3? 11.♕d5 ♕e7 12.♖:h4 c6 13.♕:f7+ ±) 11.e:d6 c:d6 12.♗b5+ ♔f8 13.♗f4 ♗e7 14.♕d4 ♘f6 15.♘c3 ± (Δ ♘d5, ♖d1) .

8.♗:f4 ♕e7

8...♗g7 9.♘c3! d:e5 10.♕:d8+ ♔:d8 11.0-0-0+ ♗d7 12.♗e3± Bilguer (1847).

9.♗b5+

Or *(oder)* 9.e:d6 ♕:e4+ 10.♕e2 ♕:e2+ 11.♗:e2 ♗:d6 12.♗:d6 c:d6 13.♘c3 ±.
Black's lack of development and numerous weaknessess are more than sufficient compensation for the pawn.
Der schwarze Entwicklungsrückstand sowie diverse Schwächen stellen eine mehr als ausreichende Kompensation für den Bauern dar.

9...c6 10.e:d6 ♕:e4+ 11.♕e2

± (Bhend)

B

(1.e4 e5 2.f4 e:f4 3.♘f3 g5 4.h4 g4 5.♘e5 ♘c6 6.d4)

6...♕e7 7.♘c3 ♘:e5 8.♘d5 ♕d6 9.d:e5 ♕:e5 10.♗:f4 ♕:e4+ 11.♕e2 ♕:e2+ 12.♗:e2 ±

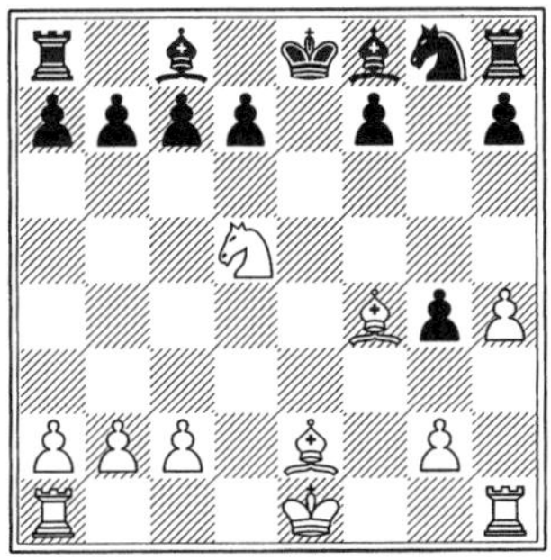

Isn't it just amazing how quickly and ridiculously easy White achieves a gigantic lead in development!?
Ist es nicht spaßig zu beobachten, wie schnell und erschreckend einfach Weiß riesigen Entwicklungsvorsprung erhält?

C

(1.e4 e5 2.f4 e:f4 3.♘f3 g5 4.h4 g4 5.♘e5 ♘c6 6.d4)

6...♗e7 7.♗:f4 ♗:h4+ 8.g3 ♗f6

8...♗g5 9.♘:g4.

9.♗c4 ♕e7 10.♘:f7 ♕:e4+ 11.♕e2 ♕:e2+ 12.♔:e2 ♘:d4+ 13.♔d2 ± ♘e6 14.♘:h8 ♗:b2 15.♗:e6

15.♘c3.

15...d:e6 16.♖:h7 ♗:a1 17.c3 ♘f6 18.♖:c7 ±

D

(1.e4 e5 2.f4 e:f4 3.♘f3 g5 4.h4 g4 5.♘e5 ♘c6 6.d4)

6...♘:d4?

This insane knight sac is supposed to give Black equality?! (According to some source quoted by Leach).
Ein hirnrissiges Springeropfer, welches dem Schwarzen - gemäß einiger von Leach zitierter Quellen - Ausgleich geben soll?!

7.♕:d4 ♗g7 8.♗:f4?

White should play the obvious
Auf der Hand liegt
8.♕d5! (Δ ♘:g4) +–.

8...d6 9.c3 d:e5 10.♗:e5 ♕:d4 11.♗:d4 ♘f6 12.♗c4 0-0 13.e5 ♘h5 14.0-0 =

This is a good reminder to always check other's analysis, for yourself!
Prüfen Sie stets die "Empfehlungen" anderer, bevor Sie sie selbst anwenden!

E

(1.e4 e5 2.f4 e:f4 3.♘f3 g5 4.h4 g4 5.♘e5 ♘c6 6.d4)

6...♕f6 7.♘c3 ♗b4 8.♘d3!? ♕:d4 9.♘:b4 ♘:b4 10.♗:f4 ♕:d1+ 11.♖:d1

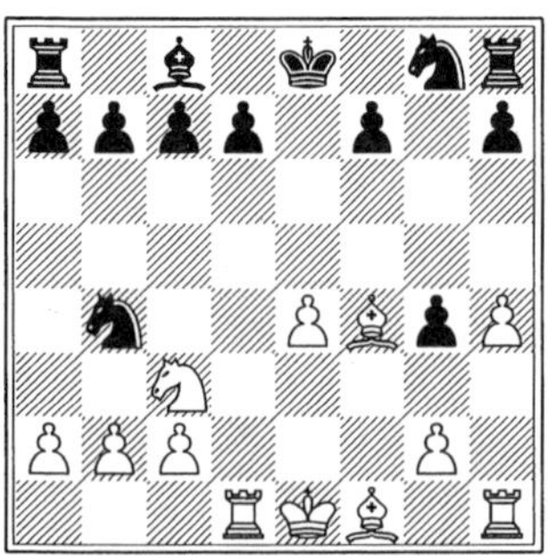

11...d6

11...♘:c2+ 12.♔f2 (Δ a3) ♘b4 13.♘b5→.

12.a3 ♘:c2+ 13.♔f2 g3+ 14.♗:g3 ♘f6 15.♗e2 ♖g8 16.♗f4 ♗g4 17.♗f3 ♘h5 18.♗h2 c5 19.♘b5 ♘d4 20.♘:d4 c:d4 21.♖:d4 ♖c8 22.♖hd1 ♘f6 23.♖:d6 ♗e6 24.♗f4 ♘g4+ 25.♔e1 ♘f6 26.♗g5 ♘d7 27.♗h5 ♖c6 28.♖:c6 b:c6 29.♖d6 ♔f8 30.♖:c6 ♔g7 31.♗f4 ♖e8 32.♔f2 a5 33.♗e2 ♖d8 34.b4 a:b4 35.a:b4 ♘f6 36.♗e5 ♔g6 37.♗:f6 ♔:f6 38.♔e3+– (1:0/63.), Nunn - Piket, Melody Amber (blindfold - *Blindpartie*) 1995.

IV

(1.e4 e5 2.f4 e:f4 3.♘f3 g5 4.h4 g4 5.♘e5)

5...h5 ♥

The Long Whip. This is an extremely common waste of time.
Die "Lange Peitsche" - eine sehr verbreitete Art der Zeitverschwendung.

6.♗c4

This simple threat is almost always good if Black doesn't have a knight on f6 supporting 6...d5 7.e:d5 ♗d6 constipating White's counter-play.
Dieser simple Überfall ist stets angebracht, wenn Schwarz über keinen ♘f6 zur Unterstützung des Stopfmanövers 6...d5 7.e:d5 ♗d6 verfügt.

A

6...♖h7 7.d4

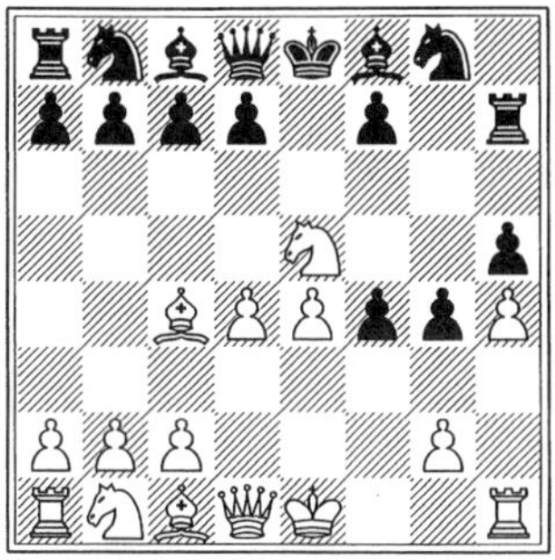

• **7...♗h6 8.♘c3 ♘c6 9.♘:f7! ♖:f7 10.♗:f7+ ♔:f7**

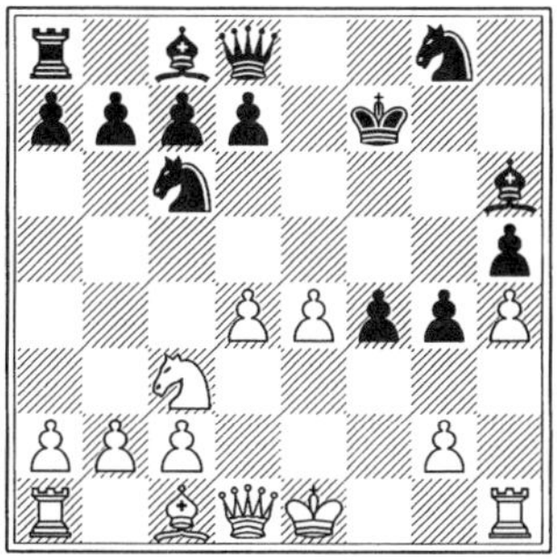

11.♗:f4!
A quite useful tactical device to open the lethal f-file!
Ein sehr nützlicher taktischer Schlag! Die todbringende f-Linie wird nun geöffnet.
11...♗:f4 12.0-0 ♕:h4
As usual this is a waste of valuable time.
Wie gewöhnlich nur mit dem Verlust wertvoller Zeit verbunden.
13.♖:f4+ ♔g7 14.♕d2 d6 15.♖af1 ♘d8 16.♘d5 ♗d7 17.e5!
Taking the c-pawn would only aid Black's development.
Den c-Bauern zu schlagen würde lediglich die schwarze Entwicklung begünstigen.
17...d:e5 18.d:e5 ♗c6 19.e6! ♗:d5 20.♖f7+ ♘:f7 21.♖:f7+ ♔h8 22.♕c3+ ♘f6 23.♖:f6 ♕:f6 24.♕:f6+ ♔h7 25.♕f5+ 1:0, Bronstein - Dubinin, Leningrad 1947.

• **7...d6 8.♘:f7 ♖:f7 9.♗:f7+ ♔:f7 10.♗:f4 ±**
What follows is an excellent example of how to exploit the f-file.
Es folgt ein Musterbeispiel zur Ausbeutung der geöffneten f-Linie.
10...♗h6! 11.0-0 ♗:f4 12.♖:f4+ ♔g7 13.♘c3 ♕:h4 14.♘d5!
14.♕d2 ♗e6!.
14...♘a6 15.♕d3 c6 16.♖af1 ♗e6
16...c:d5 17.♖f7+ Δ e:d5 +–.
17.♘e3 ♘b4 18.♕a3 c5 19.dc5 ♘:a2 20.♕:a2 ♗:a2 21.♘f5+ +–, Anderssen - Kieseritzky, London 1851.

• **7...♗e7 8.♗:f4 ♗:h4+?**
8...d6.
9.g3 ♗g5 10.♖:h5! ♖:h5 11.♗:f7+ ♔f8 12.♗:h5 ♗:f4 13.♘g6+ ♔g7 14.♘:f4 ♘f6 15.♘c3 ♕e7 16.♘fd5 ♘:d5 17.♕:g4+ ♔h8 18.♘:d5 +–
A fine illustration of how potentially crushing White's game plan is!
Demonstriert sehr schön die dem weißen Spielplan innewohnende verheerende Kraft!

• **7...f3**
A sensible idea, closing the devastating f-file!
Eine feinfühlige Idee - die gefahrbringende f-Linie wird geschlossen.
8.g:f3 d6 9.♘d3 ♗e7 10.♗e3 ♗:h4+ 11.♔d2 ± ♗g5
11...g:f3 (Inconsistent, the f-file is still very useful for White - *inkonsequent, die f-Linie ist nach wie vor äußerst nützlich für Weiß*) 12.♕:f3 ♗g4 13.♕f4 ♘c6 14.♘c3 ♘:d4 15.♖af1 ♗f6 16.♘d5 ♗h8 17.♕:g4! (The start of a

formidable massacre! - *Beginn eines Massakers)* 17...h:g4 18.♖:h7 ♘f3+ 19.♖:f3 g:f3 20.♖:h8 +– Jänisch.

12.f4 ♗h6 13.♘c3!

Avoiding 13.♖:h5 ♘f6.

Umgeht 13.♖:h5 ♘f6.

13...♗g7

The bishop has to drift on for the fifth time since the ♙h5 really was hanging this time.

Da der ♙h5 nun tatsächling hing, muß der Läufer zum fünften Mal ziehen.

14.f5! ♘c6 15.♕g1 ♗d7 16.♖e1 ♘a5 17.♗b3 ♘:b3 18.a:b3 ♗c6 19.♘f4! ± ♘f6 20.♔c1 ♗h6 21.e5! ♗:h1 22.e:f6 ♗f3 23.♘fd5! ♔f8

23...♗:e3+,

and the simplest win seems to be

und am einfachsten gewinnt wohl

24.♖:e3+ ♔f8 (24...♔d7 25.♖e7+ Δ ♘:c7 +–) 25.♘e7 (Δ ♖:f3) ♗c6 26.d5 ♗d7 27.♕g3 (Δ ♕h4-g5).

24.♗:h6+ ♖:h6 25.♕e3 ♖:f6 26.♕g5 ♖g6 27.♕:d8+ +– (1:0/52.), Kolisch - Anderssen, Paris 1860.

- **7...♕f6 8.♘c3 c6 9.0-0 ♗h6**

9...♕:h4? 10.♖:f4 ♘h6 11.♕f1 ♕e7 12.♖f6 d6 13.♗g5 ♕c7 14.♗:h6 d:e5 15.♗:f8 ♔:f8 16.d:e5 ♕e7 17.e6 ♘a6 18.e:f7 ♘c7 19.♖g6 ♖g7 20.♖h6 +–, Alekhine - Geisch/Ollisevich, corr. 1905.

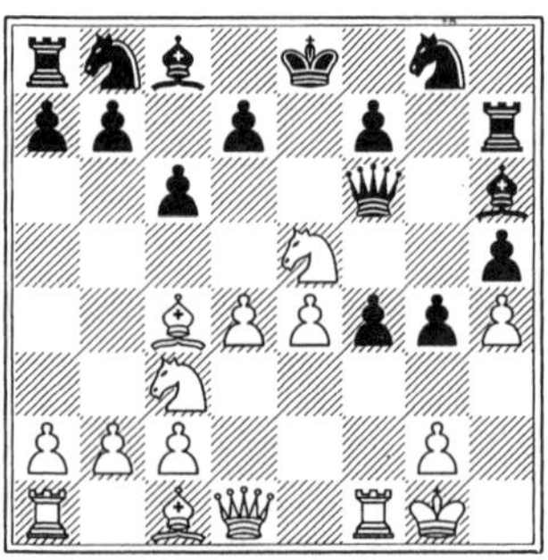

10.♗:f4!

All ways of opening the f-file are excellent, except the boring ones!

Mit Ausnahme der Allerlangweiligsten vielleicht ist jedwede Methode zur Öffnung der f-Linie toll!

10...♗:f4 11.g3 ♗e3+ 12.♔g2 ♕h8 13.♘:f7 ♖:f7 14.♗:f7+ ♔d8 15.e5 d5 16.♕d3 ± (16.e:d6 +–), Linden - Lequesne, Paris 1864.

B

(1.e4 e5 2.f4 e:f4 3.♘f3 g5 4.h4 g4 5.♘e5 h5 6.♗c4)

6...♘h6 7.d4

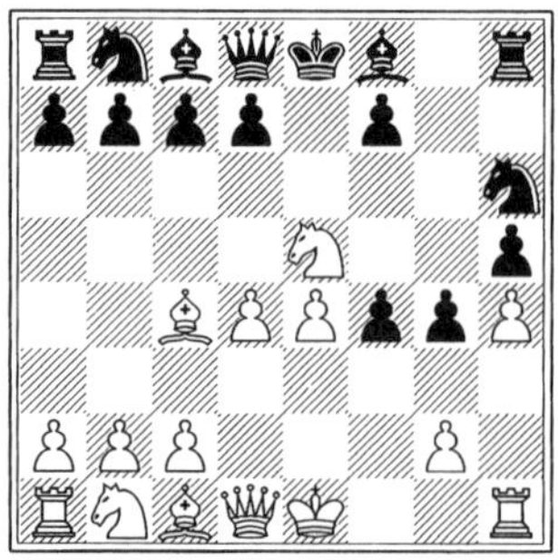

- **7...♕f6 8.0-0!**

Another strong option is:

Eine weitere starke Möglichkeit ist:

8.♘c3! c6 9.0-0 ♕:h4 10.♖:f4 ♖h7 11.♕f1 ♕e7 12.♖f6 ±.

8...♕:h4

The h-pawn seems to have some fatal attraction, since the second players rush to take it with the determination of lemmings rushing off a cliff!

Der h-Bauer scheint ein süßlich-verführerisches Gift zu versprühen - wie anders wäre zu erklären, daß sich die Schwarzspieler seinethalben gleich reihenweise ins Verderben stürzen!

9.♖:f4 ♗d6 10.♘f3! ♕g3 11.e5 ♗e7 12.♘h2 ♕h4 13.♘c3 ♗d8 14.♘e4 ♘c6 15.♘f3 g:f3 16.♖:h4 ♗:h4 17.♕:f3 ♘:d4 18.♕h5 ♘df5 19.♗:h6 d5 20.♗:d5 ♖:h6 21.♕:f7+ ♔d8 22.♕f8+ 1:0, Hebden - Benjamin, London 1987.

- **7...d6 8.♘d3 f3**

8...♕e7 9.♘c3 ♘f5 (9...c6 10.♘:f4 d5 11.♗:d5!? c:d5 12.♘f:d5 ♕d8 13.♗g5 ±, 1:0/27., Johansson - Madison, Karlskrona 1994) 10.♘:f4 c6 11.♘fe2 ♘:h4 12.0-0 ♖h7 13.♘g3 f6 14.e5, Blackburne - Amateur (1:0/23.).

9.g:f3 g:f3

9...♗e7 10.♗f4 ♗:h4+ 11.♔d2 g:f3 12.♕:f3 ♗g4 13.♕e3±, Morphy - Amateur.

10.♕:f3 ♗g4 11.♕f2 ♕d7

11...♕e7 12.0-0 ♖h7 13.♘c3 c6 14.e5! ♘f5 15.♗g5 ♕d7 16.♘e4 (16.e6!) ♗g7 17.♘:d6+ ♘:d6 18.e:d6 ♗e6 19.♘c5 ♕:d6 20.♘:e6 f5 21.♖ae1 ♔d7 22.♘c5+ 1:0, Gossip - Marston.

12.♘c3 c6 13.♗g5 ♘a6 14.♔d2 ♗g7 15.♖af1

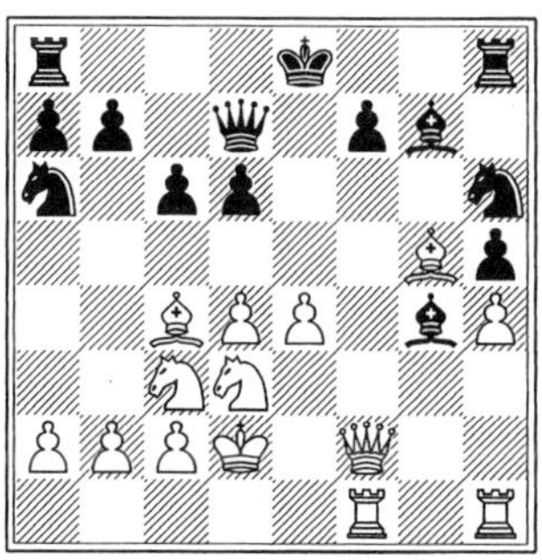

15...0-0 16.♕e3 +–, Peev - Atanasov, Bulgaria 1954.

V

(1.e4 e5 2.f4 e:f4 3.♘f3 g5 4.h4 g4 5.♘e5)

5...d5

The Brentano defence.
Die Brentano-Verteidigung.

6.d4!

Another thematic idea, White is frequently ready to give his e-pawn for the f4-pawn since the f-file is important to get active play. Here it's partly a trap too, since 6...d:e4 gives the whitefielder the strong diagonal c4-f7.
Eine weitere thematische Spielidee. In Anbetracht der Bedeutung der offenen f-Linie ist Weiß zu einem indirekten Abtausch ♙e4 gegen ♙f4 bereit. Hier könnte man es gleichzeitig als eine Art Fallenspiel bezeichnen, zumal das sofortige 6...d:e4 unangenehme "Nebenwirkungen" auf der Diagonalen c4-f7 nach sich ziehen würde.

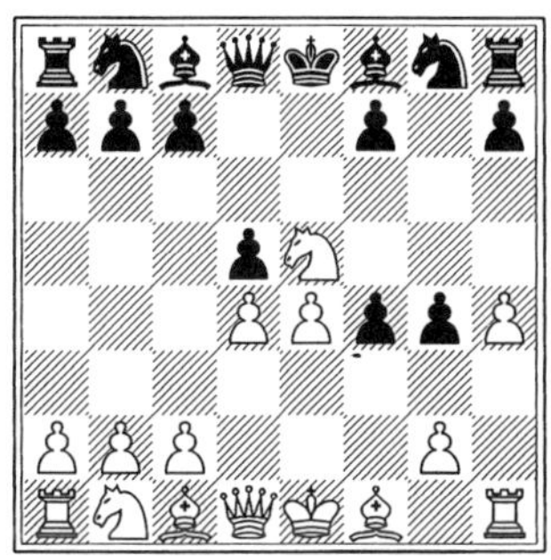

6...♘f6

Black's bad alternatives are rounded up below:
Zweitklassige Alternativen in Kürze:

- 6...d:e4 7.♗c4 ♘h6 8.♗:f4 f6 9.0-0! ±

This knight sac is standard in the Brentano, when the knight isn't sacrificed on f7 instead, that is!
Ein Springeropfer ist Standard in der Brentano-Verteidigung - wenn nicht per Einschlag auf f7, dann eben auf diese Weise!
9...f:e5 10.♗:e5 ♕:h4 11.g3 ♕h3 12.♖f2.

- 6...f6

This is usually a patzer's move, but strangely enough it's not all that easy in this position:
Gewöhnlich ein Patzerzug, doch merkwürdigerweise liegen die Dinge hier nicht ganz so einfach:
7.♘:g4 (7.♗:f4 f:e5 8.♗:e5 ♘f6 9.e:d5 ♗e7 Δ 0-0 is nothing for White - *bringt Weiß nichts ein*) 7...d:e4 8.♘f2 (8.♗:f4 ♗d6!) 8...e3 9.♕h5+ ♔e7 10.♘d3 ♕:d4 11.♘c3 ♗h6 12.♘e2 ♕d6 13.♕f3 ♘c6 14.♘d:f4 ♗:f4 15.♕:f4 ♕:f4 16.♘:f4 ♘d4 17.♘d5+ ♔d8 18.♘:e3 ♘e7 19.♗d3 ±
White still has castling rights, his bishops and slightly better pawn structure.
Weiß darf noch rochieren, hat das Läuferpaar sowie die etwas bessere Bauernstruktur.

- 6...f3 7.g:f3 ♗e7 8.♗e3 ♗:h4+ 9.♔d2 ±.
- 6...h5?! 7.♗:f4 ♗h6 8.♗:h6 ♖:h6 9.e:d5 ♕:d5 10.♘c3 ♕a5 11.♕d2 ♗e6 12.d5! ♗f5 13.♕g5 ♗h7 14.♕g7 +–

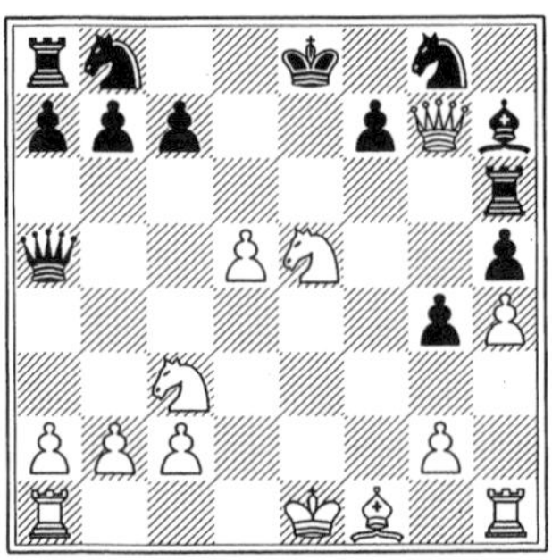

Johansson - Thomasson, Malmö 1994 (1:0/20.).

7.♗:f4 ♘:e4

7...♘h5 8.♕d2 ♗e7 9.e:d5±, e.g. *(z.B.)* 9...♗:h4+ 10.♔d1 ♘g3? 11.♗:g3 ♗:g3 12.♕e3 +–.

8.♘d2!

Just like in the Falkbeer we must challenge Black's control of e4 or suffer the consequences!
Genau wie im Falkbeer-Gegengambit muß Weiß unverzüglich den schwarzen Zugriff auf e4 unterminieren, oder er hat mit betrüblichen Konsequenzen zu rechnen!

8...♘:d2

Black is forced to give up his outpost and help White's development since the alternatives below are even better for White!
Der Nachziehende ist gezwungen, seinen Vorposten aufzugeben und damit der weißen Entwicklung voranzuhelfen, da die Alternativen noch ungünstiger wären:

- 8...♕f6 9.g3 ♗h6 10.♘:e4 d:e4 11.♘:g4! ♗:g4 12.♕:g4 ♗:f4 13.g:f4 (13.♕:f4 ♕:f4 14.g:f4 ±) 13...♕:d4 14.♖d1 ± ♕e3 (14...♕b2 15.♕c8) 15.♗e2 ♘c6 16.♖h3 (Δ ♕d7).
- 8...♗g7 9.♘:e4 d:e4 10.♗c4 0-0 11.c3 ♘d7

[see diagram next page]

12.♘:f7!
Always keep an eye out for an early knight sac on f7 in the Brentano!
In der Brentano-Verteidigung sollten Sie stets die Möglichkeit eines frühen Springeropfers auf f7 im Auge behalten!

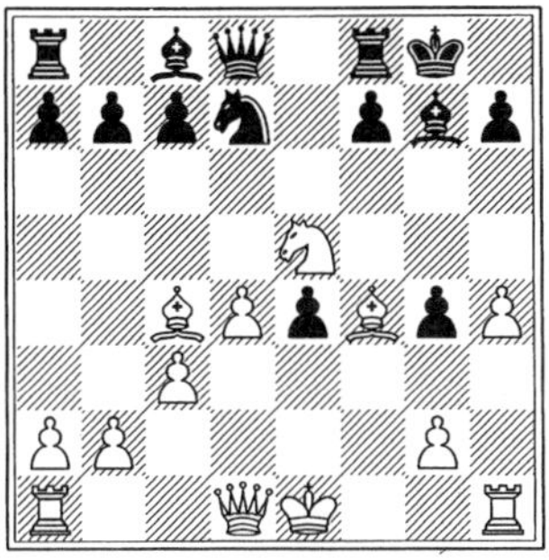

12...♖:f7 13.♗:f7+ ♔:f7 14.♕b3+ ♔e7 15.0-0-0 c6 16.d5! ±, Lutikov - Shakh-Zade, Taschkent 1950.

- 8...f5 9.♘:e4 f:e4 10.♗b5 (10.♘:g4!? ♖g8 11.♘e5 Δ ♕h5) 10...c6 11.0-0! ♗e6 (11...c:b5 12.♘f7!) 12.♗e2 ±, Bobekov - Pelitov, Sofia 1967.
- 8...♗f5 9.♘:e4 ♗:e4 (9...d:e4 10.♗c4) 10.♕:g4 ±.

9.♕:d2

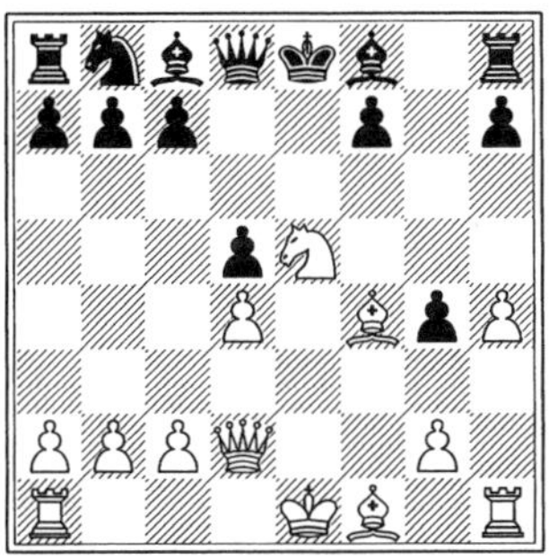

A

9...♗g7 10.♗h6!

Getting rid of the main defender of the black holes around the king.
Beseitigt den wichtigsten Verteidiger der schwarzfeldrigen Löcher rund um den schwarzen König.

10...♗:h6?!

10...0-0 11.0-0-0 ⩲, 11.♗e2 ⩲.

11.♕:h6 ♗e6 12.♗d3 ♘d7

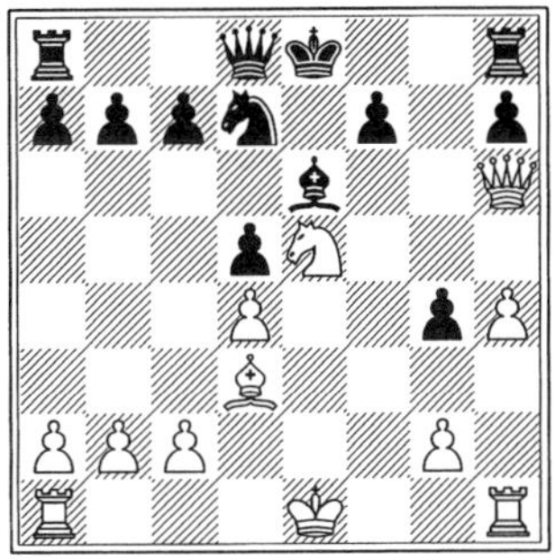

13.♘:f7!

Totally disrupting the harmony in Black's camp!
Zerstört jedwede Ordnung im schwarzen Lager!

13...♗:f7

13...♔:f7 14.0-0+ ♔e7 (14...♘f6 15.♖f4) 15.♖ae1 ♕g8 16.♗f5 ♘f8 17.♗:e6 ♘:e6 18.♖f6 +–
And all losses are restored!
Und Weiß gewinnt das Material mit Zinsen zurück!

14.0-0 ♘e5 15.♖ae1 1:0, Teschner - Dahl, Berlin 1946.

B

(1.e4 e5 2.f4 e:f4 3.♘f3 g5 4.h4 g4 5.♘e5 d5 6.d4 ♘f6 7.♗:f4 ♘:e4 8.♘d2 ♘:d2 9.♕:d2)

9...♗e6 10.0-0-0 ♘d7 11.♖e1 ♗g7

11...♗e7 12.♕e2
The idea behind this move will soon be revealed!

Die Idee hinter diesem Zug tritt gleich zutage!
12...♖g8

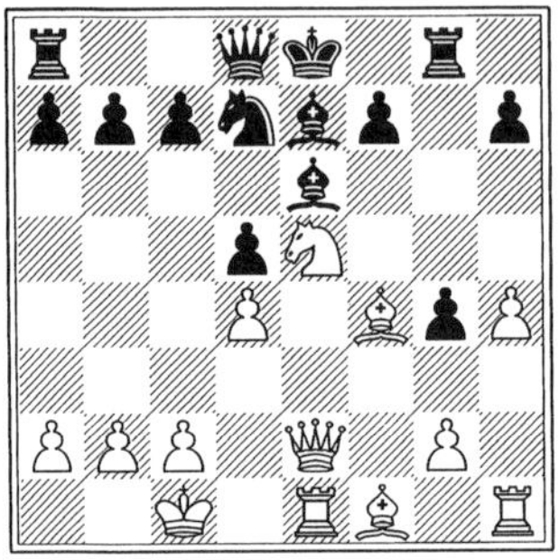

13.♘:f7! ♗:f7 14.♗:c7!+–, Cleemskerk - Rhyn, corr. 1896.

12.♘:g4 0-0 13.♗g5 ♘f6

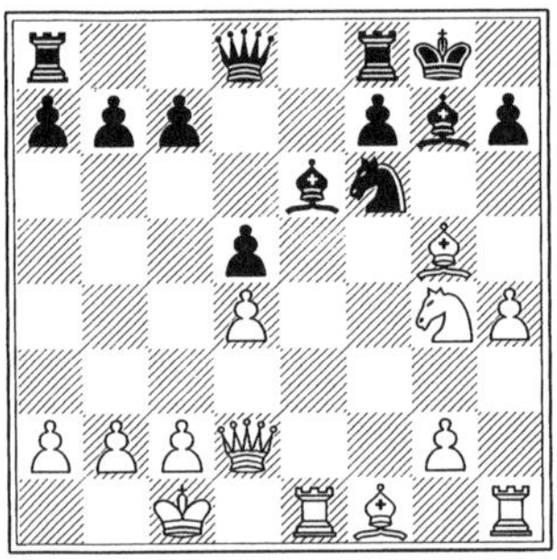

14.♘:f6+ ♗:f6 15.♗d3 ♔h8 16.♕f4 ♗e7 17.♗:e7 ♕:e7 18.♕e5+ ♔g8 19.♖e3 f6 20.♕:e6+ +– (1:0/45.), Caro - Schiffers, Berlin 1897.

C

(1.e4 e5 2.f4 e:f4 3.♘f3 g5 4.h4 g4 5.♘e5 d5 6.d4 ♘f6 7.♗:f4 ♘:e4 8.♘d2 ♘:d2 9.♕:d2)

9...♗d6 10.0-0-0 ♗e6 11.♗d3 f6?!

11...♘d7 12.♖de1 ♘:e5 13.♗:e5 ♗:e5 14.♖:e5 ♕d7 15.♕g5! ♕e7 16.♗f5 ♕:g5+ 17.h:g5 ± Keres.

12.♖de1!

The Black king will be stranded on two highways to hell, the e- and f-file!
Gleich auf zwei Gleisen - der e- und der f-Linie - rast der schwarze König der Hölle entgegen!

12...f:e5

12...♗:e5 13.♗:e5! (13.d:e5 f5) ♔d7 14.♗:f6! ♕:f6 15.♖hf1 ♕g7 16.♖:e6! ♔:e6 17.♗f5 ♔e7 18.♕b4+ +–.

13.♗:e5 ♔d7 14.♕h6!

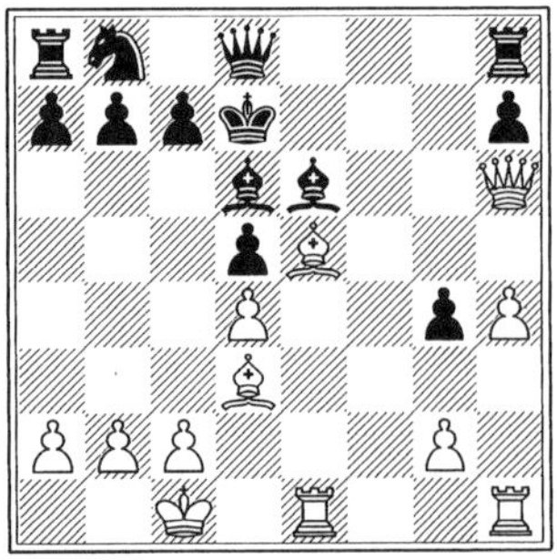

- **14...♗:e5 15.♖:e5 ♖e8 16.♖:e6 ♖:e6 17.♗f5.**
- **14...♗f8 15.♗g7 ♕e7 16.♗:f8 ♖:f8 17.♖:e6!.**
- **14...♖e8 15.♗:d6 ♔:d6 16.♗f5 ♕d7 17.♖e3!**

Black is defenceless against the doubling of the rooks.
Schwarz ist wehrlos gegen die drohende Turmverdoppelung.
(17...♘c6 - Δ ♘d8 - 18.♕f4+ +–, Gallagher)

VI

(1.e4 e5 2.f4 e:f4 3.♘f3 g5 4.h4 g4 5.♘e5)

5...♗g7

The Paulsen defence not so long ago this was thought to be Black's best defence ...
Noch vor nicht allzu langer Zeit wurde die Paulsen-Verteidigung als stärkste schwarze Verteidigung erachtet.

6.d4 ♘f6

6...d6 7.♘:g4 ♗:g4 8.♕:g4 ♗:d4 9.♘c3! ♘f6 10.♕f5!? (10.♕:f4) ♕e7 11.♗d3 ♖g8 12.♗:f4 ♖:g2 13.0-0-0 ±, Gallagher - Sanchi, Paris 1989.

7.♘c3! d6

7...d5? 8.♗:f4 ♘:e4 9.♘:e4 d:e4 10.♗c4 0-0 11.c3 ♘d7 12.♘:f7 ♖:f7 13.♗:f7 ♔:f7 14.♕b3 +
Play has transposed to 8...♗g7 in the Brentano.
Mit Überleitung zur Brentano-Verteidigung mit 8...♗g7.

8.♘d3

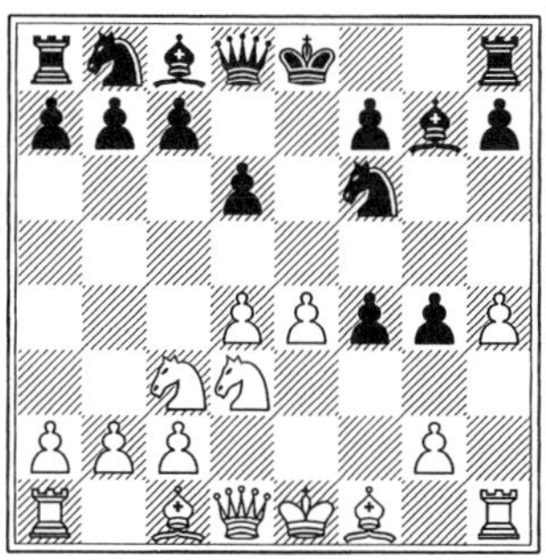

A

8...f3?! 9.g:f3 ♕e7 10.♗g2 h6 11.♗e3 ♘c6 12.♕e2 ♘h5 13.♕f2 f5 14.f:g4 f:g4 15.0-0-0 ♖f8 16.♕e1 ♘:d4 17.♘d5 ♕d7 18.♖f1 ♘f3 19.♗:f3 g:f3 20.e5! c6? 21.e6

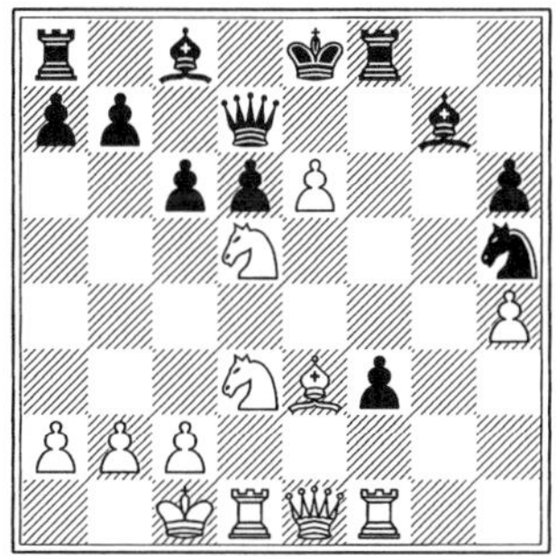

1:0, Blackburne - Greenwell, Newcastle 1889.

B

(1.e4 e5 2.f4 e:f4 3.♘f3 g5 4.h4 g4 5.♘e5 ♗g7 6.d4 ♘f6 7.♘c3 d6 8.♘d3)

8...♘h5 9.♘:f4 ♘g3

This isn't as disturbing as it looks. On the contrary, White often sneaks up on an unprepared second player and suddenly finishes him off!
Längst nicht so beunruhigend wie es den Anschein hat. Im Gegenteil, häufig schleicht sich Weiß an den gutgläubigen Schwarzspieler heran und bläst ihn dann plötzlich vom Brett!

10.♖h2 0-0 11.♗e2 f5

11...♘:e2 12.♘c:e2 f5 13.c3 f:e4 14.♕b3 + ♔h8 15.♗e3 Δ 0-0-0 ± Euwe.

12.♗c4+ ♔h8 13.h5 ♗f6 14.♕d2 ♗g5 15.♘g6+! h:g6 16.h:g6+ ♔g7 17.♕:g5 ♕:g5 18.♗:g5 ♔:g6 19.♗f4 ♘h5 20.♘d5 ♘c6 21.0-0-0 f:e4 22.♗e3 ♗d7 23.♖dh1! (23...♖h8 24.♖:h5 Δ ♘f4; 23...♘g7 allows a mate in three with - *erlaubt ein Matt in drei Zügen beginnend mit* 24.♘e7+) 1:0, Nimtz - Goerens, corr. 1990.

C

(1.e4 e5 2.f4 e:f4 3.♘f3 g5 4.h4 g4 5.♘e5 ♗g7 6.d4 ♘f6 7.♘c3 d6 8.♘d3)

8...0-0 9.♘:f4!

Stopping Black's intended ♘h5-g3 and allowing the queen to defend d4.
Verhindert das ins Auge gefaßte ♘h5-g3, gleichzeitig ist der ♙d4 nun von der Dame gedeckt.
9.♗:f4? ♘c6 10.♘f2 ♘h5 11.♗g5 f6 12.♗e3 ♘g3 13.♖h2 f5 ∓ Levenfish.

9...♘:e4 10.♘:e4 ♖e8 11.♔f2! ♖:e4 12.c3 ♕f6 13.g3 ♗h6 14.♗d3 ♗:f4 15.♗:f4 ♖:f4

Retreating the rook gives White time to start an attack.
Ein Rückzug des Turmes gäbe Weiß die Gelegenheit zur Einleitung eines Angriffes.

16.g:f4 ♕:f4+

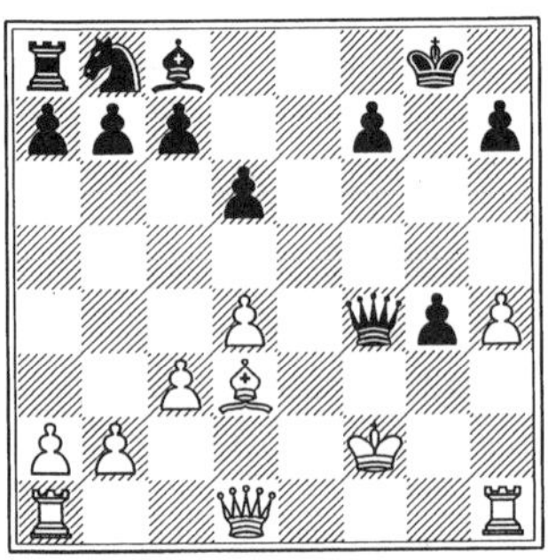

17.♔e2!

Rubinstein's discovery, probably refuting Black's exchange sacrifice.
Diese Entdeckung von Rubinstein widerlegt vermutlich das schwarze Qualitätsopfer.
(17.♔g2 b5!)

17...g3

17...♗d7 18.♕f1 ♕:f1+ 19.♖a:f1 h5 20.♗c4 1:0, van der Kooij - Alberts, corr. 1982.

18.♕d2! ♕f2+

18...♗g4+ 19.♔e1 g2 20.♕:g2 ♘c6 21.♗e2 ♖e8 22.♖f1! ±.

19.♔d1 g2

19...♗g4+ 20.♔c2 ♕:d2+ 21.♔:d2 g2 22.♖hg1 ♘d7 23.♖:g2 1:0, van der Kooij - Eigenman, corr. 1982

20.♕g5+ ♔f8 21.♖e1± ♕f3+ 22.♔c1 ♗e6 23.♗:h7 ♕g4 24.♕:g4 ♗:g4 25.♗e4 ♘c6 26.♗:g2 ♖e8 27.♔d2 f5 28.♖:e8+ ♔:e8 29.♗:c6+ b:c6 30.♔e3 ♔f7 31.♔f4 ♔f6 32.♖h1 ♗h5 33.♖g1 ♗g4 34.♖:g4 1:0, Schmelz - Geese, corr. 1988.

VII

(1.e4 e5 2.f4 e:f4 3.♘f3 g5 4.h4 g4 5.♘e5)

5...d6

The Hungarian defence. Variations A-C are old tries, the main action takes place in variation D where Black has come up with a few new ideas.
Die Ungarische Verteidigung. Die Abspiele A-C sind ziemlich alt, im Brennpunkt des Geschehens steht heute die Variante D, wo der Nachziehende mit

einigen interessanten neuen Ideen aufwarten konnte.

6.♘:g4

Bangiev's provocative 6.♘d3!? is an interesting try to liven things up a bit. Especially in blitz I've found that it works very nicely indeed, due to the surprise factor.

Das provozierende 6.♘d3!? von Bangiev scheint geeignet, ein wenig Bewegung in die Dinge zu bringen. Dank des Überraschungsfaktors funktioniert - wie ich herausgefunden habe - dieser Zug besonders gut in Blitzpartien.

6.♘d3

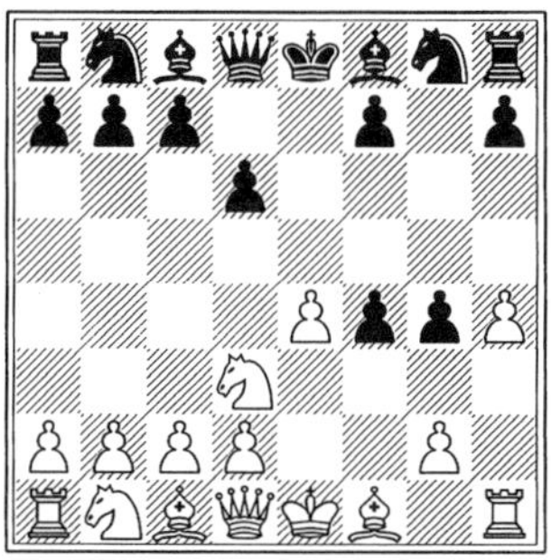

• 6...♗e7 (6...♗h6 7.b3!, 6...♕f6 7.b3 ♕:a1 8.♗b2) 7.♘:f4 ♗:h4+ 8.♔e2

• • 8...g3 9.♔e1 ∞ (Bangiev), e.g. *(z.B.)* 9...♘c6 10.d4 ♗g5 11.♘c3 ♘f6 12.♗b5 (12.♘fd5!?) ♗d7 13.♘e6!? with an annoying pin coming up after *(mit einer sehr unangenehmen Fesselung nach)* ♗:g5.

• • 8...♘h6 (Δ g3, ♘g4/♗g4) 9.♘d5! (Δ ♘:c7/♖:h4) 9...♗g5 10.d4 ♗:c1 11.♕:c1 ♘g8 12.♘bc3 ±.

• • 8...f5 9.d3 ♘c6 10.♗e3 ♗f6 11.♘c3 f:e4 12.d:e4 (12.♘:e4!?) ♗:c3 13.b:c3 ♘f6 14.♔e1!? ♘:e4 15.♗d3 ∞

• 6...♘f6! (Δ ♘:e4/♘h5)

Ay, there's the rub! By exploiting White's inability to both defend e4 and step up the pressure on f4, Black is ensured of equality.

Aha, der Haken! Weiß ist nicht imstande, gleichzeitig e4 zu decken sowie den Angriff auf f4 aufrechtzuerhalten, was Schwarz zumindest Ausgleich sichert.

7.♘:f4 ♘:e4 8.♕e2 ♕e7 9.♘d5 (9.♘h5? ♘c6 10.♔d1 ♗f5 11.d3 ♗g6!) 9...♘g3 10.♘:e7 ♘:e2 11.♘:c8 =/∞.

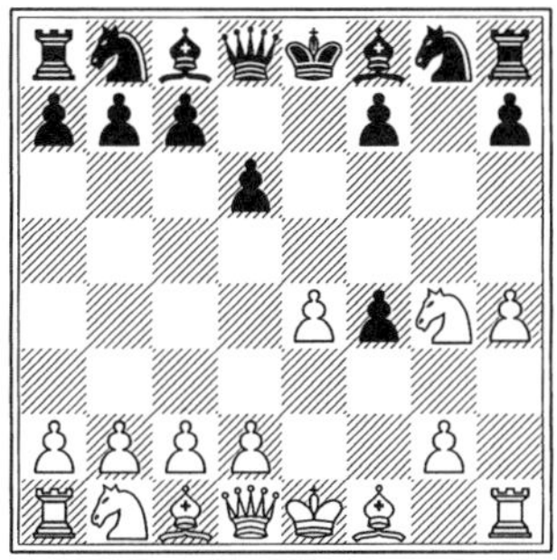

Position after 6.♘:g4/*Nach 6.♘:g4*

A

6...h5

Black attempts to make g4 a strong point but White keeps an advantage if he consistently plays to stop this by chopping off all enemy pieces setting their foot there.

Der Nachziehende versucht, aus g4 einen starken Vorposten zu machen, doch Weiß bleibt in Vorteil, indem er beharrlich jede feindliche Figur zerhackt, die ihren Fuß dorthin zu setzen wagt.

6...♘h6 7.♘f2!, × ♙f4.

7.♘f2 ♘f6 8.d4 ♗h6 9.♗e2 ♘c6 10.♘c3 ♘g4 11.♘:g4 ♗:g4

11...h:g4 12.♘d5 ♗g5 13.g3!.

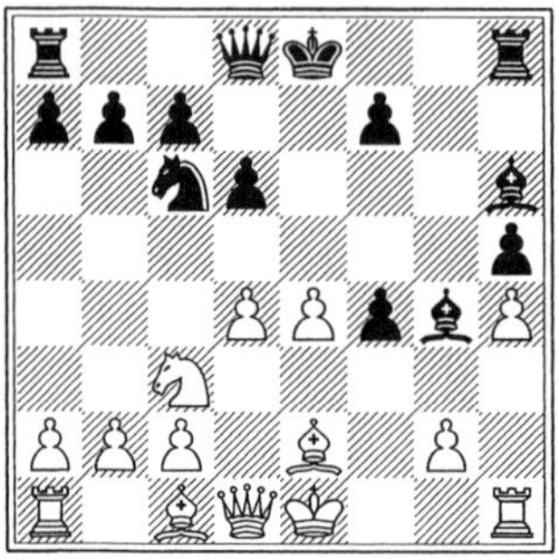

- **12.♗:g4 h:g4 13.♘d5 f3 14.g3** ± (Keres).
- **12.♕d3 ♗:e2 13.♘:e2 ♕f6 14.♗d2** ± (Glaskov).

B

(1.e4 e5 2.f4 e:f4 3.♘f3 g5 4.h4 g4 5.♘e5 d6 6.♘:g4)

6...f5 7.♘f2 ♘f6 8.d4 f:e4 9.♗:f4 d5?!

9...♗e6 10.♘c3 d5 11.g4 ± (Δ g5).

10.g4!

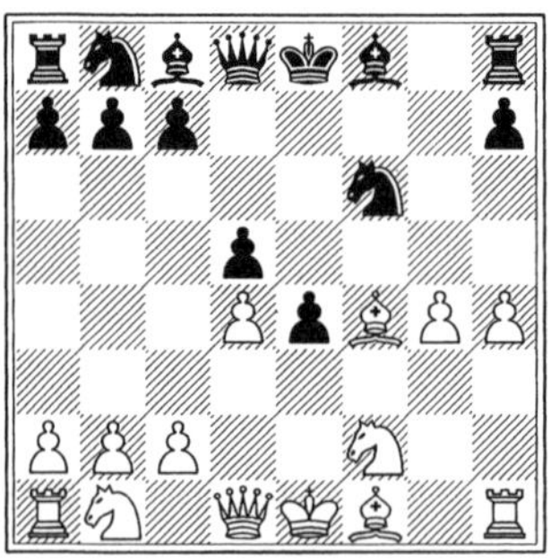

This supposedly weak pawn is suddenly a force to be reckoned with!
Dieser vermutete Schwächling erwacht zu einer respekteinflößenden Kraft!

10...♗e6 11.g5 ± ♘fd7 12.♕h5+ ♗f7 13.g6 ♗:g6 14.♕:d5 +–

C

(1.e4 e5 2.f4 e:f4 3.♘f3 g5 4.h4 g4 5.♘e5 d6 6.♘:g4)

6...♗e7 7.d3!

7.d4?! ♗:h4+ 8.♘f2 ♕g5! 9.♕f3 ♘c6! 10.♕:f4 ♗:f2+ 11.♔:f2 ♕:f4+ 12.♗:f4 ♘:d4 13.♘c3! ♗e6! 14.♘b5 ♘:b5 15.♗:b5+ ♗d7 =/∞.

7...♗:h4+ 8.♘f2 ♕g5 9.♕d2! ♗g3 10.♘c3 ♘f6 11.♘e2!

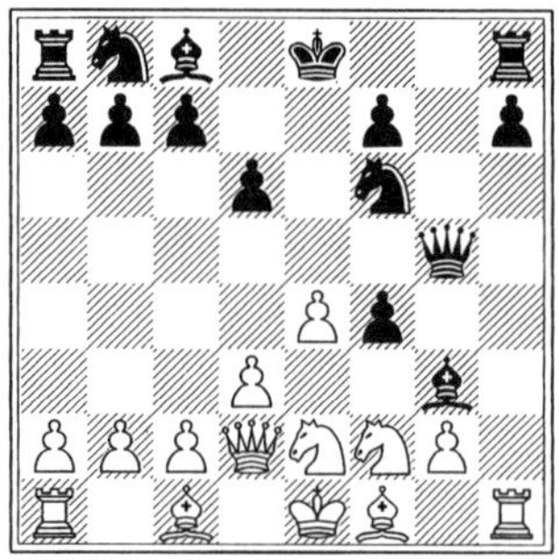

White just keeps on bombarding f4 until something gives way!
Weiß schießt einfach so lange auf f4, bis irgend etwas fällt.

11...♗:f2+ 12.♔:f2 ♘g4+ 13.♔g1 ♘e3 14.♘:f4 ♘:f1 15.♔:f1 ±

However, the game Winants - Z. Almasi, Wijk aan Zee 1995, saw the novelty:
In der Partie Winants - Z. Almasi, Wijk aan Zee 1995, kam jedoch die folgende Neuerung aufs Brett:

11...♕e5!? 12.♘:g3 f:g3 13.♘h3 ♘c6 14.♕c3 ♖g8 15.♗f4 ♕:c3 16.b:c3, and Black was more than O.K. *(und Schwarz war mehr als o.k.).*

I think White should have preferred:
Meines Erachtens sollte Weiß spielen:

14.♘g5! ♗g4 15.♖h6

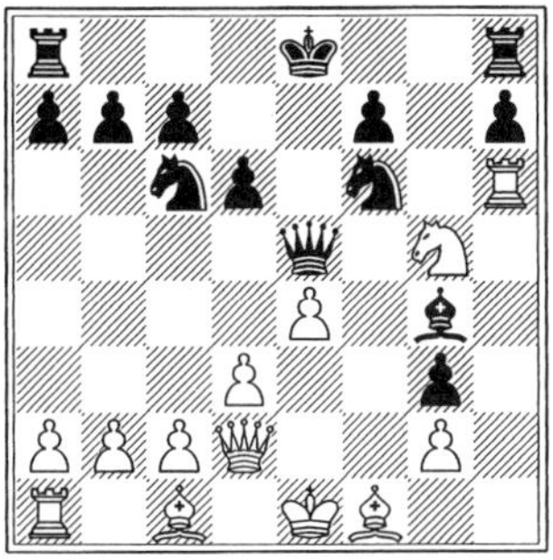

with the following possibilities:
mit den folgenden Möglichkeiten:

• 15...♘d4 16.c3 ♘e6 17.♕e3!
• • 17...♘:g5 18.♕:g5 ♕:g5 19.♗:g5 ♘d7 (19...♘g8 20.♖h4 h5 21.♗e2 ±) 20.♗e2 ±.
• • 17...♘h5 18.♘:e6 f:e6 19.♗e2 ♗:e2 20.d4! ♕f4 21.♕:e2 ♕f2+ 22.♕:f2 g:f2+ 23.♔:f2 0-0+ 24.♔e2 ±.
• • 17...♘g7 18.♘f3 ♕e7 19.♕d4 ♘7h5 20.♗g5 c5 21.♗:f6 c:d4 22.♗:e7 ♔:e7 23.♘:d4 ±/±.

• 15...♗h5 16.♕f4 ♘d4?! 17.♕:e5+ d:e5 18.c3 ♘c2+ 19.♔d2 ♘:a1 20.♖:f6 ♔e7 21.♖h6 ♗g6 22.b3 ±.

• 15...♘d7!? 16.♖h4!? (It's important to be able to eliminate Black's bishop - *Es ist wichtig, bei Bedarf den schwarzen Läufer eliminieren zu können.* 16.♕f4 ♘d4 17.♕:f7+? ♔d8 18.♕c4 ♕a5+!! 19.b4 ♕b6 –+ Δ ♘f3+, 17.♕:e5+ d:e5 =/∞) 16...h5 17.♕f4 ♘d4!? (Will this work again? - *Ob dies hier auch funktioniert?*) 18.♕:f7+ ♔d8 19.♕c4 ♕a5+ 20.b4 ♕b6 (20...♕:b4+ 21.♕:b4 ♘:c2+ 22.♔d2 ♘:b4 23.♘f7+ ♔e7 24.♘:h8 ♖:h8 25.♔c3 ±, 25.♗e2 ±) 21.♖:g4 ♘f3+ 22.♔d1

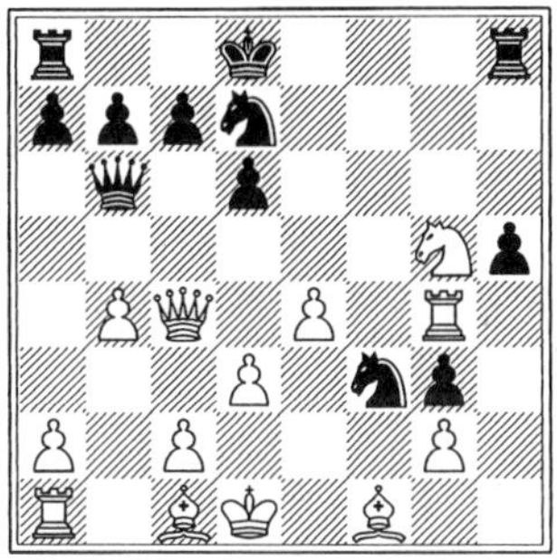

• • • 22...♕f2 23.♘e6+ ♔e8 24.♘:c7+ ♔d8 25.g:f3 ♕:f1+ 26.♔d2 h:g4 27.♔c3! +– ♘f6 28.♘:a8 g2 29.♕e6! ♘d7 30.♔b2! +–.

• • • 22...h:g4 23.g:f3!

• • • •23...♘e5 24.♘f7+ ♘:f7 25.♕:f7 g:f3 (25...♕d4 26.♗g5+ Δ ♗f6 ±) 26.♕e6! c5 27.b:c5 ♕:c5 28.♕f6+ →.

• • • •23...d5 (Δ 24.e:d5 ♖h1!) 24.♕:d5 g2 25.♗:g2 ♕g1+ 26.♔d2 ♕:g2+ 27.♔c3 ♔c8 28.♗f4!? g:f3 29.♕c4 →.

• • • •23...g2 24.♘e6+! ♔c8 (24...♔e8 25.♗:g2 ♕g1+ 26.♔d2 ♕:g2+ 27.♔c3 ± e.g. - *z.B.* - 27...♘e5 28.♕:c7 ♖h2 29.♘d4 ♘:f3 30.♕:b7 ♖d8 31.♕c6+ ♔e7 32.♘f5+ ♔f8 33.♔b2 ±) 25.♗:g2 ♕g1 26.♔d2 ♕:g2+ 27.♔c3 c6 28.♗f4 ± g3 (28...d5 29.♕d4 ♖g8 30.f:g4 ±, 28...♖e8 29.♘g7! d5 30.♕d4 ♖g8 31.♘f5 ±) 29.♕d4 ♖h2 30.♖c1 d5 31.♕g7! b6 32.♕e7 +–.

D

(1.e4 e5 2.f4 e:f4 3.♘f3 g5 4.h4 g4 5.♘e5 d6 6.♘:g4)

6...♘f6 7.♘:f6+

7.♘f2?!

There isn't time for this manoeuvre since Black hasn't wasted any time moving pawns.

Für ein solches Manöver fehlt hier die Muße, alldieweil der Nachziehende hier keine Zeit mit überflüssigen Bauernzügen vertan hat.

7...♖g8 8.d4 ♗h6 9.♘c3 ♕e7 10.♘d3 ♗g4 11.♗e2 ♗:e2 12.♕:e2 ♘c6 13.e5 d:e5 14.d:e5 ♘d4! 15.e:f6 ♕:e2+ 16.♘:e2 ♘:c2+ 17.♔d1 ♘:a1 18.♗:f4 0-0-0! 19.♔d2 ♖g3 20.♘:g3 ♗:f4+ 21.♔c3 ♗:g3 22.h5 ♖d5 –+, Alonso - Calderin, Cardenas 1988.

7...♕:f6 8.♘c3

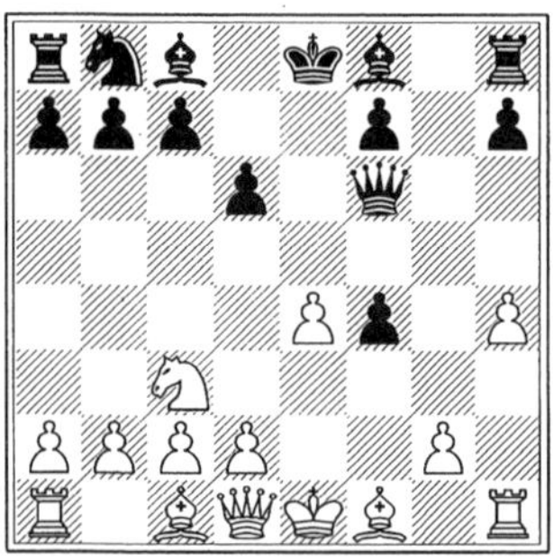

a

8...c6?!

Black can't really afford any more weakening pawn moves, considering his already rotten kingside pawn structure.

In Anbetracht seiner zerrütteten Bauernstruktur am Königsflügel darf sich Schwarz eigentlich keine weiteren schwächenden Bauernzüge mehr leisten.

9.♗e2!

9.d4 ♖g8 10.♕d3 ♖g3!.

9.♕f3

however, is an alternative.

ist allerdings eine Alternative.

9...♖g8

9...♘a6 10.♗f3 ♗d7 11.d4 0-0-0 12.♕d2 ♗h6 13.♕f2 ♗g7 14.♘e2 ♘b4 15.♔d1 ♗h6 16.♗d2 c5 17.♗c3 ♕e7 18.d5 ♔b8 19.a3 ♘a6 20.♖e1 ♖he8 21.♘g1 ♘c7 22.a4 ♕f8 23.♘h3 f5 24.e5 d:e5 25.♗:e5 ♖:e5 26.♖:e5 ♗g7 27.♖e2 ♗:b2 28.♖b1 ♗d4 29.♕e1 ♗:a4 30.♘:f4 ♗d7 31.♖e7 ♗c8 32.♖:c7 ♔:c7 33.♕a5+ ♔b8

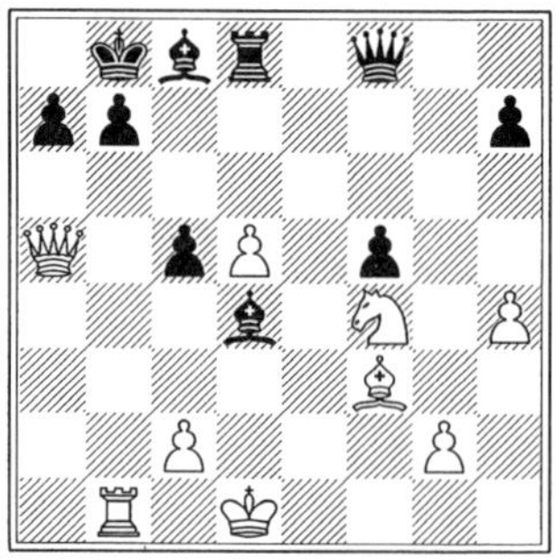

34.♘e6! ♗:e6 35.♖:b7+ ♔:b7 36.d6+ 1:0, Bangiev - Borisov, corr. 1990.

10.♗f3

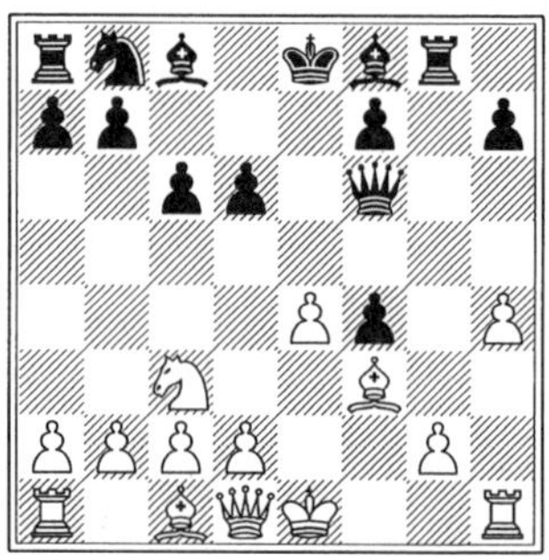

• 10...♗g7 11.d3 ♗e6 12.♕d2 ♗h6 13.d4 ♘d7 14.♕f2± ♘b6 15.♗d2 ♘c4

16.0-0-0 b5? 17.e5! d:e5 18.♗:c6+ ♔e7 19.♘e4 1:0, Kashutin - Laptev, corr. 1986.

• 10...♗d7 11.d4 ♘a6 12.♕d2 ♗h6 13.e5 d:e5 14.♘e4 ♕e7 15.d:e5 0-0-0 16.♕d6 ♕f8 17.♗d2 ♖g6 18.♕:f8 ♖:f8 19.0-0-0 ♘c7 20.♗b4 1:0 Sabel - Osipov, corr. 1979.

• 10...♗h6 11.d4 ♘a6 (Δ ♘c7-e6) 12.e5!

This, followed by White's next, is a typical device when Black has weakened d6 by moving his c-pawn.

Nach Schwächung von d6 durch Aufzug des c-Bauern ist dies - in Verbindung mit dem folgenden Zug - ein typischer Schlag.

12...d:e5 13.♘e4 ♕e7 (13...♕d8 14.d:e5 ♕:d1+ 15.♔:d1 ♔e7 16.b3 ±) 14.0-0

• • 14...e:d4 15.♕:d4 ♖g6 16.♗d2 ♗d7 17.♖ae1 ±.

• • 14...♕:h4 15.de5 ♗g7 (15...♖g6? 16.♘f6+ +–, 15...♔f8 16.♕d6+ ♔g7 17.♘f6 +– Δ ♘h5, ♕:h6) 16.♖e1 ± Δ ♘f6/♘d6 (Kortchnoi)

• • 14...♗e6 15.d:e5 ♖d8 16.♘f6+ ♔f8 17.♗d2 ♖g7 18.♗e4 ⩲ (Δ ♕h5)

b

(1.e4 e5 2.f4 e:f4 3.♘f3 g5 4.h4 g4 5.♘e5 d6 6.♘:g4 ♘f6 7.♘:f6+ ♕:f6 8.♘c3)

8...♘c6!? 9.♘d5!

The consistent move, entering some complications as Black tries to set up a perpetual.

Der folgerichtige Zug. In den entstehenden Verwicklungen versucht Schwarz, ein Dauerschach zu erreichen.

The stem game went:

In der Stammpartie geschah hingegen:

9.♗b5?!

But this bishop belongs on f3 or f1, guarding some squares on the g-file.

Der Läufer gehört aber eigentlich nach f3 oder f1, wo er einige Schwachpunkte in der g-Linie überdeckt.

9...♖g8 10.♕f3 ♔d8! 11.♗:c6 b:c6 12.d3 ♗h6 ∓ (0:1/39.), C. Chandler - Williams, England 1976.

Or the risky *(oder das gewagte)* 9.d4?! ♕:d4 10.♕f3 (10.♗d3 ♕g7 11.♕f3 ♘d4 12.♕f2 ♘e6! 13.♖f1 ♖g8 14.♘d5 ♗e7 ∓) 10...♗h6 11.♘d5 ♘b4 12.♘:b4 ♕:b4+ 13.c3 ♕c5 14.g3 ♖g8 15.g:f4 ♗g4 16.♕f2 ♕c6 17.♗g2 ♗f5 18.♕f3 ♔f8 (18...0-0-0! e.g: - *z.B.* - 19.e:f5 ♖:g2 ∓) 19.♖h2 ♗:e4 20.♕h5 d5 21.♗:e4 d:e4 22.♗e3 ♖g3 23.♖e2 ♖e8 24.♖d1 ♕f6 (24...♗:f4!? 25.♗:f4 ♖g1+ 26.♔f2 ♖:d1 ∓ Bangiev) 25.♖d5 ♕g6 26.♔d1 ♕:h5 27.♖:h5 ♖g6 28.♗c5+ ♔g8 29.f5! ♖e5 30.♗d4 ♖d5 31.♖:e4 ♖g1+ 32.♔e2 ♖g2+ 33.♔f3 1:0, Hector - Heine Nielsen, Copenhagen 1995.

9...♕g6

9...♕g7 10.g4!?

Thanks to the potential fork on f6, Black will have to take this pawn 'en passant' which involves closing his own g-file.

Wegen der latenten Springergabel auf f6 kann Schwarz diesen Bauern nur "en passant" schlagen, was bedeutet, daß er sich selbst die g-Linie versperrt.

10...f:g3 11.♗g2 h5 (11...♔d8 12.d3 h6 13.0-0 ↑) 12.0-0 (12.♘:c7+?! ♔d8 13.♘:a8 ♗g4 14.♗f3 g2 15.♖g1 ♘d4 ∓) 12...♗g4 13.♕e1 0-0-0 14.d3 ♗e7 15.♘:e7+ ♘:e7 16.♗g5 ⩲ (Bangiev).

10.d3

10.♔f2!? ♕g3+ (10...♗g7 11.c3 ♕:e4 12.♕e2! ♕:e2+ 13.♗:e2 ♔d8 14.d4±, but not - *aber nicht* - 12.♘:c7+?? ♔d8 13.♘:a8 [±Bangiev] 13...♗d4+!! 14.c:d4 ♕:d4+ 15.♔e1 [15.♔f3 ♘e5+ 16.♔e2 ♘d3] 15...♖e8+ 16.♗e2 ♗g4 −+) 11.♔g1, and now *(und nun)*:

11...♘d4 12.d3 (12.c3?! f3 13.♕a4+ c6! = 14.♘f6+ ♔d8 15.♕:d4 f:g2 Δ ♕e1+ =) 12...f3 13.♖h2 (13.♗e3? ♘e2+ −+) f:g2 14.♗:g2 ♘e6 15.d4 ♗e7 16.♘:e7±.

11...♗g7 12.c3 ♗g4 13.♗e2 ♘e5 14.♗:g4 ♘:g4 15.♕e2 (Δ ♖h3) f3 16.♕:f3 ♕e1+ 17.♕f1 ♕:e4 18.♘:c7+ ♔d8 19.♘b5 a6 20.d3 ♕d5 21.♕f3± (Bangiev).

10...♕g3+ 11.♔d2 ♗e6

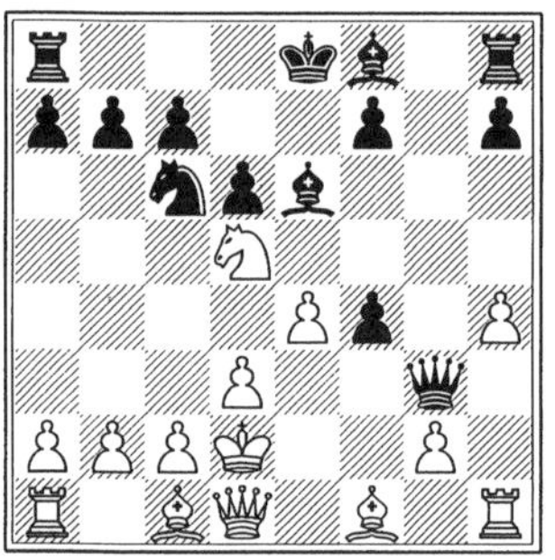

White's best now is definitely not
Mit Sicherheit nicht das Beste ist nun
12.♘:c7+ ♔d7 13.♘:e6 f:e6 14.♖h3 ♕f2+ 15.♕e2 (⩲ Bangiev)
since *(da)* 13...♕e3+ 14.♔c3 ♗g7+! ensures Black of a draw at least.
dem Schwarzen mindestens Remis sichert.

12.c3 0-0-0 13.♔c2 ♗:d5 14.e:d5 ♘e7 15.♕h5 ♕g6 16.♕f3 ♗h6 17.♗:f4

17.h5 ♕g5! (17...♕f5 18.c4 Δ ♖h4) 18.g3 ♕:d5 19.♗g2 =.

17...♗:f4 18.♕:f4 ♘:d5 19.♕f3 ♕e6 20.g3 ♘e3+

In Kristiansen - Heine Nielsen, Danish Ch. 1995, a draw was agreed in this position. A year later another Dane revealed his homework:
In Kristiansen - Heine Nielsen, Dänische Meisterschaft 1995, wurde an dieser Stelle Remis vereinbart. Ein Jahr später brachte ein anderer Däne seine Hausarbeit auf den Tisch:

21.♔d2 ♘:f1+ 22.♖h:f1 ♖df8?

This is too passive, after 22...♖de8 23.♖fe1 ♕g6 24.♕f4 White has only a minimal advantage.
Zu passiv, nach 22...♖de8 23.♖fe1 ♕g6 24.♕f4 hätte Weiß nur geringen Vorteil.

23.♖fe1 ♕h6+ 24.♔c2 f5 25.♖e7 ♕g6 26.♖ae1 ♖hg8? 27.♖:c7+! ♔:c7 28.♖e7+ ♔b6 29.♖:b7+ ♔a5 30.b4+ ♔a4 31.♕c6+ 1:0, Aagard - Rasmussen, Copenhagen 1996.

C

(1.e4 e5 2.f4 e:f4 3.♘f3 g5 4.h4 g4 5.♘e5 d6 6.♘:g4 ♘f6 7.♘:f6+ ♕:f6 8.♘c3)

8...♗e6

This seems to be the current main line in the Hungarian defence.
Dies darf derzeit als Hauptvariante der Ungarischen Verteidigung gelten.

9.♕e2!?

With the idea ♕f2 to strengthen the black squares on the kingside, ♕b5+ and ♘d5 are two additional threats making sure Black walks the line.
Planend ♕f2 mit Überdeckung der dunklen Felder am Königsflügel. Zusätzlich sorgen die Drohungen ♕b5+ und ♘d5 dafür, daß dem Schwarzen das Leben schwer gemacht wird.

9.d4!?
This move isn't mentioned in most books, perhaps because the d4-pawn may be hard to defend in the long run. However, the two practical test below were in White's favour:
Dieser Zug wird in den meisten Büchern nicht einmal erwähnt - vielleicht deswegen, weil der ♙d4 auf Dauer schwer zu verteidigen sein wird. Die beiden vorliegenden praktischen Beispiele verliefen indes zugunsten von Weiß:
9...♗g7 (9...♖g8 10.♕d3 ♖g3 11.♕b5 ♘d7 12.♘e2 ±/±) 10.♘b5 ♘a6 11.c3 ♗d7 12.♕f3 c6 13.♘a3 ♘c7 14.♗:f4 0-0-0 15.♘c4 d5 16.♘d6 ♔b8 17.e5 ♕e6 18.0-0-0 ♖df8 19.♗d3 f6 20.♗f5 ♕e7 21.e6 ♗:e6 22.♖de1 ♕d7 23.♗:e6 ♘:e6 24.♘f7+ ♘:f4 25.♕:f4+ ♔a8 26.♘:h8 ♖:h8 27.h5 f5 28.♖e2 ♖g8 29.♖he1 ♗f6 30.♔c2 ♗g5 31.♕:g5 1:0, Al-Shamma - Lonsdale, Lera 1992.
9...♗h6 10.♕f3?! (Better alternatives are - *bessere Alternativen sind* - 10.♕d3!? or 10.♗e2!? Δ ♗f3) or maybe even - *oder vielleicht sogar* - 10.♘b5!? ♘a6 11.♗d2 Δ ♗c3, d5, ♘d4) 10...♖g8? (10...♘c6 11.♗e3 [11.♗b5 0-0-0] 11...♘:d4 12.♗:d4 ♕:d4 ∓/∓) 11.e5 d:e5 12.♕:b7? (12.♘e4) e:d4? (12...f3! 13.♗b5+ ∞) 13.♕:a8 +– (Finally putting an end to this comedy of errors! - *Womit dieser Komödie der Irrungen und Wirrungen endlich ein Ende bereitet wäre!*), Gossip - MacDonnell, London 1873 (1:0/23.).

9...♘d7

9...♘c6 10.♘d5! ♗:d5 11.e:d5+ ♘e7 12.♕b5+ ∞ ♔d8 13.♕:b7 ♕e5+ 14.♗e2 ♕:d5 15.♕:d5 ♘:d5 16.♗f3 ±.

9...♖g8 10.♘d5 (10.♕b5+!?) ♗:d5 11.e:d5+ ♗e7 12.d3 ♘d7 13.♕f3 ± (Bangiev).

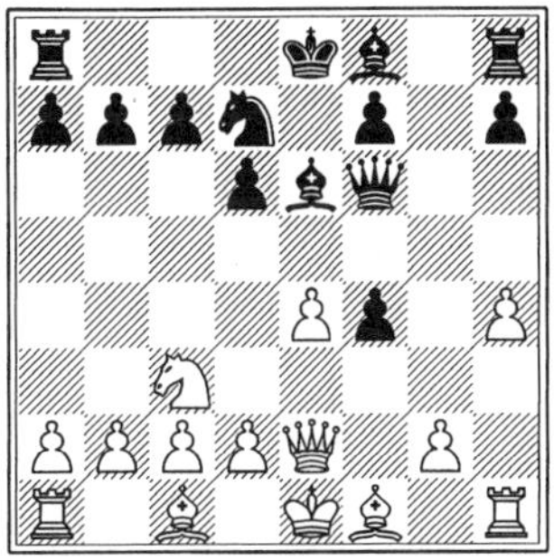

Position after 9...♘d7/*Nach 9...♘d7*

• 10.b3 ♖g8 11.♗b2
•• 11...0-0-0 12.0-0-0! ♗g4 13.♕f2 ♗:d1 14.♕:a7 ♗g4 15.♗a6! ♘c5 (15...b:a6 16.♕:a6+ ♔b8 17.♘b5 +–) 16.♗b5 c6 (16...♘d7? 17.♘d5 ♕e6 18.♗c6! +– Gallagher) 17.♗:c6 b:c6 18.♘a4 ♕:b2 19.♘:b2+ ♗e6 20.d4 ♘b7 21.♕b6 ±/±

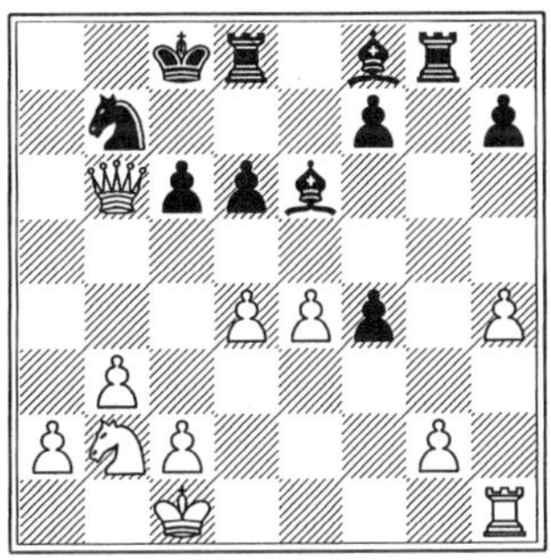

Will Black be able to get his act together before the a-pawn wins the day?
Wird es Schwarz gelingen, seine Kräfte zu vereinen, bevor der a-Bauer den Tag entscheidet?

• • 11...♗g4! 12.♕f2 d5! 13.♗e2! ♗c5 14.♕f1 ♗:e2 15.♕:e2 0-0-0 16.0-0-0 d:e4 17.♘:e4 ♕g6 18.♕c4! (18.♘:c5 ♘:c5 19.♕f2 ♕c6! =) ♘b6?! (18...♗e7 19.♘g5±, 18...♗b6 19.♘g5±) 19.♕:c5 ♕:e4 20.♖he1 ♕d5 (20...♕:g2 21.♕f5+ Δ ♕:f4) 21.♕f2 ♖g4 22.♕f3!? ± (½:½/34.), de la Villa - Fernandez, Barcelona 1990.

• 10.♕f2! ♖g8 11.d4 ♗h6 12.♗e2 0-0-0 13.♗d2 ± Δ 0-0-0 (Bangiev).

VIII

(1.e4 e5 2.f4 e:f4 3.♘f3 g5 4.h4 g4 5.♘e5)

5...♘f6

The Berlin defence.
Die Berliner Verteidigung.

6.d4!

White's best move, as usual!
Wie gewöhnlich der beste Zug für Weiß!

Löwenthal's 6.♘:g4? is obviously a desirable move - isolating three black pawns in one move and setting up some flashy cheapos - but after a few cold blooded defensive moves Black is out of harm's way, unfortunately one can't say as much for White:
Löwenthals 6.♘:g4? wäre natürlich ein wünschenswerter Zug - die schwarzen Bauern werden zersplittert, und Weiß stellt ein paar augenfällige Drohungen auf -, doch nach ein paar kaltblütigen Verteidigungszügen ist der Nachziehende außer Gefahr, was man leider von Weiß nicht gerade behaupten kann.

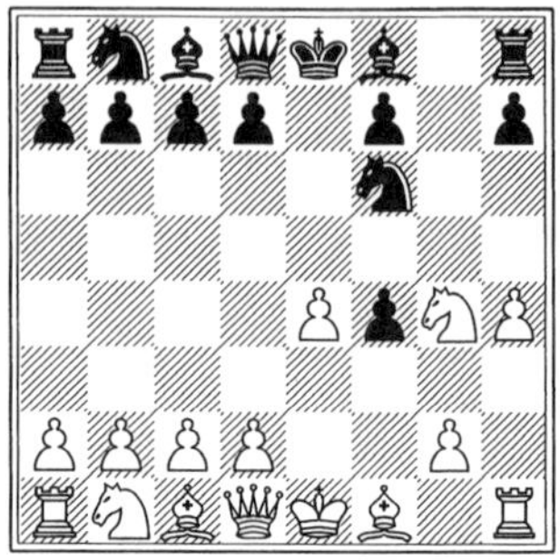

6...♘:e4! 7.d3 (7.♘c3 ♘g3 8.♘d5 ♗g7!, 7.d4 ♗e7!) 7...♘g3 8.♗:f4?! (a fifty fifty gamble - *äußerst spekulativ.* I held some hope for 8.♖h3 but it's unfortunately also accident prone, e. g. - *Ich hatte einige Hoffnungen mit 8.♖h3 verbunden, doch leider ist dies ebenso katastrophenträchtig, z.B.:* 8...d6 9.♗:f4 ♘:f1 10.♔:f1 h5!) 8...♘:h1! (8...♕e7+? 9.♗e2 ♘:h1 10.♗g5 ♕b4+ 11.c3 ♕:b2 12.♘f6+ ♔e7 13.♕a4! +–/±), and now *(und nun)*:

9.♕e2+ ♕e7 10.♘f6+ ♔d8 11.♗:c7+ ♔:c7 12.♘d5+ ♔d8 13.♘:e7 ♗:e7 14.♕g4 d6 15.♕f4 ♖g8 ∓, Hebden - Littlewood, Hastings 1982/83.

9.♗g5? ♗e7 10.♕e2 h5! 11.♕e5 f6 12.♗:f6 d6 13.♕e4 ♗:g4 14.♗:h8 ♔d7 15.♗d4 ♗:h4+ 0:1, Hebden - Stean, Marbella 1982.

6...d6 7.♘d3 ♘:e4

As usual, Black has some inferior alternatives:
Wie üblich hat Schwarz einige minderwertige Alternativen:

• 7...♘c6 8.d5 ♘e5 9.♗:f4 ♕e7 (9...♘:e4? 10.♘:e5 d:e5 11.♗:e5 ♕e7 12.♕d4 ♘g3 13.♗b5+ ♔d8 14.♔d1 +–) 10.♘c3 h5 11.♕d2 ♗d7 12.♗:e5!? (Bangiev prefers 12.♘:e5 d:e5 13.♗g5 with some pressure - *Bangiev bevorzugt 12.♘:e5 d:e5 13.♗g5 mit leichtem*

Druck) 12...d:e5 13.♕g5 ± (1:0/40.), Hartmann - Bettermann, corr. 1990.

• 7...f3 8.g:f3 ♘c6 9.c3 (9.d5 ♘d4!) 9...♗e7 10.♗g2 ♖g8 11.♗g5 h6 12.♗:f6 ♗:f6 13.h5 d5 14.♕e2 ♔f8 15.♘d2 d:e4 16.♘:e4 ♗g5 17.f4 ♗h4 18.♔d2 a5 19.♘ec5 ♗f6 20.♖ae1 ± (½:½/25.), Spassky - Xie Jun, Monaco 1994.

8.♗:f4

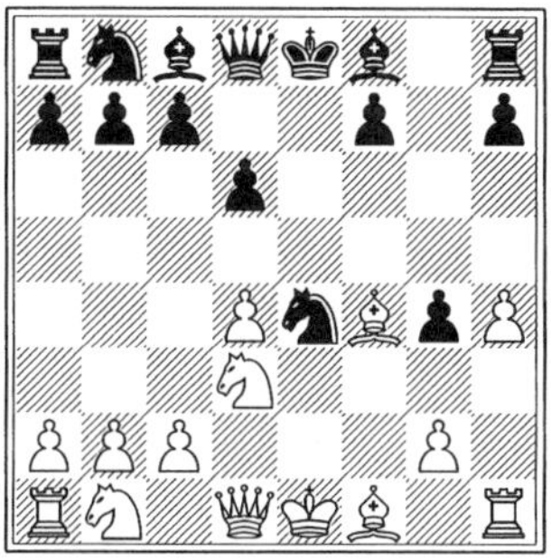

8...♕e7

Preparing a fast evacuation of the king to the queenside, which seems to be Black's best and definitely his most common plan.

Bereitet eine rasche Flucht des Königs zum Damenflügel vor - mutmaßlich der beste, und auf jeden Fall der beliebteste schwarze Plan.

• 8...♗g7 9.c3 0-0 10.♘d2 ♖e8 11.♗e2!? (A new move, since the old is refuted below - *ein neuer Zug, der ältere wird wie folgt widerlegt*: 11.♘:e4?! ♖:e4+ 12.♔f2. Was thought to be good for White until - *Wurde als gut für Weiß erachtet bis* - 12...c5!!, Δ c4, c:d4, came along in - *entdeckt wurde in* - Belotti - Arlandi, Reggio Emilia 1991; e.g. - *z.B.* - 13.d:c5 d:c5 14.♕d2 c4 15.♘b4 ♕b6+ 16.♔g3 ♗e6 17.♘d5 ♕c5 18.♖d1 ♘c6 19.b4 c:b3 20.a:b3 ♖d8 21.c4 ♖:f4! 0:1, de Wit - van der Sterren, Netherlands Team-Ch. 1994) 11...♗f5 12.♘:e4 ♗:e4 13.0-0 ♕:h4 (13...♗:d3 14.♗:d3 ♕:h4 15.g3!) 14.♗:g4 ♘c6 (14...♗:d3 15.g3 ♗c2 16.g:h4 ♗:d1 17.♖a:d1 ♘c6 18.♗h5 ±) 15.♘f2 ♗f5 16.♗:f5 ♕:f4 (In general, opposite coloured bishops tend to favour the one with the initiative - *im Allgemeinen begünstigen ungleichfarbige Läufer die Seite, die die Initiative besitzt*) 17.♕d3 h5 18.♘e4 ♕h6 19.♖f3 d5 20.♘g3 (For once it's the white squares that are weak! *Für diesmal sind es die weißen Felder, die schwach sind!*) 20...h4 21.♘f1 ♘e7 22.♘e3 ♖ad8 23.♖af1 c5 24.♘g4 ♕h5 25.♘e5 ♗:e5 26.d:e5 ♘c6 27.♕e2 (27.e6!? ♘e5 28.♗g4 ±) 27...♕h6, Gallagher - Arlandi, Forli 1992.

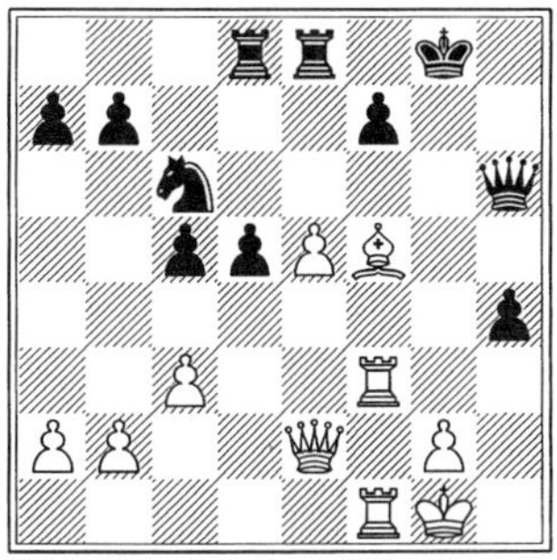

And now White should play, as pointed out by Gallagher himself: *(Und nun sollte Weiß, wie von Gallagher selbst dargelegt, spielen:)* 28.e6! ± (+− Gallagher) 28...f:e6 29.♗c2 d4! 30.♖f6 ♕e3+ 31.♕:e3 d:e3 32.♖g6+ ♔h8 33.♖f4 ±.

• 8...h5 9.♘d2 ♗f5 10.♕e2 ♕e7 11.0-0-0 d5 12.♘:e4 ♗:e4 13.♘c5 c6 14.♘:e4 d:e4 15.♕e3 ♘d7 16.g3 f5 17.♔b1 ♗g7 18.♗e2 ♘b6 19.c4 ♔f7 20.c5 ♘d5 21.♗c4 ♔g6 22.♗:d5 c:d5

(It looks like White has exchanged the wrong bishop, but f5 and g5 turns out to be extremely weak - *es hat den Anschein, als hätte Weiß den falschen Läufer weggegeben, doch f5 und g5 stellen sich nun als äußerst schwach heraus)* 23.♗d6! ♕d8 24.♖hf1 ♖h7 25.♕f4 ♕f6 26.♗e5 ♗h6 27.♗:f6 ♗:f4 28.♖:f4 ♔:f6 29.♖df1 ♖e8 30.♖:f5 ♔g7 31.♖:d5 e3 32.♔c2 e2 33.♖g5+ ♔h8 34.♖e1 1:0, Campora - Giertz, San Bernadino 1991.

- 8...♘c6

9.c3! (Δ d5) seems most prudent, transposing to the main line below.
9.c3! (Δ d5) mit Überleitung zur Hauptvariante scheint nun am umsichtigsten.
Punishment attempts seem to rebound, e.g: - *Widerlegungsversuche scheinen zu scheitern, z.B.:* 9.d5?! ♕e7 10.♗e2 ♘d4 11.0-0 ♘g3 ∓, and the pawn sac *(und das Bauernopfer)* 9.♘c3?! ♗f5 10.♗e2 ♘:d4 was a disaster for White after *(führte zu einem weißen Desaster nach)* 11.♘:e4 ♗:e4 12.♘f2 ♘:c2 13.♔f1 ♕f6 −+, Chapman - Solomon, Melbourne 1996.

9.♗e2!?

The new approach recommended by Gallagher in 'Winning with the King's Gambit', where 9.♗e2 was first analysed in any depth.
Ein neuer Versuch, empfohlen von Gallagher in seinem Buch "Winning with the King's Gambit", wo 9.♗e2 erstmals tiefgründig untersucht worden ist.

The old 9.♕e2 seems to give White an equal ending at best, my database is filled with black miniatures after
Das alte 9.♕e2 gibt Weiß bestenfalls ein gleiches Endspiel. Meine Datenbank ist voll von schwarzen Kurzsiegen nach

9...♘c6 10.c3 ♗f5 11.♘d2 0-0-0 12.0-0-0 ♖e8 and now White has to avoid: *(und nun darf Weiß keinesfalls spielen:)* 13.g3?/13.d5?/13.♕e3?, which are all answered by *(worauf jeweils folgt)* 13...♘:c3!, 13.♖e1? ♕e6!.
Relatively best is
Verhältnismäßig am besten ist
13.♘:e4 ♕:e4 ∞/∓,
which is not much to write home about...
worüber man nicht viele Worte zu verlieren braucht...

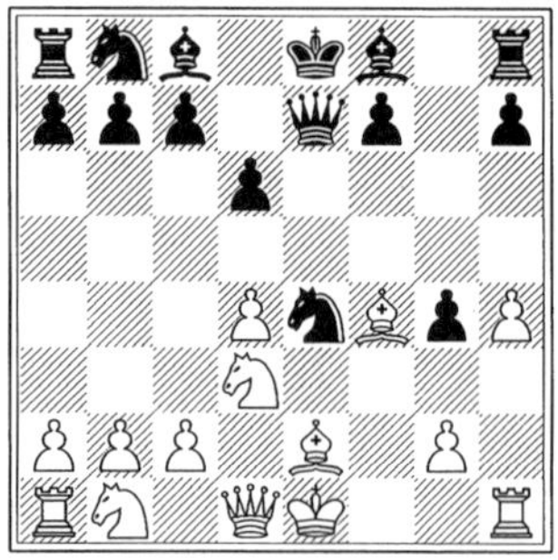

Position after 9.♗e2/*Nach 9.♗e2*

A

9...h5 10.♘d2 ♗f5 11.0-0

White doesn't have to sac the h-pawn yet, he could try sacrificing the d-pawn instead!
Weiß ist nicht gezwungen, den ♙h4 zu opfern - er kann stattdessen den ♙d4 anbieten!
11.♘:e4 ♕:e4 (11...♗:e4 12.0-0 ♕:h4 13.♘f2 transposes to the main line - *leitet zur Hauptvariante über*) 12.0-0!? ♕:d4+ 13.♔h2 (13.♔h1 ♘d7 doesn't alter much but the king feels safer at h1 - *ändert nicht viel, obgleich sich der König auf h1 sicherer fühlt*) 13...♘c6 (13...♘bd7 looks better, keeping f6

under control - *macht einen besseren Eindruck, weil es f6 unter Kontrolle behält:* 14.♗g5 ♗:d3 15.♗:d3 ♕:b2 16.♗c4 ♘e5 17.♖b1 ♕c3 18.♗d5 c6 19.♗f6 ♖h7 20.♗e4 ♖h6 21.♖:b7 d5! when it's doubtful if White has full compensation - *wonach zweifelhaft ist, ob Weiß volle Kompensation hat*) 14.♗g5 f6 15.c3 ♕d5 16.♗:f6 ♖g8 17.c4 ♕e6 18.♗g5 ♗g7 19.♕d2 ♔d7?? 20.♘c5+ 1:0, Gibajdulin - Zikeyev, corr. 1990.

11...♕:h4

Now White must be careful not to get mated and Black must be even more careful not to have his queen trapped.
Weiß muß nun aufpassen, um nicht mattgesetzt zu werden - und Schwarz noch viel mehr, damit seine Dame nicht gefangen wird!

Declining the h-pawn doesn't guarantee Black an easy life either:
Auf den h-Bauern zu verzichten, garantiert Schwarz noch viel weniger ein leichtes Leben:
11...♘d7 12.♘:e4 ♗:e4 13.♕d2 ± e.g. *(z.B.)* 13...♕:h4 14.♘f2 f5 (14...g3 15.♘h3 Δ ♗g5, 14...♗g6? 15.♗g5 Δ ♘h1) 15.♗g5 ♕g3 16.♘:e4 f:e4 17.♗c4 ♖h7 18.♖ae1 +−.

12.♘:e4 ♗:e4 13.♘f2!

- **13...♗c6 14.d5 ♗d7 15.♕d4 ♖g8 16.g3** (Δ ♖ae1) →

- **13...♗f5 14.♗d3!?**

- **13...♗g6 14.♗b5+ c6**

14...♘d7.
15.♕d2!
• • 15...c:b5? 16.♗g5 ♕g3 17.♖ae1+ (Δ ♖e3) or the miserly *(oder das geizige)* 17.♘h1 +−.
• • 15...g3 16.♘h3 c:b5 17.♖ae1+ ♔d7 18.♗g5 ♕g4 19.♖f4.
• • 15...♕f6 16.♖ae1+ ♔d7 17.♗g5 ♕g7 18.♗a4 →.

- **13...g3 14.♘h3**

And Black seems to be in trouble e.g.
Und Schwarz scheint sich in Problemen zu befinden, z.B.:
14...♗h6 15.♕d2 ♗:f4 16.♖:f4 ♕e7 17.♗b5+ ♔d8 18.d5
or *(oder)*
14...♕e7 15.♗g5 ♕d7 16.♗f6 Δ ♘g5.

B

(1.e4 e5 2.f4 e:f4 3.♘f3 g5 4.h4 g4 5.♘e5 ♘f6 6.d4 d6 7.♘d3 ♘:e4 8.♗:f4 ♕e7 9.♗e2)

9...♘c6 10.c3

10.d5? ♘d4.

10...♗f5

10...h5 11.♘d2 ♗f5 12.♘f2!? (An interesting alternative to giving up the h-pawn by castling - *eine interessante Alternative zur Rochade samt Aufgabe des ♙h4)* 12...♗h6 13.♗:h6 ♖:h6 14.♘f:e4 ♗:e4 15.♘:e4 ♕:e4 16.0-0 g3 17.♕b3 0-0-0 (17...♕:h4? 18.♕:f7+ ♔d8 19.♕f8+ ♔d7 20.♖f7+ ♔e6

21.♕:h6+ ♔:f7 22.♖f1+ ♔e7 23.♕h7+ +– or - *oder* - 20...♘e7 21.♖:e7+ ♕:e7 22.♗b5+ c6 23.♕:a8 ♕e3+ 24.♔h1 c:b5 25.♕:b7+ ±) 18.♗f3 ♕:h4 19.♖fe1 ♖f6 20.♕d5 ♕h2+ 21.♔f1 h4? (Burning the ships behind Her Majesty - *verbrennt alle Brücken hinter Ihrer Majestät)*

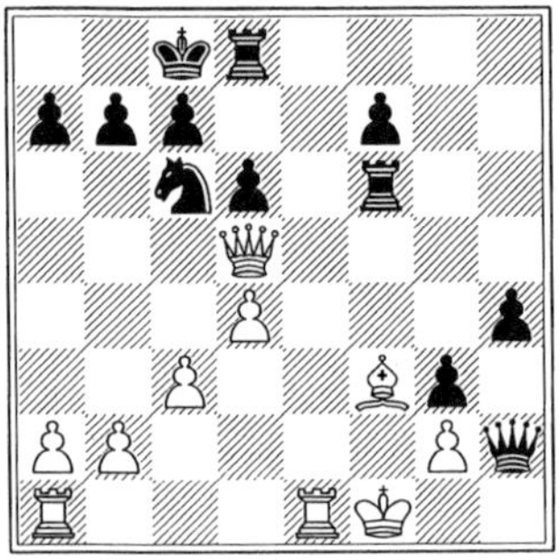

22.♔e2 ♖e8+ (22...♖e6+ 23.♔d3 ♖:e1 24.♖:e1 ♔b8 25.♗g4 and Black will have to show some ingenuity to avoid White's intended - *und Schwarz bräuchte einigen Einfallsreichtum, um das geplante ♗h3, ♕g5, ♕c1, ♖h1 zu verhindern)* 23.♔d3 ♖:e1 24.♖:e1 ♔d8(?) 25.♕g5 1:0, Myers - Haag, corr. 1987.

11.d5!

Creating some life in the position!
Bringt Leben in die Bude!
11.0-0!?.

11...♘b8

The knight is obliged to make a restart.
Der Springer muß einen neuen Anlauf nehmen.
However 11...♘e5 isn't as easily disposed of as one might think:
11...♘e5 wäre jedoch längst nicht so leichtfertig wie es den Anschein hat:
12.♗:e5 d:e5 13.♗:g4 (13.♕a4+? ♕d7 14.♕:d7 ♗:d7 15.♘:e5 ♘g3 ∓) 13...♘d6!? 14.♗:f5!? (Drastic measures requires drastic solutions! The knight on d6 must be displaced for a moment - *drastische Lösungen sind gefragt! Der ♘d6 muß für einen Moment abgelenkt werden.* 14.0-0 ♗:d3! 15.♕:d3 ♕:h4, 0:1/35., was very good for Black in - *war sehr gut für Schwarz in* - Jaulin - Caruso, Cannes 1995) 14...♘:f5 15.♕a4+ ♔d8 16.♘d2 (Δ 0-0-0) ♘e3 17.g4 ♗g7 (17...♘g2+ 18.♔d1 ♘:h4 19.♔c2 ↑ e.g: *z.B.* - 19...♘g6 20.♖ae1 ♗g7 21.♘c4 f6 22.d6 c:d6 23.♘b6 →) 18.♖h3
with a strong initiative largely due to the disharmony in Black's set-up, for example:
mit starker Initiative, in erster Linie wegen des mangelnden Zusammenwirkens der schwarzen Kräfte, zum Beispiel:
18...♘:d5 19.0-0-0 f6 20.♘e4 ♗h6 21.♔b1 ♘e3 22.♖:e3 ♗:e3 23.♘b4 ♔c8 24.♘d5 ±.

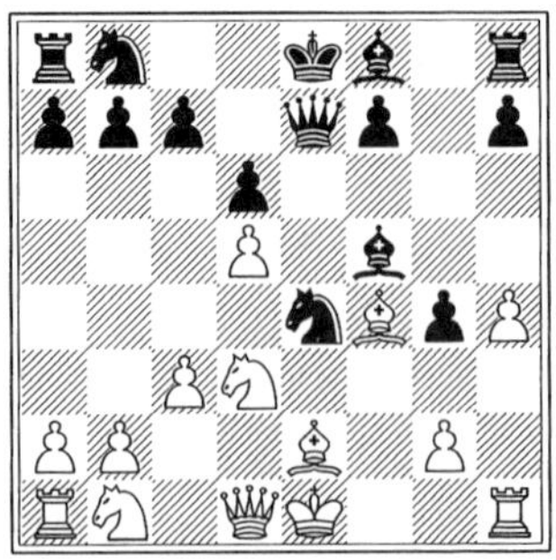

Position after 11...♘b8/*Nach 11...♘b8*

a

12.♘a3!? ♘d7

12...a6 13.♘c2 Δ ♘d4.

13.♘b5! ♘dc5

13...♘df6 14.♘d4 (14.♕a4!? ∞) 14...♗d7 15.♕b3 0-0-0 16.0-0-0 ⩱ Bangiev.

14.♘:c5 ♘:c5 15.0-0

15.♗g5! f6 (15...♕d7 16.♘:c7+!) 16.♗:f6 ♕:f6 (16...♘d3+ 17.♕:d3 ±) 17.♘:c7 ±.

15...0-0-0 16.♘d4 ♗d7 17.♗g5 f6 18.♖:f6 ♕e4 19.b4 ♘a4 20.♖f4 ♕:d5 21.♗:d8 ♘:c3 22.♕c2 ♘:e2+ 23.♕:e2 ♗g7 24.♖d1 ♔:d8 25.♘f5 ♕e5 26.♕:g4 ♖f8 27.♖df1 ♖:f5 28.♖:f5 ♗:f5 29.♕:f5 ♕d4+ 30.♕f2 ♕:b4 31.♕g3 ♕d4+ 32.♔h1 ♗e5 33.♕g8+ ♔d7 34.♕:h7+ ♔c6 35.♖c1+ ♔d5 36.♕f7+ 1:0, Wortel - Jenni, Rimavsk 1996.

b

(1.e4 e5 2.f4 e:f4 3.♘f3 g5 4.h4 g4 5.♘e5 ♘f6 6.d4 d6 7.♘d3 ♘:e4 8.♗:f4 ♕e7 9.♗e2 ♘c6 10.c3 ♗f5 11.d5 ♘b8)

12.♕b3!? ♘g3

12...c6 13.♘d2 ♘g3 14.♗:g3 ♗:d3 15.0-0-0 ♗:e2 16.♖he1 ⩲.

13.♗:g3 ♗:d3 14.0-0 ♗:e2 15.♖e1

15.♕:b7!? ♗:f1 16.♔:f1 ♕e3 17.♕:a8 ♕c1+ 18.♗e1 ♕:b2 19.♘a3 ♕:a1 20.♕:b8+ ♔d7 21.♘b5 ⩲.

15...♗h6

15...♘d7 16.♕c2 ♗g7 17.♖:e2 ♘e5 18.♘a3 =/∞.

16.♕c2 0-0 17.♖:e2 ♕f6

17...♕d7!?.

18.♖e4 ♕g6 19.♕e2

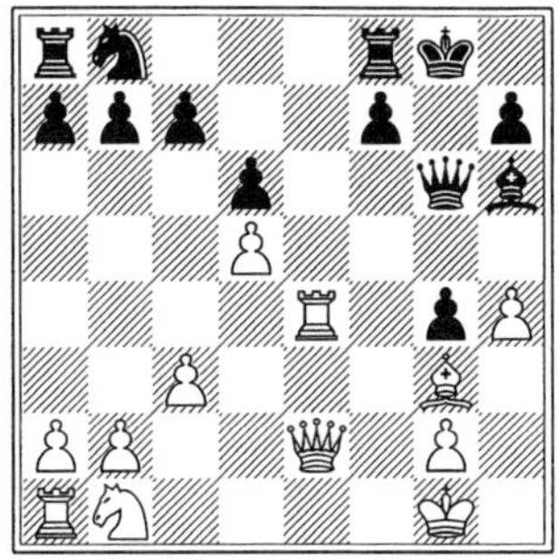

⩱ (Gallagher)

c

(1.e4 e5 2.f4 e:f4 3.♘f3 g5 4.h4 g4 5.♘e5 ♘f6 6.d4 d6 7.♘d3 ♘:e4 8.♗:f4 ♕e7 9.♗e2 ♘c6 10.c3 ♗f5 11.d5 ♘b8)

12.0-0 ♕:h4 13.♘d2 g3

13...♘:d2 14.♕:d2 ♗e7 (14...g3 now is met by - *wird nun pariert mit* - 15.♕e3+) 15.♖ae1 ♘d7?! (15...g3 16.♗:g3 ♕:g3 17.♖:f5 ♖g8 18.♗h5 ±) 16.g3! ♕f6 (16...♕h3 17.♖f2, 16...♕h5 17.♖f2 ♕g6 18.♗f1 ⩲) 17.♗:g4! ♗:g4 18.♗g5! +−.

14.♘f3 ♕h5!

14...♕e7 15.♘d4 ♕h4 (15...♗g6!?) 16.♗:g3! ♘:g3 17.♘:f5 ♕h1+ 18.♔f2 ♘:f1 19.♕a4+ ♔d8 20.♗g4! → Paralysing the ♘b8 with the threat ♘g3 Δ ♕d7# and also preparing to round up the queen in the corner with ♗h3 etc. *Der ♘b8 ist nun angesichts der Drohung ♘g3 Δ ♕d7# festgenagelt, außerdem droht die schwarze Dame in der Ecke festgesetzt zu werden (♗h3 usw.).*

15.♕a4+

15.♕b3 ♗g4 16.♖fe1! (16.♕a4+ ♔d8 17.♕:e4 ♗:f3 18.♗g5+ f6!) 16...♘bd7 17.♕:b7 ♖b8 18.♕:c7 ♕:d5 19.♘d4±; but 15...b6 is a better move
besser ist 15...b6
16.♕c4 ♔d8!
and White needs a plan ...
und Weiß braucht einen Plan ...

15...♘d7 16.♖ae1

Δ ♗d1 ± Gallagher.

16...0-0-0! 17.♗d1?

17.♕:a7 ♗g4 18.♗d1 f5∓.

17...♗g7?

17...♘:c3! 18.b:c3 ♗:d3 –+.

18.♕:a7

18.♖:e4? ♘b6.

18...♘d2! 19.♘b4 ♘:f3 20.♖:f3+ ♕h2+ 21.♔f1 ♕h1+ 22.♕g1 ♕:g1+ 23.♔:g1 ½:½, Sanchez - Rodriguez, Havanna 1993.

Black's strong outpost on e4 compensates for his pawn structure. White may have to abandon 12.0-0 due to 16...0-0-0, but 12.♘a3 seems to be a good replacement.

Zusammenfassend sei gesagt, daß der starke Vorposten auf e4 den Nachziehenden hinreichend für seine zerrüttete Bauernstruktur entschädigt. Möglicherweise sollte Weiß von 12.0-0 Abstand nehmen wegen 16...0-0-0, doch 12.♘a3 scheint ein guter Ersatz.

C

(1.e4 e5 2.f4 e:f4 3.♘f3 g5 4.h4 g4 5.♘e5 ♘f6 6.d4 d6 7.♘d3 ♘:e4 8.♗:f4 ♕e7 9.♗e2)

9...♗f5 10.♘c3
10.c3 is an alternative.
10.c3 ist eine Alternative.

10...♘:c3 11.b:c3

And White will gain some time attacking the f5 bishop, and now we've gotten rid of the irritating monster on e4.
Weiß wird Zeit durch Angriff auf den ♗f5 gewinnen, und wir sind das störende Monster auf e4 los.

D

(1.e4 e5 2.f4 e:f4 3.♘f3 g5 4.h4 g4 5.♘e5 ♘f6 6.d4 d6 7.♘d3 ♘:e4 8.♗:f4 ♕e7 9.♗e2)

9...♗g7 10.♘c3!?

As we've seen before, sacrificing a second pawn for activity is by far White's most interesting way to deal with the otherwise rather static positions springing from the Berlin defence.
Wie wir bereits gesehen haben, stellt das Opfer eines zweiten Bauern für Initiative eine sehr interessante Behandlungsweise der anderenfalls ziemlich statischen Stellungen der Berliner Verteidigung dar.

a

10...♗:d4 11.♘d5 ♕d8

11...♕d7 12.c3 ♗g7 13.h5! h6 14.♘f2! ♘:f2 15.♔:f2± Bangiev.

12.c3 ♗e6

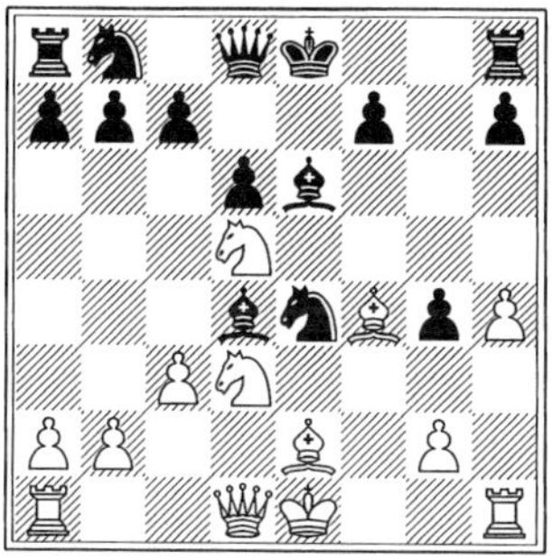

13.♕a4+!

A strong improvement on the game below:
Eine klare Verstärkung im Vergleich zu folgender Partie:
13.c:d4 ♗:d5 14.♗:g4 ♘d7 15.♘b4 c6 16.♘:d5 c:d5 17.0-0 ♕:h4 18.♗:d7+ ♔:d7 19.♕b3 ♔e6 20.♖ae1 f5 21.♕:b7 ♖ab8 22.♕c7 ♕e7 23.♕c3 ♖hg8 24.♖e2 ♖g4 25.♗h2 ♖bg8 26.♕f3 ♕f6 27.♔h1 ♖h4 28.♕a3 ♕e7 29.♔g1 ♖g5 30.♗g3 ♖hg4 31.♖f3 ♕c7 32.♖c3 ♕b6 33.♕a4 ♔f6?? (The losing moving. Black should have called White's bluff with 33...♖:g3! e.g. - *Der Verlustzug. 33...♖:g3! hätte den Bluff entlarvt, z.B.:* 34.♕e8+ ♔f6 35.♕f8+ ♔g6 36.♖:g3 ♖:g3 37.♕g8+ ♔f6 38.♕f8+ ♔g5 39.♕g7+ ♔h5 40.♕:h7+ ♔g4 41.♕g6+ ♘g5 −+) 34.♗e5+! (Forcing the king back into the pin he just escaped - *zwingt den schwarzen König in die Fesselung zurück, derer er sich gerade entkommen glaubte*) 34...♔e7 35.♖c6 ♕b7 36.♗:d6+ (Finally getting through to the king! - *Womit sich Weiß schließlich zum König durchgeschlagen hätte!*) 36...♔d8 37.♖c7 ♖:g2+ 38.♖:g2 ♖:g2+ 39.♔:g2 ♕:b2+ 40.♖c2 1:0, Reindermann - Winants, Wijk aan Zee 1993.

13...♘c6 14.c:d4

14.♘5b4? ♘:c3.

14...♗:d5 15.♘b4! ♘f6

15...♗e6 16.♘:c6 ♕d7 17.d5 ♘c5 18.♕d4 +−.

16.♗g5! ♗:g2 17.♖h2

17.0-0-0 h6!.

17...h6 18.♗:f6 ♕:f6 19.♖:g2 ♕:h4+

19...♕:d4 20.♗b5 +−.

20.♔d2 ♕g5+ 21.♔d1 h5 22.♘:c6 ♔f8 23.♘b4 g3 24.♕d7 h4 25.♖c1 h3 26.♖:c7 ♕f4 27.♕e7+ ♔g7 28.♖:g3+ 1:0, Henris - Goosens, Charleroi 1994.

b

(1.e4 e5 2.f4 e:f4 3.♘f3 g5 4.h4 g4 5.♘e5 ♘f6 6.d4 d6 7.♘d3 ♘:e4 8.♗:f4 ♕e7 9.♗e2 ♗g7 10.♘c3)

10...♘:c3 11.b:c3 ♘c6

11...c5?!
In Spassky - Fischer, Mar del Plata 1960, this was a good move, but in that game the Black queen was on d8 and the bishop on e2 was on f1, and since ♕e7 is more of a liability in this position, White has gained at least one tempo over that game.
In Spassky - Fischer, Mar del Plata 1960, bewährte sich dieser Zug in einer ganz ähnlichen Situation. In jener Partie befand sich die schwarze Dame auf d8 und der weiße Läufer auf f1, und in Anbetracht dessen, daß die Damenstellung auf e7 eher eine Belastung darstellt, hat Weiß hier faktisch mindestens ein Mehrtempo im Vergleich zu dieser Partie.
12.0-0 c:d4 13.♗:g4 ♗:g4 14.♕:g4 0-0 15.♖ae1 ±.

12.h5!

Targeting the g4-pawn for termination by cutting off its auxiliary forces.
Nimmt den ♙g4 aufs Korn, indem er diesen von möglichen Hilfstruppen abschneidet.

12...♗e6

12...h6 13.♔d2! ♗e6 14.♗:g4 ±.

13.h6 ♗f6 14.♔d2 ♗g5 15.♖h5

15.♗:g4? ♗:f4+ Δ ♕g5.

15...♖g8 16.g3

16.d5?! ♗:d5 17.♗:g4 ∞.

16...0-0-0 17.♕h1 ⩱

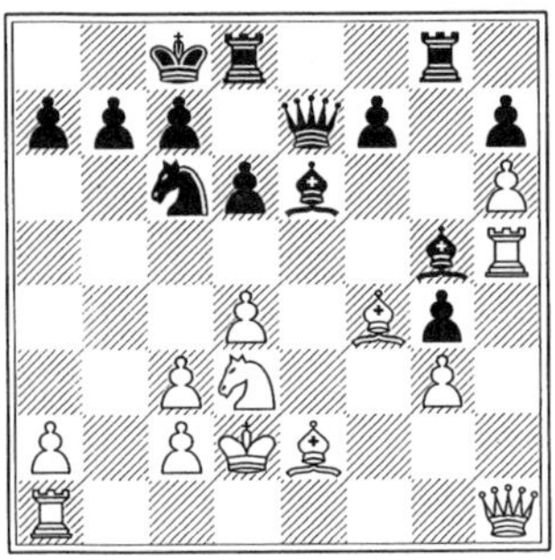

- 17...♗:f4+?! 18.♘:f4 Δ 19.d5, 19.♗b5, 19.♗d3 (Bangiev).
- More critical is
Eher kritisch ist:
17...♖de8 18.♖e1! ♗:a2 19.♗:g4 (19.d5 ♘e5!) 19...♗e6 20.♗h3 d5 21.♕:d5 ♗:f4 22.♘:f4 ♘d8 23.♖he5 ±.

C

(1.e4 e5 2.f4 e:f4 3.♘f3 g5 4.h4 g4 5.♘e5 ♘f6 6.d4 d6 7.♘d3 ♘:e4 8.♗:f4 ♕e7 9.♗e2 ♗g7 10.♘c3)

10...f5 11.♘:e4 ♕:e4

11...f:e4 12.♗g5 ♗f6 13.♗:f6 ♕:f6 14.♘f2 ± Bangiev e.g. *(z.B.)* 14...e3 15.♘e4 ♕f4 16.♗d3 d5 17.♖f1 ♕h2 18.♘f6+ ♔d8 19.♕e2 ♕:h4+ 20.♔d1 ±.

12.c3 ♕:g2 13.♔d2

Δ ♕b3.

13...♕d5 14.♕f1

Δ ♘b4, ♗c4, ♖e1+.

14...♘c6 15.♖e1 ♗e6 16.♘b4 ♘:b4 17.♗c4

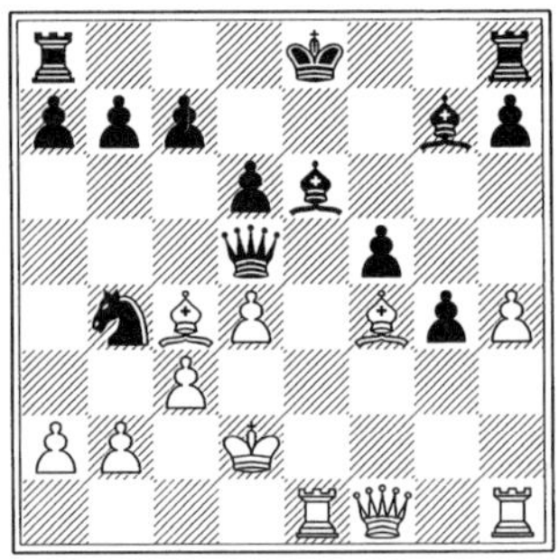

± (Bangiev)

When studying the Kieseritzky I suggest that you place the emphasis on 5...♘f6 which is critical, but not all that common. And on 5...d6 which is very common among those who have studied some theory, since it's easy to remember because it limits White's options.
Bei meiner Beschäftigung mit dem Kieseritzky-Gambit gewann ich den Eindruck, daß man sich mehr mit 5...♘f6 beschäftigen sollte, was kritisch erscheint, allerdings nicht so gebräuchlich ist. Und mit 5...d6, zu welchem Zug Spieler gerne greifen, die sich ein wenig mit der Theorie beschäftigt haben. Der Grund hierfür ist, daß dieser Zug leicht zu lernen ist, da die weißen Möglichkeiten einschränkt sind.

Chapter VI *Kapitel VI*

The Becker Defence
Die Becker-Verteidigung

1.e4 e5 2.f4 e:f4 3.♘f3 h6

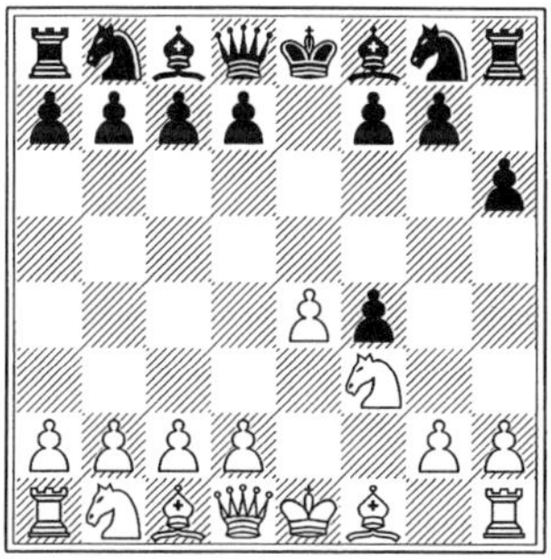

Black wants to play ...g5 without being forced to weaken his structure by White's h4 e.g. 4.d4 g5 5.h4 ♗g7. By the way, 4.h4 may stop ...g5 but it exposes White's kingside too much, e.g. ♘f6-h5-g3 is a strong manoeuvre.

Schwarz möchte ...g5 spielen, ohne gezwungen zu sein, nach h4 seine Bauernstruktur zu schwächen, z.B. 4.d4 g5 5.h4 ♗g7. Apropos, 4.h4 mag zwar ...g5 verhindern, würde aber den eigenen Königsflügel zu stark aufreißen, beispielsweise wäre danach das Manöver ♘f6-h5-g3 stark.

4.b3!?

This is a relatively new way of trying to take advantage of the black kingside squares. The bishop is given a new tempting diagonal and ...h6 looks like a waste of time since ...g5 no longer looks like a good idea. White's main idea is to quickly complete his development and then open some lines on the kingside with the g3 thrust.

Eine neuere Idee - Weiß versucht, auf die schwarzen Felder am Königsflügel einzuwirken. Mit der langen Diagonalen erhält der Läufer einen vielversprechenden Wirkungskreis, und ...h6 sieht jetzt nach reinem Zeitverlust aus - ...g5 wäre nun kaum mehr ein guter Einfall. Die grundsätzliche weiße Spielidee besteht in einem raschen Abschluß der Entwicklung und anschließender Linienöffnung am Königsflügel mittels des Hebels g3.

Most of Black's 4th move options utilize many of the ideas and set-ups from Black's 3rd move main lines, so be sure to do some cross references between them to discover the pros and cons of b3 and ...h6.

Die meisten der schwarzen Möglichkeiten in Zug 4 greifen Ideen bzw. Formationen der schwarzen Hauptvarianten in Zug 3 auf. Seien Sie mithin auf diverse Querverweise zum Pro und Contra von b3 und ...h6 gefaßt!

I

4...d6 5.♗b2

5.♗c4

would transpose to the Fischer defence.

würde zur Fischer-Verteidigung überleiten.

5...♘f6

5...♗g4 6.♘c3 ♘f6 7.♕e2 ♘bd7 8.0-0-0 ♕e7 9.♕b5 0-0-0 10.♕a5 d5 11.♘:d5 (11.♘b5 ♘b6 12.♘e5!? looks interesting - *macht einen interessanten Eindruck*) 11...♘:d5 12.e:d5 ♔b8 13.♖e1 ♕d6 14.♘e5 ♗h5 15.d4 ± Djakov - Rozkhov, corr. 1990.

A

6.♘c3!?

A more flexible move order compared with 6.♕e2, the queen can go to d2 or e2 and the ♗f1 gets a chance to evacuate before Her Majesty blocks the way.
Im Vergleich zu 6.♕e2 die flexiblere Zugfolge, die Dame behält sich d2 oder e2 vor, und der ♗f1 erhält die Chance zum Ausbruch, bevor Ihre Majestät ihm den Weg verstellt.

a

6...♘c6

6...♗e7 7.d4 0-0 (7...d5 8.e:d5 ♘:d5 9.♘:d5 ♕:d5 10.♕d2 ⩱) 8.♕d2 ♘c6 9.♕:f4 ⩲ (9.0-0-0!? ⩱) Bangiev.

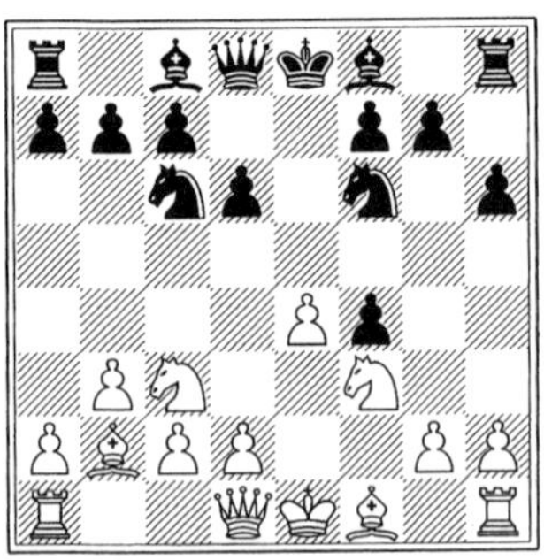

• 7.d4!? d5 (7...♗g4 8.♕d2 ♗:f3 9.g:f3 g5 10.0-0-0 ⩱ Bangiev) 8.♕e2 (8.e:d5 ♘:d5 9.♘:d5 ♕:d5 10.♕d2 ∞) 8...d:e4 9.♘:e4 ♘:e4 10.♕:e4 ♕e7 ∓ Bangiev.

• 7.♕e2 ♗g4 8.0-0-0 ♕d7 9.h3 ♗h5 10.♕f2 0-0-0 11.♖e1 ♔b8 12.♗b5 ♗:f3 13.♗:c6 b:c6 (13...♕:c6 14.♕:f3 ♗e7 15.♕:f4 ±) 14.♕:f3 ♗e7 15.♕:f4

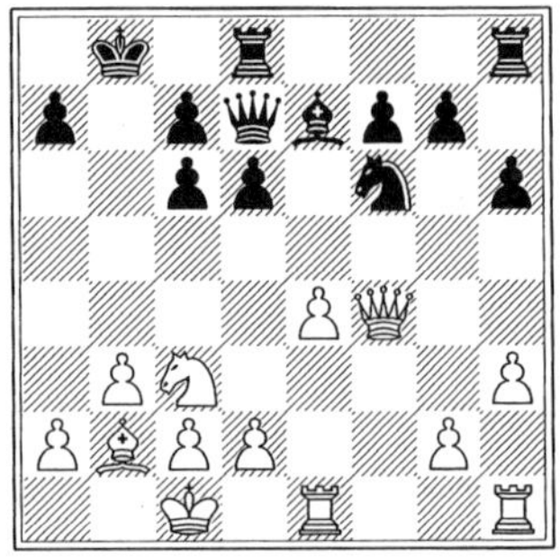

It almost looks like if White has been playing a reversed (and mirrored) Dragon, and a very healthy one too!
Es sieht fast so aus, als spiele Weiß einen farb- (und seiten-) vertauschten "Drachen" - und einen überaus gesunden noch dazu!
15...♖he8 16.♘e2 d5 17.e:d5 c:d5 18.d3 ♗d6 19.♕h4 ♖e6 20.♘d4 ♖:e1+ 21.♖:e1 ♖e8 22.♘f3 ♖:e1+ 23.♕:e1 ♘e8 24.♗e5 f6 25.♗:d6 ♘:d6 26.♕b4+ ♔a8 27.♘d4 c6 28.♕c5 ♔b7 29.b4 ♘c8 30.♘b3 ♕d6 31.♕a5 ♘b6 32.b5 (1:0/42.), Reinderman - Macieja, Pardubice 1993.

b

(1.e4 e5 2.f4 e:f4 3.♘f3 h6 4.b3 d6 5.♗b2 ♘f6 6.♘c3)

6...g6?! 7.d4 ♗g7 8.♕d2 g5

Black ought to have a losing position if he is forced to squander another tempo like this!

Wenn Schwarz schon gezwungen ist, solchermaßen ein weiteres Tempo zu verschleudern, sollte er auf Verlust stehen!

9.0-0-0 ♘c6 10.♗b5 ♗d7

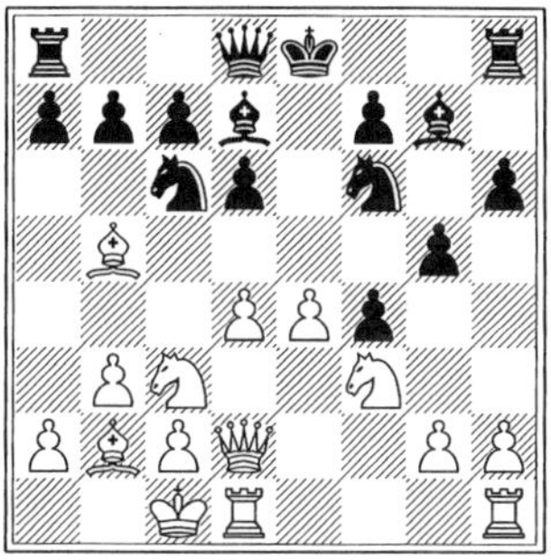

- 11.h4 ∞, Bangiev - Jürgens, Celle 1994.

I believe that White has two better moves here, either going for the white squares with
Meines Erachtens verfügt Weiß hier über zwei stärkere Züge, entweder das weißfeldrig betonte

- 11.d5!? ♘e5 12.♘d4 (Δ ♘f5) ♗:b5 13.♘f5 ♗d7 (13...♗f8 14.♘:b5 - Δ h4, Δ ♗:e5, ♕c3 - 14...♘:e4?! 15.♕e2 ♘f6 16.♗:e5 d:e5 17.♕:e5+ +–) 14.♘:g7+ ♔f8 15.♘f5 ♗:f5 16.e:f5 (Δh4, g3);

or going for the throat with
oder sofort den Finger in die Wunde zu legen mit

- 11.e5! d:e5 12.d:e5 ♘g4 13.♘d5 (Δ h3 to keep the e-file open by stopping ...♘e3 from blocking it - *Δ h3, um ...se3 mit Verstopfung der e-Linie zu verhindern*) 13...♘c:e5 14.♘:e5 ♘:e5 15.♗:e5 ♗:e5 16.♖he1 ♗:b5 (16...f6 17.♗:d7+ +–) 17.♖:e5+ ♔f8 18.♕c3! →.

B

(1.e4 e5 2.f4 e:f4 3.♘f3 h6 4.b3 d6 5.♗b2 ♘f6)

6.♕e2

The usual move. But as we've seen above 6.♘c3 is just as strong and often transposes to this line.
Der gebräuchlichste Zug. Indes ist, wie wir gesehen haben, 6.♘c3 genauso gut und leitet öfters zur vorliegenden Variante über.

6...♗e7 7.♘c3 0-0 8.0-0-0

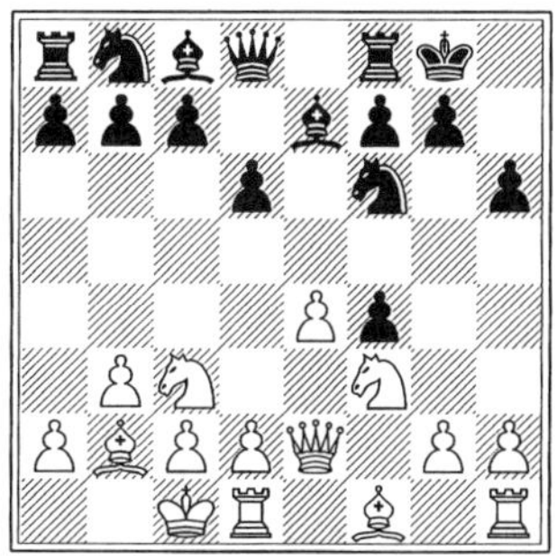

- **8...c6 9.g3! f:g3 10.♖g1**

10.♕g2!
10...♖e8 11.♖:g3 ♗f8 12.d3
12.♕e3!?
12...♘bd7 13.♕d2 ♘e5 14.♗e2 g6
And now White should have played the natural 15.♖dg1! with the initiative.
Nun sollte Weiß das natürliche 15.♖dg1! mit Initiative spielen.
Hebden - Romanishin, Moscow 1986 (0:1/56.)

- **8...♘c6 9.g3 ♗g4**

9...f:g3 10.♕g2!.
10.♕f2 ♘e5 11.♗e2 f:g3 12.♕:g3 ♘h5 13.♕f2 ♗:f3 14.♗:f3 ♗h4 15.♕f1

White is practising a kind of Judo strategy, expecting to be able to turn Black's desperate activity against himself.
Weiß praktiziert eine Art Judo-Strategie - die verzweifelte Aktivität seines Gegners soll sich gegen ihn selbst wenden.
15...♘f4 16.♖g1 c6 17.♗g4 ♘fg6
Trading pieces would emphasise White's open f and g-files, similar to the 'Benko gambit'.
Figurenabtausch würde - ganz analog zum Wolga-Benkö-Gambit - die weiße Stärke auf der f- und g-Linie betonen.
18.♗f5 ♗g5 19.♔b1 ♘e7 20.d4 ♘5g6 21.♗c1!
Getting rid of the corner-stone of Black's defence.
Beseitigt den Eckpfeiler der schwarzen Verteidigung.
21...♗:c1 22.♔:c1 d5 23.e5 ♘:f5 24.♕:f5 ♘e7 25.♕g4 g6 26.♖df1 ♕c8 27.♕h4 ♘f5 28.♕f6 ♔h7 29.♘e2

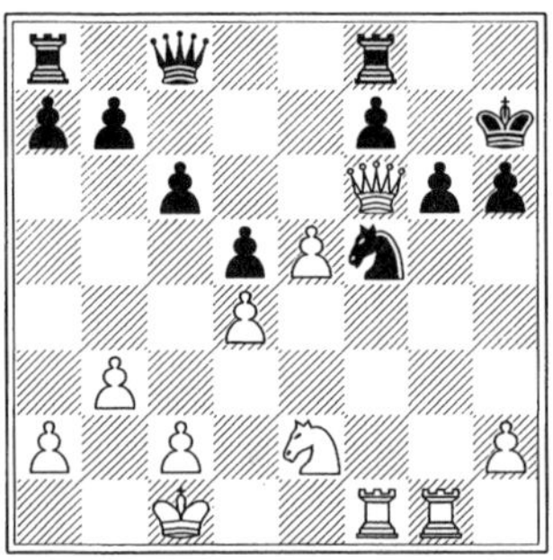

Black is completely tied up, awaiting execution!
Völlig festgezurrt wartet der Nachziehende hilflos auf seine Exekution!
29...♕e6 30.♖:g6! ♕:f6 31.♖:f6 ♘g7 32.♖:f7 ± (1:0/69.), Bangiev - Karolyi, Kecskemet 1987.

II

(1.e4 e5 2.f4 e:f4 3.♘f3 h6 4.b3)

4...d5 5.e:d5 ♗e7 6.♗b5+

6.♗c4 ♗h4+ 7.♘:h4 (A necessity here since the bishop can retreat and regain a tempo with ♗f6. In the Cunningham, however, ♔f1 would be preferable - *Notwendig, weil der Läufer anderenfalls mit Tempo nach f6 zurückgezogen werden könnte. In der Cunningham-Verteidigung wäre hingegen ♔f1 vorzuziehen*) 7...♕:h4+ 8.♔f1 (Δ ♕e1) ♕f6 9.d4 ♘d7 10.♘c3 ↑ (Bangiev); I would prefer to speed development with 9.♘c3 e.g. *(ich würde lieber mit 9.♘c3 die Entwicklung beschleunigen, z.B.:)* 9...♘e7 10.♗a3 0-0 11.♕e2 ♖e8 12.♖e1 ♔f8 13.♘e4 (Δ d6 +−).

6...c6 7.d:c6 b:c6 8.♗c4 ♗h4+ 9.♘:h4 ♕:h4+ 10.♔f1 ♘e7 11.♗b2 0-0 12.♕e1 ♕:e1+ 13.♔:e1 ♗f5 14.d3 ♘d7 15.♖f1 ♖fe8 16.♔d2 g5 17.h4 ♘g6 18.h:g5 h:g5 19.♘c3 ♘de5 20.♘e2 ♘h4

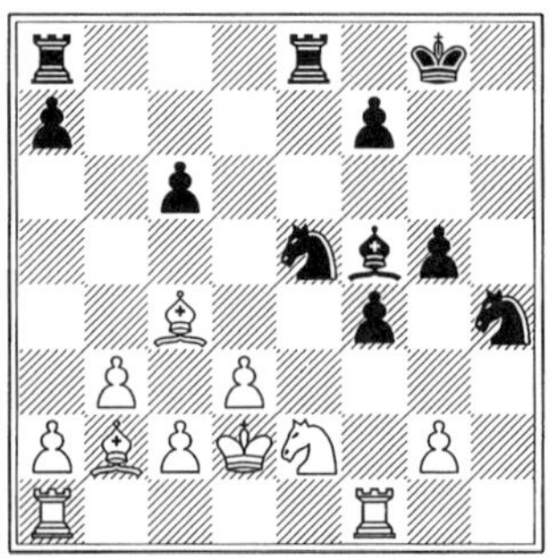

21.♘:f4 g:f4 22.♖:f4 ♘eg6 23.♖af1 ♗e6?

23...♘:f4 24.♖:f4 ♘g6 25.♖:f5 ♖e7 Gallagher.

24.♖:f7! ♗:f7 25.♖:f7

Δ 26.♖f5+ ♔h7 27.♖h5#.

25...♘e5 26.♗:e5 1:0, Basman - Griffiths, Wolverhampton 1968.

III

(1.e4 e5 2.f4 e:f4 3.♘f3 h6 4.b3)

4...♘f6!?

A

5.e5

A recommendation from Gallagher, which led to some interesting complications in our example.
Eine Empfehlung von Gallagher, die in unserem Partiebeispiel zu interessanten Verwicklungen führte.

5...♘e4!?

The ♙f4 is not as weak here as it is in the Schallopp, which gives the knight a chance to go sight-seeing.
Der ♙f4 ist hier nicht so schwach wie in der Schallopp-Verteidigung, was dem Springer die Gelegenheit zu einer Spritztour gibt.
The conventional 5...♘h5 seems less critical, e.g.
Das hergebrachte 5...♘h5 scheint weniger kritisch, z.B.:
6.♕e2 ♕e7 7.♘c3 ↑ Bangiev.

6.♕e2 ♘g5 7.♗b2

It's hard to improve White's play, e.g. 7.d4 as in the Schallopp would run into 7...♘:f3+ 8.♕:f3 ♕h4+ 9.g3 f:g3 10.h:g3 ♕:d4 and here 11.♖h4 would be idiotic; I looked at the tempting 11.♗c4 hoping for ......♕:a1 12.♕:f7+ ♔d8 13.♗g5+ h:g5 14.♖:h8 +− but 11...♕:e5 12.♔d1 ♕d4 13.♗d2 f6 seems quite safe for Black.

Es ist schwer, hier das weiße Spiel zu verbessern, beispielsweise würde 7.d4 analog zur Schallopp-Verteidigung in 7...♘:f3+ 8.♕:f3 ♕h4+ 9.g3 f:g3 10.h:g3 ♕:d4 hereinlaufen, und 11.♖h4 wäre nun ziemlich blödsinnig. Angesehen habe ich mir auch das verlockende 11.♗c4 in Hoffnung auf ...♕:a1 12.♕:f7+ ♔d8 13.♗g5+ h:g5 14.♖:h8 +−, doch 11...♕:e5+ 12.♔d1 ♕d4+ 13.♗d2 f6 macht einen sicheren Eindruck für Schwarz.

Preventing Black's queen check with 7.g3 is too slow e.g:
7.g3 zwecks Verhinderung des Damenschachs auf h4 ist zu langsam, z.B.:
7...f:g3 8.h:g3 ♘:f3+ 9.♕:f3 d6 10.e:d6 ♗:d6 11.♗b2 0-0 12.♘c3 ♖e8+ 13.♗e2 ♘c6 14.0-0-0 ♘d4 ∓.
7.♘c3 of course just transposes to *(ist natürlich nur eine Zugumstellung zu)* 8.♘c3.

7...♘c6 8.d4?

Missing Black's 10th.
A safer alternative would be
Übersieht den 10. Zug von Schwarz. Sicherer war
8.♘c3 ♘:f3 9.♕:f3 ♕h4+ 10.g3 f:g3 11.h:g3 ♘d4 (11...♘:e5 12.♕g2 ∞) 12.0-0-0! ♘:f3 13.g:h4.
White seems to have good compensation for the pawn since the f3 knight is in peril of being caught.
Weiß dürfte gute Kompensation für den Bauern haben, zumal der ♘f3 in Gefahr schwebt, gefangen zu werden.

8...♘:f3+ 9.♕:f3 ♕h4+ 10.g3

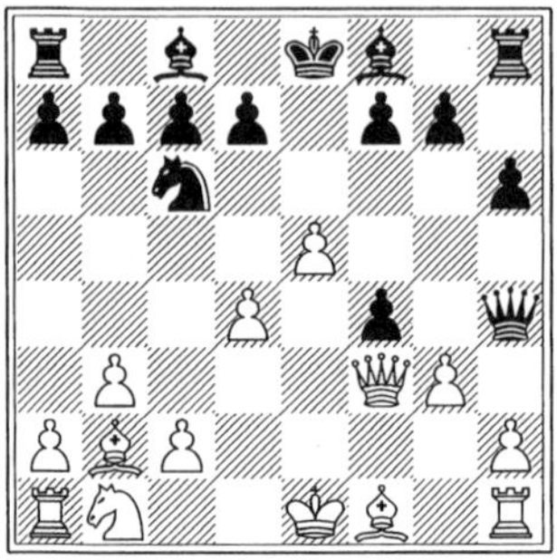

10...♘:d4! 11.♕e4 f:g3 12.♕:d4 g2+ 13.♕:h4 g:h1♕ 14.♘d2 ♕g1 15.0-0-0 ♗e7 16.♕e4 ♕g6 17.♕f3 d5 18.e:d6 ♗:d6 19.♗b5+ ♔f8 20.♖e1 ♗e6 21.♗d3 ♕g4 22.♕f2 ♔e7 23.♗c4 ♖hf8 24.♖e4 ♕g6 25.♗d3 ♕g5 26.♔b1 ♗c5 27.♕e1 ♕g1 28.♕:g1 ♗:g1 29.♗a3+ ♔d7 30.♘f3 ♗b6 31.♘e5+ ♔e8 32.♗b5+ c6 33.♘:c6 a6 34.♗a4 ♖h8 35.♘d4+ ♔d8 36.♘:e6+ f:e6 37.♖:e6 ♗c7 38.b4 b5 39.♗b3 ♖e8 40.♗b2 ♖:e6 41.♗:e6 ♔e7 42.♗d5 ♖d8 43.c4 g5 44.h3 h5 45.♔c2 g4 46.h:g4 h:g4 47.♔d3 g3 48.♗d4 ♖f8 49.♗b7 ♖f1

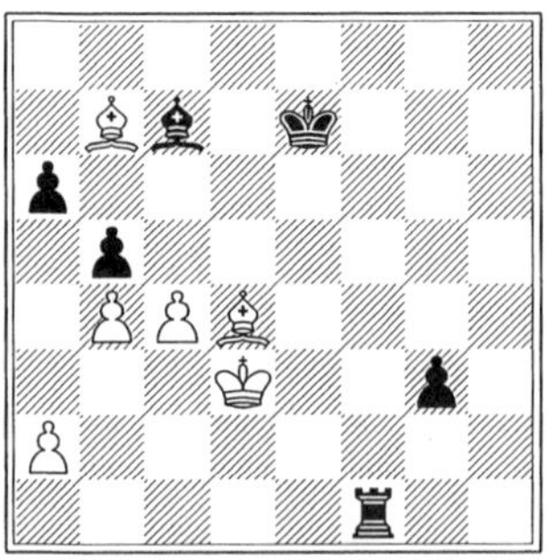

50.♔e2 ♖f4 51.♗e3 ♖:c4 52.♗:a6 ♖c2+ 53.♔f1 ♖:a2 54.♗:b5 ♗d6 55.♗g5+ ♔f8 56.♗h6+ ½:½, Shaw - Nunn, Isle of Man 1994.

A study-like draw, which I couldn't bring myself to deprive you!
Eine studienhafte Remis-Rettung, die ich Ihnen unmöglich vorenthalten konnte!

B

(1.e4 e5 2.f4 e:f4 3.♘f3 h6 4.b3 ♘f6)

5.♕e2?!

This seems to land White in some theoretical difficulties, although he scored a quick win ...
Ungeachtet des raschen Gewinns in unserer Partie scheint Weiß danach in theoretischer Hinsicht in Schwierigkeiten ...

However, 5.♘c3!? looks very natural although it's unmentioned by the experts. If Black should try to transpose to Hebden - Pein with 5...d5 White can avoid this by
Sehr natürlich sieht allerdings 5.♘c3!? aus, was jedoch nirgendwo erwähnt wird. Wenn Schwarz mit 5...d5 zu Hebden - Pein überleiten will, kann Weiß dies wie folgt verhindern:
6.e:d5 ♗e7 (6...♘:d5 7.♘:d5 ♕:d5 8.♗c4 ♕h5 [8...♕e4+? 9.♔f2! ♗e6 10.♖e1 ♕f5 11.d4 c6 12.♖e5 ♕f6 13.♕e2 ♘d7 14.♗:e6 ♘:e5 15.♗h3 ±] 9.♗b2 ∞) 7.♗c4 or *(oder)* 6.♘:d5!? e.g. *(z.B.)* ♘:e4 7.♘:f4 ♗d6 (7...♕d6 8.g3 ♗e7 9.♕e2 ∞) 8.♘h5 0-0 9.♗b2 ♖e8+ 10.♗e2 ♗f8 11.0-0 ±/∞.
The only practical test I've seen went:
Der einzig mir bekannte praktische Versuch lief wie folgt:
5...g5?! 6.♗c4 d6 7.♗b2 ♗g7 8.♕e2 ♗e6?! 9.♗:e6 f:e6 10.e5!, Simon - Hansson, Malmö 1996.
White enjoyed a clearly better position although he eventually went down.
Weiß konnte sich klaren Vorteils erfreuen, obgleich er letztendlich unterlag.

5...d5!

Opening the e-file to exploit White's artificial queen placement.
Öffnet die e-Linie, um die gekünstelte weiße Damenstellung auszunützen.
5...g5?! 6.♗b2 ♗g7 7.♘c3 c6? 8.e5! (A thematic thrust whenever Black weakens d6 and White can get a knight at e4 - *Der thematische Vorstoß, sobald Schwarz d6 geschwächt hat und der weiße Springer bereit zum Sprung nach e4 steht*) 8...♘h7 9.♘e4 d5 10.♘d6+ ♔f8 11.0-0-0 ♘a6 12.♘d4 ♘c7 13.♕h5 ♕d7 14.♘4f5 ♕e6 15.♗a3 ♔g8 16.♘:c8 1:0, Popovych - Karklins, US Open 1989.
A crushing demonstration of why Black so seldom plays ...g5 in this variation!
Belegt eindrücklich, warum Schwarz in dieser Variante so selten ...g5 spielt!

6.e:d5+ ♗e7 7.♗b2 0-0 8.♘c3 ♖e8 9.0-0-0 ♘:d5 10.♕e5 ♘:c3 11.d:c3 ♗d6 12.♕h5 ♘d7?!

12...♘c6 13.♗c4 ♕f6 14.♖he1 ♗d7 ∓, 13.c4 ♕e7 14.♗d3 ♗a3 15.♖he1 ♗:b2+ 16.♔:b2 ♕f6+ ∓ Gallagher.

13.♗c4 ♕f6 14.♖he1 ♖e3 15.♖:e3 f:e3 16.♖f1 g6 17.♕a5

17.♕:h6? ♗f4.

17...♕f5 18.♕a4 c6 19.♘d4 e2 20.♘:f5 ♘b6 21.♗:e2 1:0, Hebden - Pein, London 1987.

IV

(1.e4 e5 2.f4 e:f4 3.♘f3 h6 4.b3)

4...♗e7!?

As far as I know, only played once, fifty years ago. Perhaps it's so rare because 3...h6 is a way of avoiding large main-lines, which means that you don't want to transpose into something you know nothing about. And, of course, if you know a main-line there's no need to play 3...h6.
White entered something resembling the Cunningham with:
Meines Wissens kam dies nur in einer einzigen, fünfzig Jahre alten Partie vor. Vielleicht ist dieser Zug deswegen so selten, weil 3...h6 ja eigentlich mit der Intention verbunden ist, weitschweifigen Hauptvarianten auszuweichen - was bedeutet, daß der Anwender kaum die Absicht hat, in eine Hauptlinie überzuleiten, mit welcher er nicht vertraut ist. Und andererseits besteht natürlich, wenn man eine der Hauptverteidigungen beherrscht, keinerlei Anlaß, 3...h6 zu spielen.
In unserer Partie betrat Weiß Cunningham-ähnliche Gefilde mit:

5.♗c4 ♘f6

5...♗h4+ 6.♔f1 (I guess the original Cunningham gambit is even more unsound due to ...h6 and b3, i.e.: - *ich vermute, das eigentliche Cunningham-Gambit ist mit dem zusätzlichen ...h6 und b3 noch weniger korrekt:* 6.g3 f:g3 7.0-0 g:h2+ or - *oder* - 7...d5!?) 6...d5 7.♘:h4 d:c4 (7...♕:h4 8.e:d5 transposes to II above - *leitet zu II über*) 8.♘f3 ±.

6.♕e2

6.e5!?, 6.♘c3?! ♘:e4 7.♘e5 ♘g5 (7...♘d6 may be better since ♗b3 isn't available - *7...♘d6 dürfte in Anbetracht dessen, daß ♗b3 nicht möglich ist, vorzuziehen sein*) 8.♕h5 0-0 ∓.

6...0-0 7.0-0?!

It feels better to go for the usual set-up with ♗b2, ♘c3, 0-0-0 etc. without which b3 looks pointless and more

harmful to White's position than ...h6 is for Black's.
The rest of the game is an illustration of this, 19...♘:c5 wouldn't be so devastating with the b-pawn on b2.
Eine Normal-Aufstellung mit ♗b2, ♘c3, 0-0-0 scheint eher angebracht. Andernfalls ist b3 zwecklos und richtet in der weißen Stellung mehr Schaden an als ...h6 bei Schwarz.
Der weitere Verlauf der Partie bestätigt dies, auch das spätere 19...♘:c5 wäre mit dem b-Bauern auf b2 nicht so wirkungsvoll.

7...c6 8.e5 d5 9.e:d6 ♗:d6 10.d4 ♖e8 11.♕d1 ♗g4 12.♘c3 ♘bd7 13.♘e2 ♕c7 14.♗d3 ♘d5 15.c4 ♘e3 16.♗:e3 ♖:e3 17.c5 ♗f8 18.♕d2 ♖ae8 19.♘c3

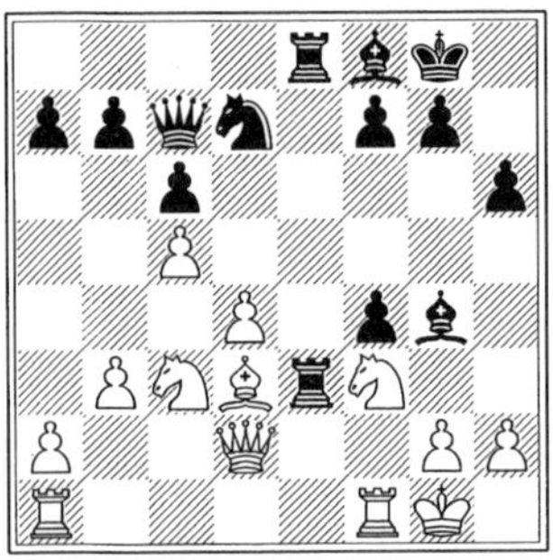

19...♘:c5! 20.d:c5 ♗:c5 21.♔h1 ♖d8 22.♘e1 ♗b4 23.♕c2 ♗:c3 24.♕:c3 ♗e2 0:1, Korning - Nielsen, corr. 1949.

V

(1.e4 e5 2.f4 e:f4 3.♘f3 h6 4.b3)

4...♘c6 5.♗b2 d5?!

Black will lose too much time on having his queen kicked around!
Danach wird die schwarze Dame herumgescheucht, was den Nachziehenden zu viel Zeit kosten wird!

5...d6 6.♗b5 ♗d7 7.d4 a6 8.♗:c6 ♗:c6 9.♘c3 Bangiev.

6.e:d5 ♕:d5 7.♘c3 ♕h5 8.♕e2

8.♗b5!?.

8...♗e6 9.♘e4 0-0-0 10.0-0-0 f5 11.♘c3 ♕e8 12.♕f2 a6 13.♗e2 g5 14.d4 ♗g7 15.d5 ♗:c3

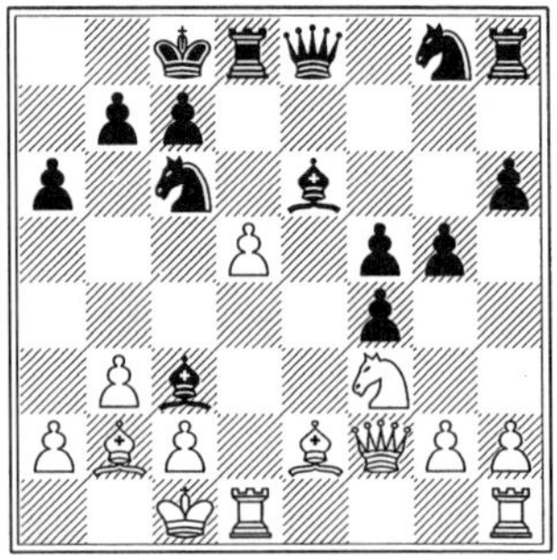

16.d:c6! ♕:c6 17.♕a7 ♗:b2+ 18.♔:b2 1:0, Kurbanov - Satsynerov, corr. 1990.

VI

(1.e4 e5 2.f4 e:f4 3.♘f3 h6 4.b3)

4...♘e7 5.♗b2

A

5...♘g6 6.♘c3 d6 7.♕e2

7.h4 ♗g4 8.h5 ♘h4 9.♕e2 ∞, 7.d4 ♗g4 8.♕d2 ♗:f3 9.g:f3 ♕h4+ 10.♕f2 ♗e7 11.♘d5 ⩱ Bangiev.

7...c6 8.0-0-0 ♗g4 9.d4 ♘d7 10.h3?!

10.g3 (Δ h3) f:g3 11.h:g3
looks preferable since it is more in the spirit of the variation, i.e. opening files on the kingside!
ist viel eher im Geiste der Variante

(Linienöffnung am Königsflügel!) und dürfte daher vorzuziehen sein.

10...♗h5 11.e5!? d:e5 12.d:e5 ♗:f3 13.g:f3?!

Opening the g-file, but giving up the thematic possibility of g3 which would open the f- or the h-file too.
Öffnet zwar die g-Linie, vergibt aber gleichzeitig die Option auf das thematische g2-g3, womit die f- bzw. h-Linie ebenfalls geöffnet würde.

13...♗c5

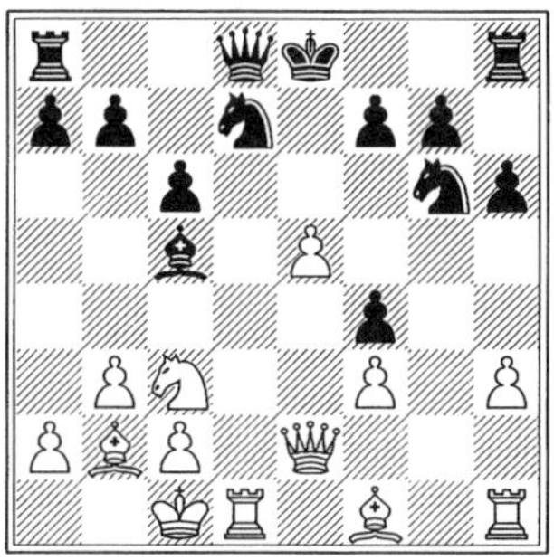

14.e6!

A necessity, to justify White's 13th move, but White is forced to play with very narrow safety margins although White's position certainly looks very threatening.
Nur so ist der 13. Zug zu rechtfertigen. Indes ist Weiß nun gezwungen, ohne Netz und doppelten Boden zu spielen, auch wenn seine Stellung einen drohenden Eindruck macht.

14...♗e3+ 15.♔b1 f:e6 16.♘e4 0-0 17.♕g2 ♔h7 18.♗d3 ♘de5 19.♖hg1 ♗:g1 20.♖:g1 ♕e7 21.♘f2 ♖f5 22.♗:f5 e:f5 23.♘d3 ♖e8 24.♖e1 ♕h4 25.♗c3?! ♖e7 26.♖g1 ♕g3 27.♕:g3 f:g3 28.♘:e5 ♘:e5 29.♖:g3 f4 30.♖g2 ♘:f3 0:1, Popovych - Sagalchik, Philadelphia 1993.

B

(1.e4 e5 2.f4 e:f4 3.♘f3 h6 4.b3 ♘e7 5.♗b2)

5...d5 6.♘c3 c6 7.♗d3 ♘d7 8.e:d5 ♘c5 9.♕e2 ♘:d3+ 10.c:d3!

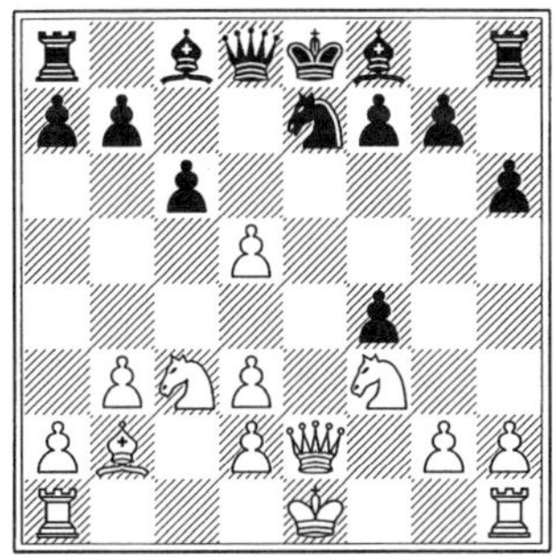

An interesting way to control some potentially weak centre squares.
Eine bemerkenswerte Möglichkeit, Kontrolle über einige wichtige Zentrumsfelder zu erlangen.

10...c:d5 11.♘b5 a6 12.♘bd4 ♗g4 13.0-0 ♖c8 14.♖ae1 g5 15.h3 ♗:f3 16.♕:f3 ♖g8 17.♘f5 ♖c6 18.♘:e7 ♗:e7 19.♖e5 ♔f8 20.♖:d5 ♕c8 21.♖e1 ♗f6 22.♗:f6 ♖:f6 23.♖de5 ♔g7 24.♖e7 b5 25.♕e4 ♕c5+ 26.d4 ♕f5 27.♕e5 ♖c8 28.♖a7 ♔g6 29.a4 b:a4 30.b:a4 ♖c2 31.♖e2 ♖c1+

31...f3 32.♕:f5+ ♖:f5 33.♖:a6+.

32.♔f2 ♕b1 33.♕e4+ ♕:e4 34.♖:e4 ♖c4 35.a5 ♖a4 36.♔e2 ♖:a5 37.♔d3 ♖a3+ 38.♔c4 ♖g3 39.♖e2 f3 40.g:f3 ♖g:f3 41.d5 ♖:h3 42.♖c7! ♖h1 43.♔d4 ♖b1 44.♖c6 ♖b8 45.♖f2! ♖:c6 46.d:c6 g4 47.♔c5 h5 48.d4 g3 49.♖g2 h4 50.d5 ♖b1 51.d6 ♖c1+ 52.♔b6 ♖d1 53.d7 1:0, Olesen - Hvenekilde, Copenhagen 1996.

Chapter VII *Kapitel VII*

The Fischer Defence
Die Fischer-Verteidigung

1.e4 e5 2.f4 e:f4 3.♘f3 d6

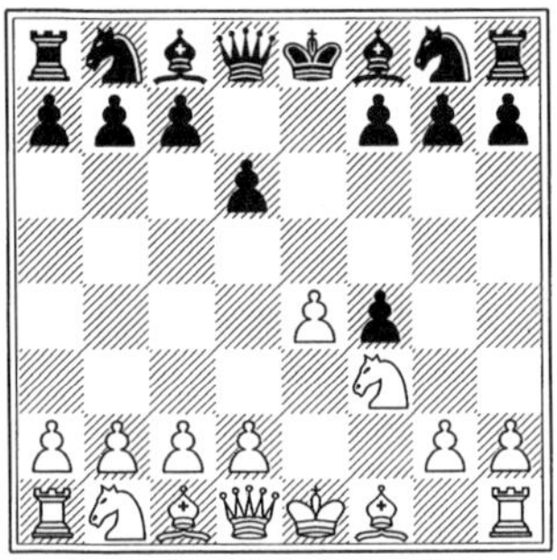

Black wants to play ...g5 but first he makes sure to avoid the Kieseritzky by taking away the ♘e5 possibility.
Schwarz möchte ...g5 spielen, will aber zunächst das Kieseritzky-Gambit ausschalten, indem er ♘e5 verhindert.

4.♗c4

This is usually dismissed as leading to the Hanstein gambit after 4...h6 5.d4 g5 6.0-0 which is good for Black. However, we have no intention of playing 5.d4?!.

Dieser Zug wird normalerweise verworfen, da er angeblich nach 4...h6 5.d4 g5 6.0-0 zum aus schwarzer Sicht sehr annehmbaren Hanstein-Gambit führt. Wir beabsichtigen indes keinesfalls, 5.d4?! zu spielen.

By the way, 4.d4 g5 5.h4 g4 6.♘g1 (not 6.♘g5? because of 6...f6!) is the most popular variation, but I don't think that I can recommend it. Partly because I have a horrendous score in it myself and partly because I've come to feel that it's against the spirit of the King's Gambit since White gives up his lead in development, which usually represents an important part of the compensation for the pawn. Besides, this is the variation people often prepare for you if they know you play the King's Gambit, so why allow your opponents to 'stand on the shoulders of giants', when you can make them think for themselves with 4.♗c4!

4.d4 g5 5.h4 g4 6.♘g1 (nicht 6.♘g5? wegen 6...f6!) ist, nebenbei gesagt, die beliebteste Variante, welche ich allerdings kaum empfehlen kann. Zum Teil deswegen, weil meine eigene Bilanz damit fürchterlich ist, und zum anderen Teil weil dies meines Empfindens nach dem Geist des Königsgambits zuwiderläuft - Weiß gibt seinen Entwicklungsvorsprung auf, welcher normalerweise einen beachtlichen Teil seiner Kompensation für den Gambitbauern darstellt. Außerdem ist diese Variante häufig Gegenstand der Vorbereitung, wenn Ihrem Kontrahenten bekannt ist, daß Sie das Königsgambit spielen. Also warum sollten Sie Ihren Gegner an der "Schulter der Giganten" ruhen lassen, wenn Sie ihn mit 4.♗c4 zum selbständigen Denken zwingen können!

Reserving d4 for the Knight and giving the e4-pawn some protection with 4.d3 also seems interesting though, e.g:
Interessant scheint auch 4.d3, um dem Springer das Feld d4 zu reservieren sowie den ♙e4 zu überdecken, z.B.:

4...g5 5.h4 g4 6.♘d4

- 6...♗g7 7.c3 ♕f6 8.♕b3 ♘e7 9.♕b5+ ♘bc6 10.♘:c6 ♘:c6 11.♕g5 ♕:g5 12.h:g5 f3 13.g:f3 g:f3 14.♘d2 ♗g4 15.♔f2 = Kortchnoi, 15.♖h4! looks stronger *(scheint stärker).*
- 6...♕f6 7.♘b5 ♘a6 8.♗d2 f3 9.♗c3 ♕f4 10.♗:h8 ♕g3+ 11.♔d2 f:g2 12.♗:g2 ♕:g2+ 13.♔c3 ∞ (Kortchnoi).
- 6...♗h6 7.♗d2 ♘f6 8.h5 d5 9.e5 ♕e7 10.♕e2 ♘fd7 11.♘f5 ♕e6 12.♘:h6 ♕:h6 13.g3 ± (Kortchnoi).

Due to the small amount of games and analysis on 4.d3 there should be plenty of room for improvements for both sides.
Da nur wenig Partien und Analysen zu 4.d3 vorliegen, gibt es hier reichlich Spielraum für Verbesserungen auf beiden Seiten!

4...h6!

The correct move order, thereby avoiding immediate disaster!
Die richtige Zugfolge. Nur so wird ein rasches Desaster vermieden.

- 4...g5? (This is an extremely common mistake, especially in blitz, when people are in a hurry to complete their black-squared fortress with g5 and h6 - *ein sehr häufig vorkommender Fehler; insbesondere in Blitzpartien, wo die Leute gern etwas zu hektisch an ihrer schwarzfeldrige Bauernkette f4/g5/h6 basteln)* 5.h4! g4 6.♘g5 ♘h6 7.d4 f6 8.♗:f4 ♘c6 (Suddenly turning chicken, but the alternative doesn't give Black that much - *wendet plötzlich das Fähnchen, doch die Alternative verheißt ebenfalls nichts Gutes:* 8...f:g5 9.♗:g5 ♕d7 10.0-0 →) 9.0-0 ♕e7 10.♘c3 ♕g7 11.♘e6 ♗:e6 12.♗:e6 ♔e7

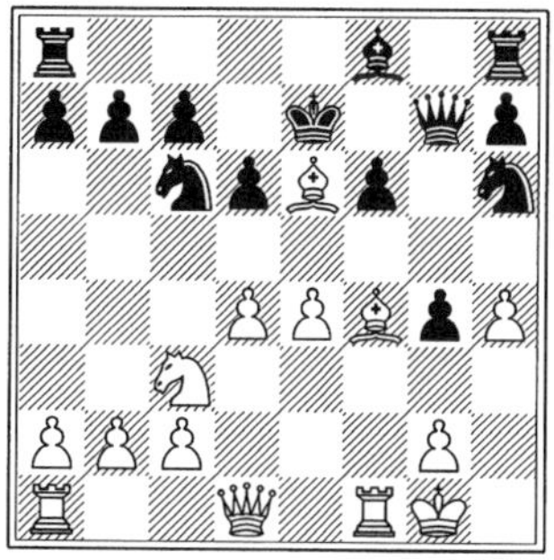

13.♘d5+! ♔:e6 14.♗:h6 ♕:h6 15.♕:g4+ ♔f7 16.♖:f6+ ♕:f6 17.♘:f6 ♔:f6 18.♖f1+ ♔e7 19.♕g5+ ♔d7 (19...♔e8 20.♕f6 ♖g8 21.♕f7+) 20.♕f5+ ♔e8 21.♕f7+ ♔d8 22.♕f6+ ♘e7 23.♕:h8 ♘g6 24.♖:f8+ 1:0, Morphy - Tilghman, Philadelphia 1859.

- 4...♗e7 5.d4 ♘f6 (5...♗h4+ transposes to a Cunningham where Black has played the inferior ...d6 instead of ...d5 - *5...♗h4+ leitet zu einer Cunningham-Verteidigung mit dem minderwertigen ...d6 anstelle von ...d5 über)* 6.♘c3 0-0 7.♗b3 ± d5 8.e5 ♘e4 9.♘:d5 ♗h4+ 10.♔f1 b6 11.c4 ♘c6 12.♗:f4 ♘f2 13.♕e1! (This is a standard reply to the knight fork in the Cunningham, after taking the rook, the knight on h1 will never see the light of day again! - *Wie in der Cunningham-Verteidigung die Standard-Reaktion auf die Springergabel. Nimmt Schwarz auf h1, so wird dieser Springer nie wieder das Tageslicht erblicken!)* 13...♗a6 14.♘:h4 ♘:h1 15.♔g1 ♘:d4 16.♖d1 c5 17.♔:h1 ♔h8 18.♘f3 ♘:b3 19.a:b3 ♕c8 20.♕e4 h6

21.♗:h6! ♕e6 (21...g:h6 22.♘f6 +–) 22.♗e3 ♖fd8 23.♘g5 1:0, Arnason - G. Kuzmin, Reykjavik 1978.

• 4...♗e6?! ♥

(Also very common - *gleichfalls sehr verbreitet*) 5.♗:e6 f:e6 6.d4

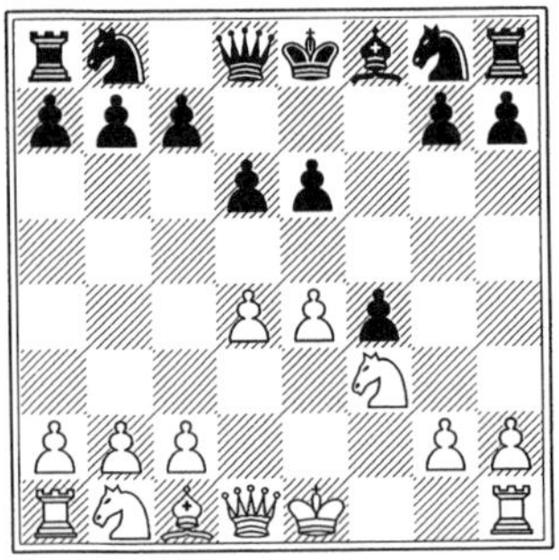

• • 6...♘f6?! 7.♘c3 d5 8.e5! ♘h5 (One might think that Black has achieved a 'good French structure' here since he's been relieved of his bad bishop. But his inability to challenge e5 with ...f6 condemns him to a cramped position - *Man möchte meinen, daß Schwarz eine recht vorteilhafte "Französisch"-Struktur erlangt hat, da er seinen schlechten Läufer abgetauscht hat. Schwerer wiegt indes der Umstand, daß er nicht mehr mit ...f6 das weiße Zentrum anknabbern kann, was ihn zu einem beengten Spiel verurteilt*) 9.♘e2 g5 (9...c5 10.g4 f:g3 11.h:g3 g6 12.♗g5 ♗e7 13.♕d2 ±) 10.g4 ♘g7 11.h4 ♗e7 12.h:g5 ♗:g5 13.♕d3 ♔f7 14.♖:h7 ♖:h7 15.♕:h7 ♕e7 16.♗:f4 ♗:f4 17.♘:f4 ♘c6 18.0-0-0 ♖f8 19.♕g6+ ♔g8 20.♘g5 1:0, Duratti - Folz, Noumea 1995.

• • 6...♕f6 7.♘c3

• • • 7...♘e7?! (7...♘a6 ±) 8.♕e2! ± (This queen activation is very important if you want the advantage! - *solchermaßen die Dame zu aktivieren, ist beim Kampf um Vorteil sehr bedeutsam!*) 8...c6? 9.e5 d:e5 10.♘e4! (I hope you recognize and remember this typical manoeuvre by now! When Black weakens d6 this is always a possibility to strive for, although it isn't usually the **coup de grace** it is in this position! - *Ich hoffe, Sie erkennen und erinnern sich inzwischen an dieses Motiv! Wenn Schwarz d6 geschwächt hat, sollten Sie stets nach dieser Möglichkeit Ausschau halten, auch wenn es nicht immer gleich wie hier der* **coup de grace** *ist!*)

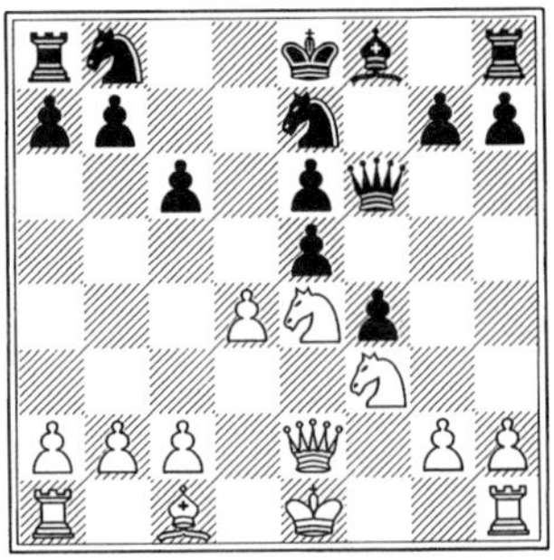

1:0, Junejev - Klovan, Odessa 1981.

• • • 7...g5 8.e5 ♕f5 9.♕e2! a6?! (9...g4 looks more critical, e.g: - *erscheint eher kritisch, z.B.:* 10.♘h4 ♕h5 11.g3 f3 12.♕b5+ ♘d7 13.♕:b7 ♖b8 14.♕:c7 d:e5 15.d5!? e:d5 16.♘:d5 e4 [16...♗c5 17.♗e3] 17.♗e3! ♕:d5? 18.♖d1 ♕b5 19.c4 +–) 10.d5 d:e5 11.♘:e5 ♘f6? 12.g4!! f:g3? (12...f3 13.g:f5 ±) 13.♖f1 ♕h3 (13...g2 14.♖:f5 g1♕ 15.♖f1 Δ ♖:f6) 14.♖:f6 g:h2 15.♖:e6+ ♗e7 (15...♕:e6 16.♕h5+ +–)

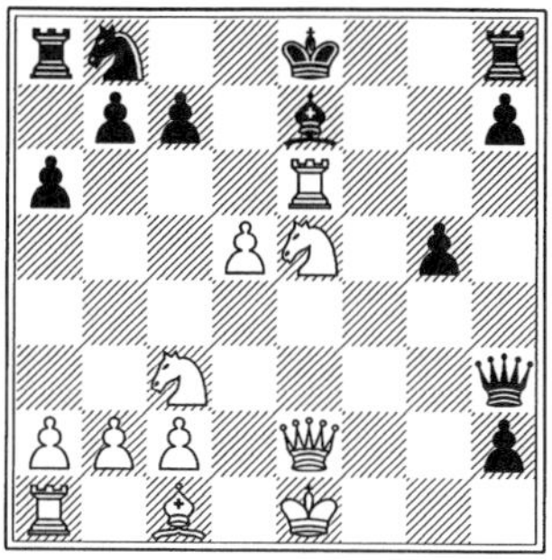

16.♖:e7+ ♔:e7 17.♗:g5+ ♔d6 18.♘e4+ ♔:d5 19.0-0-0+ ♔e6 20.♘f2 ♕g2 21.♘g6+ 1:0, Johansson - Nilsson, Malmö 1997.

• 4...♗g4 5.d4 g5?! 6.h4 ♘c6 7.c3 g:h4 8.♗:f4 ♕f6 9.♗g5 ♕g6 10.♘bd2 ♘f6 11.♕b3 ♗:f3 12.♕:b7! ♕:g5 13.♕:c6+ ±, Nazarenus - Giretti, Budapest 1996.

• 4...♘c6 5.d4 ♗g4 6.♗:f4 ♘f6 7.♘c3 ♗e7 (7...♘:e4?! 8.♗:f7+ ♔:f7 9.♘:e4 ♗:f3 (9...♗e7 10.0-0 ±) 10.♕:f3 ♘:d4? 11.♕h5+ ♔e6 12.0-0-0 g6 13.♘c5+ ±) 8.♕d3 0-0 9.0-0-0 ♘a5 10.h3 ♗:f3 11.g:f3 ♘h5 12.♗d2 ♗g5 13.♗b3 ♘:b3+ 14.a:b3 c6 15.♖hg1 ♗:d2+ 16.♕:d2 ♕f6 17.♕g5! ± ♕:g5+ 18.♖:g5 g6 19.d5 c5 20.♘b5 ♖fd8 21.e5 f6 22.♖:h5 g:h5 23.♘:d6 ♖d7 24.♘e4 1:0, Westerinen - Kraidman, Gausdal 1995.

• 4...♘f6 5.d3!? (Spending a tempo to avoid worrying about the knight trick. 5.♘c3 will probably transpose to Westerinen - Kraidman above - *Spendiert ein Tempo, um sich über ein mögliches Scheinopfer auf e4 keine Gedanken mehr machen zu müssen. 5.♘c3 dürfte zur ebengesehenen Partie Westerinen - Kraidman führen*) 5...♗e7 6.0-0 ♗g4 7.♗:f4 ♘bd7 8.♘c3 ♘h5 9.♕d2 0-0 10.d4 ♗e6 11.♘d5 c6 12.♘:e7+ ♕:e7 13.d5 c:d5 14.♗:d5 ±, Sage - Windey, Viborg 1996.

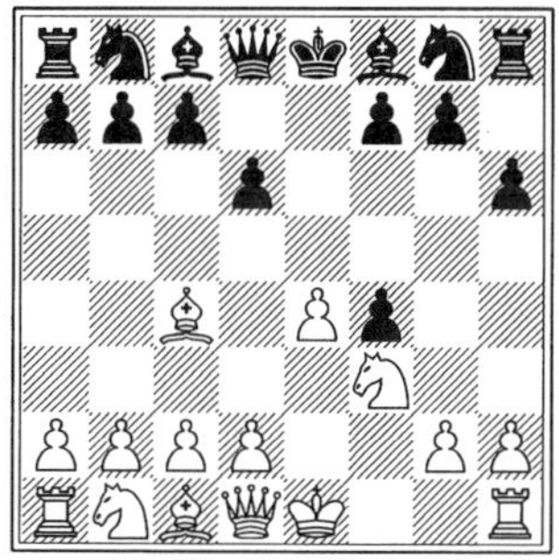

Position after 4...h6/*Nach 4...h6*

White now has two interesting options: *Nun hat Weiß zwei interessante Möglichkeiten:*

I

5.b3!?

This looks quite natural when you've studied 4.b3 in the Becker, but it may have quite some impact on your opponent, since after 4.♗c4 he was expecting a Hanstein and an advantage. Instead, after 5.b3 he finds himself in a dynamic and fluid position and if he doesn't know the Becker he'll know zilch about the position in front of him! *Nach Betrachtung von 4.b3 in der Becker-Verteidigung wirkt dies recht natürlich. Einen gewissen Eindruck auf den Geger, der auf Vorteil im Hanstein-Gambit rechnete, wird dieser Zug dennoch nicht verfehlen. Nach 5.b3 findet dieser sich stattdessen in einer dynamischen und wandlungsfähigen Stellung wieder, über die er nicht das geringste Wissen haben wird, wenn er die Becker-Verteidigung nicht kennt!*

A

5...♘c6 6.♗b2 ♘f6 7.♘c3 ♗e7 8.♕e2 ∞ 0-0

8...♗g4 9.♘d5 ♘e5 10.♘:f4 ♘:c4 11.♕:c4 ♕d7 12.0-0 (Castling queenside is not quite as essential here since Black can't open the position as easily with ...d5 as he could in the Becker - *Zur langen Rochade besteht hier keine Notwendigkeit; Schwarz kann hier die Stellung nicht so leicht wie in der Becker-Verteidigung mit ...d5 aufbrechen*) 12...♗e6 13.♘:e6 f:e6

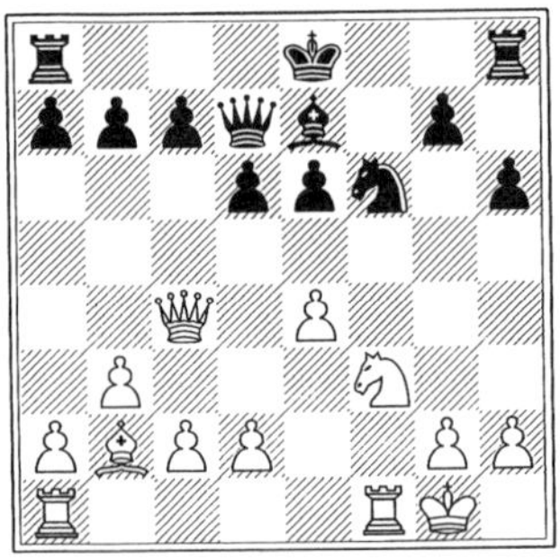

14.e5! d:e5 (Trying to close the position with 14...d5 leaves the e6-pawn weak - *Der Versuch, die Stellung mit 14...d5 abzuschließen, würde einen schwächlichen ♙e6 zurücklassen:* 15.♕e2 ♘e4 16.♘d4 Δ ♕g4, ♕h5+) 15.♘:e5 ♕d5 16.♕:d5 ♘:d5 17.♘g6 ♖g8 18.♘:e7 ♘:e7 19.♖ae1 0-0-0 20.♖:e6 ♘c6 21.♗c3 ♖d7 22.♖f4 ♔d8 23.♖g4 h5 24.♖g5 ♘d4 25.♗:d4 ♖:d4 26.d3 h4 27.♖eg6 ♖d7 28.♖h5 1:0, Sabel - Weissleder, corr. 1985.

9.0-0-0

But this is certainly the more consistent Royal hide-away.
Hier indes gewiß das programmgemäße königliche Versteck.

9.0-0 ♗g4 10.♘d5 ♘:d5 11.e:d5 ♘e5 12.♕e4 ♗:f3 13.g:f3 ♘:c4 14.♕:c4 ♗f6 15.♗:f6 ♕:f6 16.♔h1 ♖ac8 17.♖ae1 c6 18.c3 ♖fd8 19.♖g1 c:d5 20.♕:d5 ♖c6 21.♕a5 ♖a6 22.♕d5 ♖:a2 23.♖a1 ♖:a1 24.♖:a1 ♖e8 25.♕:b7 ♕h4 26.♖f1 ♕h3 27.♕a6 ♖e5 28.b4 h5 29.♕c4 g6 30.♕a6 ♔g7 31.♕c4 a5 32.b5 a4 33.b6 ♖c5 34.♕d4+ f6 35.♕f2 ♖b5 36.♖g1 ♖b2 37.♕e2 ♔h6 38.♕d3 g5 39.♖a1 d5 40.♕:d5 ♖:b6 41.♔g1 a3 42.♕d4 ♖c6 43.♕f2 ♖a6 44.♕e2 ♖b6 45.♕d3 ♕e6 46.♔f2 ♖d6 47.♕e2 ♕b3 48.♕d1 ♕b2 49.♔e2 ♖:d2+ 50.♕:d2 ♕:a1 51.♕d8 ♕:c3 52.♕h8+, ½:½/56., Mulder BP - COMP Rex, Computer World-Ch, 1989.

9...♘e5

9...♗g4 10.d4 ♘d7 11.♔b1 ♘b6 12.♘d5 ♘:d5 13.e:d5 (It definitely looks wrong to block both one's bishops just to regain the pawn - *Es ist mit Sicherheit verkehrt, sich selbst beide Läufer zu blockieren, nur um den Bauern zurückzugewinnen.* 13.♗:d5 ♘b4 14.♗c4 looks more interesting - *scheint interessanter*) 13...♘b8 14.♕e4 ♗g5 15.♖de1 ♘d7 16.♘:g5 h:g5 17.h4 ♖e8 18.♕:e8+ ♕:e8 19.♖:e8+ ♖:e8 20.h:g5 ½:½, Wennström - Lindfors, corr. 1978.

10.d4 ♘:c4 11.b:c4

11.♕:c4 ♘:e4=.

11...♘g4

11...c6 12.e5 (12.g3!? f:g3 13.♕g2 g:h2 14.♖:h2 →, 12...d5 13.c:d5 c:d5 14.e5 ♘h5 15.♕g2 (Δ g4) g6 16.♘e2 ⩱) 12...♘g4 ⩱ 13.d5 d:e5 14.d:c6 ♕a5 15.c:b7 ♗:b7 16.♖d7 ♗:f3 17.g:f3 ♗a3

18.♘d5 ♗:b2+ 19.♔:b2 ♖ab8+ 20.♔a1 ♕a3 21.c3 ♘e3 23.♖c7 ♖fd8 23.♖b1 ♖:b1+ 24.♔:b1 ♖b8+ 25.♔a1 ♕c1+ 0:1, Sabel - Airas, corr. 1984.

12.♖dg1

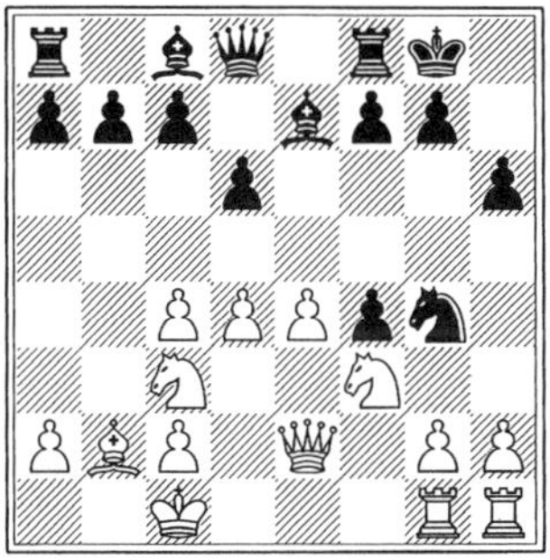

An admirably consistent approach, aim everything at the king and something will turn up!
Ein in seiner Folgerichtigkeit bemerkenswerter Ansatz: Alles wird auf den gegnerischen König geworfen, und irgend etwas wird sich dabei schon ergeben!

12...f5 13.g3 f:e4 14.♘:e4 ♗f5 15.g:f4 ♗:e4 16.♕:e4 ♕d7 17.♖g2 ♖ae8 18.♖hg1 h5 19.h3 ♗g5 20.♕d5+ ♔h8 21.♕:g5+ 1:0, Memphis Chess Club - Nashville Chess Club, corr. 1981.

B

(1.e4 e5 2.f4 e:f4 3.♘f3 d6 4.♗c4 h6 5.b3)

5...♗g4 6.♗b2 ♘d7 7.0-0

White has two interesting alternatives:
Weiß verfügt hier über zwei interessante Alternativen:

- 7.♘c3!? (Δ ♕e2, 0-0-0)
- • • 7...♘b6 8.0-0.
- • • 7...c6 8.♕e2 ♘e5 9.0-0-0.
- • • 7...♘e5? 8.♘:e5! ♕h4+ 9.g3 f:g3 10.♗:f7+ ♔d8 11.♕:g4 +−.
- 7.d4!?
- • • 7...♗e7 8.♘c3 ♗h4+ 9.♔f1 ± (White can lay f4 under siege with ♘e2 and ♕d2 or open files with ♘e2, ♕d3, g3 - *Weiß kann f4 belagern mit ♘e2 nebst ♕d2 oder aber Linien öffnen durch ♘e2, ♕d3, g3).*
- • • 7...♗:f3 8.♕:f3 ♕h4+ (This is just what White has been dreaming about! - *Genau das hat sich Weiß erhofft!*) 9.g3 f:g3 10.h:g3 ♕f6 11.♕d3 → Δ ♖f1, ♘c3, 0-0-0 (11.♕e3 ♘b6 ∞).

7...c6 8.♔h1?!

This must be an enormous waste of time, hiding the king from invisible perils when he could spend the time to build up for the thematic e5-break.
Was für eine Zeitverschwendung! Weiß schützt seinen König vor nicht erkennbaren Gefahren, wo er doch seine Zeit zur Vorbereitung des thematischen Vorstoßes e5 nützen könnte!

8...♕e7 9.h3?

A weakening waste of time, it's a miracle that White doesn't lose this game!
Diesmal nicht nur überflüssige Zeitverschwendung, sondern zugleich eine Schwächung seiner eigenen Stellung! Es ist ein Wunder, daß Weiß diese Partie nicht verliert.

9...♗h5 10.♕e1 ♘e5 11.♘h4!? f3 12.g:f3 ♘:c4 13.b:c4 ♕e6 14.♘f5 ♘e7 15.♘c3 0-0-0 16.♘e2 ♘:f5 17.♘f4 ♕d7 18.♘:h5 ♘e3 19.♕:e3 ♕:h3+ 20.♔g1 ♕:h5 21.♕:a7 ♕g5+ 22.♔h1, and Black used his checks to draw *(und Schwarz nahm die Gelegenheit zum Dauerschach wahr)* ½:½, Yurmayev - Timoshenko, Tbilisi 1980.

C

(1.e4 e5 2.f4 e:f4 3.♘f3 d6 4.♗c4 h6 5.b3)

5...♗e6

I haven't found any example of ...♗e6 on move five or later. Generally speaking I think White should continue his usual build-up with 6.♕e2 etc and if Black trades bishops the pawn recapture b:c4 looks preferable, to control d5. Especially if Black is planning to castle queenside it will come in handy since he will have to expose his king with c6 if he wants to achieve the d5-break, which looks like the only way for Black to get counter-play.

Zu ...♗e6 - jetzt oder später - konnte ich kein einziges Beispiel finden. Ein paar allgemeine Erwägungen: Weiß sollte mit seiner üblichen Aufstellung - 6.♕e2 usw. - fortfahren, und falls Schwarz zum Läufertausch greift, mit b:c4 (zwecks Kontrolle von d5) zurückschlagen. Dies wird insbesondere dann gelegen kommen, wenn Schwarz zum Damenflügel rochiert. Um den Durchbruch ...d5 zu verwirklichen - was andererseits die einizige Gegenspielmöglichkeit zu sein scheint -, müßte er dann seinen König entblößen.

II

(1.e4 e5 2.f4 e:f4 3.♘f3 d6 4.♗c4 h6)

5.d3!?

Another new idea of Gallagher's which also keeps the position highly dynamic! The King's knight can now go to d4 instead of having to start afresh from g1, and e4 is securely defended. The downside is that the knight will need some support from the c-pawn slowing down the other knight's development.

Eine weitere neue Idee von Gallagher, mit welcher Weiß das Spiel dynamisch hält! Anstelle des im Hanstein-Gambit notwendigen Neustarts von g1 aus kann der Königsspringer nach d4 ausweichen, und der ♙e4 ist zuverlässig geschützt. Ein Manko ist, daß der Springer des Schutzes durch den c-Bauern bedarf, was die Entwicklung des Damenspringers verzögert.

5...g5 6.g3!

The pawn chain should be challenged before it's consolidated!

Weiß sollte die Bauernkette angreifen, bevor diese sich konsolidiert hat.

6.♗d2!? ♗g7 7.♗c3 ♘f6 (7...♗:c3 8.♘:c3 ♘f6 9.h4 ♖g8 10.h:g5 h:g5 11.g3! f:g3 12.♕d2 ♘g4 13.♖h7 ±) 8.h4 g4 9.♘g1 (9.♘d4, 9.e5!?) 0-0! 10.♘e2 f3 11.g:f3 g:f3 12.♘f4 ♗g4 13.♕d2 h5 14.♖g1 ∞.

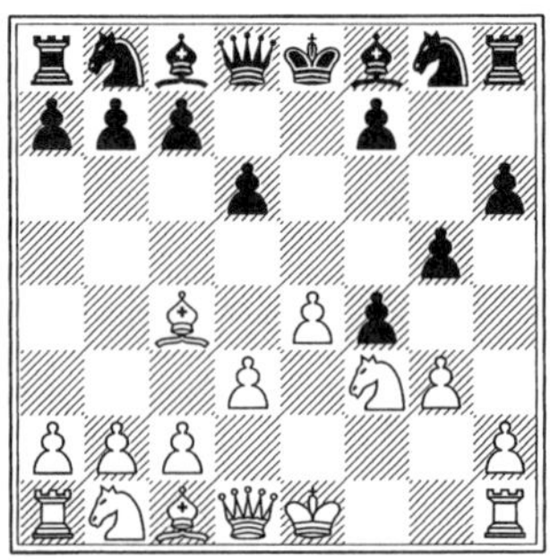

A

6...f:g3 7.h:g3 ♗g7

7...♗g4 8.♗:g5! h:g5 9.♖:h8 ♘h6 10.♘c3 ♕f6 11.♖:f8+ ♔:f8 12.♘d5!, Bhend - Issler, corr. 1970.

8.♘:g5 h:g5 9.♖:h8 ♗:h8 10.♕h5 ♕f6 11.♘c3 c6 12.♗:g5 ♕g7 13.0-0-0

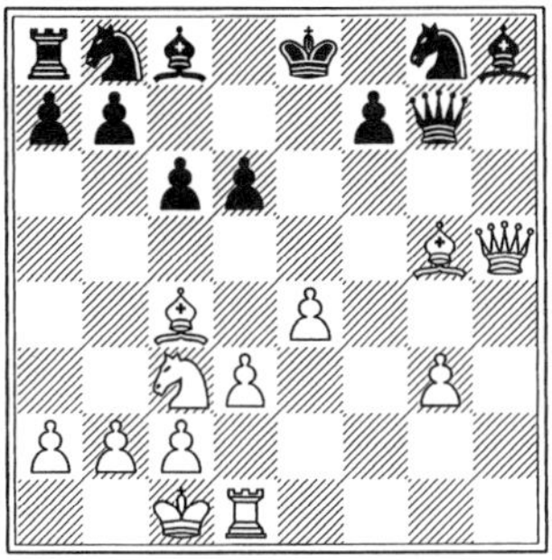

± (Gallagher)

B

(1.e4 e5 2.f4 e:f4 3.♘f3 d6 4.♗c4 h6 5.d3 g5 6.g3)

6...♘c6 7.g:f4 g4

7...♗g4 8.♖g1! ♘f6 9.f:g5 ♘e5

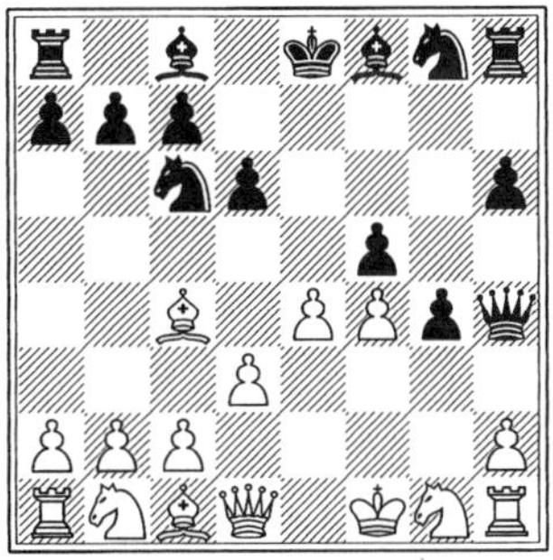

10.♘:e5! (Gallagher), e.g. *(z.B.)*: 10...♗:d1 11.♗:f7+ ♔e7 12.g:f6+ ♔:f6 13.♖g6+ ♔:e5 14.♔:d1 ♕h4 15.♗e3 ♕h3 16.♔d2 ♖h7 17.♘c3 ♕:h2+ (17...c5? 18.♖af1 +−) 18.♘e2 ♕:e2+ 19.♔:e2 ♖:f7 20.♗:h6 ♗:h6 21.♖:h6 and the presence of two rooks each, gives White a good chance of converting his pawn plus to a full point *(und da sich jeweils noch zwei Türme auf dem Brett befinden, hat Weiß gute Chancen, sein Bauernplus in einen vollen Punkt umzumünzen).*

8.♘g1 ♕h4+ 9.♔f1 f5!?

9...♘f6 10.♔g2 ♘h5 (10...♖g8 11.♘c3 g3 12.h3 h5 13.♘ce2) 11.♘c3 g3 12.♕e1! ♖g8 13.h3 ± (Gallagher).

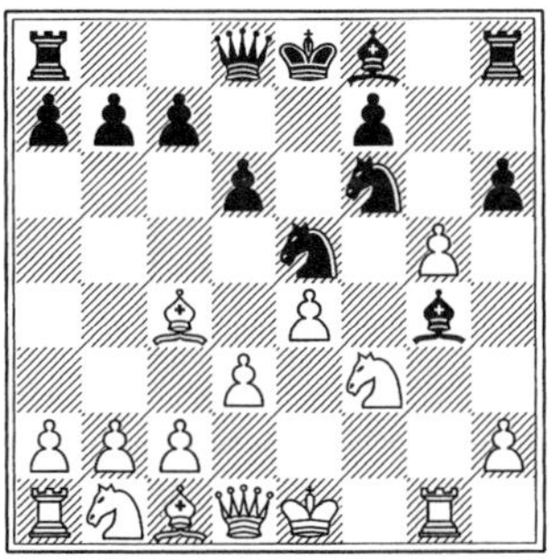

10.♘c3!?

Showing no fear for his reputed opponent, I would probably have preferred 10.♕e1.
Zeigt keinerlei Respekt vor dem großen Namen seines Gegners. Ich hätte wahrscheinlich 10.♕e1 bevorzugt.

10...♘f6 11.♔g2 f:e4 12.d:e4 ♗d7 13.h3 ♘h5 14.h:g4 ♕g3+ 15.♔f1 ♘:f4

15...♗:g4 16.♕d5 ∞.

16.♕f3 ♕:f3+ 17.♘:f3 ♘g6 18.g5 ♗g4 19.♗e2 0-0-0 20.g:h6 ♗e7 21.♖g1 ♗h5 22.♗e3 ♖df8 23.♔e1 ♘f4 24.♘d4 ♘:e2 25.♘c:e2 ♘e5 26.♖h1 ♗g6 27.♘g3 ♘g4 28.♔e2 ♘:e3 29.♔:e3 ♗g5+ 30.♔e2 ♖e8 31.♘df5 d5 32.♔f3 d:e4+ 33.♘:e4 ♗e7 34.♘:e7+ ♖:e7 35.♘g5 ♖f8+ 36.♔g4 ♖e2 37.♖ag1 ♗f5+ 38.♔g3 ♗:c2 39.h7 ♗:h7 40.♖:h7 ♖:b2 41.♖c1 c6

42.♘e4 ♔b8 43.♘c5 ♖g8+ 44.♔f3 a5 45.♖d1 ♖g5 46.♖c1 ♖b5 47.♘e4 ♖g8 48.♖c5 ♖b4 49.♖:a5 ♖f8+ 50.♔e3 ♖e8 51.♖h4 b5 52.♖a3 ♔c7 53.♖c3 ♖a4 54.♖c2 = ½:½/64.), Belotti - Beliavsky, Reggio Emilia 1996.

This game illustrates both the importance of keeping a cool head in the complications however threatening it looks and the resilience of White's seemingly shaky position from the opening.

Diese Partie zeigt zweierlei: Zum einen, daß es notwendig ist, in verwickelter Lage kühlen Kopf zu bewahren - ganz gleich, wie bedrohlich die Situation erscheint. Zum anderen demonstriert sie eindrücklich die der löchrig scheinenden weißen Stellung innewohnende Spannkraft.

C

(1.e4 e5 2.f4 e:f4 3.♘f3 d6 4.♗c4 h6 5.d3 g5 6.g3)

6...♗h3 7.♕e2

Or *(oder)* 7.♕d2 (Lane).

7...g4 8.♘h4 f3 9.♕f2
± (Gallagher)

D

(1.e4 e5 2.f4 e:f4 3.♘f3 d6 4.♗c4 h6 5.d3 g5 6.g3)

6...g4 7.♘d4 ♗g7

7...f3 8.c3 ♘c6 9.♗f4!? (9.♕b3 ♘e5 10.♗f4 ♘:c4 ∞)

- 9...♘a5 10.♘d2 ♘:c4 11.♕a4+.
- 9...♘:d4 10.c:d4 ♗g7 11.♕b3 ♕e7 12.♘c3 c6 13.d5!? b5 14.♗:b5 ∞.

8.c3 f3 9.♕b3 ♕d7

9...♕e7? 10.♘f5 ♗:f5 11.♕:b7 ♘f6 12.♗b5+ +– Gallagher.

10.♗f4 ♘c6

10...d5 11.♗:d5 ♗:d4 (11...c6 12.♗:b8 c:d5 13.♘f5 →) 12.c:d4 c6 13.♘c3! ± Gallagher.

11.♘f5 ♗e5 12.♘d2 ♘a5 13.♕b4 ♘:c4 14.♘:c4 ♗:f4 15.g:f4 ♘e7 16.♘ce3 ♘:f5 17.♘:f5 c5! 18.♕b5! ±/∞

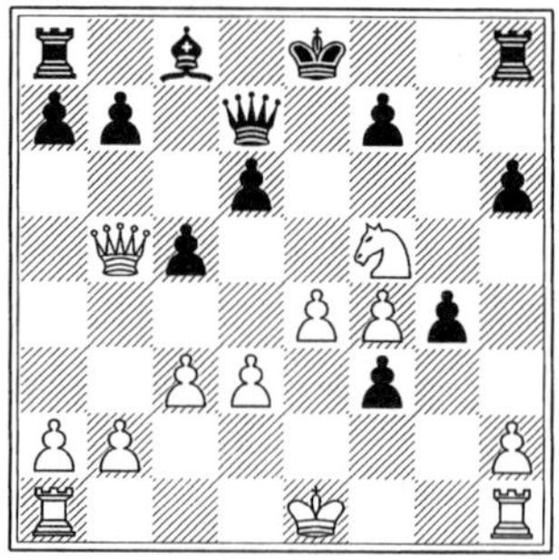

Gallagher - Flear, Paris 1990 (½:½/30.).

E

(1.e4 e5 2.f4 e:f4 3.♘f3 d6 4.♗c4 h6 5.d3 g5 6.g3)

6...♗g7 7.g:f4

7.c3 should transpose to **D** above.
*7.c3 sollte zu **D** überleiten.*

7...g4 8.♘g1 ♕h4+ 9.♔f1??

White's affairs seem to be in order after
Die weiße Sache scheint o.k. nach
9.♔e2! g3 10.♘f3 ♗g4 11.c3 g2 12.♖g1 ♕:h2 13.♔f2!?

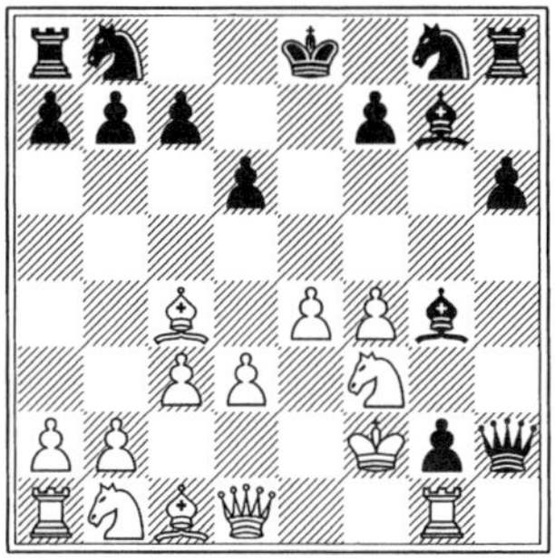

White's centre and better pawn structure gives him the advantage. If you're going to play 5.d3 I must advice you to be very careful where you put your king!
Zentrum und bessere Bauernstruktur geben Weiß den Vorteil. Wenn Sie 5.d3 spielen möchten, so muß ich Sie warnen, sich jeden Schritt mit dem König genau zu überlegen!

9...g3 10.h3 g2+! 11.♔:g2 ♗d4! –+

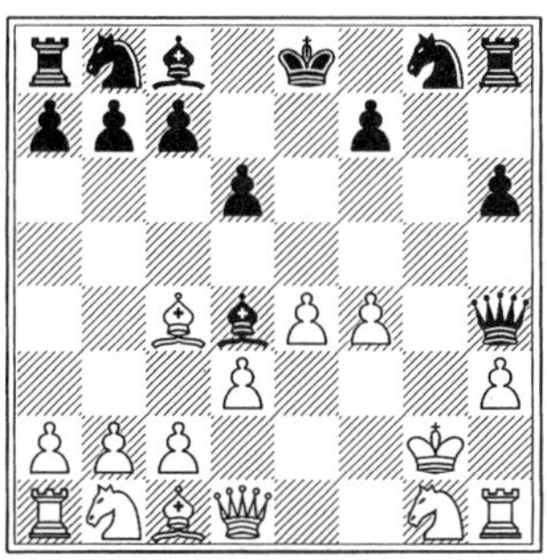

12.♖h2 ♘f6 13.♘f3 ♖g8+ 14.♔h1 ♕h5 15.♕f1 ♕:f3+ 0:1, Johansson - Bergström, Karlskrona 1996.

If you find yourself preferring White's set-up against the Fischer to the one used against the Becker, it may be possible to transpose between these, e.g:
Falls Ihnen die hier gezeigte weiße Aufstellung mehr zusagt als die gegen die Becker-Verteidigung empfohlene, so sind eventuell Überleitungen möglich, z.B.:

3...h6 4.♗c4 g5 (4...d6 is of course the Fischer - *wäre natürlich die Fischer-Verteidigung*) 5.♘e5 ♖h7 6.d4 (An hypersharp alternative is - *eine hyperscharfe Alternative ist* 6.0-0 d6 7.♘g6!? ♗g7 8.♕h5 ♘f6 9.♗:f7+ ♔:f7 10.♘e5+ ♔g8?? 11.♕f7+ ♔h8 12.♘g6#, Nyman - Arasola, Helsinki 1952, the only practical test I've found; after 10...♔e6 I guess White intended 11.♕f7+ ♔:e5 12.d4+ with an attack that better be decisive ... - *das einzige praktische Beispiel, das ich finden konnte; nach 10...♔e6 beabsichtigte Weiß wohl 11.♕f7+ ♔:e5 12.d4+ mit Angriff, der hoffentlich auch durchschlägt* ...) 6...d6 7.♘d3! ♘f6 8.♘f2! d5 9.e:d5 ♘:d5 10.0-0 ♗e6 11.♖e1 ± (Schlechter).

By the way, if you feel like trying the b3 systems but your opponents won't give you the chance, you might want to practise with something similar against the Sicilian!
That is:
1.e4 c5 2.b3 ♘c6 3.♗b2 e5 4.f4 e:f4 5.♘f3 which supposedly is good for Black according to Gallagher in 'Beating the Anti-Sicilians'.
I can't say that I understand the logic in this, since the only advantage of c5 is that it makes d4 less attractive, but as we've seen above d4 is hardly of top priority for White. The drawbacks of c5 seems more important to me, it weakens d5 and d6 and it takes away some

'transposing' opportunities for Black, like declining the gambit with ...♗c5 or playing ...d5 and ...c6 á la Nimzowitsch.
I propose that you meet 5...♘f6 with 6.♘c3 (6.e5 ♘e4!? 7.♕e2 ♘g5) 6...♗e7 7.♗c4 ♘h5 8.♕e2 ♗h4+ 9.g3 f:g3 10.0-0-0 which looks promising for White ...

Ich schlage vor, daß Sie 5...♘f6 mit 6.♘c3 beantworten (6.e5 ♘e4!? 7.♕e2 ♘g5), was nach 6...♗e7 7.♗c4 ♘h5 8.♕e2 ♗h4+ 9.g3 f:g3 10.0-0-0 aussichtsreich für Weiß aussieht.

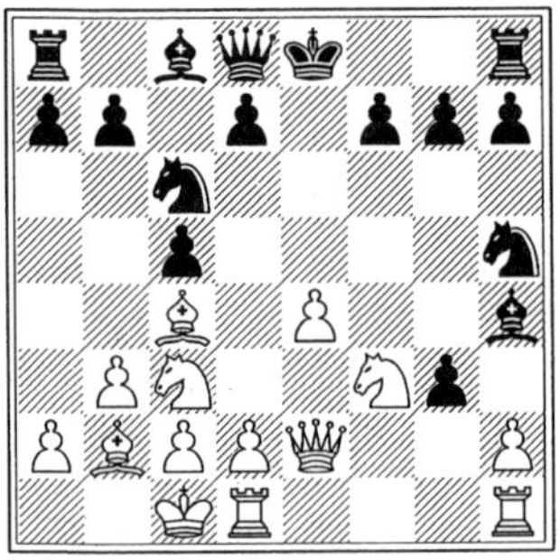

Nebenbei, wenn Sie gerne b3-Systeme ausprobieren würden, Ihr Gegner Ihnen jedoch nicht die Möglichkeit dazu gibt, könnten Sie vielleicht etwas Ähnliches gegen die Sizilianische Verteidigung versuchen!
Und zwar:
1.e4 c5 2.b3 ♘c6 3.♗b2 e5 4.f4 e:f4 5.♘f3, was laut Gallaghers "Beating the Anti-Sicilians" gut für Schwarz sein soll. Ich vermag Ihnen jedoch nicht zu sagen, aufgrund welcher Logik dies so sein soll: Der einzige Vorteil von c5 ist, daß hiernach d4 weniger attraktiv ist, doch wie wir gesehen haben, ist d4 ohnehin kaum erste Wahl von Weiß. Die Nachteile von c5 scheinen mir schwerwiegender, d5 und d6 sind geschwächt, und außerdem sind diverse Abweichungen unmöglich, wie z.B. die Ablehnung des Gambits mit ...♗c5 oder ...d5 und ...c6 á la Nimzowitsch.

Chapter VIII *Kapitel VIII*

The Nameless 3...♘c6 Defence

Die Verteidigung 3...♘c6

1.e4 e5 2.f4 e:f4 3.♘f3 ♘c6

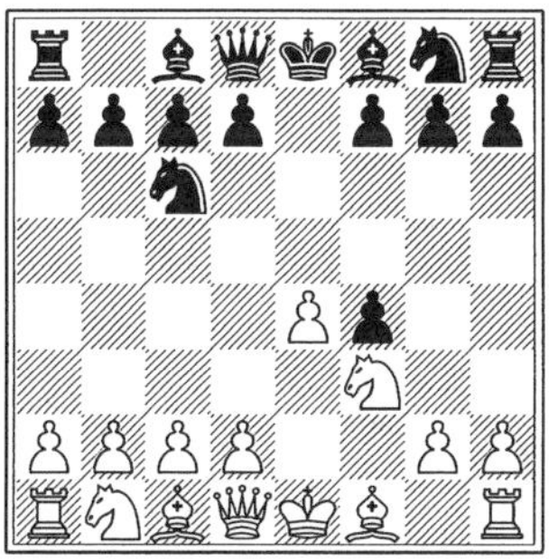

This is actually one of Black's better defences, which makes it a bit peculiar that it's mainly employed by lower rated players. But this will probably change since it is already played frequently in correspondence chess.

Dies ist tatsächlich eine der stärkeren schwarzen Verteidigungen, was es ein wenig merkwürdig erscheinen läßt, daß sie hauptsächlich von schwächeren Spielern angewandt wird. Dies wird sich wahrscheinlich jedoch schon bald ändern, im Fernschach wird 3...♘c6 bereits häufig gespielt.

4.d4!?

This natural move is in fact a rather new approach, traditionally White has usually chosen to transpose to the Vienna with 4.♘c3 but this entails learning loads of theory and also involves a knight sacrifice in either the Hamppe-Allgaier Gambit:

Dieser natürliche Zug ist tatsächlich ein ziemlich neuer Versuch. Die herkömmliche Antwort ist 4.♘c3 mit Überleitung zur Wiener Partie, doch dies erfordert ein umfangreiches Theoriestudium, beinhaltend ein Figurenopfer entweder im Hamppe-Allgaier-Gambit:

4...g5 5.h4 g4 6.♘g5 h6 7.♘:f7 ♔:f7 8.d4

or the Pierce Gambit:

oder aber im Pierce-Gambit:

4...g5 5.d4 g4 6.♗c4 g:f3 7.0-0 ♘:d4 8.♗:f4 (8.♕:d4? ♕g5 –+).

4...d5!

This is the only critical move.

Die einzig kritische Antwort.

- 4...g5 5.d5! g4 6.d:c6 g:f3

Here Bilguer gives *(Bilguer gibt hier an:)* 7.c:d7+ ♗:d7 8.♕:f3 ♕h4+ 9.g3 f:g3 10.h:g3 ♕g4 =; but I think White can do better, e.g *(doch m.E. kann Weiß stärker spielen, z.B.)* 7.♕:f3 d:c6 8.♗:f4 ♗g7 9.♗c4! ± (if - *falls* - 9...♗:b2 10.♗e5 +–).

- 4...♘f6 5.e5 ♘d5 6.♗c4 ♘b6 7.♗b3 d6 (This is reminiscent of an Alekhine's defence, except that f7 is much weaker here since Black can't blunt the a2-f7 diagonal with e6 anymore - *Dies erinnert an die Aljechin-Verteidigung - mit dem Unterschied, daß f7 hier viel anfälliger ist, da Schwarz die Diagonale a2-g8 nicht mehr mit e6 verstopfen kann)*

• • 8.♗:f4 d:e5 9.♗:e5 ♘:e5 10.♕e2 ♘bd7 11.0-0 f6 12.d:e5 ♗c5+ 13.♔h1 ♕e7 14.e6 ♘f8 15.♖e1 c6 16.♘c3 ♗d6 17.♖ad1 ♗b4 18.♘h4 g6 19.♘f3 ♗a5

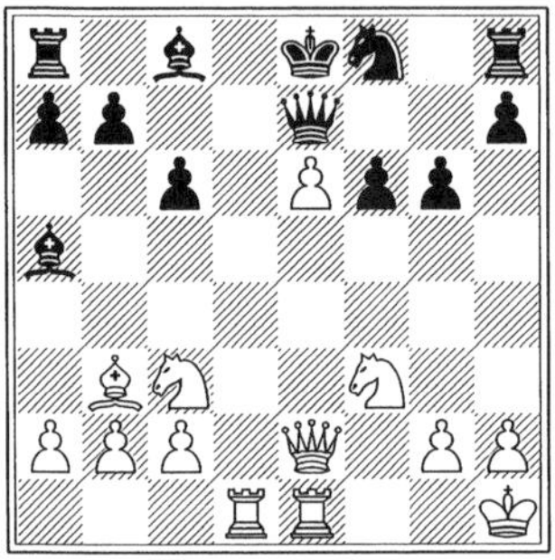

20.♘d5! c:d5 21.♕b5+ ♘d7 22.e:d7+ ♗:d7 23.♖:e7+ 1:0, Uzunov - Bogaev, Donetzk 1974.

• • 8.0-0 ♘a5 9.♗:f4 ♘:b3 10.a:b3 ♗e7 11.♕e1 0-0 12.♕g3 ♔h8 13.c4±, Fongers - Cleven, Duisburg 1992.

5.e:d5 ♕:d5

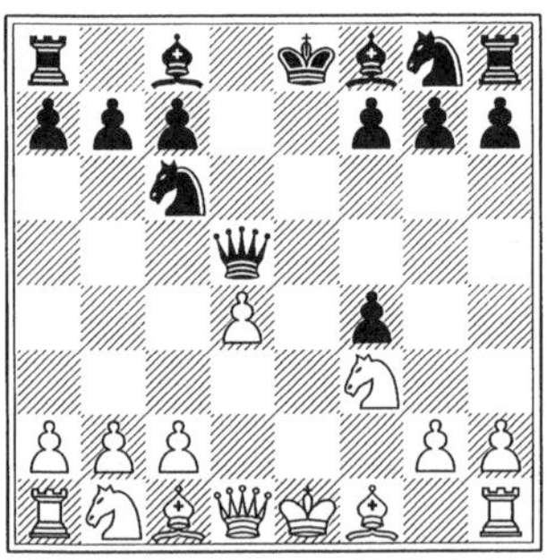

Black hopes he's got an improved Scandinavian and White reckons he'll get the bishop pair in an open position.
Schwarz hofft ein verbessertes Skandinavisch zu erhalten, und Weiß meint, er erhält das Läuferpaar in einer offenen Stellung.

I

6.♗:f4 ♗g4

Just like in the Scandinavian, Chigorin's and Nimzowitsch's defence both sides have to make strong, natural and obvious developing moves for a while.
Wie in der Skandinavischen, Tschigorin- und Nimzowitsch-Verteidigung führen beide Seiten eine Zeitlang natürliche, starke und auf der Hand liegende Entwicklungszüge aus.

6...♗d6 7.♗:d6 ♕:d6 8.♘c3 ♘f6 9.♗c4 ♗e6 10.d5 ♕b4 11.♕e2 ♕:b2 12.0-0! ♕:c3 13.d:e6 0-0 14.e:f7+ ♔h8 15.♖ab1 ♘a5 16.♗e6 ♘c6 17.♖b3 ♕c5+ 18.♔h1 ♘d8 19.♘e5! ♘:e6 20.♖h3! 1:0, Pinto - Barroso, corr. 1988.

7.♘c3

Perhaps 7.♗e2 0-0-0 8.♘c3 ♗b4 9.0-0 is a more exact move-order, since Black will only have the option ...♗:c3 once here and this will open the b-file against his king.
Vielleicht ist 7.♗e2 0-0-0 8.♘c3 ♗b4 9.0-0 die genauere Zugfolge - Schwarz hat dann nur einmal die Gelegenheit zu ...♗:c3, und dies wird bereits die b-Linie gegen den eigenen König öffnen.

7...♗b4

7...♕e6+ 8.♕e2 ±.

8.♗e2 0-0-0

8...♗:c3+ 9.b:c3 ♕a5 10.0-0!? ♕:c3 ∞.

9.0-0 ♕d7

9...♕a5 10.♘g5 ♗:e2 11.♘:e2 ±.

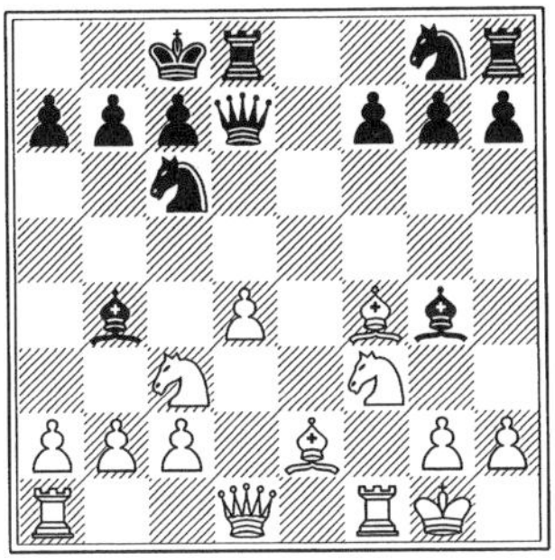

10.d5!?

Δ 10...♘ce7 11.♘e5.

Maybe White shouldn't force an endgame, and instead aim for a build up on the queenside with 10.♘b5!?:
Vielleicht sollte Weiß kein Endspiel erzwingen, sondern ein Spiel am Damenflügel aufbauen mit 10.♘b5!?:

- 10...♗a5 11.c3 a6 12.♘a3 ♗b6 13.♘c4 ♗a7 14.b4 ⩲ (14.♘ce5 ⩲)
White's pawn storm will roll on and all he has to watch out for is a good piece sac on d4 by Black, but a bad one is of course quite welcome!
Der weiße Bauernsturm wird weiterrollen, in Acht nehmen muß er sich lediglich davor, daß der Nachziehende unter günstigen Umständen eine Figur auf d4 opfert (ein Opfer unter ungünstigen Umständen wäre natürlich willkommen!).
- 10...♗:f3 11.♗:f3 ♘:d4 12.♘:d4 ♕:d4 13.♕:d4 (Δ ♗e5) ±.
- 10...a6 11.♘:c7 ♗:f3 12.♖:f3!? ♘:d4 13.♖d3 ♗c5 (13...♘f6 14.♘:a6! b:a6 15.♖c3+) 14.♔h1 ♘e7 15.c3 ♘g6 16.♗g3 ♘:e2 17.♖:d7 ♘:g3+ 18.h:g3 ♖:d7 19.♘d5 ♖hd8 20.c4 ⩲.

10...♗:c3

10...♗:f3 11.♗:f3 ♗c5+ 12.♔h1 ♘d4 13.♗e3 ± Gallagher, e.g (*z.B.*): 13...♘:f3 14.♗:c5 ♘e5 15.♗:a7; Bangiev prefers *(gibt den Vorzug)*: 13.♗g4 f5 14.♗e3 f:g4 15.♗:d4 ♗:d4 16.♕:d4 ♔b8 17.a4 ♘f6 18.♘b5 →.

11.d:c6 ♕:c6

11...♕:d1 12.♖a:d1 ♗f6 13.c:b7+ ♔:b7 14.♖:d8 ♗:d8 15.♗c4 ±.

12.♘e5!!

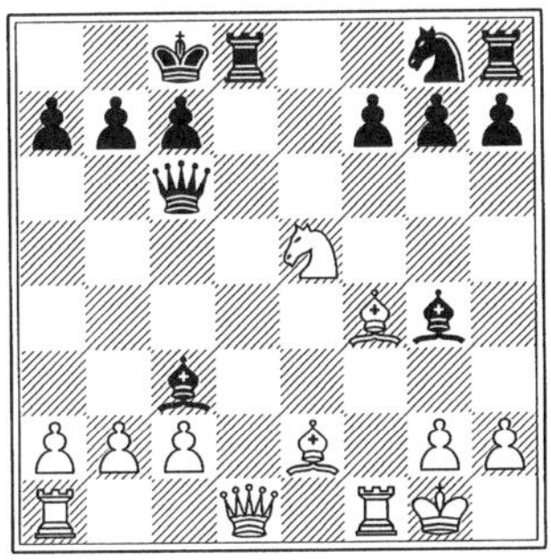

- **12...♗:e2 13.♘:c6! ♖:d1**

13...♗:d1 14.♘:a7+ (14.♘:d8 ♗d4+ 15.♔h1 ♗h5 ∓) 14...♔b8 15.♘b5! ♗e2 16.♗:c7+ ♔c8 17.♘:c3 ♗:f1 18.♗:d8 ♗:g2 19.♔:g2 ♔:d8 20.♖d1+ ♔c8 21.♘d5 ⩲ Gallagher.

14.♘:a7+ ♔b8 15.♖f:d1 ♔:a7

15... ♗:d1 16.♘b5 ♗:c2 17.b:c3 ±.

16.♖d8! ⩲ (Gallagher)

White's activity compensates for the material deficit, e.g: *(die weiße Aktivität kompensiert das materielle Defizit, z.B.:)* 16...♗f6 17.♗e3+ b6 (17...♔a6 may be better, but after 18.♖a8+ it takes some time for Black to get his troops out - *17...♔a6 ist vielleicht stärker, obgleich es nach 18.♖a8+ einige Zeit dauern wird, bis Schwarz seine Truppen ins Spiel bringen kann)* 18.♖d7 ♗e5 (not - *nicht* - 18...♗:b2 19.♖b1 ♗e5 20.♖:b6 +–) 19.♖:f7 ⩲.

- **12...♕c5+ 13.♔h1 ♗:e2**

13...♗e6 14.♘d3, 13...♖:d1 14.♗:g4+

♔b8 15.♖a:d1 ♘f6 16.b:c3 +–.
14.♕:e2 ♗:e5
14...♗:b2? 15.♘d3!.
15.♗:e5 ♘f6 16.♗:f6 g:f6 17.♖:f6 =/∞
If White could trade queens he may have some winning chances in the rook ending thanks to the weak f-pawn, e.g:
Wenn es Weiß gelingen würde, die Damen zu tauschen, hätte er vielleicht dank des schwachen ♙f7 Gewinnchancen im Endspiel, z.B.:
17...♖he8 18.♕f2 ♕a5 19.♖:f7 ♖d2 20.♖e1 ♖ed8 21.♕g3 Δ h3, ♖ee7. Black should certainly not get too optimistic, for example: *(Schwarz sollte nun keinesfalls zu optimistisch agieren, etwa:)* 21...♖d1?? 22.♕g4+ ♖1d7 23.♖e8 +–.

• **12...♕b6+ 13.♔h1 ♗:e2**
13...♗e6 14.♘d3 ♗f6 15.a4 ↑.
14.♕:e2 ♗:e5 15.♕g4+ ♕e6 16.♕:e6+ f:e6 17.♗:e5 ♘f6 18.♖:f6! g:f6 19.♗:f6 ♖hf8 20.♗:d8 ♖:d8 21.♖f1 ∞ **♖d2 22.h4 ♖:c2 23.♖f7 ♖:b2 24.♖:h7 c5 25.h5 c4 26.h6 c3 27.♖h8+ ♔d7 28.h7** +– (Gallagher).

II

(1.e4 e5 2.f4 e:f4 3.♘f3 ♘c6 4.d4 d5 5.e:d5 ♕:d5)

6.c4!? ♗b4+

Black must try to stand his ground or be bullied around the board:
Schwarz muß versuchen, sein Revier zu verteidigen, oder er wird rund um das Brett gescheucht:

• 6...♕f5?! 7.♗d3 ♕f6 8.d5 ♘e5 (8...♗b4+ 9.♔f1 ♘e5 [9...♘ce7 10.♕a4+] 10.♘:e5 ♕:e5 11.♕a4+ ±] 9.♕e2 ♗d6 10.c5 ±.
• 6...♕d6 7.d5 ♘e5 8.♕e2 f6 9.♗:f4±.

7.♘c3

No one mentions 7.♘bd2!? it may look clumsy but White retains his pawn structure, blackfielder and castling rights and also threatens 8.d5 ♘ce7 9.♕a4+, which forces Black to either defend the bishop with his queen or trade it for our 'clumsy' knight, e.g:
Nirgendwo wird 7.♘bd2 erwähnt, was plump anmuten mag, doch Weiß behauptet damit eine gesunde Bauernstruktur, den Angriff auf die schwarze Dame sowie sein Rochaderecht und droht auch 8.d5 ♘ce7 9.♕a4+, was den Nachziehenden zwingt, entweder seinen Läufer gedeckt zu halten oder aber den "plumpen" Springer abzutauschen, z.B.:

• 7...♕d6 8.d5 ♘e5 9.♕e2 f6 10.a3 ♗:d2+ 11.♗:d2 ♘ge7 12.♗b4 (12.♗:f4 ♘7g6 13.♗:e5 =/∞) 12...♘:f3+ 13.♕:f3 ♕e5+ 14.♗e2 ♕:b2 15.0-0 ∞ ♘g6 16.♗d3 ♘e5 17.♖ae1 ♕d4+ 18.♔h1 ♔d8 19.♖:e5! f:e5 20.♕h5 h6 21.♕f7 ♗d7 22.♕:g7 ♖e8 23.♗g6 ♕:c4 24.♖e1 f3 25.g:f3 ±.
• 7...♕e4+ 8.♗e2 (Consistently keeping ♕a4+ as a potential threat making 8...♘:d4 impossible. 8.♕e2 ♘f6 may be alright too - *hält konsequenterweise die Drohung ♕a4+ aufrecht und macht damit 8...♘:d4 unmöglich. 8.♕e2 ♘f6 mag gleichfalls in Ordnung sein*) 8...♘f6 9.d5 ♘e5 10.♘:e5 ♗:d2+ 11.♕:d2 ♕:e5 12.♕:f4 ♕e7 13.♕e3 ♘e4?! (13...♕:e3+ 14.♗:e3 0-0 15.♗d4 ⩲) 14.0-0 0-0 15.b3 b6 16.♗b2 ♖e8 17.♕d4 ♘f6 18.♔h1 ♖b8 19.♗d3 b5 20.♗c3 b:c4 20.b:c4 ±, Johansson - Computer (blitz).

The other 7th move alternatives for White isn't too exciting:
Andere 7. Züge reißen nicht vom Hocker:

7.♔f2 ♕d8 8.a3 ♗e7 ∓.
7.♗d2 ♕e4+ 8.♕e2 ♗f5 9.d5 ♗:d2+ 10.♘b:d2 ♕:e2+ 11.♗:e2 ♘b4 12.♘d4 ♘d3+ =/∞, Schotzig - Leisebein, corr. 1985.

7...♕a5

- 7...♕f5 8.♗d3 ♕a5 9.0-0 ±.
- 7...♕h5 8.d5 ♘e5 (8...♗:c3+ 9.b:c3 ♘e5 10.♗:f4 ♘:f3+ 11.♕:f3 ♕:f3 12.g:f3) 9.♕a4+ ♗d7 10.♕:b4 ♘:f3+ 11.g:f3 ♕:f3 12.♕:b7 ± (Bangiev).

8.♗:f4 ♗g4

8...♗:c3+ 9.b:c3 ♕:c3+ 10.♗d2 ♕a3 11.d5 ♘b4 (11...♘ce7 12.♘d4 ♗d7 13.♖b1 0-0-0 14.♗b4 ± Bangiev. On 14...♕:a2 I guess White intends 15.♕c1 e.g: - *Auf 14...♕:a2 beabsichtigt Weiß wie ich vermute 15.♕c1, z.B.* 15...♘f5 16.♖a1 ♖e8+ 17.♗e2 ♖:e2+ 18.♘:e2 ♕b3 ±) 12.♖b1 a5 (12...♘d3+ 13.♗:d3 ♕:d3 14.♔f2 ♕:c4 15.♖e1+ ♘e7 16.♗b4 ±) 13.♘d4 ♕:a2 14.♘b5 (Δ ♘:c7/♘c3) Bangiev.

9.♗e2 0-0-0

- 9...♗:f3?! 10.♗:f3 ♗:c3+ 11.b:c3 ♕:c3+ 12.♔f2 0-0-0 13.♗:c6 b:c6 14.♕g4+ ♔b8

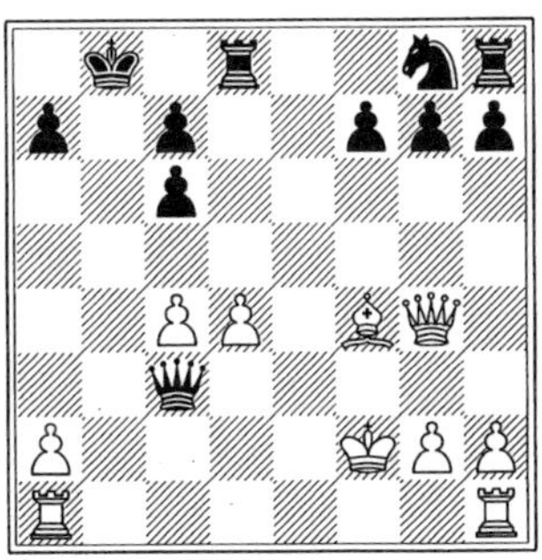

15.♖hd1! (Keeping the rook check in reserve, since the Black king is more vulnerable on b8 - *hebt sich das Turmschach auf, zumal der König auf b8 mehr gefährdet ist*) 15...♘f6 16.♕:g7 ♘h5 17.♗:c7 ♔:c7 18.♕e5 ♔b7 19.♖ab1 1:0, Arizsch - Leisebein, corr. 1988.

- 9...♘f6 10.0-0 0-0 11.♘b5 (Δ ♗:c7, a3) ↑.

10.d5 ♗:f3 11.♗:f3 ♗:c3+ 12.b:c3 ♕:c3+ 13.♔f2

13.♗d2 ♕e5 (13...♕:c4 14.d:c6 ♖e8+ 15.♔f2 ♕c5+ 16.♔g3 ±) 14.♔f1 ♘ce7 15.♖b1 ↑.

13...♕d4+ 14.♕:d4 ♘:d4 15.♗e5 ♘f5 16.♗g4 ♘ge7 17.♗:g7 ♖hg8 18.♗:f5+ ♘:f5 19.♗e5 ± (Bangiev)

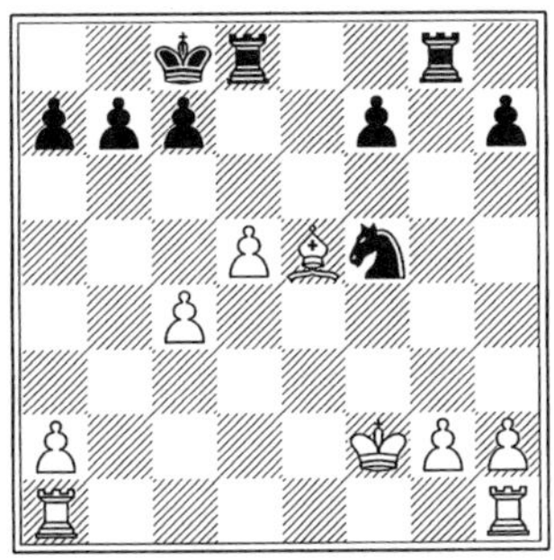

With pawns on both wings, the bishop is usually superior to the knight.
Mit Bauern auf beiden Flügeln ist der Läufer in der Regel dem Springer überlegen.

Chapter IX *Kapitel IX*

The Schallopp Defence
Die Schallopp-Verteidigung

1.e4 e5 2.f4 e:f4 3.♘f3 ♘f6

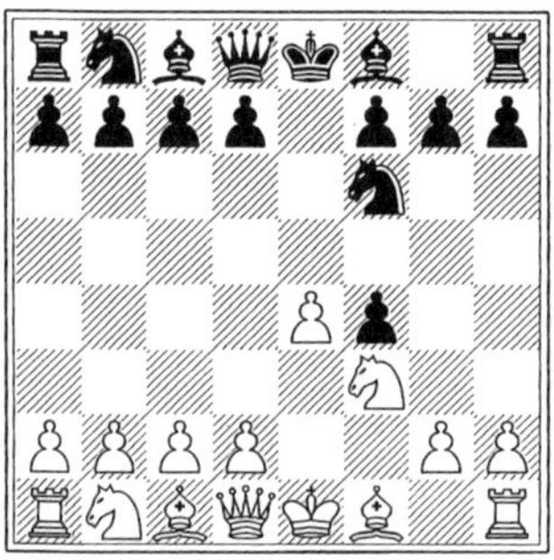

Trying to get counter-play by attacking the ♙e4.
Versucht durch Angriff auf den ♙e4 Gegenspiel zu erlangen.

4.e5!

Forcing the issue is White's best option here. As can be seen below, Black has plenty of opportunities to go wrong now.
Weiß forciert am besten die Ereignisse. Wie wir gleich sehen werden, hat Schwarz hiernach viele Möglichkeiten fehlzugreifen:

• 4...♘g4?! 5.d4 g5 6.h4 ♗e7 7.♘:g5 ♘e3 8.♗:e3 (Most books give - *die meisten Bücher empfehlen* - 8.♘:f7 ♘:d1 9.♘:d8 ♖f8 10.♔:d1 ±, but the simple 9...♘e3 –+ spoils the picture - *doch das einfache 9...♘e3 –+ zerstört das schöne Bild*) 8...f:e3 9.♕h5 or *(oder)* 9.♗c4 ±

As usual quick pressure on f7 is a good remedy against cavalier play by Black.
Wie üblich ist Druckspiel gegen f7 eine gute Maßnahme gegen "generöses" Spiel von Schwarz.

• 4...♘d5?! 5.c4 ♘b6 6.d4 g5 (6...♗b4+ 7.♘c3 d5 8.c5 ♘6d7 9.♗:f4 ±) 7.h4 g4 8.♘g1 (8.♘g5!?) ♗e7 9.♗:f4 ♗:h4 10.g3 ♗g5 11.♕:g4 ±.

• 4...♕e7?! 5.♗e2 ♘d5 (5...♘g4 6.d4 ♘e3 7.♗:e3 f:e3 8.♘c3, 5...♘h5 6.♘c3 g6 7.d4 ♗h6 8.♘d5 ♕d8 ± This must be extremely close to winning for White, e.g: - *dies muß schon fast eine Gewinnstellung sein, z.B.:* 9.g4 c6 10.♘c3 ♘g7 11.♘e4 ♘e6 12.♘d6+ ♔f8 13.h4 - White's position is so good that it might be taxable! - *die weiße Stellung ist so stark, daß der Tribut bald fällig sein müßte!*) 6.c4 ♘b6 7.d4 g5 8.0-0 h6 9.♘c3 c6 10.♘e4 ± (Bilguer).

• 4...♘e4 5.♕e2!

The most forcing move, not giving Black time to entrench his knight on the e6 square.
Die zwingendste Fortsetzung. Weiß gibt dem Gegner keine Zeit, seinen Springer auf e6 zu etablieren.

5...♘g5

• • 6.d4 ♘:f3+ 7.♕:f3 ♕h4+ (7...d6 8.♗:f4 ±/∞, 8.♗c4!? d:e5 9.d:e5 ♕h4+ 10.g3 f:g3 11.♗:f7+ ♔d8 12.h:g3 ♕b4+ 13.♘c3 ♗e7 14.♕d3+ ±) 8.g3 f:g3 9.h:g3 ♕:d4 10.♖h4 ± (Bhend)

This is the old continuation, however I'm not quite sure White really has enough for the pawns, analysis with a computer gave the following 'main line':
6.d4 ist die hergebrachte Fortsetzung, dennoch bin ich mir nicht sicher, ob Weiß hier überhaupt genug Spiel für den Bauern hat. Analysen mit einem Computer ergaben die folgende "Hauptvariante":
10...♕c5 11.♘c3 ♘c6 12.♗e3 ♘:e5 13.♕f2 ♕e7 14.♘d5 ♕d8 15.♗g5?! ♕:g5 16.♘:c7+ ♔d8 17.♘:a8 ♗c5, and Black seems to be on top of things ... *(und Schwarz dürfte Herr des Geschehens sein ...)*
• • 6.♘c3!
Instead of giving up the variation I found this alternative which seems quite strong:
Anstatt die gesamte Variante aufzugeben, verfiel ich auf diese Alternative, die recht stark zu sein scheint:
6...♘c6 (what else? - *was sonst?) 7.*♘d5 ♘:f3 8.g:f3!
• • • 8...♗c5 9.c3 ♕h4+ 10.♔d1 ♗b6 11.d4 ♘e7 (11...g5 12.♖g1!) 12.♘:e7 ♕:e7 13.♗:f4 ±.
• • • 8...♘d4 9.♕e4 ♕h4+ 10.♔d1 ♘e6 11.d4 ♕f2 12.c3!? (or just - *oder einfach* - 12.♗:f4 ±) c5(?!) 13.♘:f4 ♘g5 14.♕e3 ♕:e3 15.♗:e3 ♘:f3?? This pawn is not for the taking ... *(dieser Bauer ist nicht zum Verzehr gedacht ...)* 16.♘d5 ♖b8 17.♗e2 ♘h4 18.♗g5 +–.

4...♘h5

Finally, we've arrived at the main line!
Womit wir schließlich und endlich bei der Hauptvariante angelangt wären!

5.d4

One of the many alternatives White has tried over the years. 5.♗e2 is the main alternative, not treated in this book since one good alternative is quite enough against this unpopular variation!
Eine der verschiedenen Alternativen, die Weiß im Laufe der Jahre probiert hat. 5.♗e2 ist die Hauptalternative, welche wir jedoch nicht besprechen wollen - eine gute Möglichkeit gegen die nicht gerade sehr verbreitete Verteidigung 3...♘f6 genügt ja voll und ganz!

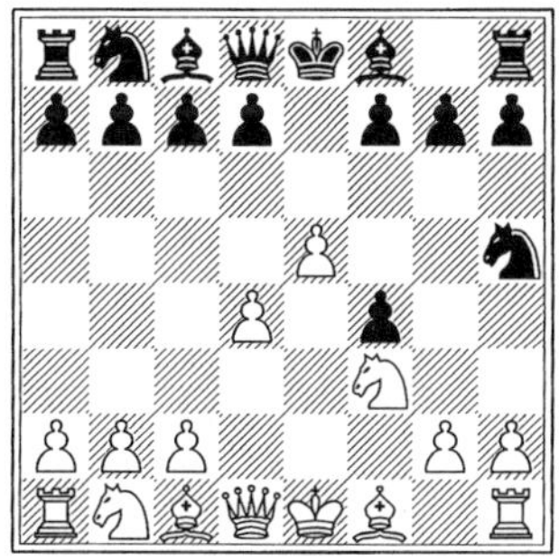

I

5...g5 6.g4!

A typical thrust in the Schallopp!
Ein typischer Schlag in der Schallopp-Verteidigung!
6.♘fd2 is not so clear e.g: *(ist nicht so klar, z.B.:)* 6...♘g7 7.h4 ♗e7 8.♘e4 d5 9.e:d6 c:d6 10.♗b5+ ♔f8 11.h:g5 d5 12.♘f6 ±/∞, Pachman - Lakes, Prague 1948.

6...♘g7

6...f:g3 7.♘:g5.

7.h4 ♗e7

7...g:h4 8.♗:f4 d5 9.♖:h4 h5 10.g:h5 ♖:h5 11.♖:h5 ♘:h5 12.♗g5 ♗e7 13.♗:e7 ♕:e7 14.♘c3 c6 (14...♕b4 is of course met by - *wird natürlich beantwortet mit* - 15.a3) 15.♕d2 ±, Shofman - Poliak, Kiev 1945.

8.h:g5 ♗:g5 9.♘:g5 ♕:g5 10.♕f3 d6 11.♗:f4 ♗:g4 12.♗:g5 ♗:f3 13.♖g1 ♘d7

13...d:e5? 14.♗f6 +–, Cheglakov - Orekhov, corr. 1972.

14.♘d2 ±

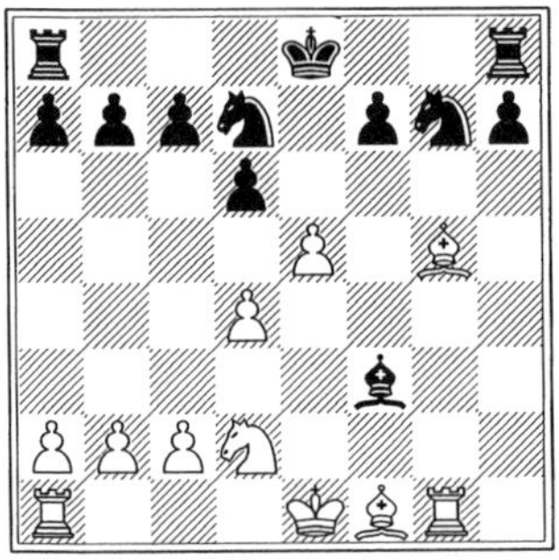

II

(1.e4 e5 2.f4 e:f4 3.♘f3 ♘f6 4.e5 ♘h5 5.d4)

5...g6 6.♗e2 ♗g7 7.0-0 d6 8.e:d6 c:d6

8...♕:d6?! 9.♘e5 ♗:e5 10.d:e5 ♕:e5 11.♗:h5 ±.

9.♘c3

According to Bangiev 9.♘e1! is more precise, not giving Black the chance to play 9...♗g4 ∞; and 9...♘f6 10.♗:f4 0-0 11.♘c3 transposes to Gallagher - Curran below.
Gemäß Bangiev ist 9.♘e1! genauer, was Schwarz nicht die Möglichkeit zu 9...♗g4 ∞ gibt. 9...♘f6 10.♗:f4 0-0 11.♘c3 leitet zur nachstehenden Partie Gallagher - Curran über.

9...0-0 10.♘e1 ♘f6 11.♗:f4 ♘c6 12.♗g5 h6 13.♗h4 d5 14.♗b5 ♕d6 15.♗g3 ♕d7 16.♗e5 ♘e8 17.♘d3 a6 18.♗:g7 ♔:g7 19.♘e5 ♕d6 20.♗:c6 b:c6 21.♕d2 ♘f6 22.♖f4 ♘d7

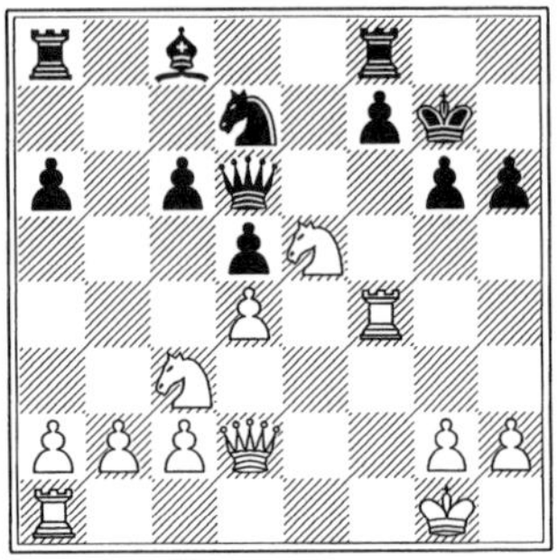

23.♖:f7+! ♖:f7 24.♕:h6+ ♔g8 25.♕h8+ 1:0, Gallagher - Curran, Lyon 1993.

III

(1.e4 e5 2.f4 e:f4 3.♘f3 ♘f6 4.e5 ♘h5 5.d4)

5...d6 6.♕e2!

Black is forced to make up his mind concerning what to do with his d6-pawn, since 6...♗e7 would allow White to play 7.e:d6 and 8.♕b5+ picking up the horse on the limb!
Schwarz ist nun gezwungen, sich bzgl. des ♙d6 zu erklären, zumal Weiß nach 6...♗e7 7.e:d6 und 8.♕b5+ das Pferd auf h5 beim Schwanz packen würde!

6...d5

6...d:e5 7.♕:e5+ (This seems to be a simple route to modest happiness! A more exciting alternative is: - *Der einfachste Weg zu einem kleinen Glück! Eine aufregendere Alternative wäre:* 7.♘:e5 ♕h4+ 8.g3 ♘:g3 9.h:g3 ♕:h1 10.♗:f4 ♗e7 11.♘c3 0-0 12.0-0-0 ♗h3 13.♗:h3 ♕:h3 14.♕e4 ♕e6!? ∞) 7...♕e7 8.♗e2 ♕:e5 9.♘:e5 ♘f6

10.♗:f4 ♗d6 11.♘c3± (11.c4 ♘c6 =/∞) e.g *(z.B.)* 11...♘c6 12.♘b5 ♘e4 13.♗f3.

7.c4!

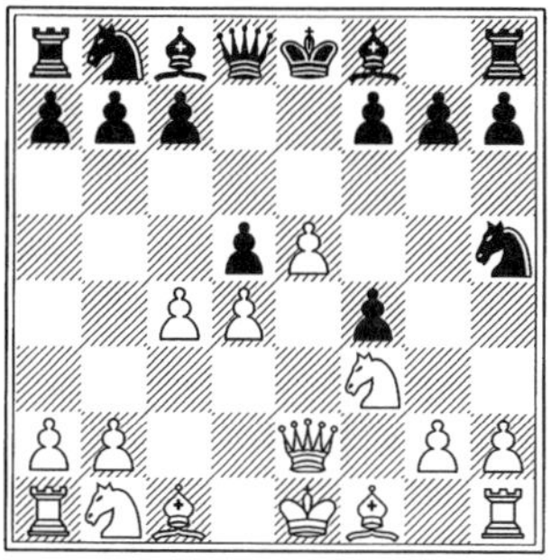

7...♗e6

• 7...d:c4!?
This might be the future main line.
Womöglich in Zukunft die Hauptvariante.
8.♕:c4 ♗e6 9.♕b5+
• • 9...♕d7 10.♕:b7 ♗d5 11.♕b5 ♘c6 12.♗e2 ♖b8 (12...♗:f3 13.♗:f3 ♘:d4 14.♕:d7+ ♔:d7 15.♗:a8 ♘c2+ 16.♔d1 ♘:a1 17.♗f3 Bangiev) 13.♕d3 g6 (Defending the knight since ...♕h4+ isn't available, 13...♘b4 or 13...♗b4+ looks obvious but does it yield anything to Black? - *Überdeckt den Springer, zumal ja ...♕h4+ nicht zur Disposition steht. 13...♘b4 oder 13...♗b4+ drängen sich auf, doch ist fraglich, was damit erreicht werden soll*) 14.♘c3 ♗:f3 15.♗:f3 ♘:d4 16.♗:h5 g:h5 17.0-0 (17.♗:f4?! ♖:b2 −+: 18.0-0 ♘e2+, 18.0-0-0 ♗a3; 18.♘e4 ♘c2+) 17...♘e6 (17...f3!? 18.g:f3 ♖g8+ 19.♔h1 ♕h3 20.♖f2 ♘f5 21.♘e4 ♗c5!? 22.♘f6+ ♔f8 23.♗h6+! ♘:h6 24.♘d7+ ♔e8 25.♘:c5 ♘f5 26.♕d7+ ♔f8 27.♖g1 ±) 18.♘d5 (18.♕f5!?) ♗g7 19.♖d1!? ♕d8 (19...♕c6 20.b3 ♗:e5 21.♗a3 ♗:a1 22.♖:a1 →) 20.♕f5 ⩱ Δ ♘f6, b3, ♗a3.

• • 9...♘c6!? 10.♘c3 (The alternative is the immediate - *die Alternative wäre das sofortige* 10.♕:b7 ♗d7 11.♘c3 ♖b8 12.♕a6 ♘b4 13.♕e2 ♗g4 14.a3 ♘c6 15.d5 ♕h4+ 16.♔d1 ♘d4 17.♕c4 ♕f2 18.♗e2 ♘:e2 19.♕:e2 ∞) 10...a6 11.♕:b7 ♘b4 12.♕e4 g6 13.♕e2 ♗g4 14.a3 ♗:f3 15.g:f3 ♘c6 16.d5 ♘d4 17.♕e4 (Δ d6) ♕h4+ 18.♔d1 ♗c5 19.♘e2 ∞.

• 7...♘c6 8.♘c3 ♗b4 9.c:d5 ♕:d5 10.♗d2 ♗:c3 11.b:c3 ♗g4 12.♕d3 (12.♕f2 could be worth a try, since the queen doesn't seem too happy on d3 - *12.♕f2 wäre einen Versuch wert, zumal die Dame sich auf d3 nicht sonderlich wohl fühlt*) 12...0-0 13.♗e2 g6 14.0-0 ♖ad8 15.c4 (What else? If 15.♔h1 or 15.♗d1 ♘:e5! and 15.♕c2 ♘:d4! isn't any better - *Was sonst? Auf 15.♔h1 oder 15.♗d1 folgt 15...♘:e5!, und 15.♕c2 ♘:d4! ist auch nicht besser*) 15...♕d7 16.d5 ♗:f3 17.♕:f3 ♘:e5 18.♕b3 ∞, Grudsky - Medvedev, Leningrad 1987.

8.c:d5

8.♘c3!? Gallagher.

8...♗:d5 9.♘c3 ♘c6 10.♗d2! ♗b4

10...♗:f3 11.♕:f3 ♕h4+ 12.g3! f:g3 13.0-0-0 g2 14.♕:g2! (This, keeping the ♗f1 flexible and the g-file unobstructed, seems simpler and thereby better than the stem game which also was good for White! *Hält dem ♗f1 alle Türen offen und verstellt auch nicht die g-Linie - mithin scheint 14.♕:g2 noch einfacher und stärker als 14.♗:g2 wie in der Stammpartie, welche sich gleichfalls zugunsten von Weiß gestaltete:* 14.♗:g2 ♗e7 15.♘d5 0-0 16.♖he1 g6 17.♖e4 ♕:h2 18.♖h1 ♕g3 19.♕e2 ♗g5 20.♖h3 ♘:d4 21.♖:d4 ♗:d2+ 22.♖:d2 ♕g5

23.♕e3 ♕:e3 24.♖:e3 ♖fe8 25.♘:c7+−, Leisebein - Schneider, corr. 1990)

- 14...♗e7 15.♘d5! ±
- • 15...0-0-0 16.♘:e7+ (Δ ♗g5, ♕g4).
- • 15...♖c8 16.♘:e7 ♘:e7 17.♗g5.
- • 15...0-0 16.♗e2 ♗d8 17.♖hg1 g6 18.♗e1 ±.
- 14...♕:d4 15.♗b5
- • 15...♕d7 16.♗g5 ♕e6 17.♘d5+−.
- • 15...♕b6 16.♕h3 g6 17.♗e3 ♗c5 18.♕d7+ ♔f8 19.♗h6+ ♘g7 20.e6 ♘e5

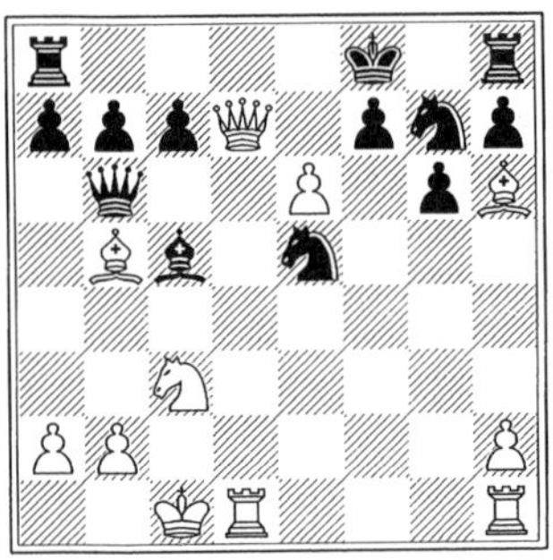

21.♖hf1! ♘:d7 (21...♗e3+ 22.♔b1 ♗:h6 23.e7+ +−) 22.♖:f7+ ♔g8 23.♖:g7+ ♔f8 24.♖:d7+ ♔e8 25.♘d5+−.

11.♘:d5 ♕:d5 12.0-0-0! ♕:a2

12...0-0-0 13.♕c4 ♗:d2+ 14.♖:d2 ♕:c4+ 15.♗:c4 f6 16.♗e6+ ♔b8 17.♗g4 g6 18.♗:h5 g:h5 19.e6 ±.

13.d5!

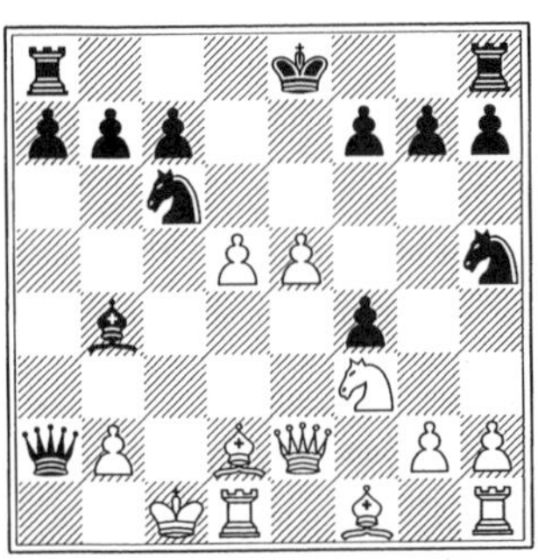

- **13...♕a1+ 14.♔c2 ♕a4+ 15.♔b1 ♘e7**

15...♗:d2 16.d:c6!.

16.♕b5+

16.♘d4 also looks interesting, e.g. *(macht gleichfalls einen interessanten Eindruck, z.B.)* 16...♗:d2 17.♖:d2 g6 18.♕:h5! g:h5 19.♗b5+ ♕:b5 20.♘:b5 0-0-0 21.♖c1 ♘:d5 22.♘d6+ ♔b8 23.♘:f7+ ♘c3+ 24.♖:c3 ♖:d2 25.♘:h8 ♖:g2 26.♖f3 ±.

16...♕:b5 17.♗:b5+ c6 18.♗:b4

With compensation for the pawns according to Kortchnoi. Black's king is far from secure, although he has managed to reach the endgame! e. g:

Mit Kompensation für den Bauern gemäß Kortchnoi. Der schwarze König ist noch längst nicht in Sicherheit, auch wenn er sich in ein Endspiel gerettet hat! z.B.:

18...c:b5 19.♘g5 ♖d8 20.♘e4 ♖:d5 21.♘d6+ ♔d7 (23...♔f8 22.♘f5) 22.♘:f7 ♖c8 23.e6+ ♔:e6 24.♖he1+−.

- **13...♗:d2 14.♘:d2 ♕:d5 15.♕:h5 ♕:e5 16.♕:e5 ♘:e5 17.♖e1 f6 18.♘c4 0-0-0 19.♘:e5 f:e5 20.♖:e5 ♖he8 21.♖:e8 ♖:e8 22.♗d3** ⩲ (Kortchnoi).

IV

(1.e4 e5 2.f4 e:f4 3.♘f3 ♘f6 4.e5 ♘h5 5.d4)

5...d5 6.c4!

This looks even stronger here, with the queen on d1, since there won't be any difficulty recapturing at c4 now!

Mit der Dame auf d1 macht dies einen noch stärkeren Eindruck, da Weiß problemlos auf c4 zurückschlagen kann.

A

6...g5 7.g4!

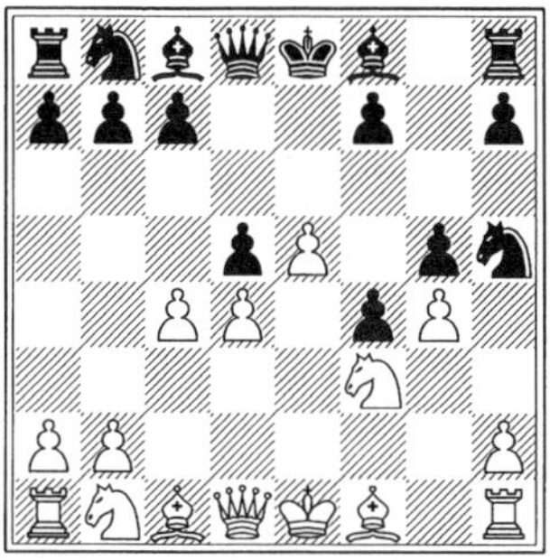

Black is immediately pushed back into a passive position because he can't afford to open the g-file with all his fifth rank weaknesses.
This kind of position is characteristic of the King's Gambit, in what other opening can you find seven pawns in midfield combat after only seven moves!?
Damit wird Schwarz auf der Stelle in eine passive Position gedrängt. Die g-Linie zu öffnen, könnte er sich aufgrund seiner zahlreichen Angriffspunkte auf der fünften Reihe nicht leisten.
Eine für das Königsgambit bezeichnende Position - in welcher Eröffnung finden Sie nach nur so wenigen Zügen sieben Bauern im Infight?

7...♘g7

A sad necessity for Black.
Eine traurige Notwendigkeit.
7...f:g3 8.♘:g5, 7...♗:g4 8.♖g1 f5 (8...♗:f3 9.♕:f3 ♘g7 c:d5) 9.h3 ♘g3 10.h:g4 f:g4 11.♘:g5 ♕:g5 12.♖:g3 ♕h4 13.♗:f4 ± Bangiev.

8.♘c3 ♗b4 9.♖g1!

White takes some time off to consolidate his territorial conquest. When his forces are properly co-ordinated, Black will have a hard time just avoiding being pushed off the board! (9.c:d5 h5! with counter-play)
Weiß nimmt eine kleine Auszeit zwecks Konsolidierung seiner territorialen Errungenschaften. Wenn der Anziehende erst einmal seine Truppen zusammengeschweißt hat, wird Schwarz mit dem Rücken zur Wand stehen. (9.c:d5 h5! mit Gegenspiel)

9...h5

9...c6 10.c:d5 c:d5 11.♕b3 ♗:c3+ 12.b:c3 h6 13.c4 d:c4 14.♗:c4 ↑ Bangiev.

10.h3

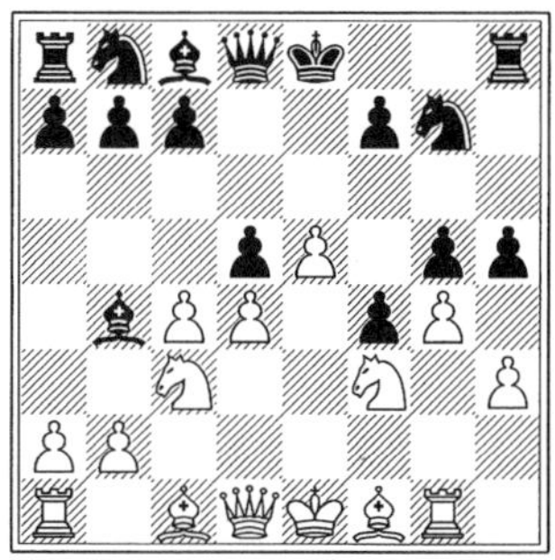

10...d:c4?! 11.♗:c4 c5 12.d5 ♘d7 13.♗d2 ♘b6 14.♕e2 h:g4 15.h:g4 ♗d7 16.a3 ♗a5 17.♘e4 ♗:d2+ 18.♘f:d2 ♕e7 19.d6 1:0, Bangiev - Podrezov, corr. 1986/87.

B

(1.e4 e5 2.f4 e:f4 3.♘f3 ♘f6 4.e5 ♘h5 5.d4 d5 6.c4)

6...♗b4+ 7.♘c3 ♘c6 8.♗e2 0-0 9.0-0 ♗:c3

9...d:c4 10.d5 ♗c5+ 11.♔h1 ♘e7 12.♘g5 ♘f5 13.♘ce4 ♗e7 14.♗:h5 ♗:g5 15.♘:g5 ♕:g5 16.♗:f4 ♕e7 17.♗e2 ±.

10.b:c3 ♗g4 11.♘e1

11.c:d5 ♕:d5 12.h3! ♗c8 13.♘g5 ♘g3 14.♖:f4 ±.

11...♗:e2 12.♕:e2 g6 13.♗:f4 ±

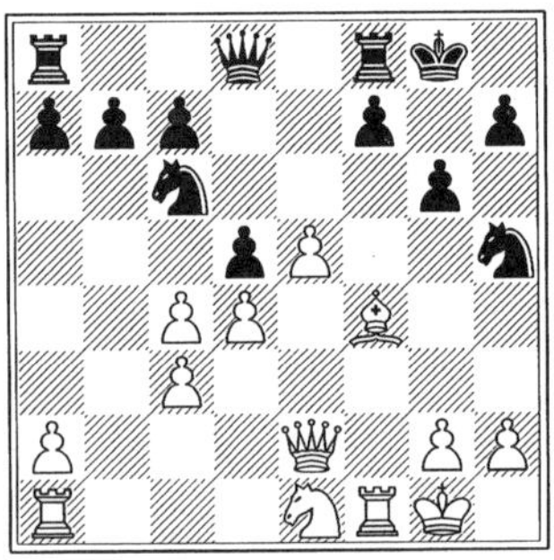

Mutchnik - Dshalalov, Moscow 1952

C

(1.e4 e5 2.f4 e:f4 3.♘f3 ♘f6 4.e5 ♘h5 5.d4 d5 6.c4)

6...♗e7

An ambitious move, but it allows White to speed ahead in development like a cyclist hitching a ride from a colleague and then pushing himself forward stealing the other's momentum!
Ein ehrgeiziger Zug von Schwarz, welcher indes dem Anziehenden erlaubt, ihn in der Entwicklung zu überflügeln - etwa wie bei einem Radrennfahrer, der sich im Windschatten seines Kollegen versteckt hält, dann aber im entscheidenden Moment unter Mitnahme dessen Schwungs nach vorne prischt!

7.♗e2 ♗h4+ 8.♔f1 ♗e7

8...♗g4 9.c:d5 0-0 10.♘c3 ± see under *(siehe unter)* **E**, 6...♗g4.

9.c:d5 ♕:d5 10.♘c3 ♕d8 11.d5 ♗g4 12.♘d4 ♗:e2+ 13.♕:e2 g6 14.♕b5+

14.♕e4 ± Gallagher.

14...♘d7 15.e6 f:e6 16.d:e6 c6 17.e:d7+

17.♕:b7!?

17...♕:d7 18.♕e5 0-0-0

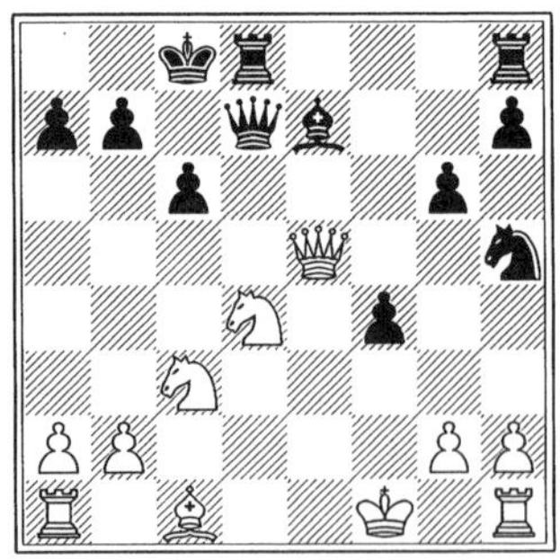

Horst - Postura, corr. 1990
And I doubt that Black has full comp for the piece after 19.♕e6.
Und ich habe meine Zweifel, ob Schwarz nach 19.♕e6 ausreichende Kompensation für die Figur hat.

D

(1.e4 e5 2.f4 e:f4 3.♘f3 ♘f6 4.e5 ♘h5 5.d4 d5 6.c4)

6...♘c6 7.c:d5 ♕:d5 8.♘c3 ♗b4 9.♗e2 ♕a5

- 9...♗g4 10.0-0 ♗:c3 11.b:c3 0-0 12.h3! (Cheremisin).
- 9...g6 10.0-0 ♗:c3 11.b:c3 ♗g4 12.h3 (12.♘g5!?) ♗f5 13.♘h4 ♘g3

14.♖:f4 ♘:e2+ 15.♕:e2 ♗e6 16.♖f2 0-0-0 17.♖b1 with some initiative for White *(mit etwas weißer Initiative)* in Grachev - Cheglakov, corr. 1990.

10.♗d2 ♗g4 11.a3 ♗:c3 12.b:c3 0-0 13.♘g5!

A well calculated knight sally!
Ein wohlerwogener Springerausfall!

13...♗:e2 14.♕:e2 g6

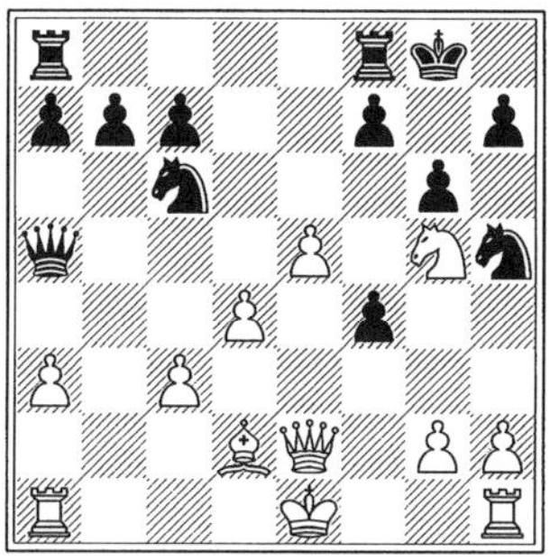

15.g4!!

This move keeps turning up, and more and more unexpectedly too!
Dieser Zug taucht wieder und wieder auf - und mehr und mehr unerwartet noch dazu!

15...f:g3 16.h:g3 ♘:g3 17.♘:h7 →, Glaskov - Maljuzhinets, Moscow 1950 for example: *(zum Beispiel:)*
17...♘:e5 (17...♘:h1 18.♘f6+ Δ ♗h6+ +–, 17...f5 18.♕g2!? f4 19.c4 ♕b6 20.♕d5+ ♔g7 21.♘:f8 ♖:f8 22.♕d7+ +–) 18.d:e5 ♘:h1 19.♘f6+ ♔g7 20.♗h6+ ♔:h6 21.♕h2+ ♔g5 22.♕g1+ ♔f4 23.♕g4+ ♔:e5 24.♘d7+! ♔d6 25.♖d1+ ♕d5 26.♕b4+ +–.

E

(1.e4 e5 2.f4 e:f4 3.♘f3 ♘f6 4.e5 ♘h5 5.d4 d5 6.c4)

6...c6

6...♗g4 7.c:d5 ♗e7 8.♗e2 ♗h4+ 9.♔f1 0-0 10.♘c3 ♘d7 11.♗d2 ♖e8 12.♖c1 ♘b6 13.a4 ♗e7 14.♕b3 ±, Freeman - Heigart, corr. 1960.

7.♘c3 ♗e6

7...♗b4 8.♕b3 a5 9.c:d5 (It looks tempting to maintain tension at least until the ♘b8 gives up all hope of reaching c6, e.g: - *es scheint verlockend, die Zentrumsspannung so lange aufrechtzuerhalten, bis der ♘b8 die Hoffnung aufgibt, jemals c6 zu erreichen, z.B.:* 9.♗d2 ♗e6 10.0-0-0!? [10.♗e2] 10...d:c4 11.♗:c4 ♗:c4 12.♕:c4 b5 13.♕e2 0-0 14.♘e4 Δ g4 ±) 9...c:d5 10.♗e2 ♘c6 11.0-0 ♗e6 12.a3 ♗:c3 13.b:c3 ± (Δ ♕:b7, Δ ♘e1), Weber - Werner, Bundesliga 1987.

8.c:d5

8.♕b3 ♕d7 9.♗e2 looks interesting too *(scheint gleichfalls interessant)*.

8...c:d5 9.♗e2 ♖g8 10.♕d3 g6 11.♕b5+ ♕d7 12.♘g5 ♘c6

Tebb - Piper, BCF 1994. Instead of *(anstelle von)* 13.♘:h7 ♗e7; White should have played 13.♗:h5 which could lead to something like this: *(sollte Weiß 13.♗:h5 spielen, was etwa folgendermaßen aussehen könnte:)*
13...g:h5 14.♗:f4 ♘:d4 15.♕:d7+ ♔:d7 16.0-0-0 ♗c5 16.g3 ± Δ ♘a4, Δ ♘:h7-♘f6+.

Chapter X *Kapitel X*

The Cunningham Defence
Die Cunningham-Verteidigung

1.e4 e5 2.f4 e:f4 3.♘f3 ♗e7

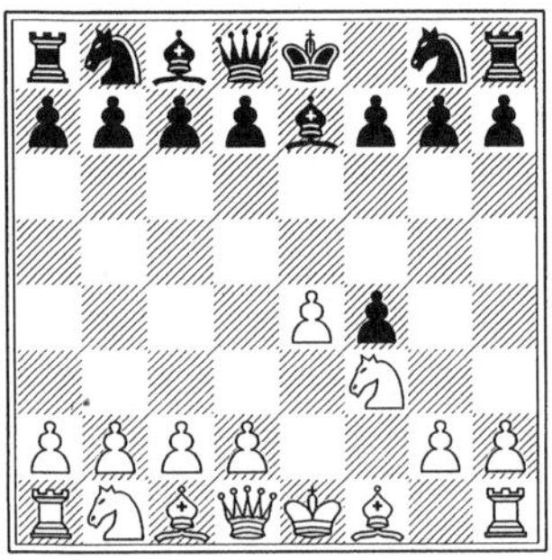

Black's intention is either to deprive White of his castling right with 4...♗h4+ or try to improve on the ideas we've already seen in the Schallopp with 4...♘f6.
Schwarz beabsichtigt, entweder dem Anziehenden mit 4...♗h4+ die Rochade zu verderben oder aber mit 4...♘f6 in verbesserter Form in die Ideenwelt der bereits betrachteten Schallopp-Verteidigung einzutreten.

The American master Anthony Edward Santasiere (1904-1977) introduced an interesting idea in the 1950s, 4.♗e2!?, which definitely deserves a better fate than it's current oblivion. Compared to 4.♗c4, 4.♗e2 has two things in favour of it, after the bishop check on h4 the bishop must retreat almost instantly since there's no pin with ...d5 and ...♗g4, the other is that 4...♘f6 can be met by 5.♘c3 since there's no fork trick with 5...♘:e4. The practical tries look good for White, and there still seems to be plenty of room for new ideas:
In den fünfziger Jahren führte der amerikanische Meisterspieler Anthony Edward Santasiere (1904-1977) mit 4.♗e2!? eine interessante Idee in die Praxis ein, welche mit Sicherheit ein besseres Schicksal verdient als ihre gegenwärtige Vergessenheit. Verglichen mit 4.♗c4 sprechen zwei Dinge zugunsten von 4.♗e2: Nach dem Schach auf h4 muß der schwarze Läufer ziemlich rasch wieder verschwinden, da die Fesselungsidee mit ...d5 und ...♗g4 entfällt. Und 4...♘f6 kann problemlos mit 5.♘c3 beantwortet werden, da der Scheinopfertrick mit 5...♘:e4 nicht geht. Die praktischen Tests hinterlassen einen guten Eindruck für Weiß, und Spielraum für neue Ideen gibt es noch dazu:

I

4.♗e2!?

A

4...♗h4+?!

This is an enormous waste of time, but this check is often the main reason why Black plays The Cunningham.
Eine enorme Zeitverschwendung. Doch das Schachgebot auf h4 stellt ja den ei-

gentlichen Grund dar, zur Cunningham-Verteidigung zu greifen?!

5.♔f1 ♗e7

5...d6 6.d4 ♗g5 7.♘:g5 ♕:g5 8.♘c3 c6 9.g3 ♗h3+ 10.♔e1 ♘d7 11.♗:f4 ♕e7 12.♕d3 0-0-0 13.♔d2 ±, Byland - Foote, Columbus 1960.

6.d4 g5 7.h4 g4

7...f6? 8.h:g5 f:g5 9.♘e5 ♗f6 10.♗c4 ♕e7 11.♕h5+ ♔f8 12.b3 b5 13.♗a3 d6 14.♗d5 c6 15.♗:d6 1:0, Fawbush - Jenison, corr. 1987.

8.♘e5 h5 9.♗c4 ♖h7

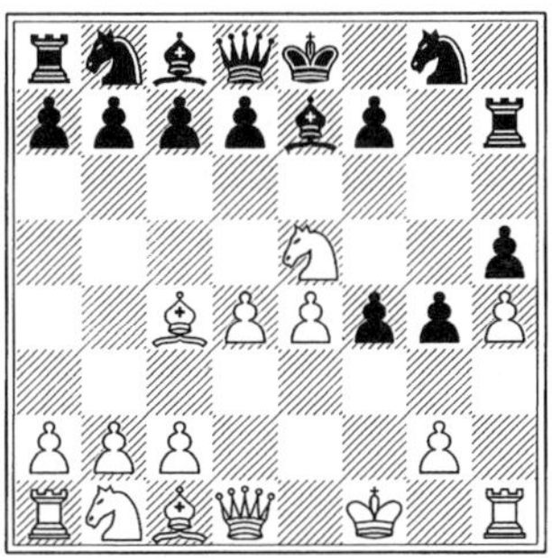

Solnzev - Vasilchuk, Moscow 1957. 10.♗:f4! ± ECO.

B

(1.e4 e5 2.f4 e:f4 3.♘f3 ♗e7 4.♗e2)

4...d5 5.e:d5 ♘f6 6.0-0

a

6...0-0 7.c4 b5

7...c6 8.d:c6 ♘:c6 9.d4 ♗g4 10.d5 ♗:f3 11.♗:f3 ♘e5 12.♗:f4 ♘:c4 13.♘c3 ± ECO.

8.c:b5

8.d3!?.

8...♘:d5 9.♘c3 ♗b7 10.d4 c5 11.♘:d5 ♕:d5 12.♗:f4 a6

12...c:d4 13.♗e5 (Kortchnoi/Zak).

13.♖c1 a:b5 14.♗:b5 ♕:a2 15.♗c4 ♕:b2 16.♖f2 ♕b6 17.♘e5 ♗a6 18.♗:f7+ +–, Heuer - Ney, Estonia 1959.

b

(1.e4 e5 2.f4 e:f4 3.♘f3 ♗e7 4.♗e2 d5 5.e:d5 ♘f6 6.0-0)

6...♘:d5 7.c4 ♘b4 8.d4 ♗f5 9.♘a3 g5 10.♘:g5! ♗:g5 11.♕a4+ ♘8c6 12.d5 ♕d6 13.d:c6 ♘:c6 14.♘b5 ♕e5 15.c5! ♕:e2 16.♗:f4 ♗e7

16...♗:f4 is answered by *(wird beantwortet mit)* 17.♕:f4 →.

17.♘:c7+ ♔d7!

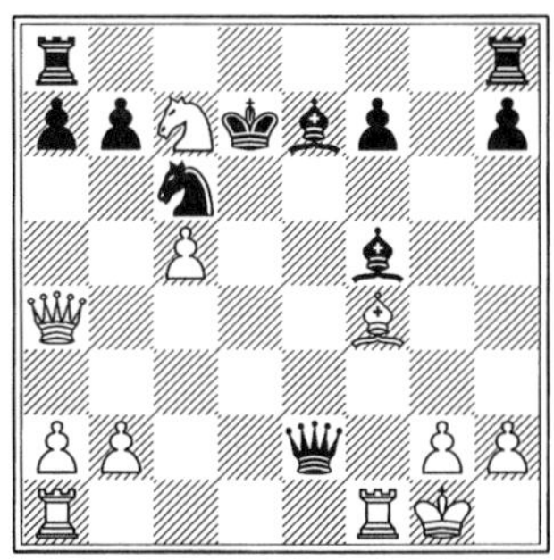

18.♖ae1! ♗:c5+ 19.♔h1 ♕g4 20.♘:a8 ♖:a8 21.♕b5 ♖c8 22.♕:c5 ♗e6 23.♕d6+ ♔e8 24.♗g5! ♕:g5 25.♖:e6+ ♘e7 26.♖e5 1:0, Hornstein - Dalk, corr. 1959.

C

(1.e4 e5 2.f4 e:f4 3.♘f3 ♗e7 4.♗e2)

4...♘f6

Black's best try, now White has two interesting continuations:
Der beste Versuch von Schwarz. Der Anziehende verfügt nun über zwei interessante Fortsetzungen:

a

5.♘c3 d5 6.e:d5 ♘:d5 7.♘:d5 ♕:d5 8.d4 ±

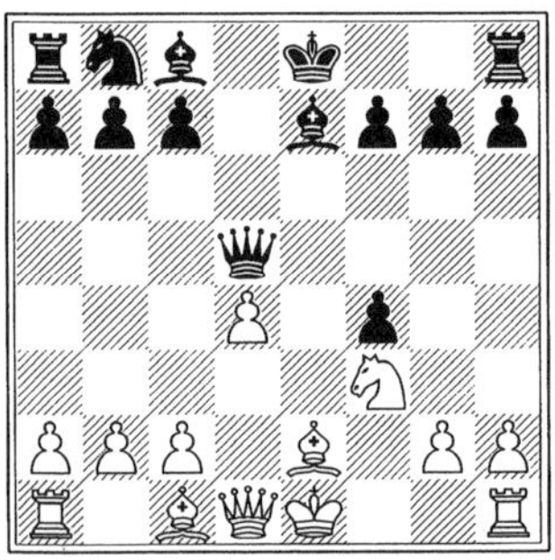

This position can arise in the Modern defence too via the move order:
Diese Stellung kann in der Modernen Verteidigung über die folgende Zugfolge entstehen:
3...d5 4.e:d5 ♘f6 5.♘c3 ♘:d5 6.♘:d5 etc.

b

(1.e4 e5 2.f4 e:f4 3.♘f3 ♗e7 4.♗e2 ♘f6)

5.d3

Surprisingly enough 5.e5 doesn't achieve more than equality due to *Erstaunlicherweise ist mit 5.e5 nicht mehr als Ausgleich zu erreichen wegen* 5...♘e4 6.d3 ♘c5 7.♗:f4 d5 Δ ♘e6 (Kortchnoi/Zak).

5...d5 6.e5 ♘g4

6...♘h5 7.0-0 g6 8.♘e1 ♘g7 9.♗:f4 = Santasiere, however this evaluation looks a bit too modest *(diese Einschätzung wirkt jedoch ein kleines bißchen zu bescheiden).*

7.♗:f4 f6

7...d4 8.0-0 h5 9.c3 ♘c6 10.c:d4 ♘:d4 11.♔h1 ♗c5 12.♗g5?! (Perhaps it would be better to give up the exchange with: *Vielleicht sollte Weiß besser wie folgt die Qualität geben:* 12.♘c3 ♘:f3 13.♗:f3 ♘f2+ 14.♖:f2 ♗:f2 15.♘e4 ♗d4 16.♕a4+ ♕d7 17.♕c4 with some comp for the material invested - *mit etwas Kompensation*) 12...f6 13.e:f6 g:f6 14.♘:d4 ♗:d4 15.♘c3 f:g5 16.♗:g4 ♗:g4 17.♕b3 ♕d7 18.♖ae1+ ♔d8 19.♕:b7 ♖c8 20.♘b5 h4 ∓, Santasiere - Ruth, US Open 1956.

8.0-0 ♘c6 9.e:f6 ♗c5+?

9...♘:f6 =/∞.

10.d4 ♕:f6 11.d:c5 ♕:f4 12.♘c3 ♗e6 13.♘:d5 ♗:d5 14.♕:d5 ♕e3+ 15.♔h1 ♘f2+ 16.♖:f2 ♕:f2 17.♗b5 +−

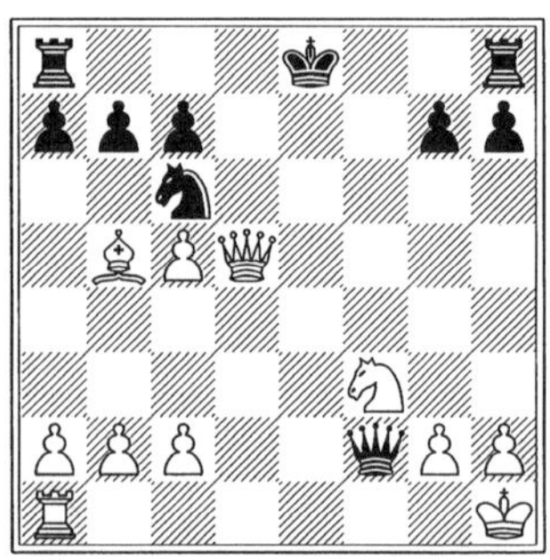

Santasiere - McCormick, New Orleans 1954.

II

(1.e4 e5 2.f4 e:f4 3.♘f3 ♗e7)

4.♗c4

Since the check can't be stopped comfortably, White develops and simultaneously prepares a safe haven for his king.
Nowadays, 4.♘c3 is most popular but after the check on h4 the king will be stranded in the centre a while, it's theoretically quite sound but it seems practically to be a bit risky.
Da das Schachgebot auf h4 nicht so ohne weiteres verhindert werden kann, entwickelt sich Weiß und schafft sich gleichzeitig eine sichere Zuflucht für seinen König.
Heutzutage ist indes 4.♘c3 am beliebtesten, doch nach dem Schach auf h4 bleibt der weiße König dann eine Weile im Zentrum hängen, was in theoretischer Hinsicht wohl spielbar ist, in der Praxis indes ein unnötiges Risiko darstellt.

A

4...♗h4+ ♥

This check has been called 'dubious' since the 1590s, but it's still as popular as ever!
Dieses Schachgebot gilt seit den Neunziger Jahren des 16. Jhdts. als "zweifelhaft", ist aber verbreitet wie eh und je!

5.♔f1

Originally, the Cunningham was a *White* gambit with 5.g3?! f:g3 6.0-0 etc, but when this gambit fell out of favour it's innovator's name gradually came to be associated with *Black's* third move.
Die ursprüngliche Idee Cunninghams war das ***weiße*** *Gambit 5.g3 f:g3 6.0-0 usw., als dieses jedoch außer Mode kam, ging der Name "Cunningham" schrittweise auf die* ***schwarze*** *Verteidigung 3...♗e7 über.*

a

5...d6

- 5...♗f6?!

Black doesn't bother trying to justify his 4th move and White seems to get a kind of accelerated Kieseritzky position for free, which must be good even with the king on f1.
Der Nachziehende versucht in aller Seelenruhe, seinen 4. Zug zu rechtfertigen, Weiß erhält aber umsonst eine Art "beschleunigter" Kieseritzky-Stellung, die auch mit dem König auf f1 gut sein muß.
6.d4! g5 7.h4 →, e.g. *(z.B.)* 7...g4 or *(oder)* 7...h6 are both met by *(werden jeweils beantwortet mit)* 8.♘e5!, Keres.

- 5...♘h6?! 6.d4 ♘g4 7.♕e2 ±.

6.d4

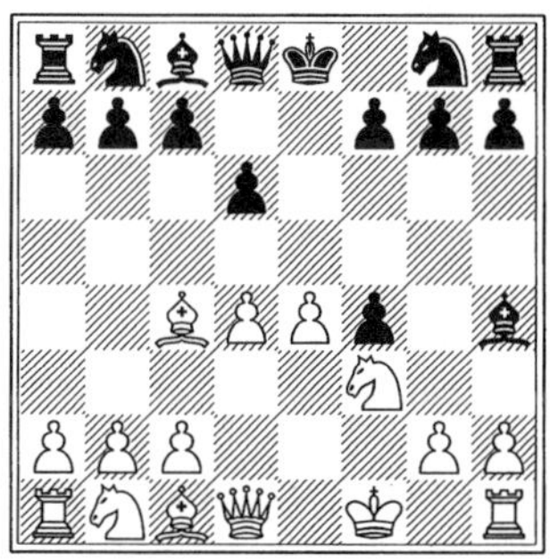

- **6...♕f6 7.e5! d:e5 8.d:e5 ♕e7 9.♗:f4 ♗g4 10.♘c3 c6 11.♘e4** ±, Morphy - McConnell, New Orleans 1849.

- **6...♗g4 7.♘c3! ♘c6 8.♗:f4 ♘ge7 9.♕d2 ♘g6 10.♘:h4 ♕:h4**

10...♘:f4 11.♕:f4 ♕:h4 12.♕:f7+ +−.

11.♗g5 ♕h5 12.h3 h6 13.♗e3 ♘ge7

13...♗d7 14.♘d5 Δ ♗e2 ±.

14.♔g1 ♗d7 15.♖f1 f6 16.♔h2 a6?

16...0-0-0.

17.b4! ± **♖f8 18.♖f2 g5 19.♖hf1 ♕g6**

19...g4 20.♗e2 ♕h4 21.♖f4.

20.♘d5 ♘:d5 21.♗:d5 0-0-0 22.a4 ♘e7 23.b5 ♘:d5 24.e:d5 f5

24...a:b5 25.♕a5! ±.

25.b:a6 b6 26.a5 ♔b8 27.a:b6 c:b6 28.♖b1 ♔a7

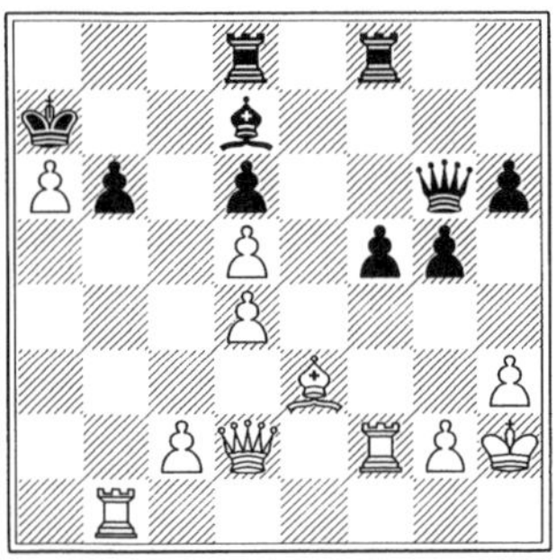

29.♖:b6! ♔:b6 30.♕b4+ ♗b5 31.c4 ♕e8 32.♖b2 ♔c7 33.c:b5 ♔d7 34.b6! ♕:e3 35.♕b5+ ♔e7 36.♖e2 +− (1:0/40.), Rabinovitch - Kieseritzky, Leningrad 1923.

- **6...♗e7**

As usual, the early bishop retreat gives White a strong centre which will allow him to build an untouchable position.

Wie gewöhnlich erlaubt der frühzeitige Läuferrückzug dem Weißen, ein starkes Zentrum und somit eine unangreifbare Position aufzubauen.

7.♗:f4 ♘f6 8.♘bd2 c6 9.♗d3 ♘bd7 10.g3 ♘f8 11.♔g2 ♘e6 12.♗e3 0-0 13.♕e2 d5 14.e5±, Levin - Zamihovsky, SSSR 1958.

b

(1.e4 e5 2.f4 e:f4 3.♘f3 ♗e7 4.♗c4 ♗h4+ 5.♔f1)

5...d5!

This is the only way Black can fight for the initiative.

Die einzige Möglichkeit für Schwarz, um die Initiative zu kämpfen.

6.e:d5!?

White consistently continues to impede the ♘g8. The most popular move is 6.♗:d5 which allows 6...♘f6 7.♗b3 ♗g4 8.d3 0-0 and it's White's bishop who's been wasting time.

Weiß hemmt konsequent den ♘g8. Verbreiteter ist 6.♗:d5, was 6...♘f6 7.♗b3 ♗g4 8.d3 0-0 ermöglicht, wonach es der weiße Läufer ist, der durch Rumziehen Zeit verliert.

6...♗g4

This pin seems quite necessary for Black:

Diese Fesselung scheint lebensnotwendig:

6...♗f6?!:

- 7.♘c3!? g5 8.♕e2 ♕e7 9.♘e4 ♗g4 10.h4 ± Hay.
- 7.d4 ♘e7 8.♘c3 0-0 9.♗:f4 b5 10.♘:b5 ♗a6 11.d6! c:d6 12.a4 ⩲, Bläss - Schoppmeyer, Bundesliga 1986/87.

b1

7.d3!

This controls the important square e4, where White would like a knight so he can play g3; another positive thing about 7.d3 is that it blocks the a6-f1 diagonal and defends the bishop. The dark squares may look weak but the c1 bishop may also profit from this, since c3 can become a very powerful outpost.

Damit nimmt Weiß das Feld e4 unter Kontrolle, wo er - zwecks Durchführung von g3 - gerne einen Springer postieren würde. Weiterhin auf der Habenseite von 7.d3 steht, daß die Diagonale f1-a6 nun geschlossen und der Läufer gedeckt ist. Zwar wirken die dunklen Felder nun etwas anfällig, doch erhöht dies auch die Wirkungskraft des ♗c1, dem auf c3 ein schöner Posten winkt.

7...g5

A risky looking move, not to everyone's taste. In blitz and speed chess many people prefer to just give up the pawn and go for practical chances:
Ein riskant aussehender Zug, der bestimmt nicht nach jedermanns Geschmack ist. Speziell im Blitz- und Schnellschach geben daher viele Spieler lieber den Bauern wieder her und suchen praktische Chancen:
7...♘e7 8.♘c3 c6 9.d:c6 ♘b:c6 10.h3 ♕b6 11.♘e4 ♗:f3 12.♕:f3 0-0 13.♕:f4 ♘g6 14.♕e3 ♕c7 15.g3 ♗e7 16.♔g2 ♔h8 17.♖f1 ♘b4 18.♕d2 f5 19.♘c3 f4 20.g:f4 ♖f5 21.a3 ♘:f4+ 22.♖:f4 ♖g5+ 23.♖g4 +– (½:½/31.), Nordström - Stolper, Stockholm 1994.

8.♘c3 ♘e7 9.♘e4

Preparing the g3 thrust, which is especially useful when Black has weakened himself with ...g5.
Bereitet den Vorstoß g3 vor, der besonders stark ist, wenn Schwarz sich bereits mit ...g5 geschwächt hat.

Perhaps it shouldn't be prepared?
Vielleicht ist jede Vorbereitung überflüssig?
9.g3!? f:g3 10.h:g3 ♗:g3 11.♘e4 ♗e5 12.♗:g5

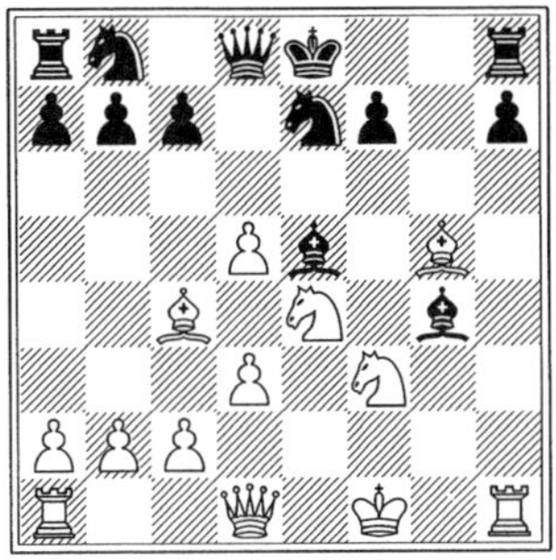

± (Hay).

9...♘f5

Stopping g3, but obstructing his bishop.
Verhindert g3, verstellt jedoch den Läufer.

10.♘f2 ♗h5 11.♕e2+ ♕e7 12.♕:e7+ ♔:e7 13.♘:h4 ♘:h4 14.g3 ♗f3

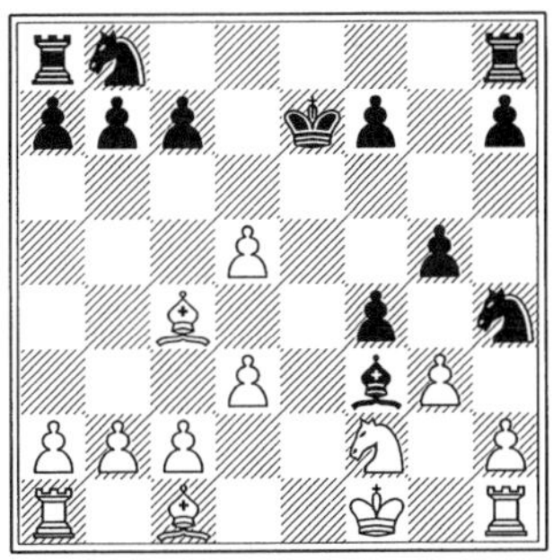

15.♖g1!?

White reckons he's gonna win a pawn anyhow, and decides to keep some pieces on the board.
Weiß glaubt, daß er schon irgendwie einen Bauern gewinnen wird, und entscheidet sich dafür, im Moment alle Figuren auf dem Brett zu halten.

15...♘g2

This looks very defeatist but Black seems to be in a bad way no matter what!

Macht einen ziemlich schicksalsergebenen Eindruck. Doch Schwarz scheint auch anderweitig schlecht zu fahren: 15...f:g3 16.♗:g5+ Δ ♖:g3, 15...♘f5 16.g:f4 ♘d4 17.c3 ♗e2+ 18.♔g2 ♗f3+ 19.♔h3 ±, 15...♘g6 16.♗d2!? c6 17.♖ae1+ ±.

16.♖:g2 ♗:g2+ 17.♔:g2 f:g3 18.h:g3 f6 19.♗d2 ♘d7 20.♖e1+ ♔f7 ±, Croll - Pupols, US Open 1955.

b2

(1.e4 e5 2.f4 e:f4 3.♘f3 ♗e7 4.♗c4 ♗h4+ 5.♔f1 d5 6.e:d5 ♗g4)

7.d4

A double-edged move, e5 is controlled but the d-pawn will require support from the c-pawn and then the ♗c1 can become a problem child, should Black manage to maintain his f4-pawn.
Ein zweischneidiger Zug. Zwar kontrolliert Weiß nun e5, doch der ♙d4 wird der Unterstützung durch den c-Bauern bedürfen, wonach der ♗c1 zu einem Sorgenkind wird, falls es dem Nachziehenden gelingt, den ♙f4 zu behaupten.

7...♘e7

7...g5 8.♘c3 ♕f6 (8...♘e7?! Black's bishop can no longer cover f6 from e5 as in the 7.d3 variation - *der schwarze Läufer kann nicht mehr wie in der 7.d3-Variante das Feld f6 kontrollieren* - 9.g3 f:g3 10.h:g3 ♗:g3 11.♘e4 ± Hay) 9.♘e4 ♕g6 10.♘f2 ⩲ (Δ ♕e1, ♘:h4), Hay - Davidovici, 1969.

8.♗:f4

- 8.♘c3 ♘g6

• • 9.♘e4 0-0 10.g3! f:g3 11.h:g3 ♗f6 and now Hay gives two options:
und hier gibt Hay zwei Möglichkeiten an: 12.♘f2 e.g: *(z.B.)* 12...♗:f3 (12...♗f5 13.g4!? Δ g5, ♘e5, ♕h5 →) 13.♕:f3 ♗:d4 14.♕h5 h6 15.♘g4 → and *(und)* 12.c3 but I think this is too slow, e.g: *(was m.E. nach aber zu langsam ist, z.B.:)* 12...♖e8 13.♘f2 ♗f5 ∞ (Δ ♗e4).
• • 9.♕e2+!? (An interesting novelty in the spirit of Steinitz's brave manoeuvres. Compare it with variation b3 below - *Eine interessante Neuerung ganz im Geiste der furchtlosen Steinzitz'schen Manöver. Vgl. mit der Variante b3 im Anschluß)* ♗e7 10.h4 h5 11.♕e4! ♘d7 12.d6 c:d6 13.♘g5 1:0, Fedorov - Heine Nielsen, Viking Games 1997.

8...0-0?!

The 'practical' approach, hoping something will turn up. And unfortunately it often does, so I advice you to study this game carefully to get a feel for how to consolidate this kind of position.
Der "pragmatische" Ansatz - hoffend darauf, irgend etwas werde sich schon ergeben. Und unglücklicherweise tut es das oft auch. Dehalb rate ich Ihnen, die folgende Partie gründlich zu studieren, um ein Gefühl dafür zu erwerben, wie derartige Stellungen zu konsolidieren sind.
8...♘:d5 9.♗:d5 ♕:d5 10.♘c3 ♕c4+ 11.♕e2+ ♕:e2+ 12.♘:e2 c6 13.h3 ⩲.

9.♘c3 ♗f6

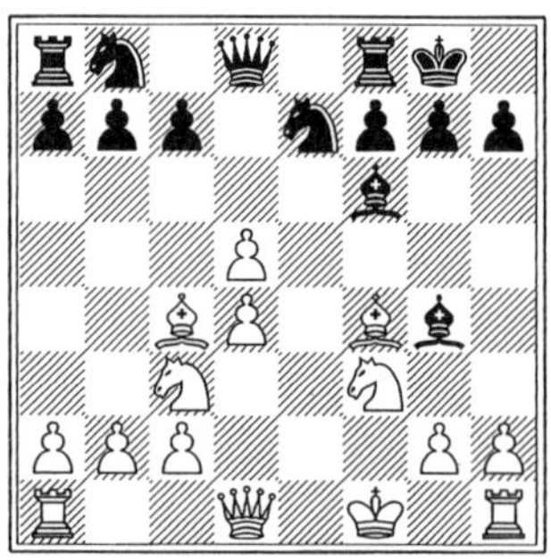

10.♔f2!

A simple, 'slow' move creating harmony in White's camp. It's very tempting to postpone a move like this until it's too late ... so Beware!
Ein schlichtes und "langsames" Manöver, mit welchem Weiß Harmonie in seinem Lager schafft. Die Versuchung ist groß, solch einen Zug aufzuschieben, bis es zu spät ist ... bewahre!

10...♗:f3 11.g:f3

A typical recapture in this kind of position, the rook gets a g-file and the king a white coloured escape square.
Eine für derartige Positionen typische Weise des Zurückschlagens. Die Türme erhalten die g-Linie und der König ein weißfeldriges Fluchtfeld.

11...♘f5 12.♘e2 b5 13.♗d3

13.♗b3 c6.

13...♘:d4 14.♘:d4 ♗:d4+ 15.♔g2 ♕f6?

15...f5.

16.♗:c7! ♕g5+ 17.♗g3 f5 18.f4 ♕d8 19.♗e2 ♗c5 20.♗:b5 g5! 21.h4! g:f4 22.♗:f4 a6 23.♗a4!

Threatening d6 and ♗b3+ and also keeping an eye on ♘b8 which otherwise might stir up some trouble given the chance.
Droht d6 nebst ♗b3+ und behält gleichzeitig den ♘b8 im Auge, der - wenn ihm die Gelegenheit dazu gegeben würde - durchaus imstande wäre, Ärger zu bereiten.

23...♗d6 24.♕d4

Centralisation is often both prophylactic and the embryo of counter-play!
Zentralisierung ist häufig gleichermaßen Prophylaxe wie auch Brutstätte des Gegenangriffs!

24...♖f7 25.♖ae1 ♖g7+ 26.♔f3! ♕c7 27.♖hg1 ♖g4 28.♗:d6 ♕:d6 29.♖:g4+ +−, Alapin - Fritz, Frankfurt 1887.

b3

(1.e4 e5 2.f4 e:f4 3.♘f3 ♗e7 4.♗c4 ♗h4+ 5.♔f1 d5 6.e:d5 ♗g4)

7.♕e2+ ♘e7 8.♕e4 ♗:f3 9.g:f3 0-0 10.d4

10.♕:f4? ♘g6 11.♕f5 ♖e8.

10...♘g6 11.♗d2 ♘d7 12.♘c3

12.♗:f4? ♘:f4 13.♕:f4 ♗g5 Δ ♗c1.

12...f5 13.♕e6+ ♔h8 14.♖g1 ♘b6 15.♗b3 c6

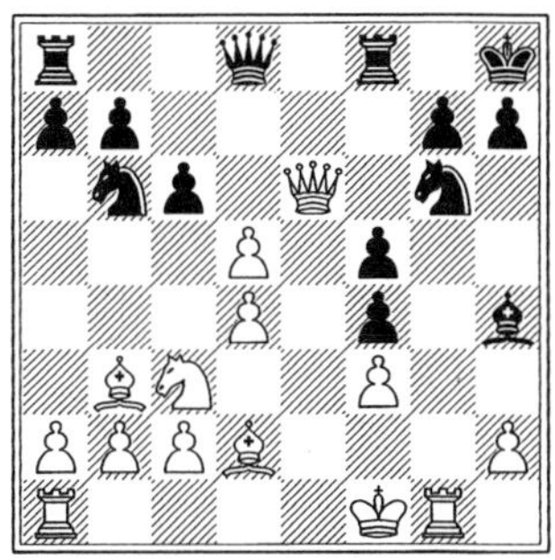

16.♖:g6 h:g6 17.♕:g6 ± (1:0/41.), Steinitz - von Scheeve, Brooklyn 1886.

b4

(1.e4 e5 2.f4 e:f4 3.♘f3 ♗e7 4.♗c4 ♗h4+ 5.♔f1 d5 6.e:d5 ♗g4)

7.♘c3

Seems to be untested, it should transpose to 7.d3 or 7.d4 but with the advan-

tage that White can choose the most favourable transposition; e.g: 7...♘e7 8.d3; 7...g5 8.d4.
Anscheinend unerprobt und sollte zu 7.d3 oder 7.d4 überleiten - doch mit dem Vorteil, daß Weiß sich die günstigste Überleitung heraussuchen darf, z.B. 7...♘e7 8.d3, 7...g5 8.d4.

B

(1.e4 e5 2.f4 e:f4 3.♘f3 ♗e7 4.♗c4)

4...♘f6 5.e5

5.♘c3 ♘:e4! =/∓.

5...♘g4

The knight will at least have some influence on the centre from here.
Von hier aus nimmt der Springer zumindest etwas Einfluß auf das Zentrum.
5...♘h5?! (Stranding the knight on the edge of the board is worse here than in the Schallopp, since Black's necessary centre thrust ...d5 will either expose the queen or lose a tempo with the bishop - *Den Springer am Brettrand stranden zu lassen, ist hier nachteiliger als in der Schallopp-Verteidigung. Nach dem lebensnotwendigen zentralen Gegenstoß ...d5 muß Schwarz entweder seine Dame exponieren oder aber ein Tempo mit seinem Läufer verlieren*) 6.♘c3 d6 7.e:d6 ♕:d6 8.d4 ♘c6 9.0-0 0-0 10.♗e2 ♗g4 11.♘e4 → (Δ ♘f2), Estrin/Glaskov.

6.d4!?

6.0-0 is the main alternative, but since The Cunningham is relatively rare there seems to be no reason to trouble our memory with another similar variation.
6.0-0 ist die Hauptalternative, doch da die Cunningham-Verteidigung eher selten vorkommt, besteht keinerlei Notwendigkeit, das Gedächtnis mit weiteren, ungefähr gleichwertigen Variante zu belasten.

6...d5

6...♗h4+ (There is absolutely no reason to worry about this check! *Es gibt keinerlei Anlaß, dieses Schachgebot zu fürchten!*) 7.♔f1 ♘e3+ (7...♘f2? 8.♕e1 +−) 8.♗:e3 f:e3 9.♕d3 0-0 10.♘c3 d6 11.♕:e3 ♘c6 and here White should have continued with *(und nun sollte Weiß folgendermaßen spielen:)* 12.♕e4! ♗e7 13.h4 →, Gallagher - Hebden, Hastings 1989/90.

7.e:d6!

Opening the centre is almost always the thing to do in this kind of structure, because White must make sure his better development counts. In this position there's no other good option, because 7.♗d3?! would allow ...♗h4+, ...♘f2, ...♘:d3 with favourable exchanges for Black.
Zentrumsöffnung ist in diesem Stellungstyp stets das Gebot der Stunde, da Weiß sicherstellen muß, daß sein Entwicklungsvorsprung auch ins Gewicht fällt. Zudem gibt es in der vorliegenden Situation keine vernünftige Alternative, so würde etwa 7.♗d3?! nach ...♗h4+, ...♘f2, ...♘:d3 für Schwarz vorteilhafte Abtauschaktionen nach sich ziehen.

a

7...♗:d6 8.♕e2+

a1

8...♕e7 9.♕:e7+ ♔:e7

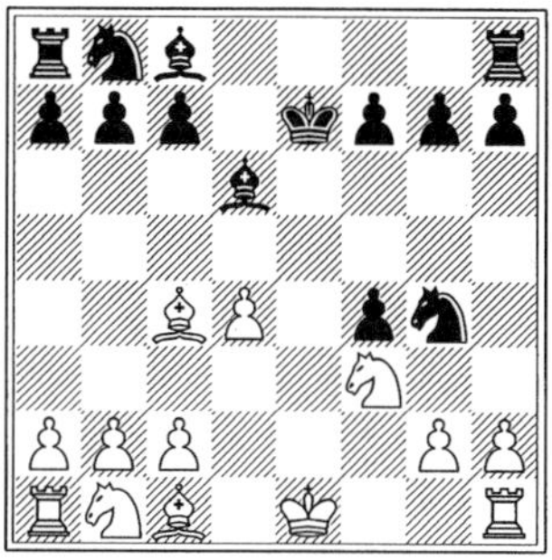

This ending appears to be at least a little better for White, which isn't all that surprising since White has gained a tempo on similar positions in the Modern defence.

Dieses Endspiel dürfte zumindest etwas besser für Weiß sein - was keineswegs überrascht, wenn man bedenkt, daß der Anziehende ein Mehrtempo gegenüber vergleichbaren Stellungen aus der Modernen Verteidigung hat.

- 10.0-0

This is supposed to lead to equality, but it doesn't look that way to me.

Dies soll zum Ausgleich führen, was mir indes nicht einsichtig ist.

10...h6 11.♘c3 ♖e8 (11...g5? 12.♘d5+ ♔d8 13.h3 c6 14.♘:f4 ±) 12.♘d5+ ♔f8 13.♘:f4 ♘e3?!

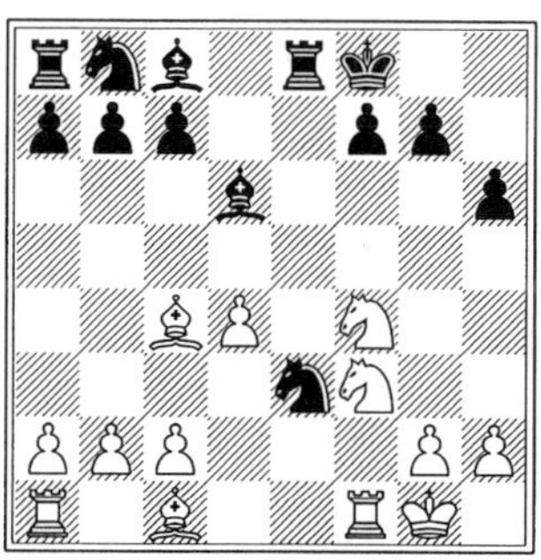

14.♘g6+!! f:g6 (14...♔g8 15.♗:f7+ ♔:f7 16.♘fe5+ Δ ♗:e3 ±) 15.♘e5+ ♔e7 (15...♘:f1? 16.♘:g6#) 16.♗:e3 ±, Chekhlov - Smulders, Riga 1986.

Tactical incidents *can* be staged even without queens!

Taktische Schweinereien ***können*** *auch ohne Damen inszeniert werden!*

- 10.♘c3 ♗e6 (10...♗f5 11.♗b3 ♖e8 12.0-0 ± Δ 13.♘d5+, Δ 13.♘b5, Δ 13.♘g5 Gallagher) 11.♗d3 ♖d8 (11...h6 12.♘e4 g5 13.h4!, 11...♘e3 12.♗:e3 f:e3 13.0-0 f5 14.♘g5 f4 15.♘e2) 12.♘e4 ♗d5 13.♘:d6 ♖:d6 14.♗:f4 ♖e6+ 15.♔d2 ♘f2 16.♖he1 ♘:d3 17.♔:d3 ♗:f3 18.g:f3 ♘a6 19.c4 ♔d7 20.♖:e6 f:e6 ± (1:0/41.), Gallagher - Wells, Islington 1990.

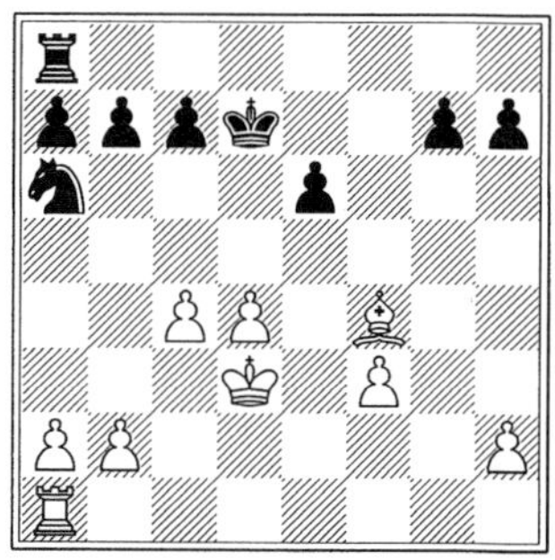

All White's pieces are better placed than their Black counter-parts and besides White's pawn structure is superior to Black's!

Alle weißen Figuren sind besser plaziert als ihre Gegenspieler, und zudem hat der Anziehende die überlegene Bauernstruktur!

a2

(1.e4 e5 2.f4 e:f4 3.♘f3 ♗e7 4.♗c4 ♘f6 5.e5 ♘g4 6.d4 d5 7.e:d6 ♗:d6 8.♕e2+)

8...♔f8 9.♘c3 ♘c6 10.0-0!? ♘:d4

- 10...g5 11.♘e4 h6 12.g3 ± Hay.
- 10...♗f5 11.♘d5 ♕d7 12.♘:f4 ♗:f4 13.♗:f4 ♘:d4 14.♕d1 ♘:c2 (14...♘:f3+ 15.♖:f3) 15.♕:d7 ♗:d7 16.♖ad1 ± e.g: *(z.B.)* 16...♗f5 17.♘h4 ±.

11.♘:d4 ♗c5

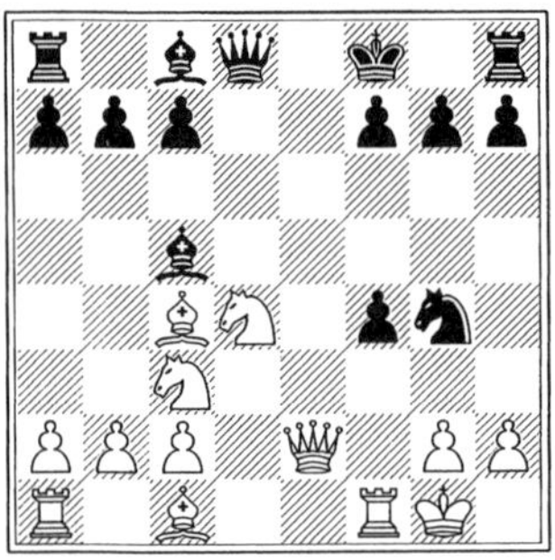

- 12.♗:f4 ♕:d4+ 13.♔h1 ♘f2+ 14.♖:f2 ♕:f2 15.♕:f2 ♗:f2 16.♖f1 → (Δ 16...♗b6 17.♗:c7!), Panov.

This variation is recommended for White by a few authorities, Euwe for example, but I'm not all that sure that White has compensation enough to maintain winning chances if Black just gives back some material, e.g:

Diese Variante wird von einigen Autoritäten (beispielsweise Euwe) empfohlen. Ich bin jedoch keineswegs sicher, daß die weiße Kompensation so stark ist, um auch dann Gewinnchancen zu behaupten, wenn Schwarz etwas Material zurückgibt, z.B.:

16...♗c5 17.♘b5 ♗b6 (17...♗f5!?) 18.♗:c7 f6 19.♗d6+ (19.♖e1 g5 is nothing special either - *ist gleichfalls nichts Besonderes*) 19...♔e8 20.♖e1+ ♔d8 21.♗e7+ ♔d7 22.♘d6 (22.♗a3 ♔c6 23.♖e7 g6 24.♖f7 ♗d8 with some initiative - *mit etwas Initiative*) 22...♔c7 23.♘f7 ♗f5 24.♘:h8 ♖:h8 =/∞.

- Since 12.♗:f4 is supposed to be so good, noone seems to have bothered looking for alternatives, anyway, here's one!

Da 12.♗:f4 als stark gilt, sollte sich niemand durch Alternativen belästigt fühlen - egal, hier ist eine!

12.♖:f4! ♗:d4+ 13.♔h1 ♘f6 14.♕d3 c5 15.♗e3 ♕b6 16.♗:d4 c:d4 17.♘a4! ♕c6 18.♖:d4 ♗d7 19.♖af1! ♗e8 (19...♕:a4? 20.♖:f6 +–) 20.♘c3 ±.

b

(1.e4 e5 2.f4 e:f4 3.♘f3 ♗e7 4.♗c4 ♘f6 5.e5 ♘g4 6.d4 d5 7.e:d6)

7...♕:d6

White should be able to pick up a tempo or two by hitting the queen, which should be enough to keep a small edge.

Weiß sollte durch Angriffe auf die schwarze Dame ein bis zwei Tempi gewinnen können, was für eine kleinen Vorteil reichen müßte.

b1

8.0-0 0-0 9.♘c3 c6? 10.h3! ♘e3

10...♘f6 11.♘e5.

11.♗:e3 f:e3 12.♘e5 ♗h4

12...♗e6 13.♘e4.

13.♖:f7 ♗e6 14.♘e4 ♗f2 15.♔h2!?

A cheeky move, voluntarily stepping into a pin Black can't exploit!
Ein kecker Zug. Weiß begibt sich freiwillig in eine Fesselung, die Schwarz nicht auszunutzen in der Lage ist!

15...♕:e5 16.d:e5 ♗:f7 17.e6 1:0, Hebden - Fassert, Guernsey 1988.

b2

(1.e4 e5 2.f4 e:f4 3.♘f3 ♗e7 4.♗c4 ♘f6 5.e5 ♘g4 6.d4 d5 7.e:d6 ♕:d6)

8.♘c3 ♗e6 9.d5!?

9.♗d3 ♘e3 10.♕e2 ♘c6 11.♘e4 ♕d7 12.♗:e3 f:e3 13.c3 0-0-0 14.♕:e3 f5 15.♘f2 ♗f6 16.0-0 h6 17.♖fe1 ♖he8 18.♘e5 ♗:e5 19.d:e5 ♗d5 20.♕f4 ♖f8 21.♖ad1 g5 22.♕a4 ♕e7 23.♗b5 ♕c5 24.b4 ♕:c3 25.♗:c6 ♕:c6 26.♕:a7 b6 27.e6 ♗:e6? (27...♖fe8 ∓) 28.♖c1 ♕d6 (28...♗c4 29.b5 +–) 29.♖:e6 ♕f4 30.♖ec6 ♖f7 31.♕a8+ ♔d7 32.♖d1+ 1:0, Horne - F. Olafsson, Hastings 1953/54.

9...♗d7 10.♕d4!?

10.♕e2?! 0-0 11.♘e4 ♕b6 12.♗:f4 ♗f5 13.♘g3 ♗g6 14.h3 ♗d6 15.♗:d6 ♕:d6 16.0-0-0 ♕f4+ 17.♔b1 ♘e3 and White was forced to give the g-pawn in *(und Weiß war gezwungen, den g-Bauern zu geben in)* Gallagher - Chiburdanidze, Biel 1990.

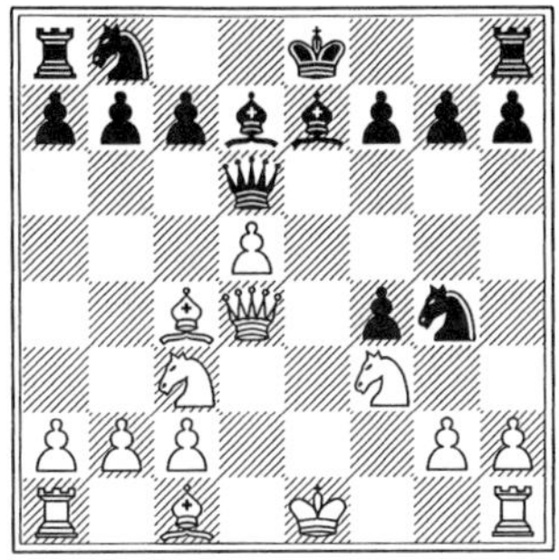

- 10...♘e3 11.♗:e3 f:e3 12.♕:e3
White has a lead in development and is ready to castle either way.
Weiß hat Entwicklungsvorsprung und kann zu jeder Seite hin rochieren.

- 10...♗f6 11.♕:f4 ♕b4 (11...♕b6 12.h3!, 11...0-0 12.♕:d6 ♗:c3+ 13.b:c3 c:d6 14.0-0 ♖c8 15.♗d3 ♖:c3 16.♘g5! ±) 12.0-0! ♕b6+ 13.♔h1 0-0 (13...♘f2+?? 14.♖:f2 ♕:f2 15.♕e4+ ♔d8 16.♗e3 +–) 14.h3 ♘f2+ 15.♔h2 ♗e7 16.♘e4! ♘:e4 17.♕:e4 ♗d6+ 18.♔h1 ♖e8 19.♕h4 h6 (19...♗f5 20.♘g5 ♗g6 21.♗d3 →) 20.♗d3 ♘a6 21.♗:h6 g:h6 22.♕:h6 f5
Both *(sowohl)* 23.♕g6+ Δ ♘g5-f7 or *(als auch)* 23.♕g5+ Δ ♗:f5 looks promising for White *(erscheint aussichtsreich für Weiß).*

- 10...0-0 11.♘e4! ♕h6 12.0-0 ♖e8 13.h3 ♘f6 14.♘eg5 ♗d6 (14...♘h5 15.♘:f7!) 15.♗:f4 ♗f5 16.♗d2 ♗:c2 17.♘:f7 ♕g6 18.♘:d6 c:d6 19.♗b4 ♘h5 20.♘h4 ♕g3 21.♕f2±.

Chapter XI *Kapitel XI*

The Modern Defence
Die Moderne Verteidigung

1.e4 e5 2.f4 e:f4 3.♘f3 d5

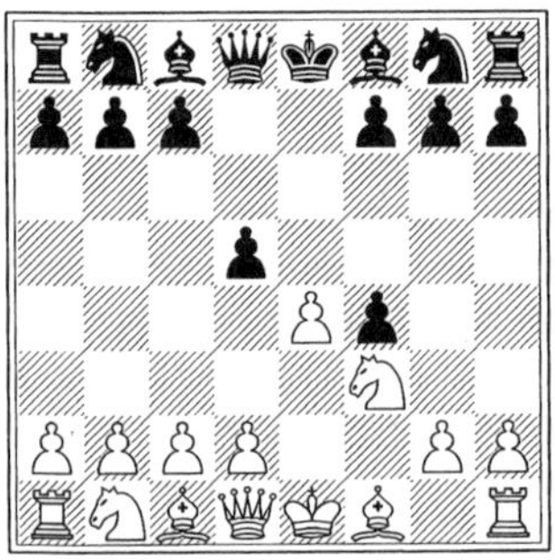

This is the most popular Black defence, because it appears to be a strong blow to White's centre, but it can turn out to have more in common with a misplayed Scandinavian defence where Black has exposed himself too much or given White a far too great lead in development!

Dies ist die am meisten verbreitete Verteidigungsmethode von Schwarz. Grund hierfür ist, daß 3...d5 nach einem schweren Schlag gegen das weiße Zentrum aussieht, doch kann im Endeffekt so etwas wie ein mißhandelter "Skandinavier" entstehen, bei welchem sich Schwarz zu viele Blößen gegeben oder sich vom Anziehenden zu weit in der Entwicklung überholen lassen hat.

4.e:d5

As usual White must open the position to prove the relevance of his better development and pressure on the f4-pawn. 4.e5? would allow ...g5 and with the centre closed it's not so easy to massage f7.

Wie gewöhnlich muß Weiß die Stellung öffnen, um die Bedeutung seines Entwicklungsvorsprungs zu unterstreichen und Druck gegen den ♙f4 auszuüben. 4.e5? würde ...g5 erlauben, und bei abgeschlossenem Zentrum wäre jeder Angriffsversuch gegen f7 illusorisch.

4...♘f6

The main variation. As usual, Black has a plethora of possibilities:

Die Hauptlinie. Wie üblich hat Schwarz eine Vielzahl von Möglichkeiten:

- 4...♛:d5?! (This is a waste of time - *pure Zeitverschwendung*) 5.♘c3 ♛e6+ (5...♛a5 6.♗c4 ♘f6 7.♛e2 ♗e7 8.d4±) Here the simple 6.♗e2 is enough for a nice edge, e.g:

Hier genügt schon das einfache 6.♗e2 für einen ansehnlichen Vorteil, z.B.:

6...♗d6 7.0-0 ♘e7 8.d4 0-0 9.♘g5 (Δ ♘ce4:d6) ±, Solnzev - Kamyshov, Moscow 1946.

But if you're not allergic to moving your king unless it's strictly necessary, then the energetic 6.♔f2!? is a harder try to totally refute Black's 4th, e.g:

Für Spieler, die keine grundsätzliche Abneigung gegen unerzwungene Königszüge haben, ist 6.♔f2!? als strengerer Widerlegungsversuch von 4...♛:d5 geeignet, z.B.:

6...♘f6 7.♗b5+ ± (Δ ♖e1) Keres.

• 4...♗e7 5.♗b5+ (This is even better than transposing to the Cunningham with: - *Noch stärker als die Überleitung zur Cunningham-Verteidigung durch:* 5.♗c4 ♗h4 6.♔f1) 5...c6 6.d:c6 b:c6 7.♗c4 ♗h4+ 8.♔f1 ♗f6 9.d3 g5 10.♕e2+ ♘e7 11.h4 g4 12.♘e5 ±

Black can forget about pawn structure and just count his blessings for every little pawn he may keep!

Seine Bauernstruktur kann Schwarz total vergessen - er muß für jeden einzelnen Bauern, den er behalten will, beten!

• 4...c6 5.d4 ♗d6 6.♘c3 or *(oder)* 6.d:c6 ♘:c6 7.♗d3!? see The Nimzowitsch Counter-Gambit *(siehe Nimzowitschs Gegengambit).*

• 4...♗d6 5.d4

White's central pawns will gain momentum by threatening the ♗d6 and if Black is not careful they may turn into a mighty tidal wave sweeping through his position!

Die weißen Zentrumsbauern werden durch Bedrohung des ♗d6 Zeit gewinnen und wenn Schwarz sich nicht vorsieht, wie eine Flutwelle über dessen gesamte Stellung ziehen!

• • 5...♘f6 6.c4 0-0 7.♗e2 ♖e8 8.0-0 c5 9.♘c3 ♗g4 10.♔h1 ±

Among other things, White is building up for the powerful thrust b4!, see Hebden - Johansen below for an example.

Neben anderen Dingen bastelt Weiß an dem kraftvollen Vorstoß b4!; siehe die gleich folgende Partie Hebden - Johansen als Beispiel hierfür.

• • 5...♘e7 6.c4 ♘g6 7.♗e2 (7.♗d3 0-0 8.0-0 c5 9.b4 b6 10.b:c5 b:c5 11.♘c3 ♗g4, Hebden - Johansen, London 1982, 12.♗:g6 f:g6 13.♘e4 ↑ Bangiev) 7...0-0 8.0-0 b6 9.♘c3 c6 10.d:c6 ♘:c6 11.♘b5 ♗e7 12.d5 ♗c5+ 13.♔h1 ♘ce7 14.♘fd4 a6 15.♘c3 ♗d6 16.♘e4 ♗e5 17.♘f3 ♗b8 18.b4 ±, Gallagher - Boulard, Paris 1990

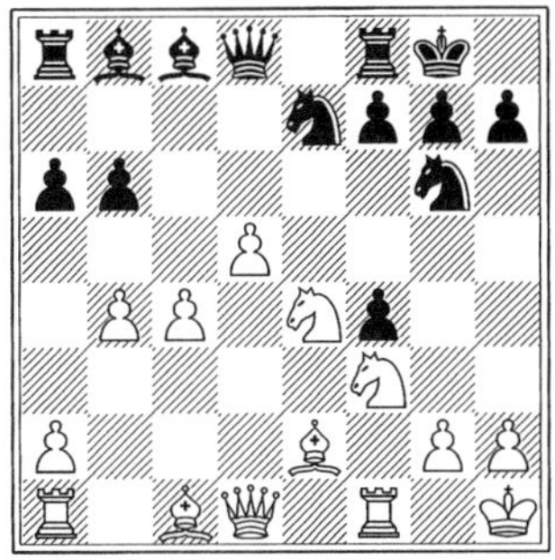

Surfs up! *(Und die ersten Wellen branden auf!)*

• • 5...g5 6.c4 b6 (6...g4 7.♕e2+ Δ ♘e5) 7.♗d3 ♗g4 8.0-0 h6 9.♕e1+ ♕e7 10.♘e5 ♗h5 11.♘c3 ± (Bangiev).

5.♗c4!?

Developing and targeting f7 at the same time, since Black will usually take on d5 which opens the diagonal for this foreseeing bishop. Now Black has two main options.

Entwickelt sich und nimmt gleichzeitig f7 aufs Korn - Schwarz wird ja normalerweise auf d5 schlagen wollen, was dann die Diagonale nach f7 für den weitsichtigen Läufer öffnet. Schwarz hat nun zwei grundlegende Optionen:

I

5...♗d6

The first main line, is an attempt to hold on to a draw with the stubbornness of a pitbull terrier. But first some alternatives:

Diese erste Hauptvariante ist ein Versuch, das Remis mit der Zähigkeit eines Pitbull-Terriers zu verteidigen. Doch zunächst einige Alternativen:

• 5...♕e7+?! 6.♗e2! ♘:d5 7.0-0

Thanks to the surprising bishop retreat, White will enjoy a harmoniously development while Black remains congested:

Dank des überraschenden Läuferrückzuges erlangt Weiß eine harmonische Entwicklung, währenddessen Schwarz im Verkehrsstau steckenbleibt:

• • 7...♗e6 8.c4

We'll see more of this typical pawn sac, trading c4 for f4 in later variations.

Dieses typische Bauernopfer - f4 wird im Austausch für c4 erobert - wird uns noch öfters begegnen.

8...♘b6 9.d4 c6 10.♗:f4 ♘:c4 11.♗:c4 ♗:c4 12.♖e1 ♗e6 13.♘c3 → (Bangiev).

• • 7...♕f6 8.c4 ♘e7 9.d4 c5 10.♘c3 c:d4 11.♘:d4 ♘g6 12.♘d5 ± ♕d8 13.♖e1 ♗c5 14.♗f3+ ♗e6 15.b4 ♗b6 16.c5 0-0 17.♘:f4 1:0, Gallagher - Orlov, Royan 1988.

• 5...♘bd7 6.d4

• • 6...♗d6 7.0-0

Note that White has no reason to trade queens with ♕e2+, as is often done after 5...♗d6, since Black can no longer quickly mobilise his forces with ...c6 d:c6 ♘:c6, or ...♗g4 followed by ...♘bd7.

Man bemerke, daß es für Weiß keinerlei Grund gibt, mit ♕e2+ die Damen zu tauschen, wie dies öfters nach 5...♗d6 geschieht. Hier nämlich hat Schwarz nicht die Möglichkeit, mittels ...c6 d:c6 ♘:c6 oder ...♗g4 nebst ...♘bd7 rasch seine Kräfte zu entfalten.

7...0-0 8.♗b3 b5 9.♘c3 a6 10.a4 b4 11.♘e2!

White intends to take a firm grip around e5 while Black will be busy restoring material equality.

Weiß bemüht sich um festen Zugriff auf e5, währenddessen Schwarz mit der Wiederherstellung des materiellen Gleichgewichts beschäftigt ist.

11...♘b6 12.♘:f4 ♗b7 13.♘e5 ♘b:d5 14.♘fd3! ♘d7 15.♕g4 ♘5f6 16.♕h4

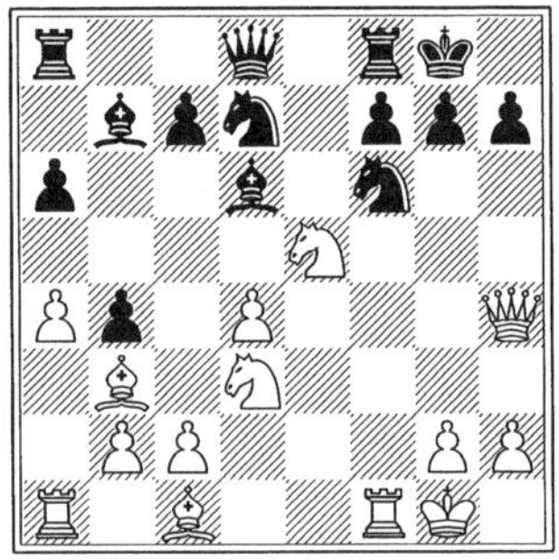

16...♗:e5?!

This presents White with the advantage of the bishop pair in an open position, which hardly is the most sensible thing to do...

Dies spielt Weiß den Vorteil des Läuferpaares in die Hand - was in solch einer offenen Stellung nicht gerade von Umsicht zeugt ...

17.d:e5 ♘e4 18.♕:d8 ♖a:d8 19.♗e3 a5?

Forgetting that White's rooks are connected now, making the following possible:

Vergißt, daß die weißen Türme nun verbunden sind, was den folgenden Schlag ermöglicht:

20.e6! f:e6 21.♗:e6+ 1:0 (21...♔h8 22.♗:d7 +–), Hebden - Boudre, Le Touquet 1987.

• • 6...♘b6 7.♗b5+!

White tries to gain time to support his centre with the c-pawn.

Weiß versucht Zeit zu schinden, um sein Zentrum mit dem c-Bauern stützen zu können.

7...♗d7 8.♕e2+ ♗e7?

Giving White the time he wanted.

Gibt dem Weißen die gewünschte Zeit.

(8...♕e7 is the only move - *ist der einzige Zug:* 9.♗:d7+ ♘f:d7 10.♘c3 ♕:e2+ 11.♔:e2 ♘f6 12.♗:f4 ♘b:d5 13.♘:d5 ♘:d5 14.♗g3 ± Gallagher)

9.♗:d7+ ♕:d7 10.c4 0-0 11.0-0 c5 (11...c6 12.d6!, 11...♖e8 12.♕d3) 12.d:c6 b:c6 13.♗:f4 ♖fe8 14.♕d3 ♗c5 15.♘bd2! ♖ad8 16.♘b3 ♗f8, Gallagher - Ferretti, Chiasso 1991, 17.♘e5 ±.

Back to 5...♗d6 *(zurück zu 5...♗d6):*

Black reckons that this plan is more appropriate now because the ♗c4 impedes the c-pawn.

Schwarz glaubt, daß dies nun eher angebracht ist, da der weiße c-Bauer hier durch den ♗c4 verstellt ist.

6.♘c3

There's nothing wrong with 6.♕e2+ entering an early endgame, but it is also what Black has been analyzing most and what he's hoping for. Besides, isn't it more fun to keep the queens on, than trying to prove White is better in a queenless middlegame or endgame with Black entrenched on the last three ranks? By the way, White shouldn't fear 6...♕e7+?! since 7.♕e2 ♕:e2+ 8.♘:e2 just adds quick pressure on f4 and allows White to support the d5-pawn with ♗b3 and c4. 8...g5 should probably be met by 9.d4! ♘bd7 10.♗b3 g4 11.♘e5!.

An 6.♕e2+ nebst frühzeitiger Herbeiführung eines Endspiels - worauf der Nachziehende hoffen mag - ist eigentlich nichts auszusetzen, doch wurde gerade dies von der schwarzen Seite am gründlichsten analysiert. Doch macht es nicht viel mehr Spaß, die Damen auf dem Brett zu behalten, als zu versuchen, einen kleinen Vorteil in einem Endspiel nachzuweisen, in welchem sich Schwarz auf den drei letzten Reihen verschanzt? Nebenbei, Weiß sollte nicht umgekehrt (6.♘c3) 6...♕e7+?! fürchten, zumal 7.♕e2 ♕:e2+ 8.♘:e2 auf der Stelle den Druck gegen f4 erhöht und dem Anziehenden gleichzeitig ermöglicht, den ♙d5 durch ♗b3 und c4 zu stützen. Auf 8...g5 ist dann vermutlich 9.d4! ♘bd7 10.♗b3 g4 11.♘e5! die richtige Antwort.

6...0-0 7.0-0

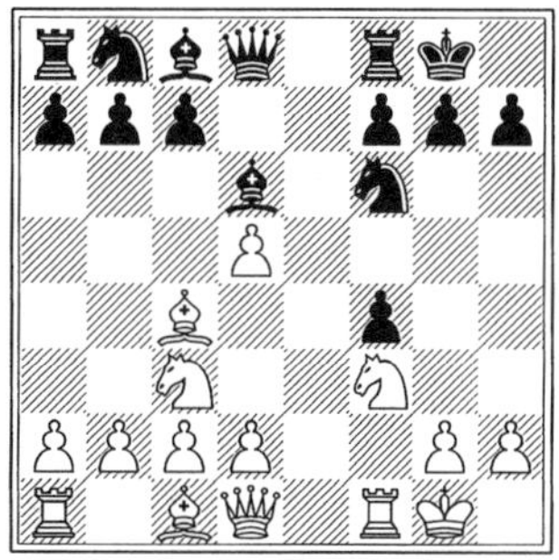

A

7...c6 8.d4 ♗g4

8...c:d5 9.♘:d5 ♗e6 10.♘:f6+ ♕:f6 11.♗e2 ± ECO.

9.♕d3 ♕b6 10.♔h1 ♗h5 11.♘h4 c:d5 12.♘:d5 ♘:d5 13.♗:d5 ♘c6 14.c3 ♖ae8 ∞, Lassahn - Wundt, corr. 1991.

B

(1.e4 e5 2.f4 e:f4 3.♘f3 d5 4.e:d5 ♘f6 5.♗c4 ♗d6 6.♘c3 0-0 7.0-0)

7...♘bd7 8.d4 ♘b6 9.♗b3 ♗g4

9...♖e8 10.♘e5 g5 11.g3 ♗h3 12.♖e1 ♘g4 13.g:f4 g:f4 14.♕f3 ♕g5!? ∞, Masserey - Cela, Mamaia 1991. Personally, I prefer White after e.g. *(subjektiv würde ich Weiß bevorzugen nach z.B.)* 15.♘e4 ♕g7 16.♔h1.

10.♕d3 a5 11.a3 a4 12.♗a2 ♗:f3 13.♕:f3 ±, Spielmann - Fahrni, Baden Baden 1914.

C

(1.e4 e5 2.f4 e:f4 3.♘f3 d5 4.e:d5 ♘f6 5.♗c4 ♗d6 6.♘c3 0-0 7.0-0)

7...♗g4 8.d4 ♘bd7 9.♗b3

9.♕d3 ♗h5 (9...♖e8 10.♗b3 ♗h5 11.♘g5 ♗g6 12.♕f3 ±) 10.♘g5 ♗g6 11.♕h3 h6 12.♘e6! f:e6 13.d:e6 ♔h8 14.e:d7 ♘:d7, Heuer - Uusi, Tallinn 1964, 15.♗d3 ±.

9...♘b6 10.♕d3 ♖e8 11.♘e5 f3 12.♘:f3 ♗h5 13.♗g5 ♗e7 14.♖ae1 ♗g6 15.♕d2 ♕d6 16.♘e5 a6 17.♘:g6 h:g6 18.♗:f6 ♗:f6 19.♘e4 ♖:e4

Desperation since *(Verzweiflung, da)* 19...♕d8 20.♘:f6+ g:f6 21.♖:e8+ ♕:e8 22.♖:f6 loses a second pawn *(einen zweiten Bauern verlieren würde)*.

20.♖:e4 ♘:d5 21.♖fe1 ♘e7 22.♕f4 ♕d7 23.♖:e7! +−, Gardner - Mac Donald, Canada 1994.

II

(1.e4 e5 2.f4 e:f4 3.♘f3 d5 4.e:d5 ♘f6 5.♗c4)

5...♘:d5

The most natural move, spending a tempo to remain a pawn up, for a while at least.

Der natürlichste Zug. Schwarz gibt ein Tempo, um sich zumindest eine Weile lang eines Mehrbauern erfreuen zu können.

6.0-0

White makes a useful move, waiting to see which bishop Black plays to the e-file, Black's other options are rarely played:

Weiß führt einen nützlichen Zug aus, um zunächst abzuwarten, welchen seiner Läufer der Nachziehende auf die e-Linie zieht. Zu anderen Möglichkeiten greift Schwarz selten:

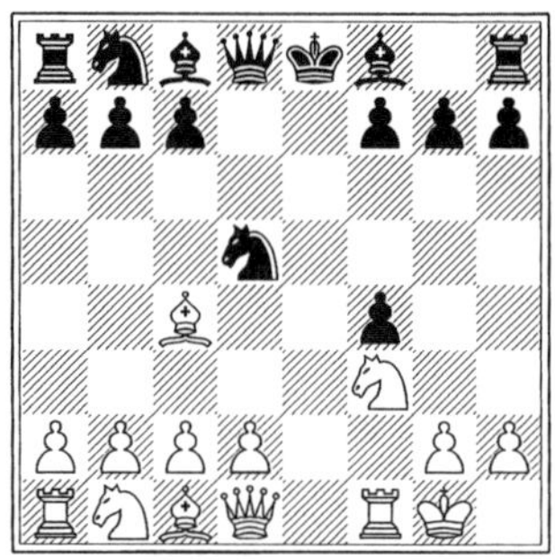

- 6...c6 7.♗b3

Preparing c4 as usual!

Bereitet wie üblich c4 vor!

7...♗d6 8.c4 ♘e7 9.d4 0-0 (9...♗g4 10.♘c3 0-0, and White's position contains a lot of attacking potential, moves like - *und der weißen Stellung wohnt ein großes Angriffspotential inne, mit Zügen wie:* c5, ♕d3, ♘g5 or - *oder* - ♘e4-f2-d3/h3 or - *oder* - ♗c2 Δ ♗:h7+, ♘g5+, - ♕d3. The white pieces are just waiting to be coordinated according to White's preferred plan of attack! - *Die weißen Figuren lauern geradezu darauf, entsprechend des gewählten Angriffsplanes koordiniert zum Einsatz zu schreiten!)*

10.♘g5!? c5
Trying to block in the b3 bishop.
Versucht, den ♗b3 einzumauern.
11.♘c3 (♕h5 isn't dangerous as long as Black has ♗f5 to defend with - *solange Schwarz ...♗f5 zur Verfügung steht, ist die Drohung ♕h5 nicht gefährlich*) 11...♘bc6 12.♘b5 ♘f5 (12...♘:d4 would unleash the ♗b3, e.g: - *12...♘:d4 würde den ♗b3 aus seinem Käfig entlassen, z.B.:* 13.♘:d4 c:d4 14.c5! →) 13.♕h5 h6 14.♘e4!

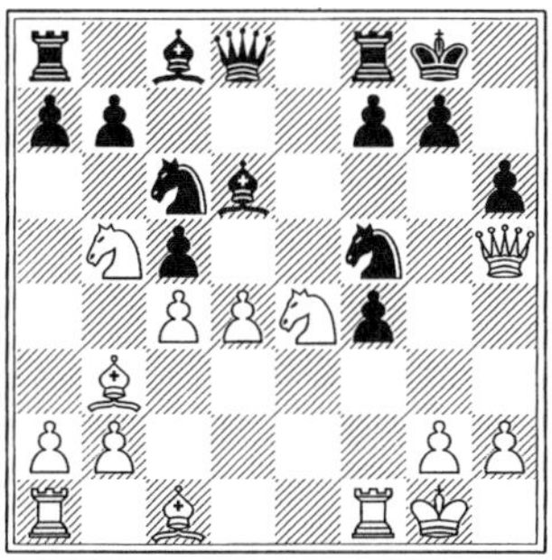

Forcing the release of the white-fielder!
Zwingt die schwarzen Abfangjäger zum Rückzug!
14...♘c:d4 (14...c:d4 would be met by exchanges on d6 and then c5! - *14...c:d4 würde mit zweifachem Abtausch auf d6 und dann c5! beantwortet*) 15.♘e:d6 ♘:d6 (15...♘:b3? 16.a:b3 ♘:d6 17.♖d1) 16.♘:d4 c:d4 17.♖:f4 ♘f5? (17...♗e6 18.♖:d4 ±, 17...♖e8 18.c5 ♖e1+ 19.♔f2 ♕a5 20.♖:f7! ♖:c1 21.♖:c1 ♕d2+ 22.♔g1 ♘:f7 [22...♕:c1+ 23.♖f1+] 23.♕:f7+ ♔h7 24.♕g8+ ♔g6 25.♗f7+ +–) 18.♖:f5 g6 19.♕:h6 ♗:f5 20.♗g5 ♕d6 21.♕h4 ♔g7

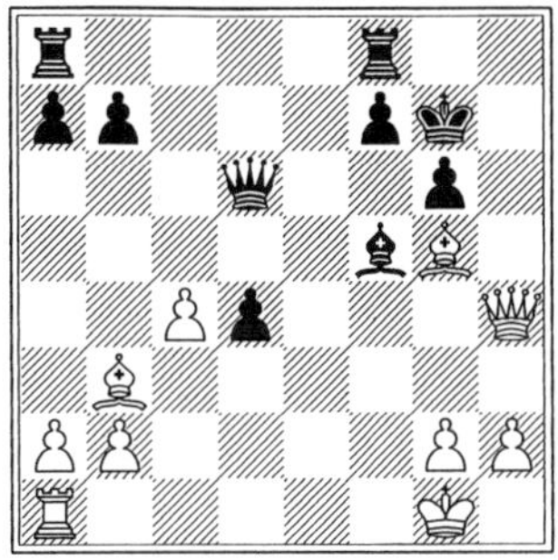

22.c5!
Finally unleashing the mighty bishop!
Schließlich wird verheerende Kraft des weißen Läufers doch noch freigesetzt!
22...♕c6 (22...♕e5 23.♖e1) 23.♗h6+ (23...♔g8 24.♕:d4) 1:0, Fedorov - Gorelov, Moscow 1995.

• 6...♘c6!?
An uncommon move, but fast development always seems to be a sound option.
Ein ungebräuchlicher Zug, doch rasche Entwicklung ist anscheinend niemals ganz verkehrt.
7.d4 (7.♗b3 with the usual pawn pushing in mind is worth considering - *7.♗b3 nebst dem üblichen Bauernvormarsch wäre der Überlegung wert.*) 7...♗g4 8.♕e1+! ♗e7 9.♘e5 (Eliminating Black's pressure on d4 - *neutralisiert den schwarzen Druck auf d4*) 9...♘:e5 10.♕:e5 ♗e6 11.♗:d5 ♕:d5 12.♗:f4 ♕:e5 13.♗:e5 0-0 14.♘c3 c6 15.♖ae1 (Bangiev).
White has a small edge due to his active and centralized pieces.
Dank seiner aktiveren und gut zentralisierten Figuren verfügt Weiß über einen kleinen Vorteil.

A

6...♗e7 7.♗:d5 ♕:d5 8.d4 0-0

Trying to hang on to the pawn is associated with a certain risk:
Der Versuch, den Bauern zu behaupten, wäre mit einem gewissen Risiko verbunden:
8...♕f5 9.♘e5 g5 10.♘c3 c6
And now White has a few interesting options which all are waiting to be tested in practice (which is usually a good sign for White!):
Und nun stehen dem Anziehenden einige interessante Möglichkeiten offen, die alle ihrer praktischen Erprobung harren (was in der Regel ein gutes Zeichen für Weiß ist!):
11.g3 ♖g8 12.g:f4 g:f4+ 13.♔h1 or *(oder)* 11.g4 ♕e6 12.♖e1 (Δ d5) or *(oder)* 11.♕e2 ♗e6 12.g3 ♖g8 (12...♘d7 13.g:f4 g:f4 14.♘e4) 13.g:f4 g:f4+ 14.♔h1 ♘d7 (14...♗b4 15.♖:f4 ♕h3 16.♖f3 ♕h5 17.♘:f7!) 15.♗:f4 0-0-0 16.♗g3 ♕h3 17.♘:c6 ♖:g3 18.♘:e7+ ♔b8 19.♕f2 ± (Glaskov).
I've taken the liberty of changing the move order of this last analysis. It's originally an analysis of 6.♗:d5.
Ich habe mir die Freiheit genommen, bei Glaskovs Analyse ein wenig die Züge umzustellen - ursprünglich galt diese Analyse dem Zug 6.♗:d5.

9.♗:f4

As usual, when White regains his gambit pawn, we can expect an edge due to our centre and development.
Wie üblich kann Weiß nach Rückeroberung des Gambitbauern auf einen Vorteil dank Zentrums- und Entwicklungsüberlegenheit rechnen.

9...c5

- 9...c6 10.♘c3 ♕h5 11.♕d2 h6 12.♖ae1 ♗e6 13.♘e5 ♖e8 14.♘e4 ♘d7 15.♘g3 ♕h4 16.♘g6! f:g6 17.♖:e6 ±, Bangiev - Alexandrov, Minsk 1987.
- 9...♕d8 10.♘c3 ♗g4 11.♕d2 ♘d7 12.♖ae1 ±.

10.♘c3 ♕c4 11.♕e1!

Δ b3.

11...♗f6

The most natural, the alternatives illustrates the strength of White's 11th move!
Die natürlichste Antwort. Nach anderen Zügen wird die Stärke des 11. Zuges von Weiß offenkundig:

- 11...c:d4 12.♕:e7 d:c3 13.♗d6 ♘d7 14.♘e5 +– (Gallagher).
- 11...♘c6? 12.b3 ♕e6 13.d5 ♕:e1 14.♖a:e1 ♗f6 15.♘e4 ♗d4+ 16.♘:d4 ♘:d4 17.c3 ♘c2 18.♖c1 ♖e8 19.♘d6 ♖e2 20.♖f2 ♖:f2 21.♔:f2 ♘a3 22.♖e1 ♗d7 23.♖e7 1:0, Mohr - Wöber, Austria 1995.

12.♗d6! ♗:d4+ 13.♔h1 ♖d8

13...♕e6? (Like a lamb to slaughter - *geht brav wie ein Lamm zur Schlachtbank*) 14.♗:f8 ♕:e1 15.♖a:e1 ♔:f8 16.♘:d4 c:d4 17.♘b5 ♘c6 18.♘c7 1:0, Gallagher - Morris, Hastings 1990/91; 13...♗:c3? 14.b:c3 ♖d8 15.♘e5 ♕e6 16.♘:f7 ±.

14.♘e4!

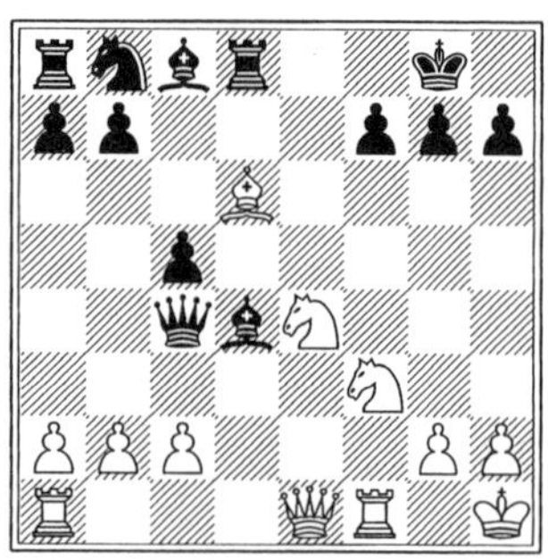

Introducing the threats of 15.c3, 15.♕h4 and 15.♕g3 (Δ ♘f6+).
Damit tauchen auf einen Schlag die Drohungen 15.c3, 15.♕h4 und 15.♕g3 (Δ ♘f6+) auf.

- **14...f5?! 15.♕h4! ♘c6**

15...♖e8 16.♘fg5 h6 17.♘f6+ g:f6 18.♕h5 +–.
16.♘e5!! ♗:e5
16...♕e6 17.♘:c6 ♖:d6 18.♘e7+ ♔h8 19.♘g5 +–, 16...♕:f1+ 17.♖:f1 f:e4 18.♕:d8+ +– Gallagher.
17.♘f6+ ♗:f6 18.♕:c4+ ♔h8 19.♗:c5 ♘e5 20.♕e2 b6 21.♗e7 ♗:e7 22.♕:e5 ♗f6 23.♕c7 h6 24.♖ae1 ♗a6 25.♖:f5 ♗:b2 26.h3 ♖dc8 27.♕e7 ♗c4 28.♕b4! ♗d4 29.♖e4 a5 30.♕d2 ♗b2 31.♖h5 ♖c6 32.♖:c4! ♖:c4 33.♖:h6+ g:h6 34.♕:h6+ ♔g8 35.♕e6+ 1:0, Gallagher - Balashov, Lenk 1991.

- **14...♕d5?! 15.♘:d4!**

15.♖d1? ♘c6 (Δ 16.c3 ♗f5! ∓), Hector - Barkhagen, Stockholm 1995/96.
15...c:d4 16.♗:b8 ♖:b8 17.♕g3!
17.♘f6+?? g:f6 18.♕g3+ ♔h8 19.♕:b8 ♖g8 Δ ♗h3 –+.
17...♕:e4 18.♕:b8 ± Grahn.

- **14...♘c6 15.c3**

When one threat is met another springs into action!
Kaum ist eine Drohung pariert, so taucht auch schon die nächste auf!
• • 15...♗f5?! 16.♘fg5!

[see diagram next column]

16...♗g6 (16...♗:e4 17.♕:e4 →) 17.b3 ♕b5 18.c:d4 c:d4 19.♗f4 h6 20.♘h3 ♖e8 21.♘d6 ±.

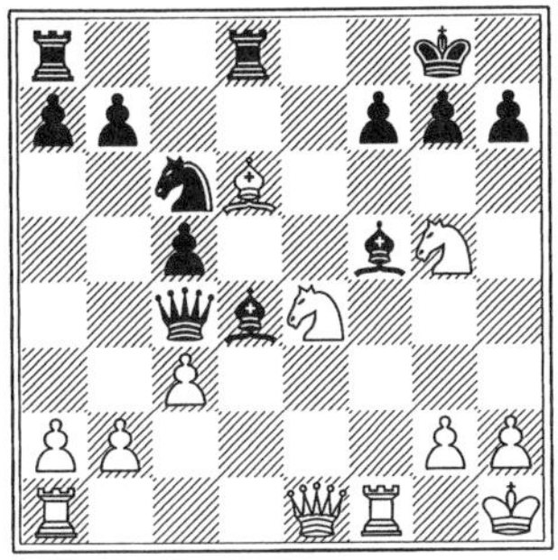

• • 15...♗f6 16.♘fd2 ♕e6 17.♘:f6+ g:f6 18.♕g3+ ♕g4 (18...♔h8 19.♖ae1) 19.♕:g4+ ♗:g4 20.♖:f6 ± Gallagher.

B

(1.e4 e5 2.f4 e:f4 3.♘f3 d5 4.e:d5 ♘f6 5.♗c4 ♘:d5 6.0-0)

6...♗e6

The most popular continuation, preparing to recapture on d5 with the bishop.
Die beliebteste Fortsetzung. Schwarz steht bereit, mit dem Läufer auf d5 zurückzuschlagen.

7.♗b3 ♗e7

Black's options include:
Außerdem kann schwarz spielen:

- 7...c5 8.d4! (Blowing the centre open! - *Legt das Zentrum frei!*) 8...c:d4 9.♘:d4 ♗c5 10.♔h1 ±.

White will regain his pawn and get a strong initiative as interest.
Weiß wird seinen Bauern zurückgewinnen und starke Initiative erlangen.

- 7...♘c6 8.d4

The usual pawn sac doesn't work here: (*das gebräuchliche Bauernopfer funktioniert hier nicht:*) 8.c4?! ♘b6 9.d4 ♘:c4 because there's no potential check

at a4 and Black already has pressure on the d4-pawn *(weil das Schachgebot auf a4 fehlt und Schwarz bereits Druck auf den ♙d4 ausübt)*
8...♘e3 9.♗:e3 ♗:b3 10.♗:f4 ♗e6 11.♘c3 ±, Gallagher - Murey, France 1990.

• 7...♗d6 8.c4!
Black's congested set-up is just asking for the c- and d-pawn treatment!
Die schwarze Figurenansammlung schreit förmlich nach der c- und d-Bauern-Behandlung!

• • 8...♘e7 9.d4 ♘g6 10.♘c3 0-0 11.c5 ♗e7 12.♗:e6 f:e6 13.♕b3 ±.

• • 8...♘b6 9.d4 ♘:c4 10.♕e2
If you compare this with with Hebden - Toth (10th move note, main line) you'll see what an enormous difference the placement of a single piece can make.
Wenn man diese Stellung mit der Partie Hebden - Toth (siehe Anmerkung zum 10. Zug von Weiß in der Hauptvariante) vergleicht, fällt auf, was für einen enormen Unterschied die Postierung einer einzelnen Figur machen kann!
10...b5 11.a4 0-0 (11...c6 12.a:b5 c:b5 13.♘c3 ♕b6 14.♘:b5! Gallagher) 12.a:b5 ♘e3 13.♗:e6 ♘:f1 14.♗d5! c6 15.b:c6 ♗c7 16.♘c3 ♘e3 17.♗:e3 f:e3 18.♕:e3 →, Gallagher - Greenfeld, Tel Aviv 1988 (½:½/50.).
It's hard to believe that Black actually survived this, but on the other hand it's good to see that miracles do occur!
Es ist kaum zu glauben, daß der Nachziehende hier tatsächlich überlebt hat - andererseits ist es gut zu wissen, daß mitunter in der Tat Wunder passieren!

8.c4 ♘b6 9.d4!?

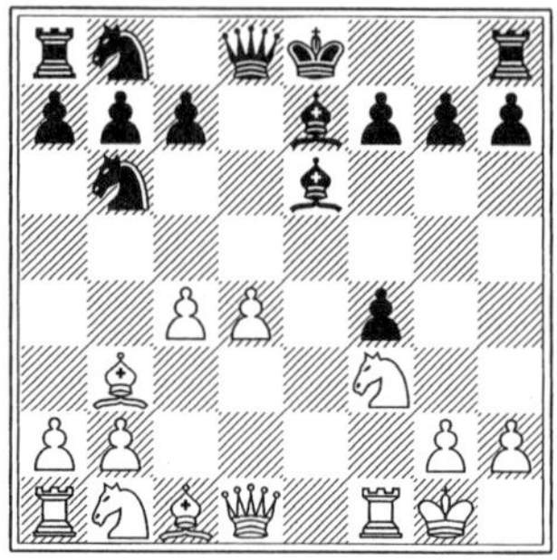

A thematic pawn sac to open files and speed development! When I began playing the King's Gambit a few years ago, I was a bit sceptical about this offer because I wasn't properly acquainted with this kind of position where one must put one's trust in the strength of the initiative and the power of one's imagination! However, I can't believe that the simple 8.d4 0-0 9.c4 ♘e3 10.♗:e3 shouldn't give White even the tiniest edge, e.g:
Ein thematisches Bauernopfer zwecks Linienöffnung und rascher Entwicklung! Als ich vor einigen Jahren anfing, das Königsgambit zu spielen, war ich diesem Opfer gegenüber zunächst ein wenig skeptisch eingestellt, zumal ich mit diesem Stellungstyp noch nicht hundertprozentig vertraut war. Und in der Tat, Vertrauen in die Kraft der Initiative sowie in die eigene schöpferischen Phantasie sind hier unablässig! Nichtsdestotrotz fällt es mir schwer zu glauben, daß das einfache 8.d4 0-0 9.c4 ♘e3 10.♗:e3 nicht den kleinsten Vorteil ergeben soll, z.B.:
10...f:e3 11.♕d3 ♗g5 12.♘c3 ♘c6 (12...f5 13.♘:g5 ♕:g5 14.♖ae1 f4 15.♕e4 ♗h3 16.♖:e3! f3 17.c5 Δ ♕:f3 +–) 13.d5 ♘b4 14.♕d4 ♗d7 15.a3 ♘a6 16.♘:g5 ♕:g5 17.♖f3 ♖ae8 18.♖e1 ±, but noone seems to mention

it at all *(was in anderen Quellen nicht einmal erwähnt wird)*. I tried it in Johansson - Kepcija but Black preferred to transpose to the gambit declined with 9...♘b6 *(ich wollte diese Linie in Johansson - Kepcija erproben, doch mein Kontrahent zog es vor, mit 9...♘b6 zur anschließend besprochenen Ablehnung 9...0-0 überzuleiten).*

9...♘:c4

If the pawn isn't accepted, White obtains a comfortable attacking position for nothing!
Wenn der Nachziehende diesen Bauern verschmäht, erhält Weiß umsonst eine gemütliche Angriffsstellung!
9...0-0 10.d5 ♗g4 11.♗:f4 ♗d6 (11...♗c5+ 12.♔h1 ♘8d7 13.♘c3 ♘f6 14.♕e1 ♘h5!? led to complications in - *führte zu Verwicklungen in* - Johansson - Kepcija, Malmö 1996, ½:½/62.; 14.♕d3! looks better and more natural too. e.g: - *doch 14.♕d3 wirkt stärker und zudem natürlicher, z.B.:* 14...♘bd7 15.♗c2 a6 16.♘g5 h6 17.♘h7 ♖e8 18.♗:c7 ♕:c7 19.♘:f6+ ♘:f6 20.♖:f6 g:f6 21.♕h7+ ♔f8 22.d6 ♕:d6 23.♘d5 +–) 12.♕d4 (12.♕d2!) ♗:f3 13.♖:f3 ♘8d7 14.♗:d6 c:d6 15.♗c2 ♘e5 16.♖h3 g6 17.♘d2 ♖c8 18.b3 f5 19.♖f1 ♘bd7 20.♖g3! ♔h8 21.♘f3 ♕b6 =/∞ (22.♔h1!), Gallagher - Dutreeuw, San Bernadino 1991.

10.♗:f4

There's no good reason to postpone this capture.
Es gibt keinen vernünftigen Grund, dieses Schlagen hinauszuzögern.
10.♕e2?! ♘e3! 11.♗:e6 ♘:f1 12.♕b5+ c6 13.♕:b7 f:e6 14.♕:a8 ♕b6 15.♗:f4 0-0 16.♘c3 ♘d7 17.♕:f8+ ♗:f8 18.b3 e5! 0:1, Hebden - Toth, Biel 1983.

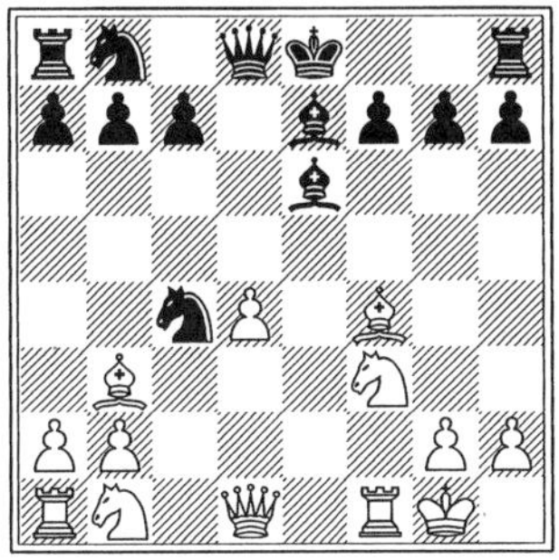

a

10...0-0 11.♕e2 b5

Black is forced to weaken his structure giving White something to latch on to.
Schwarz ist gezwungen, seine Bauernstruktur zu schwächen, um den Anziehenden irgendwie zu bremsen.

12.♘c3 a6

Another try would be:
Ein anderer Versuch wäre:
12...c6 13.a4 ♕b6!? (This might be a critical variation if it wasn't for the following analysis by Bangiev: *Dies stellt möglicherweise - und für Bangiev, von dem die folgende Analyse stammt, ganz gewiß - das kritische Abspiel dar:)* 14.♔h1 ♗f6 (14...♖e8 15.a:b5 c:b5 16.♘:b5 ♕:b5 17.♗a4 ♕f5 18.♘e5! ♖c8 19.♗c1 The queen is caught midboard! *Damenfang mitten auf dem Brett!)* 15.♘g5! ♗:g5 (15...♕:d4 16.♘:e6 f:e6 17.♕:e6+ ♔h8 18.a:b5 c:b5 19.♘:b5 ±, 15...♖e8 16.♗:c4 b:c4 17.d5 ♗d7 18.♕h5 ♗:g5 19.♗:g5 →) 16.♗:g5 ♕:d4 17.♖f4! ♕c5 18.♘e4 ♕b4 19.♗:c4 ♗:c4 20.♘f6+!! g:f6 21.♕g4 ♗e6 (21...h5?? 22.♕:h5 ♖fe8 23.♗:f6! ♖e1 24.♖f1 +–) 22.♕g3 ± (Bangiev), e.g: *(z.B.:)* 22...♕b3 23.♖f3 ♕c2 24.♗h6+ ♕g6 25.♕h4 ♗g4

26.♖g3 f5 27.♗:f8 ♔:f8 28.h3 h5 29.♕d8+ ♔g7 30.h:g4 +–.

13.a4! ♘c6 14.a:b5 ♘:d4 15.♘:d4 ♕:d4+ 16.♔h1

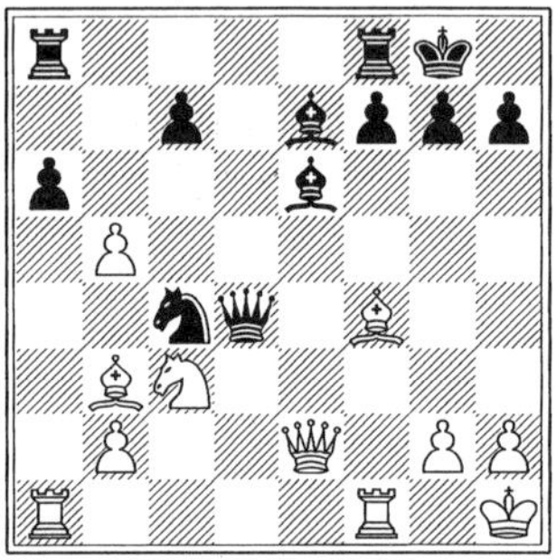

Here Black has tested two moves:
Hier wurden zwei schwarze Züge erprobt:

- 16...♘d2 17.♗:e6 (Another interesting continuation is - *eine andere interessante Fortsetzung wäre* - 17.♗e5!? e.g: - *z.B.* - 17...♕b6 18.♗:e6 ♕:e6 [18...♘:f1? 19.♗d5 ♘e3 20.♗:a8 ♖:a8 21.♗f4! +–] 19.♕:d2 ♕:e5 20.♖fe1 ♕d6 21.♕e2 ♗h4 22.♖ed1 ±) 17...♘:f1 18.♗d5 ♕:f4 19.♖:f1 ♕d6 20.♗:a8 ♖:a8 21.♕c4 (21.♕e4!? ± Bangiev) a:b5 22.♕:f7+ ♔h8 23.♘:b5 (winning the f-pawn proved to be more trouble than it was worth after: - *Auf Eroberung des f-Bauern zu spielen, brachte mehr Ärger als Nutzen, wie sich rasch zeigte nach:)* 23...♕e5 24.♕c4 ♖b8 ∓, Getta - Korney, Hamburg 1993.

- 16...♖ab8 (16...a:b5? 17.♖:a8 ♖:a8 18.♘:b5 ♕:b2 19.♗:c4 ± Gallagher) 17.♖:a6 ♗d6 18.♖a4! (Forcing favourable exchanges - *Erzwingt günstige Vereinfachungen*) 18...♗:f4 19.♗:c4 ♕d6 20.♖d1 ♕e5 21.♗:e6 f:e6 22.♖e4 ♕g5 23.g3 ♗d6 24.♖:e6 ♕f5 25.♔g2 ♗c5 26.♖d5 ♕f2+ 27.♕:f2 ♖:f2+ 28.♔h3 ♗d6 29.♖e2 ♖:e2 30.♘:e2 ♖e8 31.♘c3 ± (½:½/70.), Hebden - Geller, Moscow 1986.

b

(1.e4 e5 2.f4 e:f4 3.♘f3 d5 4.e:d5 ♘f6 5.♗c4 ♘:d5 6.0-0 ♗e6 7.♗b3 ♗e7 8.c4 ♘b6 9.d4 ♘:c4 10.♗:f4)

10...♘b6 11.♗:e6 f:e6 12.♕e2 ♘c6 13.♘c3

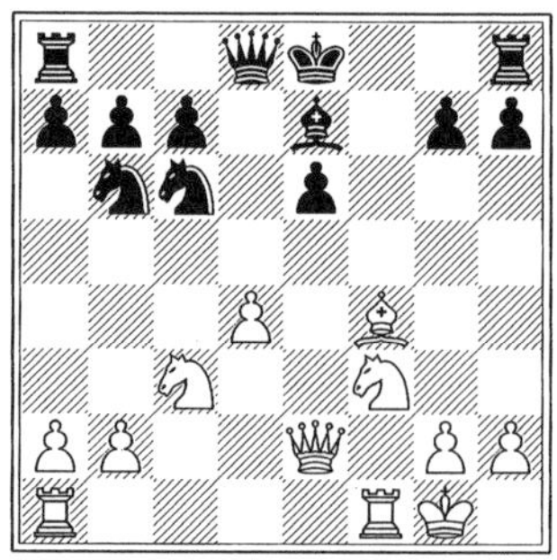

- 13...♕d7 14.♘e5 ♘:e5 15.♗:e5 ♗d6, Bangiev - Flomin, corr. 1986/87, 16.♘b5!? ♘d5 17.♗:d6 c:d6 18.♖ae1 ⩲.
- 13...♘:d4 14.♕e4!? (14.♘:d4 ♕:d4+ 15.♔h1 0-0 16.♕:e6+ ♔h8 =) 14...♘:f3+ 15.♖:f3 0-0 16.♕:e6+ ♔h8 17.♖d1 ♕e8 ∞ Bangiev, 17.♕e4!? (Δ ♖h3) could be worth a test *(könnte einen Versuch wert sein)*.
- 13...♘d5 14.♘e5 ♘:f4 15.♖:f4 ♘:e5 16.d:e5 ♗c5+ 17.♔h1 ♕e7 18.♖d1 ± (Bangiev).

Well, that's all folks! This is the end of the book and hopefully the start of your career as a King's Gambiteer!

If you play any interesting games with this repertoire or (Heaven forbid!) you suffer defeat due to some strong Black novelty, you're welcome to send me the game and if there's a second edition of this book you'll probably be in it. (You can reach me at the following email address: tjmisha@hem2.passagen.se)

Finally, I would like to thank the following people: A fellow King's Gambiteer, Erik Bäcklund for encouraging me to write this book. And Lars Norqvist and Anders Johansson for generously supplying me with games from their databases.

Thomas Johansson

So, daß wär's, liebe Leute! Dies ist das Ende des Buches und zugleich der hoffnungsfrohe Start zu Ihrer Karriere als Königsgambit-Ritter!

Wenn Ihnen mit dem hier vorgestellten Repertoire interessante Partien gelingen oder aber Sie im Gegenteil einer schwarzen Verbesserung zum Opfer fallen (Gott möge bewahren!), so seien Sie hiermit herzlich aufgefordert, mir Ihr Werk zuzusenden, und falls es dann irgendwann zu einer überarbeiteten Neuauflage dieses Buches kommt, werden Sie sich dann höchstwahrscheinlich darin wiederfinden können. Per eMail können Sie mich unter folgender Adresse erreichen: tjmisha@hem2.passagen.se

Schließlich möchte ich noch den folgenden Leuten meinen Dank aussprechen: Dem Königsgambit-Genossen Erik Bäcklund dafür, daß er mich dazu ermutigt hat, dieses Buch zu schreiben. Sowie Lars Norqvist und Anders Johansson dafür, daß sie mich großzügig mit Partien aus ihren Datenbanken unterstützt haben.

Thomas Johansson

Sources *Quellen*

Books *Bücher*

Alföldy, Laszlo: *Gambit-Eröffnungen* (Schach-Archiv Kurt Rattmann, Hamburg 1970)

Bangiev, Alexander: *Das angenommene Königsgambit* (Schach-Profi-Verlag Reinhold Dreier, Ludwigshafen 1996)

Bücker, Stefan: *Das neue Königsgambit* (Schach bei Franckh, Stuttgart 1986)

Bücker, Stefan in: Kaissiber Nr. 1 (Stefan Bücker, Nordwalde 1996)

Capablanca, Jose Raul: *My Chess Career* (Dover Publications, New York 1966)

Dahlgrün, Harro: *Königsgambit Bd. 2-4* (Kurt Rattmann, Hamburg 1977/1979/1980)

Gallagher, Joe: *Winning with the King's Gambit* (Batsford Ltd., London 1993)

Gallagher, Joe: *Trends in the King's Gambit vol. 1&2* (Trends Publications 1990/1993)

Keres, Paul: *Theorie der Schach Eröffnungen Bd. 2* (Sportverlag, Berlin 1955)

Kortchnoi, Viktor & Zak, Vladimir: *King's Gambit* (Batsford Ltd., London 1986)

Leach, Colin: *KGD: Classical Defences* (Caissa Books Ltd., London 1990)

Leach, Colin: *KGA: Allgaier and Kieseritzky Gambits* (Caissa Books Ltd., London 1990)

Leach, Colin: *KGA: Becker, Fischer and Cunningham Defences* (Caissa Books Ltd., London 1990)

Leach, Colin: *Falkbeer Counter-Gambit* (Caissa Books Ltd., London 1988)

Lukov, Valentin & Wienigk, Harry: *Königsgambit C30 - C39* (Verlag Elektronisches Schach, Deutschland 1990)

Lutes: *Cunningham Gambit* (Chess Enterprises Inc., Coraopolis 1990)

Miles, Anthony in New in: Chess Yearbook 36 (Interchess BV, Netherlands 1995)

Schiller: *Who's Afraid of the King's Gambit?* (Chess Enterprises Inc., Coraopolis 1990)

Wahls, Matthias in New in: Chess Yearbook 38 (Interchess BV, Netherlands 1995)

Magazines *Periodika*

Correspondence Chess Yearbook 12 (sl Editrice, Bologna 1994)

Sahovski Informator 1 - 70 (Chess Informant Ltd., Belgrade 1966-1997)

LGT Gambitbulletinen 4-1994 (LGT Simon Marder, Stockholm 1994)

Randspringer Nr. 1 - 75 (Hrsg. Rainer Schlenker, Tübingen/Nürnberg/Schwenningen 1982-1997)

SSKK bulletinen 6-1991 (Carl-Eric Erlandsson, Lund Sweden 1991)

Index of Variations *Variantenverzeichnis*

'♥' Variations *Die "♥"-Varianten*

Learn by heart! *Auswendig lernen!*

Index of Players *Spielerverzeichnis*

Numbers refer to pages • *Ziffer = Seite*

Schachverlag Kania

Hofpfad 32 • D-71701 Schwieberdingen
☎/Fax 07150/37098 • eMail Keilhack@aol.com

Zbigniew Ksieski **Sizilianisch mit e6 und d6** - Scheveninger System u.ä. (1998)

Band A: Mittelspielpraxis, 158 S., geb., DM 24,-
Band B: Eröffnungspraxis, 254 S., geb., DM 29,80

In *Band A* hält der polnische IM und Trainer Vorlesungen zu typischen sizilianischen Endspielen, Opferfeldern (e6, d5, c3 etc.), dem Vorstoß e4-e5 bzw. den Gegenstößen ...d6-d5/...e6-e5 usw. Ein Kurs in moderner sizilianischer Strategie.
In *Band B* werden dem Leser dann die Subsysteme wie Englischer Angriff, Keres-Angriff, Velimirovic-Angriff, Klassische Variante usw. mittels Muster- und Ergänzungspartien nähergebracht.

Paul Motwani *"S.T.A.R. Chess"* - **Sterne des Schachhimmels** (1998)

255 S., gebunden, DM 32,-

Erstmalig ein Werk des schottischen Kultautors in deutscher Fassung. Garniert mit frechen Wortspielen und schachbezogenen Denksportaufgaben bringt GM Motwani dem Leser durchschlagende (Eröffnungs-)Ideen aus der aktuellen Turnierpraxis nahe. Dies geschieht auf sehr lockere, leichtverständliche Weise; Taktik- und Motivationstraining gibt es gratis noch dazu.
Ideal für all die Leser, die ihr Spiel ohne unvertretbaren Aufwand einer "Frischzellenkur" unterziehen wollen!

Rolf Voland **Strategen im Hinterland** -
Das UdSSR-Schach 1941-45 (1998)

238 S., gebunden, DM 32,-

Rolf Voland - als ehemaliger Sportverlag-Übersetzer die "Synchronstimme" von Polugajewski, Suetin und anderen - bringt Licht ins Dunkel der Kriegsjahre, in denen die russische Schachschule das Fundament für ihre spätere Überlegenheit schuf. Text und Fotos sind ein Zeugnis für den Enthusiasmus, mit welchem damals unter schwierigsten Bedingungen Schachturniere durchgeführt wurden. Trotz ungünstiger Quellenlage schildert Voland die Dramatik der damaligen Turniere so, als hätten diese erst gestern stattgefunden. Ergreifende wie Hoffnung bereitende Schicksale russischer Schachmeister werden geschildert. 228 Partien dokumentieren die Spielkunst jener Tage.

Schachverlag Kania

Hofpfad 32 • D-71701 Schwieberdingen
☎/Fax 07150/37098 • eMail Keilhack@aol.com

A. Suetin: **Grundlagen des modernen Eröffnungsspiels** (1997)

Der neueste Leitfaden aus der Feder des Erfolgsautors und Seniorenweltmeisters von 1996 handelt vom *Wie* der Beschäftigung mit der immer komplexer werdenden modernen Eröffnungstheorie. Anhand zahlreicher Beispiele aus dem aktuellen Turnierschach weiht Suetin den Lernenden in die methodischen Geheimnisse des Eröffnungsstudiums ein. Einige Stichworte: Elementare Eröffnungsprinzipien, Geschichte der Eröffnungskunde, Spiel in typischen Stellungen, frühzeitige Verwicklungen, Zerfließen der Grenze zwischen Eröffnung und Mittelspiel usw. "Das Werk ist vom gleichen Rang wie die besten Produktionen der früheren Sportverlag-Reihe." (Stefan Bücker in *Kaissiber 5*)
255 S., gebunden, DM 29,80

G.K. Sanakojew: **"Der 3. Versuch"** - Mein Weg zum Fernschach-Weltmeister (1997)

Auf eindrückliche Weise schildert der XII. Fernschach-Weltmeister seinen leid- wie freudvollen Weg zum Gipfel. Mit 59 ausführlich kommentierten Partien sowie etlichen Tips rund um das Fernschach. "Nicht nur die glänzende analytische Seite des Werkes, sondern auch die fernschachbegeisterte Ausstrahlung sowie die Betonung des Schöpferischen haben mich tief beeindruckt. Dies ist ein Meilenstein nicht nur der Fernschachliteratur!" (Prof. Dr. Robert von Weizsäcker)
239 S., gebunden, DM 38,-

K. Trautmann: **Eine Reise über das Schachbrett** (1997)

Der Autor schickt sich an, in die Fußstapfen des unvergessenen Kurt Richters zu treten - köstlich-unterhaltsam wie lehrreich zugleich begleitet er den Leser auf seiner wundersamen Reise durch die Welt der Kombinationen. 120 Motive (wahllos herausgegriffen: Epaulettenmatt - Kreuzfesselung - Verbundene Freibauern - Wanderkönig - Unterverwandlung - Sprengpunkt e6 - usw.) werden mit einem ausführlich kommentierten Themenbeispiel vorgestellt, bevor anschließend jeweils 5 Übungsbeispiele folgen.
351 S., gebunden, DM 38,-

Schachverlag Kania

Hofpfad 32 • D-71701 Schwieberdingen
☎/Fax 07150/37098 • eMail Keilhack@aol.com

Gambit- und verwandte Literatur:

Raetzki/Tschetwerik **Albins Gegengambit** (1998)
156 S., gebunden, DM 24,-
Nonverbal, kurze Einführung in Deutsch und Englisch. 1.d4 d5 2.c4 e5 unter der Lupe zweier Spezialisten im enzyklopädischen Teil. 239 Partien, 37 davon im Informatorstil kommentiert, zeigen die spektakulären Möglichkeiten dieser Gambit-Eröffnung auf. Die Eröffnungsspezialisten aus Woronesch/Rußl. publizierten schon Theorieartikeln in den renommierten New-in-Chess-Jahrbücher.

Rainer Schlenker **Franco-Polnisch 1.e4 e6 2.d4 b5!? und anderes** (1998)
95 S., kart., DM 16,80
Über ein Jahr arbeitete der Underground-Literat an der Kreierung seines neuesten Eröffnungssystems. Hier das Resultat seiner Forschungstätigkeit. Im Rahmenprogramm dieser RANDSPRINGER-Sonderausgabe gemischte launische Beiträge, u.a. das "Keilhack-Journal".

Keilhack/Schlenker **1...♘c6! aus allen Lagen** (1995)
191 S., kart., DM 26,80
Seriöse wie experimentelle Eröffnungsvarianten rund um den "unanständigen" Rösselsprung 1...Sc6 "gegen alles". Praxisnah gestaltet anhand von 124 kommentierten Partien mit eingearbeitetem Ergänzungsmaterial. Vielfältiges Studienmaterial aus Klassik, Amateur- und Meisterpraxis; ausführliche Originalanalysen zu verschiedenen Spezialsystemen.

Bernhard Lach **Spanisch - Die Alapin-Variante** (1995)
63 S., kart., DM 13,80
Dieses Buch bringt dem Leser eine Spielweise nahe, mit denen er bis zum Exzess ausanalysierten Varianten der "Spanischen Leier" frühzeitig ausweichen kann. In positioneller Hinsicht ist der absurd anmutende Läuferzug ins Leere keineswegs ohne Sinn: Eine weiße Zentrumsbildung mit d2-d4 ist einstweilen verhindert, während der Nachziehende zu ...Sge7 und ...d5 bereitsteht.